P9-AQY-164

100 Best
FAMILY RESORTS
IN NORTH AMERICA

Seventh Edition

100 Quality Resorts with Leisure Activities for Children and Adults

JANET TICE AND JANE WILFORD

The
Globe
Pequot
Press

GUILFORD, CONNECTICUT

Text design by Nancy Freeborn
Photo layout by Sue Preneta

ISSN 1536-6170
ISBN 0-7627-2818-3

Manufactured in the United States of America
Seventh Edition/First Printing

The prices and rates listed in this guidebook were confirmed at press time. We recommend, however, that you call establishments to obtain current information before traveling.

100 Best
FAMILY RESORTS
in NORTH AMERICA

Aspen/Snowmass Village

The Resort at Seabrook Island

Grand Traverse Resort and Spa

The Breakers Palm Beach

Smugglers' Notch Resort

Club Med/Sandpiper

Grand Traverse Resort and Spa

Whistler/Blackcomb

Alisal Guest Ranch and Resort

Highland Lodge

Grand Hotel on Mackinac

Snowbird Ski and Summer Resort

Hyatt Regency Scottsdale Resort at Gainey Ranch

Squaw Valley USA

TradeWinds Island Resorts/Island Grand

Mohonk Mountain House

Smugglers' Notch Resort

The Cloister

Marriott's Grand Hotel Resort, Golf Club & Spa

Kiawah Island Golf Resort

Cheeca Lodge and Spa

Snowbird Ski and Summer Resort

Shanty Creek

Severn Lodge

The Tyler Place Family Resort

Flathead Lake Lodge

© 2003 jeff@JAGPhotoInc.com

CONTENTS

PREFACE

"Best" is a curious adjective, one that is entirely subjective. So let us define our sense of best—both what it does and what it doesn't mean.

Best is not necessarily the fanciest, the biggest, or the most expensive.

Best is not always the sleekest, the poshest, or the newest.

Best, in the context of this book, is what is best for families.

Best is variety in setting and atmosphere.

Best is variety in recreational interests and in prices.

Best is variety in geographical location. A broad selection allows you to have choices whether you want to travel far or near.

We searched for the most extensive children's programs, yet balanced this with an interest in presenting a good cross-section of North America. If we have overlooked your favorite, let us know. Please write to us in care of The Globe Pequot Press, P.O. Box 480, Guilford, CT 06437.

Janet Tice
Jane Wilford

INTRODUCTION

Although traveling with children is not a new phenomenon, many Americans these days are viewing the traditional family vacation in a different light. In past decades family vacations have most frequently been determined by the needs and wants of the children. Planning the entire vacation around the kids often left Mom and Dad feeling that they had not had a vacation at all but, rather, a trial by fire. The only option was to leave Junior behind in the care of grandparents or close family friends while the parents ventured off on their own. In an attempt to share experiences with their children, many parents, seeking middle ground, are adjusting the focus of their leisure-time plans.

Vacations these days often mean shorter and more frequent jaunts. Increasingly, they involve flying rather than loading up the family car and driving. Minivacations are becoming popular and are frequently planned to coincide with one or the other parent's business trips. On the philosophical side, current trends in child care emphasize the importance of a parent's presence, especially for the first three years, and many parents are reluctant to leave their infants and toddlers for extended periods.

The intent of this book is to identify those places where adults and children can enjoy interesting and age-appropriate activities. Baby-sitting services for infants, a ski school for three-year-olds, and a supervised recreational program for older children are some of the possibilities explored. In selecting resorts, we have taken into consideration different styles, price ranges, and diverse geographic locations. It is a representative sampling rather than an all-inclusive listing. Often we have been limited by lack of space and lack of information. This book does not highlight every Disney World and Six Flags Over Somewhere establishment in the United States. While these certainly serve an important educational function in a pleasant and exciting atmosphere for children, therein lies the catch: They

are directed primarily toward children. But parents deserve vacations, too—adult vacations with grown-up activities.

This is not, then, a book about vacations *for* kids. Rather, it is a book about vacations *with* kids, about family adventures in which adults can be adults and children can be children and in which there is common ground for sharing.

In general we are pleased with the progress we've noted in the resorts we have chosen from our previous editions. They are not resting on their laurels but seem to be enthusiastic and dedicated to making more and more improvements and providing better and better facilities and programs for families. In addition, new resorts developing exciting programs are constantly entering this family-oriented market.

If we've left out your favorite family spot, or if you own a resort and feel slighted, please write to us in care of The Globe Pequot Press. We're always glad to know of places where families find special treatment.

Costs and Caveats

Prices are noted throughout the book in the accommodations section of each resort's description. They are current as of 2003. But, just like the new car that depreciates the minute you drive away from the showroom, prices have to be adjusted for inflation the minute they're stated. Keep this in mind if your travel plans do not materialize right away but instead are put on the back burner for a couple of years. Inflation takes its toll simultaneously and universally; however, the prices quoted here can serve as a basis for comparison among resorts regardless of the year in which you consult this guide.

The problem most commonly caused by prices is sorting out just what a given price includes. In the travel industry, various pricing schedules are frequently used to identify the relationship between lodging and meals. For example:

European Plan means the rate quoted is for lodging only.

Modified American Plan means two meals a day (usually breakfast and dinner) as well as lodging are included in the daily rate.

Full American Plan means three meals a day and lodging are covered in the daily rate.

All-inclusive means that all meals, generally all activities, and other extras are included in one price.

The extent of what else is included in the daily room rate, such as use of the recreational facilities, varies widely from one resort to another. Every effort has been made to identify the extras for which no additional charge is required. If "complimentary" or "free" is not clearly stated for a service or activity, you can safely assume that there is a fee.

Certain other things may come as a shock when you check out, so be sure to investigate beforehand. For example, we have not included taxes in the rates. This varies from state to state and will be 7 percent to 17 percent additional. Sometimes occupancy taxes are also added, based on the room or on the number of people.

Recently, it's become a common practice for hotels to add a "resort fee" or "amenity fee" of $5.00 to $15.00 per night. This fee covers things that previously were "free" or included in the rate; in-room coffee and tea, daily newspapers, Internet access, or telephone charges for local or toll-free numbers, etc. Often, resorts will add this fee to include "use of the facilities"—fitness rooms, swimming pool, beach chairs—any number of things. Or it may include room gratuities. We've tried to identify these charges, but they're not always easy to find. You'll want to read the fine print, so to speak, and ask, ask, ask. No one wants a nasty shock at the end of a lovely vacation.

Although we've already discussed rates, it's a complicated issue and bears repeating, so please forgive us if you already know this. The rates that we list will not be exact. Sometimes they may be more; often they may be less.

Rates depend on many things—size of the room, day of the week, location and view, season of the year, number of adults and children—the list goes on and on. Especially now that technology is so prevalent, hotels are following the airlines' examples and using yield management techniques. This simply means that a hotel will look at its past booking patterns and its current occupancy rate (how many empty rooms are sitting there) and adjust its rates accordingly, sometimes day by day. And competition is fierce: A resort may lower or raise its rates based on what its neighbors are doing. Also, many resorts, again like the airlines, are putting lower rates on the Internet. While we often give a sample package rate in the descriptions, there may be more packages available. Sometimes it may not be labeled a family package, so don't limit yourself. The resort may be marketing the spa or other recreation, with very good rates.

Besides lodging, prices are specifically noted for children's programs. As a well-seasoned traveler, you already have a ballpark idea of the prices of lift tickets for skiing and greens fees for golf. Emphasis here is on costs of the children's activities because now you're trying to become well seasoned as a traveling parent.

Most children's programs, even if it's not stated in the descriptive entry, require children to be potty-trained. Those programs specifically for infants and toddlers, of course, do not. However, they usually do require parents to supply diapers and baby food or formula.

Reservations, reservations, reservations!! Again, we may not always list this in the entry, but it's safer to assume that reservations are required. If staffing is limited, the program may fill up—many parents plan months in advance via phone or Internet. Most resorts plan their staffing ahead of time, and if no children are signed up, there may be no program. Another caveat: Many hotels are now charging a fee if you cancel your child within twenty-four hours. Illness might not count, but capriciousness would. Advance planning may limit the spontaneity, but ultimately makes life, and certainly vacations, smoother.

PLANNING FAMILY VACATIONS

How This Book Can Help You

As your vacation rolls around, you start weighing the pros and cons of bringing the children along. You feel that you desperately need exclusive time for adult conversation with your spouse or other grown-ups. Yet you wonder if following through on that idea is fair to your kids. Vacations need not be an either/or proposition—either resigning yourself to a week or two of nonstop "Sesame Street" activities with no relief in sight or excluding the children from the few leisure weeks you have away from a demanding career. The former scenario almost always requires relinquishing your own interests, while the latter is complicated by worry and guilt over little Johnny or Susie left behind at Grandma's as you're off footloose and fancy-free. It is possible, however, to have a vacation that is fair to both you and your children.

So you're ready to plan a vacation with the kids. Though this sounds like what parents have been doing for generations, you're different from previous generations. You're better educated and fairly well traveled; you've delayed getting married and having children until your career was launched; and most likely you're older as you reach this phase of family life than were your parents. In addition, you probably have different expectations for both yourself and your children, expectations that influence how you want to spend your leisure time. While you're devoted to your children and conscious of the importance of your input into their intellectual, emotional, and social growth, you also realize that part of being a good parent is tending to your own physical and psychological well-being. You imagine that it must be feasible to share a pleasurable vacation experience with your children without denying your own interests and concerns. Well, it is!

When you've made the decision that the kids should come along this time and you know that one more carousel or one more pair of Mickey Mouse ears just might drive you crazy, then let this book help you discover the perfect vacation spot, where the whole family can be happy together.

Whether you are considering a few relaxing days at a country hideaway or a week of fun in the sun on a beach, rest assured that there are accommodations with facilities and activities that will delight both you and your children. A family vacation doesn't have to mean settling for renting the same house at the nearest beach each season for the next several years or the proverbial visit to Grandma's house year after year. Variety can be found, and if you're itching for a good game of golf, you don't have to fret over whether your three-year-old can manage walking eighteen holes or what antics he'll perform along the way. These concerns can be resolved by choosing the proper surroundings and conditions.

When a young parent once inquired about children's activities at one resort, the staff member gave her a bottle of bubbles. That would last about thirty seconds, right? Thank goodness many resorts are more enlightened, and you'll find those here.

Explore in the following pages a selection of hotels, condominiums, and resorts that offer conveniences to accommodate the needs and wishes of both adults and children. So that you can gratify your diverse and periodically changing geographical interests, you will discover that this guide includes establishments throughout the United States, with a few in Canada. The United States is at the forefront of the new approach to family vacations.

In compiling this collection, several criteria were considered: attractive surroundings;

good dining facilities, including comfortable lounges and bars; baby-sitting services; and recreational activities for both parents and children. Needless to say, some of the establishments listed here meet more of the criteria or meet them better than others. But then, your wishes and requirements may vary from one trip to the next: One year you may need just a competent baby-sitter to stay in your hotel room with your infant while you enjoy an elegant, leisurely dinner, and the next year you may need a complete day-care center/nursery school for your energetic toddler while you spend the day out on the slopes. This book does not rank resorts on how well the criteria are met; it simply describes them and all their available services. You can then pick and choose according to your personal preferences and current needs.

To make it easier to find your ideal vacation spot, the descriptive entries are grouped by geographical location, then alphabetically within these divisions; addresses, telephone numbers, and Web sites are included in the descriptions.

Following the descriptions is a standard alphabetical index of resort names to help you pull out the perfect place that a friend recently mentioned at a dinner party, the location of which eludes your recollective powers. We've also included an alphabetical index by state and province. This arrangement should afford you easiest access to the required information regardless of your perspective when designing your vacation.

Finally, a special categories index is given that lists resorts by the seasonal schedule of the children's programs.

While probably the foremost concern for your next trip is simply to make that perfect match between your personal circumstances and the most suitable resort, you may occasionally feel a bit nervous about some of the practical logistics of traveling with kids. The section on helpful hints when traveling with children may forestall a few inconveniences

that may arise when away from home; the medical information should allay some fears about illnesses and emergencies; and the segments on educating yourself and the advantages of a good travel agent may assist in ironing out the details of your vacation arrangements. In any case, they will stimulate you to analyze your own and your children's habits so that you can anticipate some of the problems and joys of traveling with youngsters.

So you're off. Good luck and happy vacation!

Helpful Hints for Traveling with Children

It can be a joy to travel with children. Sure, sometimes the preparations may seem exhausting and spurts of parental anxiety en route may be tiring as well, but the excitement and wonder of children as they encounter new experiences are worth the price of admission.

On the following pages you'll find some helpful hints for traveling with kids. Many of these suggestions may seem incredibly obvious, but stating the obvious is not always a disadvantage. And a little repetitive reinforcement may help you react more quickly or think better on your feet. One easy-to-read and practical resource book is *Trouble-Free Travel with Children* (The Book Peddler, 1996) by Vicki Lansky, author of more than twenty-five books for new parents.

Preparation, preparation, preparation! The first trick to traveling with kids is preparing them for the adventure. Talk to your child in advance; advise her where you're going and what you'll be doing. Infants (in spite of the mounds of diapers you must tote) are very portable. Even toddlers whose whole world revolves around Mom and Dad are happy as long as familiar faces are near at hand. But as a child's world expands to include friends and a wider realm of belongings, verbal preparation becomes very important. Sometimes it's easy to assume that your youngster will pick up on things by osmosis, but children don't always assimilate information about vacation plans that floats around the house in chitchat. It's necessary to explain directly to them what is in store.

Many families like to spend time together planning vacations. Encouraging participation from all family members and allowing children to help plan the trip makes them feel like "shareholders," creating cooperation and increasing satisfaction for everyone. Books and maps about your destination and route can be shared; even for very young children, maps translate the excitement of travel into a tangible form. Participation easily continues throughout the vacation when you assist children with keeping a "journal" (drawings, pictures, flowers, poems, ticket stubs,whatever!); allow them their own camera (inexpensive, of course); or encourage them to collect postcards, badges for their backpack, or follow any theme that appeals to them.

Besides detailing the fun of this new experience, reassure your child that you'll be returning home; that although your daughter may not bring along every Barbie doll and Raggedy Ann, her dolls will still be here when she gets back; and that even though your son may miss his best friends, they won't forget him. Even three- and four-year-olds can "write" postcards along the way as a means of staying connected with friends back home.

As an experienced traveler, you know the ropes of appropriate packing for trips. As a conscientious parent, you are most familiar with what your child will want or need away from home. The standard rule of thumb—don't overpack—applies just as well for children as it does for adults. The length of the trip adjusted for the dirt factor of your own child (how many outfits can he go through in a day?) should give you a reasonable handle on the amount of clothes to pack. Laundromats are never that far away, many hotels have laundry services, and kids' clothes (just by virtue of their size) are fairly easy to hand wash in a hotel bathroom. And don't take

along what your child isn't happy with. No matter how much time dear Aunt Josie spent crocheting that sweet little dress, if your daughter doesn't like it, if it's uncomfortable, it will be nothing more than an unnecessary bulge in your suitcase. We've developed a couple of packing "rules" over the years. Rule #1: Take half as many clothes and twice as much money as you think you need; and Rule #2: Pack your bag and then walk around the block with it to test it before departure!

If your child uses a bottle, a trip may not be the best time to nudge him out of it; a bottle may provide a bit of security in unfamiliar surroundings. Just be sure to pack a bottle brush: If a bottle gets lost at the bottom of a travel bag for a day or two, mysterious molds blossom, or new life forms may be discovered.

Toys, too, have to fall under the "don't overpack" rule. Remember that for children, seemingly mundane objects in new surroundings often provide considerable amusement. It's a good idea to stash away a couple of new attention-getters, but don't forget the tried and true. A cuddly doll, even if it is beginning to look somewhat old and ratty, or a special pillow is often very comforting for a little one sleeping in a strange bed for the first time. Age-appropriate books, a small ball, crayons, coloring books, scissors, construction paper, a bean bag (remember them from when you were a kid?), and small games such as a pint-size checkerboard are all packable items. Even blocks like Duplos or Legos, if arranged in one compact cube, can be packed fairly easily. Some parents cherish a Fisher-Price tape recorder or a Walkman (with earphones, please) as something akin to a gift from the gods. Terrifically totable and accompanied by a selection of tapes (anything from Disney stories to old radio shows to historical accounts of George Washington and Benjamin Franklin are on the market now), a tape recorder can effectively hold a child's attention.

For the preschooler or older child, consider investing in a backpack. Set down the rules with your child when packing: She can bring along whatever fits in the pack, and she has to carry it. This way you give your child a sense of participating in the preparations and obviate the almost inevitable whine about something Mom didn't include. And practically unnoticed you can sneak in a little lesson in responsibility. Just make sure enough room is left for new additions along the way.

A "surprise box" is a fun way to keep children interested and amused. Without divulging details, prepare "surprises" such as snacks, small toys, or other things you know your child will like. Then watch the fun as he delves into the goodies when the vacation adventure begins. A surprise box can entertain your youngster anywhere from two minutes to two hours; if you're clever, you'll be on the upper end of the spectrum.

When making plane reservations, try to secure seat assignments at the same time. Indicate the age of your young traveler, and request the bulkhead seats. These seats afford a little extra leg room and can be padded with blankets and pillows if your child decides to snooze (lucky you!). It may mean that your feet will be struck by paralysis if little Janie nestles down on her pillow and curls up on your toes, but it is an improvement over having her elbow in your drink. Also, without passengers in front of you in this seating arrangement, you won't fret over a rambunctious child's kicks disturbing other people.

If two parents are flying with a lap child (under two years old), try to reserve an aisle seat and a window seat. Regular air travelers never request a center seat, so if the plane is not full, you'll wind up with that third seat in which to spread out; if a stranger does venture into your row, it's simple enough for one parent to move over a notch. Often parents opt to purchase a ticket for the child, bringing their own safety seat.

In the past, airlines stocked onboard activity packs, and even special meals for their younger travelers. These days, you need to pack your own. Bringing a mostly disposable picnic lunch onboard can keep the whole family happy. Do take advantage of the early boarding airlines provide for families with small children—it helps to "settle in" before the crowd.

Airplanes pose additional problems: Small children often have greater difficulty than adults in adjusting to altitude changes. During takeoffs and landings, infants should be encouraged to nurse or drink a bottle; the sucking action combats blocked ear and painful sinus problems. Older children can use the same techniques as adults—yawning and chewing gum or candy.

If you plan to rent a car during your vacation, be sure to request a car seat for a child four years old and younger. While many rental agencies take this in stride, the number of car seats is usually limited, so it's important to make a reservation for this accessory in advance. Whether your mode of transportation is your own car or a rental, plan frequent stops. Cramped legs and fidgetiness set in fast for youngsters. These factors are not unknown in air travel either; even a walk down the aisle of the plane to the bathroom is a change of pace for a child.

In car travel, a small ice chest in the back seat can be a real boon. Filled with milk, juice, and fruit, it provides a source of ready refreshment and relieves frantic searches for a fast-food stop or a corner grocery. Even when traveling by air, if your luggage allotment permits, check a small ice chest (empty) along with your other bags. Once you arrive at your hotel, it can be filled with ice and drinks and can be taken along in a rental car on side trips. Or, upon arrival at your destination, make one of your first stops at a grocery, drug, or discount store and pick up an inexpensive Styrofoam cooler that can be left behind. Many accommodations include small refrigerators in the rooms, and some are equipped with kitchens, but if not, you've solved a problem before it arises. It's much easier to dig into an ice chest for a drink than to track down juice somewhere in the hotel facilities at nine o'clock at night. But if this seems too cumbersome and your child desperately needs something late at night, remember the hotel bar—it is the best place to hit, for it always has orange juice (for Screwdrivers), tomato juice (for Bloody Marys), and milk (for White Russians). It may be more expensive, but can you really afford to count pennies when Johnny refuses to go to sleep without his nightly cup of milk? It's an investment in your peace of mind.

When stocking up on drinks, buy the variety in cardboard cartons. Since they are unbreakable and need no refrigeration, they can be squirreled away in a suitcase or even tossed into a purse. On an airplane, the flight attendants never seem to pass by soon enough or often enough to satisfy little ones.

For edibles, small boxes of raisins, granola bars, and individually wrapped cheese chunks such as La Vache qui Rit (what child can resist a silly laughing cow in a red net bag?) make good nourishing snacks. Good old clever Mom can rack up some kudos when she pulls one of these treats from her bag before Susie even thinks about getting antsy.

Once you arrive at your destination and settle into your hotel, turn over an area, even if just a corner, to your child. Having his own space filled with his own stuff may mean a lot in terms of a sense of belonging, and with a bit of prodding, you may avoid having toys strewn all about.

Collecting souvenirs on a trip can be a time-consuming process or maybe even cause a headache or two. Either Joey wants everything in sight or he chooses the most inappropriate piece of junk you've ever seen. Sure, certain limits on buying have to be set, but who cares if he chooses the made-in-Japan pencil sharpener in the shape of a cannon during a visit to Valley Forge? Just as a cookbook containing three wonderful meat-pie recipes from Nova Scotia or an artistic ceramic tile made in the Southwest is something that you must have, there are special reminders of a trip that a child

feels he needs. They're just different. A few neat rocks and a couple of sticks may be the only things Joey wants to show off to his best buddy back home. Or if your little girl wants to take home a shiny red coin purse to her best friend, she doesn't care (and neither does her friend) that the same item is on the shelves in every chain store across the country, so why should you? A smattering of understanding and patience can go a long way.

Recreational activities in your new surroundings must be evaluated with a clear head and a sharp eye. Most of the resorts included here offer organized children's activities or baby-sitting services, so it may not be necessary to drag kids along on every adult event you want to investigate. Antiques hunting and long museum visits are usually not first-rate attractions for members of the kiddie league. Plan on a baby-sitter or a group activity for an afternoon that you want to spend on a grown-up outing.

And for those days that are devoted entirely to being together, alternate grown-up pursuits with juvenile ones. Remember that a child's attention span is not as refined or sophisticated as an adult's; variety is more than the spice of life—it's the key to sanity in some cases. Climbing on the cannons at an old fort is much more fun for a child than reading every historical marker; a mixture of both keeps everyone happy. All day on the beach may be too much for a three- or four-year-old, and you can take ten-to-one odds that he won't be content following your lead to relax and soak up the sunshine. Bargain with your child: a run on the beach and a few splashes in the waves, then quiet time building a sand castle; an hour of shopping or sightseeing for two hours in the swimming pool.

Many resorts have lodging with fully equipped kitchens so that you can cook family meals in a homelike setting. Many resort restaurants make an attentive effort to please children; a special dining hour for families or a children's menu certainly helps make life more pleasant. And when you grow weary of dining in restaurants, a picnic may be a reasonable alternative. Many hotels can prepare box lunches, or you can pick up some cold cuts at a small grocery for a do-it-yourself picnic. Ordering a meal through room service is often a special treat for a child.

As you skim the descriptive entries of the resorts that follow, you'll realize that most are self-contained vacation spots. Each offers a place to sleep, a place to eat, and something to do. This is intentional, as children seem to function best staying in one place. Establishing a home base, exploring the setting, and taking afternoon side trips are often preferable to being on the road constantly. Besides negating all the packing and unpacking of a traditional road trip (remember, this is not the newest rock star promoting his latest album that you're traveling with!), having a home base helps a child develop a sense of security as the new surroundings become familiar.

With a few tricks up your sleeve, some understanding, and forethought, traveling with kids can be a fun-filled family adventure. Your well-considered plans make the whole process workable and buy a lot of happiness for both you and your child. With solid pre-planning there's space for spontaneous "happenings" that make a vacation memorable.

Medical Information

Unless you can take your own family doctor or pediatrician with you, the best advice to follow is the old Girl Scout motto "Be Prepared." Keep in mind: (1) this adventure you're about to embark upon is not a trek along the shores of the East Siberian Sea, and (2) you are not the sole custodian of Band-Aids. As amazing as it may seem, doctors and pharmacies do exist out there in that twilight zone called family vacations.

Before starting your trip, consult your pediatrician for advice; she may even be able to supply names of colleagues where you'll be visiting. If you fear that your child is coming down with something as you depart on your vacation, or if he's particularly accident-prone, you can check with the resort staff upon arrival about the location of the nearest hospital and pharmacy and the availability of doctors and nurses (many resorts have medical personnel on call). Sometimes the best recommendations come from other parents, wherever you may find them. If the need is immediate, don't hesitate to ask a likely looking parent working in a car rental agency, a restaurant, a shop, or the airport. And without seeming alarmist, look up the telephone number of the local poison control center; anticipating the slim chance of ever needing it, you'll be gratified that it's handy should your child ingest a handful of your brightly colored vitamin pills. It is also a good idea to check with your medical insurance provider before you leave home for out-of-state or -country authorization/billing procedures.

Pack a medical emergency kit and try to envision the unexpected. If your child scrapes a knee at a playground or develops an earache in the middle of the night, you won't want to take time tracking down a drugstore to relieve his discomfort. You can purchase a ready-made medical kit that fits compactly in a car's glove compartment or carry-on bag, or you may prefer the do-it-yourself variety. The following list is merely suggestive; review your own medicine cabinet to fill in the gaps.

- vitamins and medications your child normally takes
- a thermometer
- children's Tylenol
- children's cough syrup
- adhesive strips
- nose drops (though most kids hate them)
- a decongestant
- an aspirator
- ear drops
- suppositories and antidiarrheal medicine (change in water and altitude or sheer excitement can affect a child's system)

- Desitin, A and D, or calendula ointment
- antibiotic ointment or spray (for cuts and scrapes)
- tweezers and a sterile needle (to remove splinters)
- Ipecac (to induce vomiting if your child overdoses on peculiar substances)
- Q-Tips and cotton balls
- sterile gauze pads (for applying direct pressure to cuts)
- insect repellent
- Band-Aids (of course)

Though this list seems long, the items take up very little space in a suitcase. Remember, you don't have to pack a lifetime supply of any of these things. A small supply will meet the immediate need and buy you time to find a drugstore.

Knowing What Questions to Ask

Sometimes it seems as if there are almost as many pricing schedules, package plans, and special programs as there are stars in the sky. There are EP, MAP, FAP, golf and tennis packages, weekend specials, and midweek discounts. Depending on geographical location, high season is winter at one resort and summer at another. Even the seasons are defined arbitrarily. Summer may be the end of June through Labor Day or, perhaps, Memorial Day through Labor Day. Christmas season starts December 15 at some places and a week later at others. All the jargon and variations on a theme can make you feel like a babe in the woods when contacting a resort about your plans. To avoid arriving someplace and getting halfway through your stay only to find out that you should have taken advantage of some special offer, you have to be savvy in the possibilities and the vocabulary. Even if you aren't familiar with the latest buzzwords, just knowing that different vacation configurations exist puts you a leg up; you can at least ask, "Are there any family discounts or package plans for _____ [fill in the blank— golf, tennis, skiing, etc.]?"

At some resorts, you walk in and pay one price. At others, every hour on the tennis court or every bicycle ride around the block is charged separately. Both approaches have redeeming aspects. To some folks, it's downright annoying to have to constantly reach for a wallet. After all, this is a vacation and they don't want to be troubled with mundane monetary matters. On the other hand, some people would rather pay as they go, laying down the cash for only the services they use. If you've had aquaphobia since childhood and don't care to be within 10 feet of a lake, much less out in the middle rocking a canoe, free boating privileges are worthless. As long as you're in the know as to a resort's practices and policies beforehand, you'll suffer no surprises and no aggravation or disappointment during your visit.

Much of a resort's terminology is self-explanatory, and acronyms may or not be a mystery to you. The most commonly used abbreviations are EP for European Plan, meaning lodging only; MAP for Modified American Plan, which includes two meals a day in the room rate; and FAP for Full American Plan, which includes three meals a day.

Knowing a resort's designation of low and high season is also crucial to your planning. If you're not absolutely wedded to certain dates and you can juggle your schedule on the home front, you might land in the low season simply by altering your plans by a week.

Moving to more detailed information, you may want to ask a resort certain specific questions. The questions outlined here can be used on the resorts described in this book for elaboration on particular points, or you can test them out on places that you discover on your own.

Lodging
Are the accommodations hotel rooms, condominium units, or cottages with kitchens?
   If they are hotel rooms:
   - Are there connecting rooms?
   - Is there a refrigerator in the room? (This is handy for chilling juice and milk and

keeping snacks fresh.)

- What is the range of prices, and is there a reduced rate for children?
- Is there a charge for a crib or rollaway bed?

Dining

What types of dining areas are there? Is there a spot to get the kids a hot dog and a place that tantalizes more refined taste buds?

Is there a dress requirement? (What a disappointment to venture into a tempting restaurant only to learn that gentlemen are required to wear jackets and you packed nothing but golf shirts!)

Is there a meal plan? Is it mandatory or optional?

Kids

Is there a supervised program for children?

- What are the planned activities, and what are the ages of the children who participate?
- When is it held—times of the year, days of the week, and hours of the day? (The level of specificity may seem a little overboard, but consider a Monday-through-Friday-morning program: It's not going to be much help if you pull in at 1:00 P.M. on Friday and leave at 10:00 A.M. Tuesday.)

What is the daily or hourly fee?

- Is there a playground or game room? (Even if you're doing the supervision, if there's something amusing for the kids, they can release some energy and you can sit on the sidelines and read the newspaper.)

Are baby-sitting services available?

- Who makes the arrangements—you or the resort staff?
- What is the average rate? (You may linger a bit longer over that fine cabernet if your baby-sitter receives $3.00 an hour rather than $6.00 an hour.)

And if you're skittish about your kid's health or proclivity toward disaster, inquire about local medical facilities.

- Is there a doctor or nurse in residence or on call?
- Where are the nearest hospital and pharmacy?

For You

If you're investigating a resort or have chosen it as a vacation destination, you no doubt have an inkling as to its recreational facilities. You're looking at it because of its beach, golf course, tennis center, or ski mountain. Besides its main attraction, you'll also want to know what secondary diversions are possible. You can't play golf sixteen hours a day—not even Tiger Woods does that. So ask:

- Is there a jogging path? Parcourse fitness trail? Hiking trails?
- Is there a spa or exercise room? Sauna, steam room, whirlpool?
- Does the tennis complex also house racquetball courts? Indoor courts?
- For golf, tennis, and fishing, is it possible to rent equipment, or is it necessary to bring your own?
- Are there any concerts, lectures, or classes?

Your interests will determine which questions to ask. Once you get a handle on what to ask, you'll find planning a vacation a lot more fun and a lot less time-consuming. You don't have to have all the answers; just being able to pose a few intelligent questions sets the ball in motion and can generate maybe even more information than you thought you wanted. As a knowledgeable consumer, you can pursue plans on your own or you can work quite effectively with a travel agent. In either case, a little self-education can certainly enhance the preparation and the end product: your leisure time.

Information, Please

Travel, like so much else today, has become increasingly complicated. Since the deregulation of the airlines, the proliferation of airfares has been phenomenal. Any given pair of cities has up to one hundred different fares, with as many rules and regulations. While this ulti-mately benefits the pleasure traveler, it also creates a certain amount of chaos. On a trip from New York to San Francisco, for example, the same seat in the airplane can cost any-where between $299 and $1,499, depending on how far in advance you book, how long you're staying, and the promotional needs of the air carrier. When one adds other factors such as the day of the week, certain airports, one-stop versus nonstop flights, or whether you're wearing polka dots, more complica-tions arise. While airlines generally give you their own lowest fares, they do not necessarily tell you about a competitor who may have even lower fares or more convenient flights.

The Internet provides what seems like an unlimited amount of information, as well as a direct and efficient system for travel suppliers to market their wares. Airlines constantly evaluate their "load factors"—how many empty seats remain on each flight. Once that airplane takes off, each empty seat is "dead" and has earned no revenue. The same is true of hotels—an empty room night cannot be profitable. Therefore, more and more, airlines are offering last-minute flights, particularly on weekends, in an effort to fill those seats. They are also offering lower fares, additional frequent-flier miles, and other incentives to encourage travelers to directly book on-line. Hotels and car-rental companies are following suit and wooing travelers with free nights, upgrades, and special offers. Developing "brand loyalty" has long been a goal of travel suppliers; the advent of the Internet has inten-sified that process.

Incredible amounts of information exist in cyberspace. You can get lost for hours, some-times pleasurably, sometimes not. Most air-lines, hotels, car-rental companies, tour companies, and cruise lines have their own Web sites. Tourist offices in many states and countries offer virtual tours. Newsletters, chat rooms, and articles abound. A search for "travel with children" quickly gets you started.

Not comfortable with surfing the Web? Ask your ten-year-old to help! Start with Fam-ily Travel Forum (www.familytravelforum.com, 888–FT–FORUM), a comprehensive site for family travel information. The site offers lots of news, deals, and ideas for free; flexible mem-bership plans begin at $3.95 a month for "armchair travelers" and include savings and discount coupons from family-friendly suppli-ers. Encourage your children to share their travel experiences by submitting articles to FTF for publication on their affiliate site, www. KidTravels.com.

Family Travel Network (www.familytravel network.com) is another extensive site for talking on-line with other parents and kids, finding tons of information, hot deals, and travel tips—all free.

Dorothy Jordon, one of the acknowledged pioneers of family travel, offers advice and a quarterly newsletter, *Family Travel Times,* at www.familytraveltimes.com. The site is fairly simple, and Jordon's approach is straightfor-ward and no-nonsense. As she says, "an hon-est publication—written by parents, for parents—based on first-hand research." Sub-scription information is found on the Web site or call (888) 822–4FTT or (212) 477–5524.

This is the age of information overkill; managing this information, sorting through the myriad possibilities, can be mind-boggling. Working with a professional travel agent can add several dimensions to this information process. An agent is a bountiful source of books, brochures, and maps; but more impor-tant are the agent's personal experience, the client base that gives feedback on pros and cons of trips, and close contact with col-leagues in the travel agency who have traveled extensively. Even something as seemingly straightforward as a hotel reservation can be complicated by weekend specials, golf or ten-nis packages, seasons, midweek, and family offers. A good agent is a whiz at interpreting brochures and deciphering the fine print. "Ocean view" does not mean on the beach; in fact, you may have to hang over the balcony with a pair of binoculars to see the ocean. "Secluded" may mean private, or it may mean you have to go 10 miles to find any other signs of life. Finally, you can capitalize on an agent's knowledge of the fares and facilities that each airline provides for children and of any special family-travel offers, such as "kids fly free" and discounts for spouses. A good agent can pull all of this together, analyze your needs, and help make your vacation dream become a coherent reality.

Travel agents provide a service. In the past there was no charge to the traveler for booking airline flights, or reserving hotel rooms and rental cars, as the travel suppliers paid commissions to travel agents. In recent years the airlines have ceased to pay commissions to travel agents. While hotel, cruise lines, and car-rental companies still pay a 5 percent to 10 percent commission to travel agents, many agencies maintain they cannot survive without charging service fees. It has become an accepted practice for agencies to charge for each service they provide. The cost varies according to the services provided—from $10 for issuing an airline ticket to $100 per hour for planning and researching a more complicated trip. If you decide to work with a travel agent, it is vital to establish the charges upfront. If the agent books a hotel abroad, do you have to pay fax or phone charges? If you change your plans, what are the change or cancellation fees? Don't be afraid to ask.

Travel agents are dealers in dreams—in charge of that very precious event, your vacation. You should pick your travel agent as carefully as you would your doctor—or your auto mechanic! It's very nice to go to your Aunt Nelly or your neighbor's first cousin, but a smart consumer considers more substantial factors. A number of people prefer to go to the travel office and talk with the agent face to face. Others are comfortable with a telephone relationship, or even with booking on-line, perhaps with an agency that specializes in family travel. It's important to identify your own particular preferences and to honor them.

Regardless of which method you choose, certain considerations are basic. What are their policies on service charges, refunds, and payments? Are they an appointed agency of the airlines, Amtrak, and the cruise lines? Airline appointments indicate a certain basic financial investment and preparation and the ability to write airline tickets. Agencies are computerized and have the capability to scan quickly for the best fares and most convenient flights, make seat assignments, and request special meals. Ask if they hold your money in an escrow account until your travel date. What insurance do they provide? What is their responsibility to you if the hotel/cruise/tour reservation is canceled or not properly delivered? In short, be proactive. This is your vacation; you should feel comfortable and ask questions—even the same one repeatedly and especially the ones you're afraid may sound dumb.

Whether you use a travel agent or do it yourself, the higher your level of involvement in planning, the more satisfaction you stand to gain from your trip. A good agent should be able to determine the broad outlines of your trip, to respond and listen to your ideas and needs, and to fill in with specific suggestions. The agent should have an idea of your lifestyle, your ideal vacation, and your budget. Your agent should ask, or you should volunteer, what seems to be personal information: How do you like to spend your days? Is shopping important to you? If you have a beach, are you happy? Will you die if you have no evening entertainment, or do you prefer a quiet stroll and a good book? What are your hobbies or special interests? Again, do not be afraid to discuss financial expectations. This can avoid a few nasty surprises—such as having to ransom one of the kids to pay for the trip!

No one knows your expectations as well as

you, so assume some of the legwork for detailed information yourself. Check with the tourist offices of the state or country you plan to visit for brochures and information on special events and attractions. The American Automobile Association (AAA) is an excellent resource for maps and detailed information if you're a member and are driving for part or all of the trip. Travel books and articles are fun for the family and often have good advice on extras or little-known attractions in the area; check your local library for these. Chinaberry Book Service, in San Diego, California (800–776–2242, www.chinaberry.com), has well-selected general books and tapes catalogued for various ages and interests. Also, talk to your friends who have been there, for those real inside tips.

Several tour operators specialize in family travel, working with both travel agents and individual clients. In Chevy Chase, Maryland, Grandtravel does escorted tours for grandparents and grandchildren, both in the United States and abroad (800–247–7651 or www.grandtrvl.com). In San Francisco, California, Rascals in Paradise (800–U–RASCAL or www.rascalsinparadise.com) offers resorts and tours all over the world. Many local agencies are becoming aware of the family market and are beginning to specialize in this field; check your local parents' paper or the travel section of the local Sunday paper for agencies in your area. Several agencies are listed on Family Travel Forum's Web site, www.familytravelforum.com.

Finally, close your suitcase, lock the door, and take off—secure in the knowledge that your advance planning, plus professional help, will make this the best trip ever!

NEW ENGLAND

Maine
Massachusetts
New Hampshire
Vermont

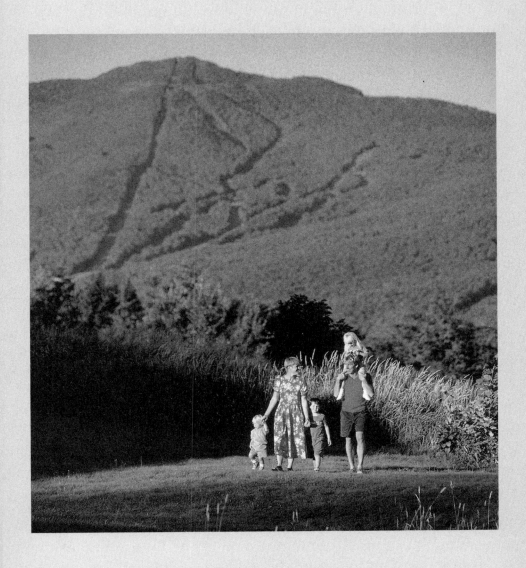

THE BALSAMS GRAND RESORT HOTEL

Dixville Notch, New Hampshire

In the fine tradition of grand old hotels, The Balsams, a 15,000-acre private estate located high in the White Mountains, has been graciously welcoming guests since 1866. The three main buildings are interconnected and quite impressive, with their white facades and red-tiled roofs. Two date from the late 1800s—the Dixville House and The Balsams Inn—and the "new" wing, the Hampshire House, was added in 1917. At the foot of three very precipitous mountains—almost entirely surrounded by steep, 1,000-foot cliffs with the Notch Road the only way in or out—and overlooking Lake Gloriette, The Balsams offers a relaxed escape in a charming atmosphere. In summer Dixville Notch is a refreshing mountain retreat; in winter, a delightful getaway for skiers.

The Balsam's all-inclusive American Plan adds all the amenities for a fun-filled vacation in a worry-free atmosphere. Golf, tennis, swimming, hiking, mountain biking, lawn games, children's day camp, fine dining, and nightly entertainment are available and—an increasingly rare practice these days—at no additional charges for use of any of the facilities. Spring and fall seem to be the seasons for groups and conventions, while the Summer Social Season (late June to early September) and winter (mid-December to late March) are more geared toward individuals and families. Winter activities include skiing, snowboarding, snowshoeing, and skating. Your needs are tended to, your interests can be pursued, and your cares can be dispelled. The resort is open from mid-December until late March, reopening for the summer season from late May to mid-October.

Accommodations: There are 204 rooms at The Balsams, many with views of the mountains or the lake. Family suites with one or two bedrooms offer ample space for youngsters; these are quite popular. The Hampshire House is configured to provide convenient adjoining rooms for family accommodation. All the rooms have been restored, creating a comfortable ambience. Rates depend on the size of the room, its location and view, and the time of the year. Summer rates, per person double, range from $219 to $259. Winter rates range from $170 to $205 (lunch not included). During Christmas season (mid-December to January), rates increase to $175 to $292. Children's rates are on a graduated scale, calculated at $10 per day multiplied by the child's age, with a minimum charge of $40. So, infants to three-year-olds are $40 per day, and so on. These rates are based on a Full American Plan and include unlimited access to all the facilities. Cribs are provided.

Dining: The main dining room serves breakfast, lunch, and dinner during the summer season, breakfast and dinner only during the winter season. And, of course, meals are included in the rates. The summertime luncheon buffet is a sumptuous display of hot and cold entrees, cheeses, fruit, and desserts; you might sample the fried Maine shrimp or the Atlantic salmon. A menu luncheon is available at the Golf Clubhouse. The dinner menu offers an entirely different selection every evening, featuring seafood dishes as well as Long Island duckling, beef, and chicken. At the dinner hour jackets for men are appropriate. Parents are advised to bring appropriate dinner clothes for older children as well.

The Cafe is open for both summer and winter seasons, 10:00 a.m. to midnight, and is perfect for lighter meals (sandwiches and grilled items). In the summer you might try

The Panorama Golf Clubhouse or the poolside bar for refreshments; both offer delightful views and a chance to soak up the beautiful scenery. In the winter warm up with a cup of cider or hot buttered rum in La Cave. Also in winter you'll be shuttling over to The Balsams/Wilderness Ski Area, where breakfast and lunch are served at the base lodge and an a la carte luncheon is served in the dining room. Evening entertainment means cocktails and floor shows in the Switzerland of America Ballroom or dancing in the Wilderness Lounge; both are in the hotel.

Children's World: The Balsams is interested in providing excellent service for its younger guests as well as its adult visitors. For children this translates into a busy schedule of fun activities. Camp Wind Whistle is available from the Fourth of July through Labor Day (seven days a week); here children ages five through thirteen meet with counselors in The Balsams Playroom for sports, games, picnics, swimming, nature walks, arts and crafts, fishing, farm visits, and movies. Outdoor activities are stressed. Children have lunch with their counselors and then, after linking up with Mom and Dad around 4:00 P.M. to share their day's experiences, they can rejoin their young group for dinner at 6:30 P.M. There is no charge for this service. Age groups are divided as follows: five to seven years, eight to ten years, and eleven to thirteen years, with age-appropriate activities. Camp Wee Whistle is a special program for younger children, ages three and four, at no additional charge; during July, call for specific dates.

The outdoor children's area features a state-of-the art fiberglass and stainless steel play structure. The indoor game room (supervised) has an array of board games, video games, and table tennis and pool tables. Open daily from 9:00 A.M. to midnight, the game room is a popular spot for youngsters to gather and make friends during both summer and winter seasons.

In winter children ages three to five can enroll in the Wee Whistle Ski School. Older

children have their own morning and afternoon lessons. The cost is approximately $40 for 1 to 1½ hours. Wintertime room rates for children at The Balsams include ski privileges, but not lessons.

From December through March a well-equipped nursery/play area in the Alpine Base Lodge welcomes children ages six months to five years. The experienced staff amuses children with a selection of games and toys from 9:00 A.M. to 4:00 P.M.; parents may want to join their children for lunch. This service is provided gratis to children of hotel guests. Individual baby-sitters (usually off-duty hotel employees) can be arranged at reasonable rates; sitters should be requested when lodging reservations are made.

Recreation: At The Balsams you can spend busy days of back-to-back events from morning to night or just relax, set an unhurried pace, and enjoy the peace and beauty of the mountains. Two golf courses await golfers. The Panorama, an eighteen-hole championship course, was designed by Donald Ross, a Scottish golf course architect famous during the early twentieth century; set in the mountains, the undulating terrain can be challenging and the views truly stunning. The nine-hole executive course, the Coashaukee, is just right for beginners or those who haven't tested their clubs in a while. There are pro shops at each course, putting greens, a practice fairway, and a pro staff on hand to help you polish your swing. The Centennial Golf School operates in June and features individualized coaching by PGA professionals. The Balsams is the only resort in New England to be named "One of the Nation's Finest Golf Courses" by *Golf Magazine*.

Tennis enthusiasts can choose to play on either red-clay courts (three) or all-weather courts (three). Sign up with the pro for group or private lessons, and stop by the tennis shop to pick up those indispensable accessories.

Swim a few laps in the Olympic-size heated swimming pool overlooking Lake Gloriette. With the mountains in the background, this is an idyllic spot for sunbathing. You might try a refreshing dip in the lake or a relaxing excursion in a paddleboat, canoe, or rowboat. Fish in a crystal-clear mountain stream, hike in the wilderness (solo or with a guided group), or take a nature walk with the staff naturalist. The hotel's natural-history program combines tours, hikes, and discussions for a good introduction to the flora and fauna of the area. The mountain biking trails are well marked and offer fun at every level. Mountain-bike rentals and repairs are available.

Lawn sports include badminton, horseshoes, croquet, volleyball, and shuffleboard; when you head indoors, there are billiards, table tennis, bingo, an aerobic-exercise room, and a movie theater. Take to the library/card room to snuggle up with a good book or play a few hands of bridge, or view wide-screen films in the movie theater. To track down that essential souvenir, drop in at the gift shop, craft shop, gallery, balloon store, and fashion boutique.

In the wintertime this wonderland is draped in snow, and The Balsams/ Wilderness Ski Area

(located on the property) is just a short shuttle ride from the hotel. There are sixteen tree-lined downhill trails and 95 kilometers of packed and groomed trails for cross-country, ranked among the top ten in North America. Wintertime also means ice-skating, snowshoeing on dedicated trails, and riding in horse-drawn sleighs. Like to stay inside? Enroll in the three-day culinary cooking class and prepare a sumptuous four-course meal for family and friends. Whether you're seeking an escape from city crowds or want an active sports-oriented vacation, The Balsams offers the attention and service to make it all possible.

THE BALSAMS GRAND RESORT HOTEL

Dixville Notch, New Hampshire 03576
(603) 255–3400, (800) 255–0600; (800) 255–0800 (in New Hampshire)
www.thebalsams.com

HIGHLAND LODGE
Greensboro, Vermont

Cross-country skiing in Vermont—it sounds so romantic and wholesome. You almost expect to see Bing Crosby round the corner of the lodge. A lovely old white-frame building with a comfortable front porch, the lodge is set on 160 acres bordering Caspian Lake. Open from Christmas to mid-March, the lodge facilities make it easy to enjoy wintertime sports; open again from Memorial Day weekend until mid-October, the lodge is a perfect spot for enjoying the fall foliage colors or for enjoying a summer trip of swimming and boating. Step back in time, relax, and enjoy.

Accommodations: Choose a guest room

in the lodge or one of the cottages just behind the main building. Tastefully decorated with nice furnishings and old-fashioned wallpaper, these accommodations can house approximately sixty guests. The cottages feature a living room, porch, bath, and one to three bedrooms; nine cottages include kitchenettes. Cribs are provided for little ones. Based on a Modified American Plan and double occupancy, rates are $202.50 to $290.00 per night. Children sharing a room or cottage with their parents are charged according to their ages, $35 to $90 a day.

Dining: Two connecting dining rooms in

the lodge serve breakfast, lunch, and dinner. For entrees you may select fresh fish, lamb, duck, veal, or prime rib with vegetables from a local farm, and sample the homemade soups and breads, but be sure to save room for what the staff boasts are sinful desserts. You might sit near the fireplace in the dining room or by the large windows to take in the view; weather permitting, dining tables are set up on the porch. A Modified American meal plan is offered, and there are children's portions and special items for youngsters.

Children's World: A swing set and a sand-box stocked with toys attract little ones. There are tennis and hiking for older children. For children of all ages, swimming at the super-vised private beach is a great way to spend the afternoon. After a busy day kids may settle into the children's library, where they'll find books, games, and puzzles. In the mornings during July and August, youngsters ages four to nine link up with the Play Lady, who devises programs of crafts, swimming, and nature hikes; this is free of charge to guests. In addi-tion, the staff can make arrangements for individual baby-sitters.

Recreation: Thirty miles of groomed cross-country ski trails meander through fields and forests and across frozen lakes. You can line up a guided tour or pick up a little instruction. Bring your own equipment or rent the neces-sary paraphernalia at the ski shop. Snowshoe trails and rentals are also available.

Enjoy the sights and sounds of nature in both summer and winter with a resident nat-uralist on guided nature walks. In warmer weather hike or jog in the adjoining Barr Hill Nature Preserve, walk the lodge's nature trail, rent a bicycle, or take to the water: swim at the beach or head out on the lake in a canoe, sailboat, or paddleboat provided by the lodge. The lake also means good fishing, par-ticularly in early summer and fall; set your line for salmon, trout, or perch.

Back on land, challenge another guest to a tennis match on the clay court and then round up a game of badminton, volleyball, or croquet on the lawn. The nearby Green Mountains and White Mountains lure guests into afternoon driving and hiking excursions. Or simply sit on the wide verandah and let it all come to you.

HIGHLAND LODGE

Caspian Lake
1608 Craftsburg Road
Greensboro, Vermont 05841
(802) 533–2647
www.highlandlodge.com

KILLINGTON SKI AND SUMMER RESORT
Killington, Vermont

Killington is the largest ski area in the eastern United States, and its vital statis-tics are indeed impressive: 212 runs on six interconnected mountains, plus Pico Mountain at Killington; more than 3,000 ver-tical feet; and a ski season that starts in mid-October and continues to June. Killing-ton boasts an average annual snowfall of 250 inches. To ensure it has the earli-est opening date and latest closing date in the East, sophisticated snowmaking techniques assist Mother Nature. Thirty-three lifts, including an eight-passenger heated gondola, get you quickly to the top.

A year-round resort, Killington is cradled in the Green Mountains of central Vermont, a setting whose beauty does not wane with the melting snow; in late spring and summer, the lush green landscape is the backdrop for tennis and golf holidays; in autumn the fall foliage colors take over.

Accommodations: There are almost 200 properties at Killington, ranging from small inns and lodges to condominium complexes and private houses. Killington Central Reservations (800–621–6867) lists more than 115 of these and publishes helpful, descriptive information clearly outlining the many package plans available. Ski-in locations include Trailside Lodge, with standard rooms/bunk beds, Trailside Village, Sunrise Village, and Spruce Glen condos. Rates are lower in summer and higher at holiday periods. Call or check the Web site for the latest rates.

Killington Resort Villages (800–343–0762) offers hotel-style and one-, two-, and three-bedroom condos, some within walking distance of the slopes, plus several other condominium complexes. The Grand Resort Hotel is 50 yards from the lift, while Sunrise Mountain Village in Bear Mountain Base Lodge has its own lift and trails. Condominiums not within walking distance but right at the base of Killington Mountain include Edgemont, Whiffletree, Highridge, Mountain Green, and Pinnacle. Studio to four-bedroom units have fully equipped kitchens and fireplaces. Some condominiums have special features, such as indoor pools or spa/exercise facilities (if you don't get enough on the slopes!). Shuttles run every fifteen to twenty minutes in winter.

Lodgings near the Snowshed Base Lodge may be the most convenient location for families, as this is one of the main lodges for adult lessons/activities and is also located across the street (connected by an underground passageway) from the Rams Head Base Lodge, where children's activities and day care are held.

Dining: In addition to the half dozen cafe-terias at the bases of and on the mountains, in the area you'll find Italian, Chinese, Mexican, and German restaurants, or perhaps you'll sample French country dinners at the Red Clover Inn, typical New England dishes at the Vermont Inn, or Continental cuisine at the Casa Bella. Open in summer, the Clubhouse Grill is located across from Snowshed Base Lodge. Pubs and nightclubs provide late-evening entertainment in winter and summer.

Children's World: Whether your child is six weeks old or twelve years old, a first-time skier or a veteran, he or she will find a niche at Killington's Children's Center. Open daily from 8:00 A.M. to 4:30 P.M., the staff orchestrates indoor and outdoor play for infants to six-year-olds. First Tracks Ski School, for four- to six-year-olds, includes ski and snowboard lessons as well as supervised play (half day $66; full day $99); the Superstars Ski Program groups seven- to twelve-year-olds by ability for a full day of ski and play. Full-day fees ($95) include lunch; half-day sessions ($74) are available for the nonskiing and introductory skiing groups. For teenagers there's a weekly under-twenty-one disco with DJ or live bands, soda, and pizza. In December and March special weeks for teens are scheduled as well. The winter children's program runs from November through the first week of April.

Summer kids' programs in July and August offer a wide variety of outdoor fun. Day care for children ages six weeks to six years is offered at the Grand Resort Hotel from 8:00 A.M. to 4:30 P.M.; cost is $69 per day or two days for $121.

Beattie's Trailside Lodge (800–447–2209; www.camptrailside.com) offers an organized summer camp program for nine- to twelve-and thirteen- to sixteen-year-olds. One-week sessions begin on Sunday and have such themes as "Up the Wall, Up the Creek," "Kids on Stage," and "Earth Avengers." Cost is $575 per week; lodgings accommodate up to five campers per room in a typical New England lodge. Campers use all of the facilities in and around Killington for mountain bikes, hikes, horseback riding, water slides, and all manner of adventure.

Recreation: Start your visit with a Meet the Mountain tour; skiers are grouped by ability and guided through a complimentary two-hour introduction to Killington's mountains. All seven mountains are accessed by the same lift ticket. All have beginner runs from their summits so that even novices can enjoy top-of-the-mountain views. From long lazy runs (one beginner's trail is 10 miles long) to steeply pitched expert terrain, every skier finds the appropriate challenge. This goes for ski and snowboard clinics too, from classes for the newest beginner to workshops in racing for the advanced skier.

Après-ski activities include free sleigh rides in the country and movies in the village, ice-skating, rock climbing, snowmobiles, puppet shows, and ice-cream sundaes. Or maybe most appropriate for the end of an active day is a quiet rest in a sauna.

Summertime brings golf on an eighteen-hole course; tennis at the Killington School for Tennis; fishing, hiking, mountain biking, and horseback riding in the mountains. There's something for everyone, from adventures with the Bungee Thing or water slides to art and antiquing.

KILLINGTON SKI AND SUMMER RESORT

4763 Killington Road
Killington, Vermont 05751
(800) 621–MTNS
www.Killington.com

THE LIGHTHOUSE INN
West Dennis, Massachusetts

An old-fashioned country inn, The Lighthouse Inn sits on the shores of Nantucket Sound. It was originally constructed in 1854 as a lighthouse called the Bass River Light, which was operative until 1914. In 1938 the Stone family purchased the Lighthouse property, and three generations later they still own and operate the inn. After being dark for 75 years, the light was relit in 1989, and is the only privately owned, privately maintained working lighthouse in the country, now recognized by the Coast Guard as the West Dennis Light. The classic Cape Cod–style main house provides a beautiful view of the ocean; sprawling out behind are nine secluded acres with additional accommodations and recreational facilities.

Accommodations: The main house offers individual rooms and suites. Alternatively, you might choose one of the cottages with one to three bedrooms. Rooms begin at $218 a night (including breakfast) in the summer season; mid-may through June and early September to mid-October, deduct $35 per person from all rates. Children sharing a room or cottage with their parents are charged a graduated rate depending on their ages: ages three to nine, $45 a day; ten and older, $65 a day. The daily rate for children includes breakfast and dinner. For adults, dinner is approximately $50 more per day. One-bedroom cottages begin at $298; two bedrooms at $447.

Dining: The dining room in the main house entices guests with fresh fish and lobster dinners and lovely views over the water. Outdoors, the oceanside deck is the setting for a la carte lunches. A snack bar adjoins the pool, serving light lunches and beverages during July and August. Once a week a poolside cookout is planned.

A really nice touch is that all children are welcomed to a special InnKids Dinner offered each evening. They may order their favorite meal in advance, eat, and play with their peers—all in a separate area from the more formal Main Dining Room, where proper attire is requested, and parents can tarry over a relaxed dinner. Evening entertainment in the Sand Bar ranges from boogie-woogie piano to jazz saxophones.

Children's World: Games, swimming, arts and crafts, sand-castle building, kite flying, miniature golf, and nature walks fill the days for InnKids. Three- and four-year-olds participate from 9:30 A.M. to noon, while children ages five and older carry on until 3:00 P.M. In the evening both groups are invited to get together from 5:30 to 8:30 P.M. for dinner and entertainment, perhaps a movie or a magician's show. The InnKids program runs from late June through August and is included in the fees for children noted above. Individual baby-sitting is available on request.

Recreation: Enjoying the soft ocean breezes may be all the activity you want during your first couple of days at The Lighthouse Inn. Renewed and refreshed, you can then jump into the swimming pool, splash in the gentle waters of Nantucket Sound, and stroll along the beach. The outdoor tennis court awaits you when you turn energetic, go golfing at one of five nearby eighteen-hole courses or fishing can be a pleasant morning outing. You can also play table tennis, pool, and shuffleboard or pursue quieter interests in the library/game room. The inn also has a great location for exploring Cape Cod.

THE LIGHTHOUSE INN

1 Lighthouse Inn Road
West Dennis, Massachusetts 02670
(508) 398–2244
www.lighthouseinn.com

MOUNT SNOW
West Dover, Vermont

Nearly fifty years ago, Walter Schoenknecht decided that music, barbecues, and outrageous special events would liven up his ski area. Since other resorts weren't even serving food, he was deemed rather eccentric. But sure enough, old Walt was right, and today that same infectious, creative spirit is not only encouraged, it's one of the core values of the resort.

A very popular New England ski resort, Mount Snow is situated in the beautiful Green Mountains of southern Vermont. Much of its popularity is, no doubt, due to its accessibility and proximity to major Northeast metropolitan areas: A four-and-a-half-hour drive

from New York and two and a half hours from Boston make this a very manageable weekend trip for residents of these cities. But Mount Snow's size and variety also account for its appeal. From gentle beginner and broad intermediate slopes to some of the steepest expert runs in the Northeast, 145 trails in all drop down from a 3,600-foot summit for 1,700 vertical feet. The average annual snowfall is about 170 inches. It is supplemented by sophisticated snowmaking that covers 76 percent of the skiable terrain; the ski season runs from about early November to late April.

Accommodations: Lodging runs the

gamut of possibilities in atmosphere, style, price, and location. From modern condominium complexes to quaint country inns, more than fifty options are within 10 miles of the mountain base. The lodging bureau (800–451–4211) will help you choose the right spot, and various package plans for lodging and lift tickets are offered.

A full-service hotel at the edge of a small lake with grand views of the mountain, Snow Lake Lodge runs free shuttles to/from the slopes. With its own restaurant, game room, and spa, it's also walking distance to evening entertainment at the Snowbarn. Two-day weekend rates range from $318 to $398 with continental breakfast. Seasons and Snow Mountain Village are condominiums near the base, where two-bedroom units start at $1,198 for a two-day weekend. These units have kitchens and fireplaces; some have balconies and mountain views.

The 200-room Grand Summit Resort Hotel is located slopeside in Mount Snow's main base area and offers a variety of rooms, ranging from standard hotel-style rooms to multi-room suites with kitchenettes. Amenities include ski-in/ski-out accommodations, valet parking, a health club, spa and fitness programs, a year-round heated outdoor pool, Harriman's Restaurant, and more. A two-day weekend ranges from $698 to $1,530.

The many country inns around the area can add a distinctly New England flavor to a ski holiday. The charming Hermitage Inn, 3 miles from Mount Snow, maintains 40 miles of cross-country ski trails. The White House of Wilmington also has cross-country trails. Vacation Services (800–245–SNOW) books many of the inns and bed-and-breakfasts.

Dining: At the base of Mount Snow are ten cafeterias and restaurants along with eight bars/lounges; at the Summit Lodge, views over the mountains complement cafeteria-style lunches. Also near the base is the Lakeside Bar and Grill, in the Snow Lake Lodge. Most of the inns and lodges of the area have their own restaurants and feature a variety, from hearty home-style cooking to the Continental cuisine typical of the Hermitage and the White House of Wilmington. Dot's of Dover is reputed to have the best breakfast in town, while TC's and Two Tannery offer fine dining. Many restaurants have children's menus.

Children's World: Throughout the year, kids have a place at Mount Snow. Child Care, a quality program for ages six weeks to six years, is located in the heart of the main base area. The program is fully licensed by the state of Vermont and is designed to be interactive, fun, and developmentally appropriate for each child's needs. Child Care is open weekdays from 8:30 A.M. to 4:30 P.M.; weekends and holidays, 8:00 A.M. to 4:30 P.M. Reservations are required (800–889–4411). A full day is $65, a two-day package is $115; snacks and lunch are provided; however you must supply diapers and infant food. A list of baby-sitters is available through Child Care.

For three-year-olds enrolled in full-day Child Care, Cub Camp offers an introduction to the fun sport of skiing through games and activities both on and off the snow. Cost for full-day child care, lunch, a one-hour snow clinic, and equipment is $87. For children four to twelve, Mount Snow offers Perfect Kids ski and snowboard clinics. Snow Camp is divided into full- and half-day sessions and is designed especially for children four through six years of age. Children are placed in small groups based upon their age and ability levels, and groups ski, take breaks, and have fun together. Full-day programs include lunch and cost $87; half days cost $52. Mountain Camp and Mountain Riders is for seven- to fourteen-year-olds; rates are $72 for a full day with lunch and $38 for half days. Rental equipment is not included and begins at $23 per day; junior lift tickets are also required. Children new to skiing or snowboarding can enjoy expanded, private learning terrain. All Perfect Kids programs are centrally located in the main base area.

Children under five ski/ride free, while kids ages twelve and under ski/ride free when their parents purchase a five-day non-holiday lift ticket. During "Teddy Bear Ski Weeks," three- to five-day vacation packages include lodging, lift tickets, and many fun family activities. The week is filled with games, activities, pancake breakfasts, ice-cream parties, fun races, and free tubing. Mount Snow also offers a new lift-served snow tubing park open every day and weekend nights. The Galaxy Arcade is open daily in the main base area and features video games, recreational games, a penny candy counter, and a lounge area.

Summer is in full swing from mid-June through August with Mount Snow's Kids Camps. The Child Care program is available, again offering individual playrooms and programs for ages six weeks to six years. Activities include arts & crafts, water play, puppet shows, mini–nature hikes, gardening, games, and music. Special rest areas are also provided for quiet time. Mount Snow's Summer Kids Camps offer children a variety of activities, adventure-themed weeks, and hands-on exploration. Junior Adventure Camp, for children ages five through eight, serves up a variety of outdoor activities including scavenger hunts, swimming, field trips to local sites and attractions, chairlift rides and nature hikes, a climbing wall, and arts and crafts. Children ages nine through twelve can enroll in Adventure Camp and do all of that plus mountain-bike and golf. Kids Camps are offered Monday through Friday from June 16 through August 30 and Saturday from July 5 through August 30. Child Care is offered Monday through Friday only. Operation times are from 9:00 A.M. to 4:00 P.M. Rates for both programs are $50 per day ($225 for five days). Reservations are required and can be made by calling (800) 889–4411.

Recreation: Almost 50 percent of the runs at Mount Snow are ranked intermediate. The rest are just about evenly split between beginner and expert. The Main Mountain has forty beginner and intermediate trails, the North

Face with its steeper terrain and moguls attracts advanced skiers, and the Sunbrook area with sunny southern exposure supports a couple of long lazy runs. The teaching staff is prepared to show you the way to improved techniques, and you have your pick of packages for various combinations of lifts, lessons, and equipment.

For cross-country skiers, four touring centers are within 10 miles of Mount Snow at the Hermitage, Sitzmark, Timber Creek, and White House. Also within this distance are three stables—Beaver Brook, Flames, and Adams Farm—where you can arrange sleigh rides. Other winter sports include snowmobiling, a tubing park, nearby snow shoeing and ice-skating. If your tastes run to being pampered, schedule a session at the Grand Summit Spa, or curl up in front of the fire with a hot drink.

When the mountains turn green, the big event is the Golf School, held on the championship Geoffrey Cornish course. More warm-weather activities include swimming, fishing, hiking, biking, and horseback riding. Sit back and enjoy the scenery from one of the scenic chairlift rides, or prowl through the unique shops that feature the crafts, pottery, wood carving, and antiques to be found only in Vermont. The whole family will love Adams Farm, a sixth-generation working farm, home to more than one hundred friendly farm animals that you can visit and interact with. Take a hayride, wander through the craft and quilt shops, or enjoy a bonfire and marshmallow roast.

MOUNT SNOW

Route 100
West Dover, Vermont 05356
(802) 464–3333, (800) 245–7669
www.mountsnow.com

THE MOUNT WASHINGTON HOTEL & RESORT

Bretton Woods, New Hampshire

Majestic Mount Washington presides over this resort, a massive complex of lodging, dining, and recreational facilities on 2,600 acres of wooded New Hampshire countryside in the White Mountains. Voted a *Better Homes and Gardens* "Favorite Family Resort," the architectural gem and focal point of this New England resort is the gracious and stately hotel. Built in 1902 by the industrialist and railroad tycoon Joseph Stickney, the hotel began welcoming visitors to a lifestyle of classic elegance and soon claimed its status among prime vacation retreats of the Northeast.

International fame came to Bretton Woods in 1944 when the hotel hosted financiers from forty-four countries who created the World Bank and the International Monetary Fund and set the gold standard at $35 an ounce (ah—the good old days). In 1978 this fine old structure—with its wonderfully spacious verandah furnished with white wicker chairs and settees, and its 150-foot-long lobby—was added to the National Register of Historic Places. Since 1986 it has held the distinction of being a National Historic Landmark. The goal of becoming a year-round resort has been realized with the resort's purchase of the popular Bretton Woods Ski Area in 1997 and the winter opening of the Mount Washington Hotel in 1999.

Accommodations: The 200-room hotel offers standard to deluxe lodging with a number of two-bedroom family suites. Nearly all have views of Mount Washington, the Willey-Rosebrook Mountain range, or the well-tended gardens. All guests in the hotel participate in a Modified American Plan, and per-person prices range from $115 to $455 for double occupancy. Children under age four stay for free, ages five to twelve are $35, and over twelve are $70. A family chamber costs $500 to $1,320 a night and accommodates up to four persons. The thirty-four rooms and suites of the Bretton Arms Country Inn, also a National Historic Landmark, offer accommodations in the atmosphere of a Victorian inn. Guests here enjoy all the facilities of the main hotel. Bed-and-breakfast prices range from $55 to $195 per person per night; children's rates are the same as the hotel's. The Bretton Arms is open year-round.

Also open year-round, The Lodge at Bretton Woods, located across from the hotel's entrance, offers contemporary accommodations at rates of $79 to $199 per night, meals not included.

For an economical alternative, the Town-homes at Bretton Woods provide ample space for parties of two to twelve people; situated on the mountainside, these one- to five-bedroom units (with full kitchens) run from $149 to $599 per night, depending on the size of the unit and the season. All guests have access to all resort recreational facilities at established guest rates. Cribs are complimentary, and cots are available at $10 a night. Inquire also about special seven-day vacation packages.

Dining: With all the different dining arrangements, your biggest problem will be deciding where to pick up your napkin. From casual, light meals to gracious, formal dinners, it just depends on how the spirit moves you. The main dining room of the Mount Washington Hotel is a large octagonal space (heaven forbid anyone should be relegated to a corner!) glimmering with crystal chandeliers and stained-glass windows. The menu changes nightly and features Continental cuisine and regional American dishes. In this elegant setting, with orchestra music and views of Mount Washington, guests are invited to regard dinner as a dress-up affair; jackets are required for men, and ladies and children should dress appropriately. Sumptuous breakfasts are also served in the dining room.

The Bretton Arms dining room is also open year-round for breakfast and dinner; here the evening meal features classic New England cuisine. For lunch and dinner, Stickney's Restaurant (located on the lower concourse of the hotel) has a cafe atmosphere and specializes in lighter fare—salads, sandwiches, and light entrees; afternoon cocktails are also served here. Darby's Restaurant in the lodge serves breakfast and dinner; guests enjoy family dining in a warm, rustic atmosphere, along with scenic views of the mountains and the hotel. For sandwiches, Italian fare, and seafood, Fabyan's Station is open year-round for lunch and dinner. A restored railroad depot from the Victorian era, Fabyan's is near the base of the ski area about a mile from the hotel. The base lodge at the ski area offers full lunch and dinner at the Slopeside Restaurant and Lounge as well as quick breakfasts and lunches cafeteria-style for those eager to hit the slopes. The midmountain Top O' Quad restaurant serves lunch with spectacular mountain views in winter.

For sipping cocktails, you may want to linger at Stickney's, Darby's, or Fabyan's. Or try the unique Rosebrook Lounge, set behind the grand staircase and serving on the porch and verandah, weather permitting. The Cave Lounge, located in the lower lobby of the hotel, offers a speakeasy atmosphere and nightly live entertainment that transports you to the Roaring Twenties. The elegant Princess Lounge is perfect for before- and after-dinner cocktails. The Pool Bar offers refreshments on warm summer days.

Children's World: Late June through Labor Day, and on holiday weekends in spring and fall, the hotel sponsors the King of the Mountain Kids Kamp for children five to twelve. Upon check-in, kids receive a special welcome pack with newsletters, the Birthday Klub—even a free T-shirt. Enroll your child for a full- or half-day program with adventures like hiking in the woods, treks to the stables,

swimming, tennis, "Cooking with the Chef," "Putting with the Pro," and crafts sessions. The program is from 9:00 A.M. to noon and from 1:00 to 4:00 P.M. The cost is $40 for full day, $25 for a half day. Lunch is available for $7.25. There's also an evening program ($15) from 6:00 to 9:00 P.M. so that parents can dine quietly alone. Guests not on the Modified American Plan pay an additional $10 for dinner. Babysitting can be arranged for children under the age of five. The resort charges a $10.00 processing fee; rates are $8.00 per hour, plus $2.00 for each additional child. Reservations are required for all programs.

In the wintertime, the Babes in the Woods nursery at the ski area lodge takes children from two months to five years for an indoor program costing $59 full day or $45 half day. Open 8:00 A.M. to 4:30 P.M. Children ages four to twelve participate in the Hobbit Children's Ski and Snowboard School, however, snowboarding is only for ages eight to twelve. Rates for lifts, two lessons, equipment, and lunch are $89 a day. Half-days are $69. Those children under age five and toilet trained, who are new to the slopes, can join a snow play and ski-readiness program at the same rates.

In 2002, *Ski Magazine* rated Bretton Woods number two in North America for family programs.

Recreation: You'll never be at a loss for things to do at Bretton Woods; your only dilemma may be trying to fit in all the activities. You may start your day jogging on one of the many marked trails ranging from 1 to 11 miles in length and graded by levels of difficulty.

Then stroll over to the first tee for a match on the eighteen-hole Donald Ross–designed championship golf course or the challenging nine-hole Pleasant Course and take in the rolling terrain and mountain views, or sharpen your skills on the putting green and driving range. The Golf Club Pro Shop can meet all your needs for equipment and accessories (including attire) and can assist in scheduling lessons.

There are two heated pools at the hotel (one outdoor and a smaller indoor one) and another indoor heated pool at the lodge; both locations have a sauna, and the lodge facility includes a Jacuzzi as well. Or you can take a refreshing dip in the Ammonoosuc River.

Tennis buffs can head over to one of twelve well-groomed red-clay courts or join the tennis program for instruction (group and private lessons) at all levels of expertise.

The horseback-riding stables mean good fun for those who want their exercise sitting down. Set in an old Victorian building, the stables offer lessons and guided trail rides on the 50 miles of picturesque trails in the woods and fields. The woods are captivating whether you choose horseback riding or hiking (maybe you'll link up with a guided tour or a nature walk).

Other diversions include trout fishing, a game of badminton, croquet, volleyball, or horseshoes; an afternoon of bicycling; a sunset carriage ride; or an hour in the game room for billiards, table tennis, and video games (particularly big with the seven- to fourteen-year-old group). Your interests may take you to a night at the movies, a fashion show, an aerobics class, a bridge tournament, or a presentation of fine culinary techniques (these often include a bit of wine, sampling a dish, and a tour of the kitchen). The activities staff is on hand full-time to plan interesting and varied events. For some private, quiet time, wander into the library or relax under the nimble fingers of an expert massage therapist.

Music is special at Mount Washington. Chamber-music recitals are held frequently in the Conservatory, live music is featured in the Cave Lounge, and the Mount Washington Orchestra will dance you off your toes nightly during dinner.

Kids love an excursion on the Mount Washington Cog Railway, the original "little train that could." Built in 1869, it was the world's first mountain-climbing cog railroad, and it remains the only one still powered entirely by steam. The (breathtaking!) round-trip takes about three hours, and you can visit the mile-high park and observation center at the top.

Stickney Street, in the lower concourse of

the hotel, is an array of shops featuring gifts, crafts, fashions, ice-cream delights, flowers, and the hotel's own post office.

Wintertime explodes in skiing events at Bretton Woods. The Bretton Woods Touring Center, housed in a Victorian-style building, is one of the finest cross-country skiing complexes in the East. There are approximately 100 kilometers (60 miles) of beautifully groomed trails among the firs and birches of the scenic countryside and the White Mountain National Forest; three different trail systems are ranked in difficulty. Head out on your own, enroll for instruction, or join a daytime guided tour or a moonlight trek. Alpine skiers and snowboarders are delighted with the expansion done in the past decade. This once modest ski area with a 1,100-foot vertical drop has added 400 vertical feet and now boasts seventy-six trails serviced by eight lifts. The addition of West Mountain makes Bretton Woods the largest ski area in New Hampshire. And it's set to become even larger with the addition in 2004 of Mount Stickney. The ski season lasts from late November to mid-April; the average annual snowfall is 200-plus inches, and 95 percent of the trails are covered by snowmaking equipment to assist Mother Nature. In addition to the children's ski school, instruction for the more advanced is also available, accommodating all skiing levels in your family.

Add snowmobiling, snow tubing, ice-skating, snowshoeing, sleigh rides, and winter hiking trails, and there's enough to keep you busy for two vacations.

THE MOUNT WASHINGTON HOTEL & RESORT

Route 302
Bretton Woods, New Hampshire 03575
(603) 278–1000, (800) 258–0330
www.mtwashington.com

SMUGGLERS' NOTCH RESORT

Smugglers' Notch, Vermont

The Green Mountains of Vermont are not just about beautiful foliage colors in the autumn and skiing fun in the winter. Smugglers' Notch Resort makes sure there's much more to enjoy all year long. This is our idea of a true "family resort." Tucked in the rolling hills and mountains of northern Vermont, Smugglers' Notch is a self-contained resort village with sports facilities and getaway relaxation potential for the whole family. In winter, when Mother Nature blankets the region in snow, skiing on the three interconnected mountains is the primary activity. Tennis, hiking, swimming, and horseback riding are favorite pastimes when the weather warms. Any time of year one can explore the natural beauty and charm surrounding this mountain village and experience family fun—guaranteed! Yes, the resort guarantees families will have fun or it refunds the activity portion of their stay. Maybe that's why for the past five years, Smugglers' Notch has been voted the number one family resort by *Ski Magazine*, and the number one family resort in the Northeast by *FamilyFun*, a Disney publication, for the past four years.

Accommodations: Almost 600 condominium units are arranged in clusters of two- and three-story, modern but rustic buildings. From these all the amenities of the village are accessible by foot or free shuttle service. Most of the units have fireplaces and private balconies, and all have completely equipped kitchens or kitchenettes. Size varies from studios to five-bedroom apartments.

The Club Smugglers' package plans cover lodging and most of the recreational activities. For example, the summertime FamilyFest program for seven days and seven nights includes accommodation in a one-bedroom condo (which sleeps four), full-day programs for children three to seventeen, guided walks and hikes, swimming and water sliding, and evening entertainment for both families and adults, from $1,759 to $2,895 (rates based on dates of stay). A winter five-day package for a family of four in the same type of lodging runs about $2,050; this includes lift tickets, lessons (Nordic, Alpine, snowboard, cross-country, telemark, and shaped skis), outdoor ice-skating, welcome parties, swimming pool, sauna, and après-ski activities. A crib or extra futon cot for two- to seven-year-olds can be provided for $20 for the entire stay.

Dining: Though you may opt to cook in your condo, there are several restaurants in the village when dining out seems better than facing a skillet. The Green Mountain Cafe and Bakery serves home-baked breakfast treats and hot lunches with fresh-roasted specialty coffees. The Mountain Grille is open for all three meals, including light fare available well into the evening and a special buffet for children. At the Hearth & Candle, parents enjoy nouveau cuisine, and at Riga-Bello's all ages savor the ever-popular Italian favorites—pizza, calzones, salads, and beverages—to eat in or have delivered to their condo. For ice-cream treats, there's the Village Creamery or Ben and Jerry's Scoop Shop, or choose refreshing drinks at the Sports Bar, with its big-screen TV.

The Mountainside Cabana is a relaxing summertime spot for lunch and cocktails. And teenagers even have their own clubhouses, the Outer Limits and Teen Alley, open daily from 5:00 P.M. to midnight, serving juice and soda. For extras, snacks, and wines stop by the Village Country Store.

Children's World: The Smugglers' Discovery Dynamos Camp operates from early December to the beginning of April. Three- to five-year-olds join their ski host for morning and afternoon ski lessons, tractor rides, movies, and arts and crafts. Skiers and boarders ages six to ten meet with the Adventure Rangers Ski or Snowboard Camp for lessons, snow soccer, and races. The Notch Squad, for ages eleven to fourteen, increases the adventure with more emphasis on improving skills. Après-ski activities include a daily bonfire at 3:30 P.M. with hot chocolate for parents and children. With lunch included, the daily rate for these programs, 9:30 A.M. to 4:00 P.M., is $95, or $69 on a Club Smugglers' package.

For teens ages fifteen to seventeen, Mountain Explorers offers challenging instruction and techniques, racing development, and a great way to make new friends. With the Outer Limits and Teen Alley teen centers and scheduled daily activities at 7:00 and 9:00 P.M., teenagers have plenty to do.

For younger, nonskiing children (six weeks to three years), Treasures is just that. Located in a quiet, sunlit slopeside area of the resort, Treasures offers ten rooms of real state-of-the-art facilities. There are kid-size bathrooms, a complete kitchen, an infant "crawler room" equipped with mirrors and soft-sculpture gym, a separate crib room for naps, a closet of costumes, radiant floor heating, and an indoor jungle gym. Open from 8:30 A.M. to 4:30 P.M. during ski season, staffed with professionals, and boasting a ratio of one caretaker to four children, it's available at $15 per hour for up to three hours, then reverts to a full-day charge of $66.

During the summer season, from the beginning of June through Labor Day, days and nights are filled with fun events: outdoor games, fishing, arts and crafts, hiking, treasure hunts, and swimming. At the playground are swings, climbing equipment, and a sandbox. The day camps are included in the price of the FamilyFest vacation. Summer Fun University allows kids to major in fun and minor in a variety of other activities like arts and crafts, nature and hiking, or adventure and games. So, they'll get the same great activities always offered in the all-day camps, plus a special focus of their own choosing. They'll join the Discovery Dynamos (ages three to five); Adventure Rangers (ages six to ten); The Notch Squad (ages eleven to fourteen); or Mountain Explorers (teens fifteen to seventeen); all from 10:00 A.M. to 4:00 P.M. daily. Teen Alley (ages thirteen to fifteen) and the Outer Limits (ages sixteen and older) provide gathering centers with all those things dear to teens—video games, Internet access, music and dancing, and no parents! Optional programs, for extra fees, include tennis camps; overnight hikes; "Wheels," clinics in mountain boarding (blending snowboard and skateboard) and "digglering" (a cross between a mountain bike and snowboard); and Video Camp, where kids learn the basics of camera operation, make their own video, and enjoy watching their directorial debut weekly at Smugglers' Vermont Country Fair. The fair is a taste of a small New England fair, with cotton candy, entertainers, and lots of family games and contests.

Treasures Child Care Center is the new fully certified, $1 million facility for children ages six weeks and older, with special features like giant fish tanks in every room, one-way mirror viewing for parents, 5,400 square feet of indoor space, and over 4,000 square feet of outdoor playground. Rates are $66 per day, or $15 per hour for up to three hours. If you prefer, individual baby-sitters are available in your condo at $9 per hour for one child, $1 per hour each additional child. Smugglers' has a great understanding of kids of all ages, and more options than it's possible to list. Check the Web site for all the details and watch your kids get super-excited.

A nice feature is Kids Night Out, when children ages three to eleven are invited to dinner and a fun evening from 6:00 to 10:00 P.M. The cost is $25 per child.

The fun doesn't end in the fall. For families with children under five, AutumnFest packages provide morning programs for children six weeks to five years (all day on Wednesday and Thursday) with family fun in the afternoons, amidst that gorgeous Vermont foliage—and at the lowest rates of the year.

Recreation: A network of seventy-two trails on three interconnected mountains is the focus of wintertime play. The ski season runs from Thanksgiving to mid-April, and the average annual snowfall of 286 inches is supplemented by snowmaking equipment covering 62 percent of the terrain. The three mountains fall more or less into novice, inter-mediate, and advanced runs, but each mountain offers skiing for all levels of expertise. The total vertical drop is just over 2,600 feet making it Northern Vermont's biggest. For the cross-country skier, 14 miles of trails roam through the mountains. Lessons in cross-country skiing, downhill skiing, and snow-boarding can help you learn as a beginner or improve your skills. Smugglers' has six Learning and Fun Parks, geared from rank beginner to expert. You might also try ice-skating with the kids or snowshoeing, an increasingly popular sport. Experience the winter woods on your own two feet, with dedicated snowshoe-ing trails, guided family tours, or for the more adventurous, a lift ride up the mountain, and a walk down.

Turning indoors, you can enjoy the benefits of The Tub Club, with an exercise room and whirlpool and sauna facilities. The FunZone offers indoor play for all ages: inflatables, rolling in the ball slides, table tennis, basketball, and jousts (very popular with teens), and even a little minigolf. Also in winter, the large, heated swimming pool is covered with a bubble, so pack your swimsuit along with your ski sweater.

In summer the bubble comes down. There's a water slide called the Flume, a baby wading pool, and a seventeen-person outdoor hot tub. Free swimming instruction is provided as part of the day-camp program, and adults can join the Aqua Aerobics for a good workout.

Notchville Park, Smugglers' newest water playground, encompasses three acres with three pools in a unique, tiered hillside setting. In addition to 5,000 square feet of water, the park includes Raven's Roost Climbing Tower, Catbird's Croquet Court, Sand Swallow's Vol-leyball Court, Peregrine's Picnic Pavilion, and the Half-Moon Bath House.

The Mountainside Pools is a third, separate water facility that includes a turtle slide (for chil-dren ages three to eight years), the Little Smug-

glers' Lagoon (a large splash pool with waterfall, tunnels, fountains, and a lazy river ride), a lap pool, and every parent's delight, the Giant Rapid River Ride—306 feet of twists and thrills on an inner tube beginning 26 feet up in the air. Bath-house, snack bar, and lounging deck with gor-geous mountain views help one recover.

Also a favorite with families is Rum Run-ner's Hideaway, a beautiful swimming lake tucked in the mountains, a short hike or drive away from the village. Access is free to resort guests for swimming, fishing, picnicking, and relaxing; canoes and paddleboats are available for rent. It's a great way to relive the old days and introduce your kids to the joys of summer days at the ole swimmin' hole.

In addition to two indoor courts, there are eight outdoor clay courts; six are lighted for evening play. The Ten Pro Tennis School, which has videotape review, just about guarantees improvement in your game.

Hiking and biking are popular ways to enjoy the mountain countryside, or try jogging on one of the cross-country trails. Head to a mountain stream for perch, pike, and trout fish-ing. Outdoor lawn games include Frisbee, bas-ketball, volleyball, soccer, and shuffleboard. If your inner artist is seeking expression, take a painting or sculpting workshop. And reserve time for a horseback ride at the Vermont Horse Park (services here are not included in the pack-age plans). For those who can't possibly leave home without their golf clubs, courses in nearby Stowe and Morrisville are open to Smugglers' guests, or take a practice time with instruction on Smugglers' own driving range.

SMUGGLERS' NOTCH RESORT

4323 Vermont Route 108 South
Smugglers' Notch, Vermont 05464-9537
(802) 644–8851, (800) 451–8752
www.smuggs.com

STRATTON MOUNTAIN RESORT

Stratton Mountain, Vermont

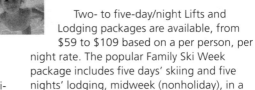

Lessons, lessons, lessons! At Stratton Mountain Resort you can have instruction and training in several major sports. Whether your interests lead you to golf, tennis, swimming, racquetball, cross-country skiing, downhill skiing, telemark skiing, snowboarding, or snowshoeing, you can participate in classes for an introduction to a new sport or for polishing existing skills and techniques.

And where could you find a better place to get into shape and sharpen your sports expertise than in southern Vermont? Stratton Mountain Resort is set on 4,000 acres in the beautiful Green Mountains of Vermont. Since its opening in 1961, the resort has expanded a number of times to enhance the facilities and to attract sports-minded visitors to return again and again. Stratton Mountain is open year-round.

Accommodations: Choose a resort hotel, an alpine lodge, or your own villa. The Stratton Mountain Inn has 125 rooms and suites and also houses a restaurant, lounge, pool, sauna, and tennis courts. Stratton Village Lodge has ninety-one rooms in the heart of the village, just a few steps away from shops, and is considered ski-in/ski-out. The Liftline Lodge offers more traditional accommodations and has its own restaurant. Winter rates at the Stratton Mountain Inn range from $99 to $349; Stratton Village Lodge ranges from $149 to $519 a night; the Liftline Lodge is $119 to $250. All rates are per room, and children under 17 stay for free. Rates vary depending on date, midweek or weekend, packages, and so on. The Stratton Condos are one- to four-bedroom condominium apartments with fully equipped kitchens; many have fireplaces and private balconies. One-, two-, and three-bedroom condos range from $239 to $600 per night.

Two- to five-day/night Lifts and Lodging packages are available, from $59 to $109 based on a per person, per night rate. The popular Family Ski Week package includes five days' skiing and five nights' lodging, midweek (nonholiday), in a two-bedroom condominium. Call for rates and other available packages.

Summer rates at the Mountain Inn begin at $49; studio and one-bedroom condos begin at $110 at the Stratton Condos and Long Trail House, the new condo/lodge with underground parking and outdoor pool. Again, check for special-interest packages.

Dining: The Stone Chimney Grille at the Stratton Mountain Inn serves hearty breakfasts, lunches, and New England cuisine dinners; savor cranberry duck or rack of lamb and pick up the recipe for your favorite dish, graciously shared by the chef. Also at the inn is the Tavern, a cozy spot to sip a hot toddy or your favorite cocktail. Tenderloins is the restaurant and lounge at the Clubhouse on the golf course.

In the winter start your day with breakfast at the base lodge, also fine for a quick lunch or try the Cafe on the Corner in Liftline Lodge for an outstanding breakfast year-round. The Mid-Mountain Restaurant (at 2,700 feet) is perfect for those who don't want to be off their skis long. The Liftline Lodge also offers dining in an old-world European atmosphere plus the Partridge in a Pantry deli. Mulligan's Tavern is a great spot for families, with a good kids' menu, fireplaces, and live music. For terrific entertainment, head back to the base lodge for live music at Grizzly's bar/restaurant. Or stroll through Stratton Village and discover multitudes of restaurants, from casual pizza to fine dining.

Children's World: The ski season lasts from mid-November into April, and during this period youngsters are well cared for and find lots of entertainment. Seven- to twelve-year-olds join the Big Cub group for full-day supervision, lunch, and ski lessons, at $95 a day. Lift tickets are extra. Stratton also offers this age group packages for private lessons ($75/hour), group lessons ($32/1¾ hours), or Magic Trax; two group lessons, equipment, and lift ticket for $95. Little Cubs take in ages four to six years for indoor games and fun as well as ski lessons (8:30 A.M. to 4:00 P.M. daily); the fee is $95 a day, including lunch; a half day is $50. And real tiny tots gather at the Stratton Childcare Center, a certified day-care facility for children six weeks to three years old. It operates year-round from 8:00 A.M. until 5:00 P.M. and offers indoor and outdoor activities. Winter rates are $95 for a full day; $50 for half-day sessions. The Stratton offers night skiing trails and Saturday night activities for ages five to twelve include pizza, tubing, mini Z's, and snowmobile rides on the menu.

The fun continues in summer with day-camp programs offered seven days a week during July and August. Kids between six and twelve years old spend from 8:30 A.M. to 4:00 P.M. busily engaged in art classes, swim and gymnastics lessons, group games, and field trips. The cost is $59 a day. The child-care center entertains ages six weeks to five years for the same hours and rate, including lunch. An intensive tennis camp for ages seven to seventeen focuses on lessons and tournaments but breaks up the day with hikes, games, and swim time. Two- and three-day Junior Golf Camps help kids from seven to fourteen improve their skills on the green.

Recreation: Skiing at Stratton Mountain is a big event. Thirty-seven miles of trails add up to ninety-two runs for all levels of downhill skiers. Mother Nature drops an average annual 170 inches of snow on this mountain—at 3,875 feet, the highest peak in southern Vermont—and is nudged along by rather sophisticated snowmaking equipment, covering 80 percent of the skiable terrain.

The Stratton Ski School holds classes for every level of ability. It prides itself on a full-day learning experience—five hours with an instructor. The Stratton Touring Center offers instruction in cross-country skiing for treks through the tall evergreens and across quiet meadows. Ice-skating is another favorite winter sport.

If you're more inclined to warm-weather sports, enroll in the Stratton Golf School. Meet fellow students and your PGA instructors in a twenty-two-acre outdoor classroom where all playing conditions can be simulated, then head to the Stratton Mountain Country Club for a round on the twenty-seven-hole championship course. Two- and three-day Junior Golf Clinics are available for ages seven to fourteen.

Attend the Stratton Tennis School for private lessons or a group clinic. There are nineteen indoor and outdoor tennis courts at the Stratton Sports Center and two courts at the inn.

At the Sports Center you can take classes in swimming and aquacise in the 75-foot indoor pool, join aerobics classes, use Nautilus equipment, play tennis, or use one of three racquetball courts. During a recess from classes, sneak into the steam room or the whirlpool for some solitary relaxation. In addition, an outdoor pool, a sauna, and three whirlpools are located at the inn. The Zone is an indoor/outdoor play area near the mountain base. Indoors is geared toward younger kids, with a play section, games, toys, arts and crafts, and a climbing wall. Outside is another climbing wall, a skate park, and volleyball. Skateboards, in-line skates, fishing equipment, and mountain bikes can be rented.

And don't forget to make time to poke around the beautiful Vermont countryside. Hike in the hills and breathe that fresh clean air, jog or bicycle (rentals available) down country roads along fields of wildflowers, horseback ride on mountain trails, or try mountain biking from the summit. When you've had your fill of exercise, join bargain hunters at a local antiques auction or crafts fair. Stratton Mountain Village, with the flair of an Alpine village, has lots of quaint shops, so finding the right memento of your trip will be an easy task.

STRATTON MOUNTAIN RESORT

Stratton Mountain, Vermont 05155
(802) 297–2220, (800) STRATTON
www.stratton.com

SUGARLOAF/USA
Carrabassett Valley, Maine

Traditional New England reserve seems to be missing at Sugarloaf/USA. The prevailing attitude is friendly, upbeat, and casually welcoming. While mainly associated with skiing and winter, Sugarloaf is fast becoming an all-season destination, with golf predominating in summer. All access is via Portland or Bangor, and once in western Maine, just about all roads lead to Sugarloaf. Route 27 is the main road to the ski area, and from the Carrabassett Valley, Sugarloaf literally stands out. You can distinguish the peak from 20 to 40 miles away, and once you leave the valley floor and start to climb, the panorama just gets better and better. Locals and repeat visitors have dubbed one particular spot "Oh-my-gosh corner," because it is so stunning as you round the corner and suddenly see the front of this impressive mountain with its seventy trails and an Alpine village set on the slope.

Accommodations: Sugarloaf has the capacity to sleep approximately 7,000 people on the mountainside. Nine hundred–plus condominiums are set in various clusters of two to twenty-eight units and offer a wide selection of design. Styles include hotel rooms, studios, lofts, and up to five-bedroom, three-bath complexes. The forty-two–room Sugarloaf Inn and the Sugarloaf Grand Summit Resort Hotel's 120-plus rooms and suites complete the lodging options. Custom packages are planned for each family's needs.

Packages generally include a health club pass and group ski lessons. A complimentary shuttle system gets you around the resort with ease.

Rates range from $128 to $678 for a hotel room, from $135 to $745 for a one-bedroom unit, and from $370 to $870 for a four-bedroom condominium. Cribs and rollaway beds are provided at a daily charge of $5.00.

Sugarloaf was one of the first ski areas to introduce the ski-in/ski-out concept; in fact, most accommodations are slopeside or within walking distance of a lift. This is great for older children, as it gives them a sense of independence and it gives everyone a sense of freedom. If you want to sleep late or linger over coffee, others in your party need not delay their skiing. Gondola Village is the largest condominium and the heart of the development, and is where you will find the nursery.

Dining: Dining in the Sugarloaf area is a fun adventure that is taken quite seriously. With fourteen on-mountain restaurants, you can have everything from burgers to bouillabaisse to haute cuisine.

Gepetto's is a slopeside restaurant with a greenhouse addition and a gourmet menu for lunch or dinner. The Seasons Restaurant at the

Sugarloaf Inn offers fresh Maine lobster every night and innovative American cuisine in a relaxed atmosphere. The Double Diamond at the Grand Summit boasts "a fab food experience" and entertainment. For après-ski the Widowmaker Lounge advertises "comfort with class," cocktails, and music you can hear yourself talk over. Upstairs at the base lodge, Avalanche provides a nonalcoholic teen center with lots of action. One of the more recent additions to Sugarloaf/USA is the Shipyard Brewhaus, located just at the base of the Birches slope. It serves fine Maine microbrews on tap, lunch daily, and pub fare after 2:00 P.M. During the summer six restaurants remain open, so there's still a wide choice.

Children's World: Sugarloaf has a terrific winter child-care program. A state-licensed child-care center at the base of the mountain accepts children from ten weeks to five years of age. Hours are from 8:30 A.M. to 4:00 P.M. Advance reservations are a must. The charges are $48 for a full day or $30 for a half day. The night nursery is available from 6:00 to 9:00 P.M. on Thursday and Saturday for $20, $15 per additional sibling. Reservations are required. A fenced-in outdoor play area adds to winter fun, and inside are toys, movies, story time, circle time, and arts and crafts—a developmentally appropriate program provided by caring professionals. The nap area is separate, with individual cribs, cots, and mats. A hot lunch is served, and snacks are given during the day. Introduction to skiing lessons for willing three-year-olds originate from the child-care center. For $63 a full day or $47 a half day, your child has the option of a thirty- to forty-minute private lesson or two-hour group experience. Price includes lifts, rental equipment, and all the components of the child-care program.

Evenings offer free supervised activities for five- to twelve-year-olds six nights a week. Included in the offerings are game nights, Movie Night, Wild Card Night, and Turbo-Tubing. Reservations are required.

Mountain Magic teaches skiing to children

ages four to six years and stresses independence, safety, and fun. The Perfect Kids system teaches walking on skis, wedge stops and turns, side-stepping, falling, and, of course, getting up. In fact, most first-timers will be skiing under their own power after the first day. Half- ($47) and full-day ($63) programs are available. The full-day program includes lots of skiing, indoor activities, a snack, and a hot lunch. Lift passes and rental equipment are included in both sessions. For three-year-olds, the morning half-day session is recommended. This allows your youngest Sugarloafers to acquaint themselves with skiing at a comfortable pace. Mountain Adventure is a program for ages seven to fourteen, where skills are perfected. These programs run from 8:30 A.M. to 3:00 P.M.; half-day ($37) and full-day programs ($49) are available. The full-day program includes lots of skiing/riding, a snack, and a hot lunch. Mountain Teen provides group clinics for ages fifteen to eighteen. Lift tickets and equipment are not included for these age groups.

Summertime brings flowers and traditional July-to-mid-August day camps. A five-week program provided by Carrabassett Valley begins in the second week of July. Kids ages four to thirteen enjoy lessons in swimming, tennis, golf, and fly-fishing, and an extensive arts program. At $120 for five days or daily rates of $30, it's a great deal. For little ones, Sugarloaf offers summer child-care Monday through Friday from 8:00 A.M. to 4:00 P.M. for ages ten weeks to five years. Reservations required, and the cost is $40 per day.

Recreation: The most impressive aspect of skiing Sugarloaf is that you are skiing a big mountain. It is a traditional mountain in that it begins gently, goes to intermediate in the middle, and gets "durn hard at the top," as a local might say. Sugarloaf has the greatest vertical drop in the East. It is possible to come almost straight down the 2,820-foot vertical drop (and even do it in an upright position if you're good) having taken only two lifts. A good beginner or low intermediate skier can take Tote Road, a 3-mile trail from the top that follows the ridge and comes safely to the base, but gives that exciting feeling of skiing at the top of the world and surviving it. At the Outdoor Center, cross-country skiers can explore 100 kilometers of trails, including some lighted for night skiing, or relax at the warm, comfortable lodge.

Other winter fun includes ice-skating, snowshoeing, turbo-tubing, and hockey. The three Family Theme weeks offer additional family activities, and Holiday Weeks are chock-full of entertainment opportunities, such as a free sleigh ride through the woods. At the foot of Sugarloaf/USA, the Carrabassett Valley Anti-gravity Recreational Complex is a 20,000-square-foot facility that boasts Maine's largest indoor skate bowl, trampolines with harness rigging, an indoor rock-climbing wall, and a multipurpose court with a running track, along with weight training and aerobics facilities.

Come summer, when there is no snow on the ground, the Sugarloaf Golf Club opens. Designed by Robert Trent Jones Jr., this course is one of the best for wilderness golf and is one of the top one hundred to play in the United States, according to *Golf Magazine*. Every tee has a spectacular view, and the mountain air is always cool. Tennis is limited to outside play, with two courts on the mountain and four in the town. The village has indoor racquetball courts, a sauna, hot tubs, a steam room, tanning beds, a climbing wall, and two swimming pools. But probably the most exciting summer sport is white-water rafting on the Kennebeck River. Sugarloaf also has a concentrated mountain-biking program, environmental programs, and guided adventures for the whole family.

SUGARLOAF/USA

RR 1, Box 5000
Carrabassett Valley, Maine 04947
(207) 237–2000, (800) THE–LOAF
www.sugarloaf.com

THE TYLER PLACE FAMILY RESORT
Highgate Springs, Vermont

Tucked away in the northwestern corner of Vermont, on Lake Champlain and just minutes away from the Canadian border, Tyler Place Family Resort rightly boasts of its beautiful setting and family-friendly atmosphere. The Tyler Place was one of the first resorts to devote itself entirely to families. The original owners, Mr. and Mrs. Edward Tyler, developed a concept that includes family time as well as time for parents to rejuvenate as a couple. And for over 60 years, the Tyler family (second and third generations) has continued to carry on the resort's family philosophy. Open from late May to mid-September, it's the kind of place that families return to again and again.

And parents and even grandparents who came here as children now bring their own kids.

Accommodations: The inn is the hub of activity, with its recreation rooms, main dining room, fireside lounge, deck, and glass-enclosed porches for visiting, relaxing, cocktails, and candlelight dining. Guest rooms—some are studios, some suites—are located in a separate wing. In addition, twenty-nine cottages, most with a fireplace in the living room and two or more bedrooms, are situated on or near the lake; these have kitchenettes and can sleep up to eight people. Many of the rooms include sleeping lofts or bunk beds; with these special attractions, it may not be difficult at all to get a youngster to go to sleep in a strange place. Cribs and high chairs for infants and toddlers are available at no extra charge.

In total, Tyler Place accommodates approximately sixty families. Based on a Full American Plan, the daily per person rate for each of the first two lodgers in a unit is $149 to $277 during July and August; children and teens are $94 daily. This rate covers lodging, all meals, sports, eight separate Toddlers to Teens programs, and most activities. Rates are $78 to $219 for adults and $58 to $84 daily for children and teens in late May, early June, and September, during hands-on Retreats for the Whole Family. Request their special leaflet and rates for infants and toddlers. The resort is closed the rest of the year.

Dining: The main dining room in the inn serves a semibuffet breakfast, lunch, and dinner. New American country cuisine is the kitchen's specialty, and since a Full American Plan is in effect, you have only to decide which delicious entree to sample. Children have earlier dining hours with their counselors, allowing parents to relax over meals. Share breakfast with your children in the family breakfast room or request a family picnic lunch basket at no extra charge.

Children's World: Outstanding, individualized, and flexible describes the children's programs at the Tyler Place Family Resort. During the entire season there's an extensive program of events geared to eight different age groups, plus infant care. From the youngest Junior Toddlers (twelve to eighteen months) to Senior Teens (fourteen- to sixteen-year-olds), children are well entertained with morning and evening activities led by energetic and enthusiastic college students. Children take meals with their group leaders, and the hours between breakfast and lunch and after supper are filled with arts and crafts, nature walks, songs, games, storytime, volleyball, swim-

ming, hayrides, fishing, movies, treasure hunts, sailing, tennis, sailboarding, kayaking, indoor pool parties—one gets out of breath just listing the activities! Busy and active, your child will no doubt be happy as well, with no chance of being "kid-starved." Afternoons (1:30 to 5:30 P.M.) are devoted to individual family time, with activities available if desired. If you can drag the kids away from friends and counselors, the staff will help you plan a day of sight-seeing or fishing and send you off with a picnic lunch.

For the very young (newborns to two and one-half years), the resort features one-on-one "Parents' Helpers" (from high-school-age to mature adult), who will care for your young child and even prepare meals. The standard fee is $5.50 to $7.50 per hour. This is a real vacation for Mom and Dad, a break from wet diapers and baby food. During Family Retreat Weeks, Parents' Helpers are available only in the evening. Mornings, the Infant Center provides care for the wee ones (with a 1:2 ratio), and toddlers are looked after in the Toddler Center (with a 1:3 ratio of caregivers to children).

During the first week of September, you're invited to bring a friend (ages six to fifteen) at no extra charge as long as the friend is in the same age group as your child.

Recreation: Beautiful Lake Champlain is the source of much of the recreation and relaxation of Tyler Place. Take off in one of the resort's sailboats, canoes, kayaks, or sailboards. Try waterskiing (with instruction), guided canoe and bike trips, yoga, aerobics (step and water), and the workout facilities. Or bait your fishing line for bass and pike. The outdoor and indoor heated pools and Jacuzzi on the lakeshore provide hours of fun. Kids and adults both get a thrill from the "banana boat ride."

Retreats for the whole family, a popular addition, started in 1998. They feature hands-on activities for all ages, including such topics as gardening, nature and outdoor skills, lakeshore studies, rural and farm life, and family wellness.

On land, six tennis courts and a fleet of bikes (one-speed, mountain, children's, tricycle, and child seats, all with helmets) are at your disposal, and the nature trails beckon hikers and joggers. For a change of pace, challenge another guest to an old-fashioned game of horseshoes, or try your hand at archery. Maybe you'll join a soccer game or start up a tennis round-robin with the folks in the neighboring cottage. Golf privileges are available at three golf courses within a fifteen- to forty-five-minute drive of the resort. Recreation fees are applied only for golf, outboard motors for fishing, waterskiing, lake cruises, and mountain bikes.

Within an hour's drive you can get a taste of Europe by visiting cosmopolitan Montreal, or take a mountain hike and an aerial tram ride at Stowe or Jay Peak. Covered bridges, waterfalls, little New England towns, country auctions, and antiques shops are even closer.

Nighttime brings other events, from dances and live jazz to guitar sing-alongs and Monte Carlo nights—pick your pleasure. What many guests like most is the hospitable atmosphere of the many and varied activities, with never any pressure to participate.

THE TYLER PLACE FAMILY RESORT

Box 1, Old Dock Road
Highgate Springs, Vermont 05460
(802) 868–4000
www.tylerplace.com

THE WHITNEY INN
Jackson, New Hampshire

If you seek the tranquillity of a winter or mountain vacation without crowds or large resorts, then a holiday at a classic country inn may do as much for the mind and spirit as the body. Sometimes, small is better. Located in the beautiful White Mountains of New Hampshire, the inn sits on fourteen acres of open fields and wooded hills, with a mountain pond and a brook. Drive through town across an old covered bridge, point your car toward the mountain, and at the end of the road, you'll find the welcoming charm of the Whitney Inn. Open year-round, the owners claim 95 percent of their clientele are families.

Accommodations: Standard and deluxe rooms are in the main inn, and family suites, particularly suited to parents and children, are close by in a separate building. Few standard rooms will accommodate families. The rate structure, based on bed and breakfast in deluxe rooms and family suites (more motel than inn style, but with more space also), is $99 to $199 per room; two children under sixteen stay free; over sixteen pay $20 per night. Rates to include dinner are available on request. A good deal, and very popular, is one of the freestanding cottages (there are only two, so reserve early) with fireplace and two bedrooms: $146 to $210 per night, including breakfast. Weekend and holiday times are when the higher rates are in effect.

Dining: Breakfast and dinner will satisfy the best appetites. Breakfasts feature hearty fare, preparing you for an outdoor, athletic day. Dinners are relaxing affairs where you'll find American regional cuisine and a wide choice of entrees. The children's menu offers youngsters their favorite dishes, such as pizza, broiled chicken, and fried fish. In winter, try the Shovel Handle for lunch fare of salads, sandwiches, and hearty soups, or stop by at the end of the day for a little après-ski action.

Children's World: The Whitney has no children's program of its own, or even baby-sitting; no special activities are planned for families as the owners feel that people come for the outdoors and to spend time together as a family. However, Black Mountain, practically ski in/ski out from the inn in winter, provides Ski and Snowboard Schools and Child Care. The Mountain Action Gang (ages nine to twelve) and Snow Busters (ages five to eight) are $65 for a half day, $79 for a full day including lunch. Tots Snow Flake for ages three and four is a half day of on-snow fun and supervision for $55. For the under threes, Day Care costs $30 for a half day and $45 for a full day with lunch. Hourly options are $8 per hour with a two-hour minimum. The oldest ski area in New Hampshire, Black Mountain (800–698–4490, 800–475–4669, www.blackmt.com) is considering a children's summer program; however, no details were available at press time.

Recreation: Skiing at the inn's back door is the primary winter activity. Of the forty downhill trails, 34 percent are ranked intermediate. The vertical drop on this sunny side of Black Mountain is 1,100 feet. From the summit, skiers look out to Mount Washington and across picturesque New England farms. Snow-making facilities on 98 percent of the mountain complement Mother Nature's efforts.

The Betty Whitney trail, named in honor of a longtime resident, provides a 2-kilometer groomed loop connecting the Whitney Inn and the village of Jackson. This is a great starting point for families who ski both cross-country and downhill.

For cross-country skiers, the Jackson Ski Touring Center is located just 2 miles from the inn; some of its 150 kilometers of trails criss-cross the inn's property. Also on the wintertime calendar, the inn has sledding, ice-skating parties, sleigh rides, and movies. The activities room offers games for the whole family, and the library is a peaceful hideaway.

In summer, mountain biking, hiking, and jogging in these beautiful mountains are favorite activities. You also can fish, swim in the heated pool, take a paddleboat on the pond, join a cookout, or play a bit of tennis, badminton, croquet, volleyball, and shuffleboard. Storyland, a very popular theme park for ages two to twelve is five minutes away from the inn. Celebrating their fiftieth season, everything is included in the pay-one-price admission of $20 per person. Under threes are free, and it's good for a full day of adventure that includes twenty rides, four live shows, multiple attractions, and free strollers on a first-come, first-served basis. Open Memorial Day to Labor Day, find more information at www.storylandnh.com.

THE WHITNEY INN

Black Mountain Road
Route 16B
Jackson, New Hampshire 03846
(603) 383–8916, (800) 677–5737
www.thewhitneyinn.com

EAST

New York
Pennsylvania

GOLDEN ACRES FARM AND RANCH

Gilboa, New York

"Old MacDonald had a farm, ee-i-ee-i-oh. And on that farm he had a cow." Well, the Gauthiers have a farm too, with at least as wide a variety of animals as Old Mac did—horses, goats, sheep, ducks, chickens, and a number of baby animals for cuddling and petting. If you like, you can begin your day by milking a cow, collecting eggs from the henhouse, or feeding the animals. Since it opened in 1950, the farm has always been family oriented and prides itself on a genuine "down-on-the-farm" experience with modern comforts. This 800-acre farm/resort is located on top of a 2,000-foot-high knoll in the Catskill Mountains and is open mid-June to Labor Day only.

Accommodations: In the main house are the dining room, the nursery, an indoor playroom, and a teen lounge. Next door is a motel complex connected to game rooms, lounges, and the indoor pool and hot tub. Across the road (a short city block away) is Gilboa Ridge, with a farmhouse and farm cottage. There are ten connecting rooms and suites. Most rooms contain a double bed and a single bed, with space for rollaways or cribs ($25 per stay per crib). Also at Gilboa Ridge are twenty-six "you cook" vacation apartments with kitchenettes (you bring your own dishes, towels, etc.) and a campground area with water and electric hookups. The farm pays particular attention to single parents and has nondiscriminatory rates for one adult traveling with a child. Weekly rates for a one-bedroom in the farmhouse begin at $520 per adult, or $660 in the main complex, and include two meals. Infants under one year old stay free, and children/teens are priced by age, ranging from $155 to $335, including three meals. Two-night packages range from $200 to $285 per adult and $110 to $175 per child. The U-Cook Apartments cost $720 to $1,025 weekly, with no meals. All accommodations and rates are clearly outlined on the Web site.

Dining: Only in the Catskills can you find fresh country meals that are also kosher. Children and adults have a joint menu and dining room for breakfast and dinner, but no adults are allowed at lunch; then the children and teens and their counselors eat all those things that are so dear to their hearts—pizza and hamburgers, along with a few fruits and vegetables. Jewish dietary laws are observed, as is Shabbos. Two snacks daily are included for the young set, and the selection at the Snack Bar hits the spot between meals. Food is fresh, locally grown, and hearty, and you can eat all you wish. The evening menu includes appetizer, salad, soup, choice of two meats or one fish entree, side dishes, and desserts. All breads and pastries are freshly baked daily in the farm bakery.

Evening activities center on the Skylite Room and the Ragtime Lounge and include happy hour, bands, and entertainment; folk and square dancing; night at the races; and other activities—some for everyone, some for adults only, and a teen lounge for special programs. After the early evening entertainment, live music and dancing continue in the Ragtime Lounge.

Children's World: The program for children varies by age, takes advantage of the farm surroundings, and is offered from mid-June through the first week of September. For the under-four set, a complete nursery service is scheduled from 10:00 to 11:45 A.M., 12:30 to 5:00 P.M., and 6:30 to 7:45 P.M. Parents collect their children for mealtimes.

For four- to twelve-year-olds, it is nonstop action throughout the day. For teens, informal activities emphasize meeting others and sharing things while maintaining freedom of action. The rec room, with its jukebox and video games, is popular with this group. Experienced and enthusiastic counselors (most of whom are studying to be teachers) supervise the events. The staff is international, with many countries represented. It's great exposure for the children, who learn games and activities from around the world.

A typical day starts at 10:00 A.M. with a tour to feed the animals, collect eggs, or visit the gardens. Then come horseback riding (teaching beginners is a specialty here), swimming, lunch, and a rest period. Afternoon activities are geared to the children's interests—berry picking, frog hunts, hayrides, crafts, games, and perhaps an excursion to the caves or a hike and cookout in the woods. A snack of milk and cookies is followed by rounding up the cows for milking.

After a break for dinner and a quick hello to the parents, evening activities such as bonfires, talent shows, or cartoons start at 7:45 P.M. Kids have another snack, then head for bed about 9:00 P.M.—and well deserved it is! Parents can go out if they want, as a "check at your door" night patrol is on duty from 9:00 P.M. to 1:00 A.M., with a sign-in sheet on each room door. If you prefer, you can hire a baby-sitter from either the staff or local listings at approximately $7.00 an hour.

Recreation: There is no charge for any of the activities. After catching your limit of fish, you might take off to one of the two tennis courts, the archery field, either of the two swimming pools, or the exercise room. The boats and floating docks at the lake make for a relaxing afternoon, or join a group for softball or volleyball. And grown-ups, too, can partake in the farm activities—feeding the animals, horseback riding, hopping aboard a hayride. A less active afternoon might include a class in macramé, copper enameling, pottery, or stained glass, or a stop by one of the recreation rooms for table tennis and pool. If the weather is uncooperative, there's an indoor riding arena, five playrooms for rainy-day activities, and a complete workout room for adults. One nice feature at the Golden Acres is the policy of allowing an early check-in and late use of the facilities when checking out.

Local sites of interest include Howe Caverns, Secret Caves, Hunter Mountain, game farms, and bird sanctuaries. Cooperstown, home of the Baseball Hall of Fame, is nearby, as is the Oneonta Soccer Hall of Fame. Golden Acres is in the center of numerous auction barns, flea markets, and roadside vegetable stands.

New this year is the addition of a nearby 400-acre farm for exploring. A thirty-five acre lake with a ten-acre island even has a land bridge to the island from shore. You'll be able to discover and explore a beautiful site, just like the early settlers.

GOLDEN ACRES FARM AND RANCH

South Gilboa Road
Gilboa, New York 12076
(607) 588–7329, (800) 847–2151,
(800) 252–7787 (in New York)
www.goldenacres.com

MOHONK MOUNTAIN HOUSE

New Paltz, New York

The wholesome peace and serenity of Mohonk Mountain House are not merely by-products of its setting in 2,200 acres of the Shawangunk Mountains, 90 miles north of New York City. The resort was founded in 1869 by twin brothers, Albert and Alfred Smiley, who, following their Quaker upbringing, regarded drinking, dancing, smoking, and card playing as unacceptable activities. Rather, they emphasized spiritual renewal as evidenced by the nature walks or prayer meetings planned for their proper clientele.

The times have indeed changed, but the gracious, quieter way of life of a bygone era still prevails at Mohonk. No discos swing until dawn here. In fact, no bar is on the premises, though guests may order cocktails with the midday and evening meals. Instead, you'll find cozy conversation lounges furnished with Victorian antiques, verandahs lined with rocking chairs, miles of hiking trails, and extensive gardens. Open year-round, the rambling wood-and-stone Victorian structure appears almost like a castle, complete with turrets and towers, and sits on the edge of a clear mountain lake a half mile long. In fact, Mohonk means "lake in the sky" in Iroquois. Though physically isolated, guests want for nothing during a stay here.

Accommodations: The 251 guest rooms are spacious and tastefully and simply decorated with period furnishings. Some have fireplaces and private balconies overlooking the lake or looking across the valley to the mountains. Some connecting rooms share a bath. On a Full American Plan (mandatory), daily rates are from $358 to $698 for a standard double guest room. The special Victorian and tower rooms command higher rates. For children occupying a room with their parents, the charge is $126 a day for those over twelve and

$76 a day for four- to twelve-year-olds; children under age four are accommodated free. There is no charge for cribs or rollaway beds. Weekly rates and package plans are available. Ask about the "kids stay free" events held throughout the year.

Dining: The main dining room where breakfast, lunch, and dinner are served is a large and elegantly simple room with highly polished woodwork and paneling rising 30 to 40 feet. The kitchen specializes in American cuisine and ingredients indigenous to America. "Healthy Choice," vegetarian, and kosher menus are also available, and the spectacular natural setting adds to the dining experience. Jackets are standard attire for gentlemen age twelve and over at the evening meal. Cookouts and clambakes are occasionally planned, and complimentary afternoon tea is served daily at 4:00 P.M. Refreshments are also available in the Ice Cream Parlor and Soda Fountain and the Tee Room on the golf course.

Children's World: On weekends and holidays throughout the year and daily from mid-June through Labor Day, Mohonk's Kids' Club divides children into two age groups: two- to three-year-olds, and four- to twelve-year-olds. Both groups have daily activities in the morning and again in the afternoon, after lunch with the family; and evening activities as well. Typical events on the agenda are hikes, nature walks, scavenger hunts, shuffleboard contests, swimming, pony rides, rock scrambles, and frog hunts. Movies, square dances, and campfires are frequently planned for evenings. Winter brings ice-skating, snowshoeing, and hot chocolate. Kids' Club is a complimentary service for hotel guests. Babysitters can be hired for younger children, with advance notice, and there are planned activities for the whole family to enjoy together.

Recreation: Discovering nature's beauty

is at the core of Mohonk's recreational activities, many of which are complimentary. More than 85 miles of hiking trails wind through the woods and along the lake; dotting the paths are one hundred gazebos where you can sit to take in the views. Explore the grounds on horseback (Western and English style) or in a horse-drawn carriage ride (extra fees), and leisurely meander through the award-winning gardens. Lake Mohonk has a small sandy beach at the west end and is stocked with trout; it is the location for swimming, fishing, and boating.

Traditional sports are tennis (lessons available) on the six courts (four clay, two Har-Tru) and the two platform tennis courts, and golfing on the nine-hole Scottish-design course and the eighteen-hole putting green. Tennis and midweek nine-hole golf are complimentary. There are tennis and golf pro shops for equipment and apparel. The fitness center, although small, offers exercise equipment and saunas. Spa services are available in Mohonk's Massage Center at an extra charge. Lawn games include shuffleboard, croquet, and lawn bowling.

During the winter months, when the lake freezes, ice-skating is a favorite sport. Mohonk's Victorian Skating Pavilion is host to skating parties on a refrigerated ice rink in fall and winter. And Mohonk maintains more than 35 miles of marked trails for snowshoeing and cross-country skiing, also included in the rates.

Throughout the year lectures, concerts, and slide shows are scheduled in the evening. Several three-day to weeklong programs are planned, covering topics such as bird watching and identification, gardening, photography, foreign languages, cooking, music, mystery and sleuthing, and stargazing; professionals in the respective fields conduct these programs.

MOHONK MOUNTAIN HOUSE

Lake Mohonk
1000 Mountain Rest Road
New Paltz, New York 12561
(845) 255–1000, (800) 772–6646
www.mohonk.com

ROCKING HORSE RANCH
Highland, New York

"Giddy-up, ole paint" and, with a tip of your ten-gallon hat, off you ride into the sunset. Located only 75 miles from New York City with a three-diamond rating by AAA, Rocking Horse Ranch has been owned and managed by the Turk family since 1958. They take pride in treating their guests as family; in fact, more than 80 percent of the guests are repeat clients. The 300 acres easily accommodate up to 450 guests while permitting a feeling of "wide open spaces." With a stable of 120 horses, mainly quarterhorse stock,

Rocking Horse stakes a claim to being one of the best family dude ranches in the East.

Accommodations: Rooms (120 in all) are located in either the main lodge or the Oklahoma Annex (motel-style units). The twenty-four connecting rooms and the ranchettes may be appropriate for large parties. The latter are similar to minisuites, with sitting areas and convertible sofa beds. Eighteen rooms have refrigerators. Summer daily all-inclusive package rates based on double occupancy are

$200 to $270 per adult; children under four are free; ages four to fifteen are $95 for the first child and $90 for other children. Less per day for longer stays! Spring, fall, and winter feature weekend and midweek stays.

Dining: Meals and entertainment are included in the resort's rates. Choose from the Longhorn Dining Room, The Cactus Grill, or during summer, poolside parties and snack bar. Adults receive breakfast and dinner while children have all three meals, enjoying lunch with the counselors. Meals are five to six courses, prepared by graduate chefs from the nearby Culinary Institute of America. Dinner selections include roast prime rib, barbecued steaks, or fillet of sole brought in fresh from a local market, complemented by a huge salad bar. At the dessert bar the chocolate blackout cake is not to be missed. The Round-Up Room Nightclub has floor shows and a live band. Two other cocktail lounges, each with a fireplace and a conversation area, are also quite inviting.

Children's World: The Fort Wilderness playground area, with swings and climbing equipment and the animal farm where Tony the Llama lives, is a favorite with kids. Year-round, children have a planned, supervised program seven days a week. The 9:00 A.M. to 5:00 P.M. schedule is filled with horseback riding, swimming, waterskiing, crafts, and games. In the evening the family fun continues with pizza parties, dances, and cookouts. On weekends during the winter, kids turn to skiing and snow tubing.

There is no charge for the day's events, which include lunch and snacks with the counselors, or for the "night patrol," set up to make rounds of corridors and, upon request, to check inside the room when parents are out. Baby-sitting can be arranged at $6.00 per hour.

Recreation: You might start your day with an early-morning horseback ride; invigorated by the sweet mountain air, lead your horse down a quiet trail through the woods. If you're a novice, you can link up with the experienced ranch staff for some basic instruction.

The rest of your day may be filled with waterskiing (instruction is free), enjoying more than 150 feet of water slide, swimming, fishing, and boating (paddleboats and rowboats) on the ten-acre lake. Play a game of tennis and hike or jog along the nature trails. A relaxing swim in one of three heated pools (two are outdoors, with one just for kids) can revive your spirits for a workout in the exercise room or a rousing game of volleyball, softball, basketball, or badminton. The climbing wall is a popular place. For an easier pace, try a round of croquet, shuffleboard, or horseshoes. An archery field and an indoor shooting range are available for aspiring marksmen, and the eighteen holes of miniature golf are fun for kids and their parents.

In the fall the social director plans hayrides and cookouts; in winter add cross-country skiing, snow tubing, and horseback riding in the snow. The 300-foot vertical ski slope is modest but has two new trails. At Rocking Horse all activities are free; the horseback riding, the use of all the sports equipment and facilities, and the entertainment are all covered in the lodging rates.

ROCKING HORSE RANCH

Highland, New York 12528
(845) 691–2927, (800) 647–2624
www.rhranch.com

THE SAGAMORE

Lake George at Bolton Landing, New York

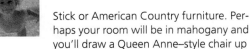

The notion of an island hideaway usually involves images of thatch-roofed huts or oceanside condominiums, palm trees waving in a gentle breeze, miles of sandy beach, and golf, tennis, sailing, and swimming. The Sagamore will take you by surprise, for it is an island resort, and it grants its guests opportunities for golf, tennis, sailing, and swimming—and then it deviates from the traditional image. You see, The Sagamore is on a seventy-acre island in Lake George in upstate New York. Surrounded by clear lake waters and the Adirondack Mountains, the tall evergreen trees and the clean mountain air set the stage here.

The Sagamore itself is different. Originally opened in 1883, it is part of another era, gracious and elegant. The main hotel building dates from 1930 and is listed on the National Register of Historic Places. After an extensive multimillion-dollar renovation, The Sagamore reopened as a year-round resort in 1985 and is a member of Preferred Hotels and Resorts Worldwide. The wings radiate from the main lobby and its semicircular, white-columned porch and seem to embrace the lawns, gardens, and lake views. Down the wings are more porches for sitting, strolling, and catching a different view of the lake. In the center, topping off this Victorian showplace, is the bell tower.

Accommodations: Of the 350 rooms and suites, 100 are in the main hotel and another 240 are distributed among the island's seven modern lodges (don't worry, modern does not denote a disturbance to The Sagamore's ambience). The remaining ten suites are part of a business executive complex. You will find attention to detail and historical accuracy in the decoration of the rooms and throughout the hotel. You'll think "charming, quaint, elegant, reserved" when you see Adirondack

Stick or American Country furniture. Perhaps your room will be in mahogany and you'll draw a Queen Anne–style chair up to the desk when writing postcards. Rocking chairs and quilted bedspreads complete the picture in some rooms. In others fireplaces or balconies capture a guest's eye. Even the bathrooms are special and true to a grand era, with their pedestal-base sinks and mahogany towel bars.

Rates vary within the main hotel and the lodges, depending on the season. Winter rates are the lowest, beginning at $169 nightly for a hotel room, or $259 for a suite. A two-bedroom family suite ranges from $349 in winter to $669 in the Adirondack season (late May to mid-October). Children to age seventeen pay only a $6.00 service charge on the room, except in July and August, when there is a $50 charge per child. The Sagamore's rates do not include meals; you may dine a la carte or arrange a meal plan for everyone over thirteen; twelve and under pay a reduced a la carte rate.

Dining: For a casual afternoon by the pool, you can have a light lunch and beverages at the Terrace. For a truly elegant and memorable dinner, the four-diamond Trillium can transport you back through time in style (coats and ties required for gentlemen). Recipes for this restaurant have been carefully researched so that you can have an adventure in history as well as in dining. In between these options are the Sagamore Dining Room, where regional favorites are served at breakfast and dinner, and the Club Grill on the mainland, where views stretch out over the golf course and the lake. At the glass-enclosed Verandah, in the lobby, guests can have continental breakfast in the morning, tea and finger sandwiches in the afternoon, and nightcaps before retiring. Mr. Brown's serves light meals in a publike setting and provides evening entertainment. May through October, the 72-foot yacht *Morgan* cruises the lake during lunch and dinner, offering its diners constantly changing scenic views. It is suggested that you make your dinner reservations when you book your room.

Children's World: Under the cheerful and watchful direction of the activities counselor, Sagamore kids take swimming lessons, play lawn games, dance, do face painting, go on boat rides, see clown shows, and unveil their hidden talents in crafts classes. In this one area The Sagamore does not follow nineteenth-century practices, which were somewhat restrictive when it came to children. Instead, in keeping with modern philosophies, The Sagamore wants its energized children to have a fun, athletic, and creative visit. The authentic 22-foot tepee gives the program its name: The Tepee Club. It runs from 9:00 A.M. to 4:00 P.M. daily, July 1 through Labor Day for ages four through twelve; a modified year-round program operates on Saturdays and holidays. Costs are $25 for a half-day session (no lunch) or $45 for a full-day session (with lunch). From 5:00 until 9:00 P.M., children can have dinner together, play, and enjoy games such as dress-ups or clown parties ($45 per session). A game room offers table tennis, a pool table, video games, and a television. Baby-sitting is available for $15 an hour for the first child, $5.00 each additional child, with a three-hour minimum required. Children under four may participate in the programs, accompanied by a baby-sitter (not an older sibling). They pay program costs plus baby-sitting costs. Registration is required, and a $25 fee applies for cancellations within 24 hours.

Recreation: Just across the bridge from The Sagamore's island, Donald Ross designed an eighteen-hole championship golf course in the Adirondack foothills near the lake's edge, complemented by the restaurant and pro shop facilities at the course's attractive Tudor-style clubhouse.

The indoor swimming pool, tennis courts, and racquetball courts help guests stay busy and active year-round. The complete health spa offers its own form of indoor workout with its Nautilus equipment and then pampers with saunas, whirlpools, and massages. Spa packages include special diets, herbal wraps, and aromatherapy.

In warm weather swim in the beautiful, clean, freshwater lake; skim across its surface sailing, waterskiing, or sailboarding; or gently stroke the waters in a rowboat or fishing boat. Jog on the trails around the island or hike the foothills around the golf course. Take a horse out for an hour-long jaunt or stay close to home for a Sunday afternoon concert on the lawn.

In the wintertime Lake George freezes; hearty souls go ice-fishing, while others snuggle together during a horse-drawn sleigh ride. Ice-skate over the frozen lake or go tobogganing and cross-country skiing on the snow-covered golf course. Downhill skiers can take advantage of nearby Gore Mountain and West Mountain, ski areas to which the Sagamore provides free bus transportation.

Saratoga is about 30 miles away and in summer shares its Performing Arts Center with interested visitors.

THE SAGAMORE

Lake George at Bolton Landing, New York 12814
(518) 644–9400, (800) 358–3585
www.thesagamore.com

SCOTT'S OQUAGA LAKE HOUSE

Deposit, New York

A reader shared this gem of a family resort with us, and described it as "warm, friendly, hospitable, fun, down to earth, great for every age, and even enchanting." We tend to agree. Six generations of Scotts have created this lovely resort, beginning in 1869. Over the years the warmth of the welcome you receive and the sense of belonging to a family has not dimmed. Set on a clear, spring-fed lake amidst the hills and woods of beautiful New York State, it is truly run for families, by a family; Mom and Pop Scott (Ray and Doris) plus daughter Patty and her family all work in different capacities at the resort. Reminiscent of the Von Trapp family, they even present a Broadway musical review! An all-inclusive policy (you never see your wallet during your stay) adds to the old-fashioned charm of this country resort—and there's no tipping! Scott's is open late-May to mid-October, so stroll up the flower-lined walk to the main house and into everyone's memory of a summer house on a lake—somewhere.

Accommodations: One hundred thirty-five rooms are set in the main lodge, various buildings, and cottages; some with two doubles or two twins, a few with king-size beds; all are simple, clean, and comfortable. Rates are per person and include room, three full meals, all recreation and entertainment, kids program, and unlimited golf, tennis, waterskiing, and all other sports and activities. July and August are the high season, but rates are only about $10 more per day; single parents pay only $30 to $40 more. Based on double occupancy, per person rates range from $104 to $130; weekly rates are $690 to $910. Two-room suites are $149 to $165 daily per person. Children under three are free; three to five are $50; six to twelve are $65; and thirteen to nineteen are $77.

Dining: Contrary to many times in our hectic lives, eating is a communal event here, showcased in the large dining room. Fresh, natural ingredients prepared simply and with care, shared family-style with fellow guests make it easy to slow down and appreciate life and good food. Choices abound, and kids may even eat their vegetables! Twice a week you can bus or hike to a sheltered pavilion for a hot lunch, with live music and dance and a spectacular view.

Children's World: Long summer days spent swimming in a lake, or watching nature in the woods, lunch with friends, lots of adventures—it's great to give your kids a taste of a slower, relaxed time. Supervised activities from 9:30 A.M. to 12:30 P.M. and again from 2:00 to 4:30 P.M. provide just that, while keeping kids from three up busy and amused. Age groups are blended nicely, and it's secure enough for kids to strike out on their own yet still be safe. A large playhouse on the lakefront, which includes a nostalgic soda fountain, pool tables, table tennis, and some old-fashioned bowling alleys, provides a focal point for fun. Teens can "hang" here, and while they'll laugh at having to set up their own pins, they'll probably secretly get a kick out of it.

Recreation: You'll experience no shortage of activities here, as the resort's nearly 1,100 acres are packed with things to do. Anything even remotely connected with sports is yours for the asking—volleyball, softball, bocce, table tennis, pool, bowling, two scenic nine-hole golf courses, a nine-hole pitch-and-putt and a putting green, and three outdoor and one indoor tennis courts. On the water, row a boat, canoe, sail, take a speedboat ride, fish, or water-ski. In the water, swim, splash, or simply lie on the floating raft and soak up the sun. Colorful Adirondack chairs line the lakefront beach, perfectly conducive to contemplating the green mountains while everyone else does all of that activity. Hike, bike, walk in the woods, or dance—your choice of ball-room, square, line, country, or folk dancing, all on a 3,200-square-foot hardwood dance floor on the lakefront. Enjoy live shows and family entertainment nightly. Ride the *Show Boat,* a tradition on Oquaga Lake for years, and you provide the sing-along show! Most of all, experience summer as you like it.

SCOTT'S OQUAGA LAKE HOUSE

Oquaga Lake, Box 47
Deposit, New York 13754
(607) 467–3094
www.scottsfamilyresort.com

SKYTOP LODGE
Skytop, Pennsylvania

The Pocono Mountains have long had a reputation as a romantic honeymoon destination. While this is certainly warranted, the Skytop Lodge will convince you that this area of northeast Pennsylvania is just right for a family vacation as well. Set on 5,500 acres of rolling hills, lakes, and rivers, the lodge is a large, rambling, stone building with a welcoming circular drive. Just 100 miles from either New York or Philadelphia, Skytop attracts many visitors with its relaxed atmosphere, hospitable charm, and recreational activities. It is open year-round.

Accommodations: Most of the rooms in the historic stone manor house have views of the gardens and grounds; some will accommodate a family of four. If a large-enough room is not available, or if parents prefer, children are given their own room at $100 off the regular rate (maximum two children; additional children are $45 each). Based on double occupancy, Full American Plan high-season (May through October) rates begin at $470 per night; winter rates begin at $350. Children under sixteen sharing their parents' room pay $30. November to April special off-season rates and packages are available; weekend and holiday rates, however, are more comparable to those in summer.

Also available are ten cottages, each with four interconnecting bedrooms. Each room within the cottage can be occupied separately or together in suites from two to four. All accommodation rates include three meals daily, outdoor picnics, health club, archery, miniature golf, winter sports, and entertainment.

Dining: Skytop's Full American Plan includes a choice of meals in the Windsor Room in the main hotel and the Lake View at the Inn; both request that gentlemen wear jackets, although ties are not required. Also included as a dining choice is the Deli, a seasonal lunch spot in warm weather, and the year-round scheduled picnics. The Pine Room, an elegant and inviting area of the lobby with floor-to-ceiling windows, is the site of afternoon tea (part of the dining plan) with musical entertainment in the summer and cozy gatherings near the fireplace in the winter. The Tap Room, offering food, cocktails, and entertainment/dancing, and the Tea Room, with light fare such as soups and sandwiches, are not included in the dining plan.

Children's World: Camp-in-the-Clouds is in session for four- to ten-year-olds daily from

July 1 to Labor Day. The morning program runs from 9:30 A.M. to 1:30 P.M., the afternoon program from 1:30 to 4:30 P.M. Each session is $12, or $20 for the full day, and covers a program of swimming, boating, hiking, golf and tennis lessons, games, and crafts. Young children also enjoy the playground and the kiddie pool, while the older ones make the most of pool, table tennis, and video games in the Recreation Room. Saturdays bring picnics for everyone and an evening dinner from 6:00 to 8:00 P.M. for children. The weekly Saturday night "Grand March" has become a tradition at Skytop. A combination parade, quadrille, and snake dance, it becomes hilarious at times, and guests and staff alike anticipate the fun. At holiday times during the rest of the year, the staff plans activities, dinners, and movies for children. Individual baby-sitters can be arranged for $10 an hour.

Recreation: The Poconos make a lovely setting for sports activities. The eighteen-hole championship golf course is a combination of lush fairways and beautiful old trees on a rolling terrain. Putting greens and a pro shop round out the golfing facility. Tennis players are invigorated by the clean mountain air; of the seven outdoor courts, five are Har-Tru and two have all-weather surfaces. Private lessons and clinics are offered.

Skytop's Fishing and Shooting Center provides fishermen with a trout-filled stream and three lakes full of bass and pickerel; novices will appreciate the Orvis School fly-fishing instruction. Others take to these waters for swimming, boating, and canoeing. There's an outdoor swimming pool, and in cool weather swimmers enjoy the large indoor pool in its solarium setting.

You can work out in the exercise room, but outdoors you can have beautiful scenery *and* all the exercise you want. Try lawn bowling on well-tended greens (tournaments are held during the summer), or practice more conventional sports like badminton, croquet, archery, shuffleboard, softball, and miniature golf. The 30 miles of trails through the woods are perfect for hiking, biking, and jogging, and the gardens are suitable for relaxing strolls. Naturalists conduct tours of the local wildlife and vegetation. In the evening you might find a bridge game, play a little pool or billiards, take in a movie, or relax in the library.

In the winter Skytop has a few gentle slopes for downhill skiing. Two poma lifts and seven trails with a vertical drop of just 275 feet make it ideal for learning. A ski pro can help with lessons. Several well-groomed trails cover acres of attractive territory for cross-country skiing. Rental equipment is available for both types of skiing, and larger ski areas are nearby at Alpine Mountain (8 miles) and Camelback (15 miles). Tobogganing, sledding, and ice-skating are also wintertime favorites.

SKYTOP LODGE

One Skytop
Skytop, Pennsylvania 18357
(570) 595–7401, (800) 617–2389
www.skytop.com

MID-ATLANTIC

Maryland
North Carolina
South Carolina
Virginia
West Virginia

FAIRFIELD SAPPHIRE VALLEY

Sapphire, North Carolina

The rolling foothills of the Blue Ridge Mountains provide the backdrop for Fairfield Sapphire Valley, a four-season resort community. The 5,700 acres, filled with the scent of pines and fresh mountain air, encompass three lakes, a golf course, a horseback-riding stable, and picturesque scenery for nature lovers and hikers. The serenity of a canoe ride on the lake, relaxing afternoon fishing from the dock, or the rigors of a tennis clinic attract vacationers to this mountain setting tucked in the southwestern corner of North Carolina. Back in 1896, finding this place meant travel by wagon or train. Today, that serene and rustic lifestyle still exists, but it's a lot easier to get there!

Accommodations: Hotel rooms, efficiencies, one- to three-bedroom condominiums, and three- and four-bedroom houses boast spectacular mountain views or are nestled among tall pines. Most of these lodgings have kitchens, and all have sundecks or balconies where you can sit to watch the sunset. Condominium rates begin at $100 for a kitchenette or $175 for a one-bedroom and go to $265 for a deluxe three-bedroom with view. Off-season (November through March) rates are $10 to $35 less, and weekly rates are available. Housekeeping services (clean towels daily) are provided only for those units with no washer/dryer. Useful items you may want to pack include napkins, paper towels, salt and pepper, coffee and coffee filters, dish soap, and laundry detergent.

Dining: Many families prepare meals in their villas, but if your idea of a vacation does not include cooking, the restaurants can relieve you of this chore—although you'll definitely want to have breakfast items and snacks on hand in the condo. The Library Restaurant offers dinner in a casual atmosphere, while Mica's Restaurant has an old-world charm and serves lunch and dinner daily with a children's menu. Sunday brunch, karaoke twice a week, and live music and dancing on Saturday nights make Mica's the center of Sapphire social life. Jimmy Mac's is family-friendly with simple, mostly Italian fare, plus soups and sandwiches. The club for the Sapphire Mountain Golf Course also houses a restaurant, which is open for lunch. The resort is located in a dry township; while no liquor, beer, or wine can be purchased on-site, brown bagging is permitted and setups are available in the area restaurants. Venture to Cashiers (3 miles) or Highlands (12 miles) for more dining selections. A car is recommended to fully enjoy the area.

Children's World: The children's program operates Monday through Friday from 9:00 A.M. to 4:00 P.M., mid-June through mid-August. Enroll your child for a full-day session of events supervised by an enthusiastic staff. A full day with lunch is $31. The program is offered for ages five to twelve.

Swimming, boat rides, tennis, nature walks, fishing, and arts-and-crafts classes are on the agenda, as are an occasional puppet show and scavenger hunt. Video games are offered for the young computer whiz in your group. The recreation staff assists in making individual baby-sitting arrangements.

Recreation: An Amenities Card ($5.00 per person for ages fourteen and over) is required to access recreation facilities; a cardholder must accompany children under fourteen. There are modest fees for most activities.

The Sapphire Mountain Golf Course is an eighteen-hole championship course. Views of the beautiful Blue Ridge Mountains provide ample inspiration for your game. Water hazards on nine holes, including a waterfall, make it a memorable experience. If you're really serious about your performance, seek private instruction at the pro shop, which also accommodates your fashion and equipment needs.

Tennis enthusiasts enjoy the Tennis Center, which includes eight Har-Tru courts and two all-weather courts (two courts are lighted for evening play), as well as a well-stocked pro shop. The resident pro can assist in improving your swing in either private lessons or clinic programs.

For hikers and nature lovers, several trails wind around the lakes and through the woods; along the Fairfield Lake Trail, information plaques describe the plants and wildlife of the area. Trek around Whitewater Falls, at 435 feet the highest waterfall in the eastern United States. At the Equestrian Center you can engage a mount for a group escorted trail ride.

For an unusual afternoon outing, you might consider gem mining. In the late 1800s the land was mined quite successfully—after all, that's where the name comes from. While you might not bring home a sapphire or a ruby, you'll no doubt have a fun excursion. Check with the Recreation Department for mining tips and equipment.

Swimmers can opt for a dip in one of the lakes or in the indoor and outdoor heated pools located at the Recreation Center. Lake Fairfield is also the setting for boating expeditions; canoes, paddleboats, rowboats, and fishing boats can be acquired on a rental basis. Fishermen head to the lakes or a quiet mountain stream for fine trout fishing. A North Carolina license is required; obtain one in Cashiers.

At the Recreation Center you'll also find basketball, volleyball, table tennis, swimming pools, miniature golf, a game room, an exercise room, Jacuzzi, and a sauna. In winter the Recreation Center becomes the focus of snow activities. Two main trails, one for beginners and one for intermediate, are covered by snowmaking and lighted for evening skiing; group and private lessons are taught at the ski school. Snowboarding and tubing have been added for more variety.

Many visitors reserve time for sight-seeing in the area. The Biltmore House and Gardens, along with its winery, certainly warrant a side trip, as do the Great Smoky Mountain Railway or the Cherokee Indian Reservation. Monday through Friday the resort schedules van trips. Local mountain crafts can be purchased in Cashiers and Highlands.

The Community Center is open from 9:00 A.M. to 8:00 P.M. There are socials, television viewing rooms, a gift shop, trip and event reservations, table tennis, the nature center, board games, puzzles, book exchange, and area information. The Starlab Dome, a portable planetarium, allows you to view the stars and constellations, and then enjoy a laser show. Sapphire Valley is making an effort to add more evening activities and special events such as summer concerts and weekly comedy nights.

FAIRFIELD SAPPHIRE VALLEY

70 Sapphire Valley Road
Sapphire, North Carolina 28774
(828) 743–3441, (800) 533–8268
www.fairfieldsapphirevalley.com,
www.sapphirevalleyresort.com

THE GREENBRIER

White Sulphur Springs, West Virginia

The Greenbrier is a 6,500-acre estate in the beautiful Allegheny Mountains. Its history dates back to just after the Revolutionary War, when early settlers discovered the sulfur springs of this area. The grand Georgian architecture of The Greenbrier with its white columned porticoes, elaborate formal gardens, and friendly atmosphere set the scene for a memorable experience of fine dining, recreation, and relaxation.

The only problem at The Greenbrier may be deciding what to do first. With a list of recreational and social activities a mile long, you may need a personal secretary to help you get organized. When planning events for your stay, though, save time for an escape to discover nature's charms along the enticing woodland trails, well marked for joggers and walkers alike. And pause among the twelve acres of formal gardens, tended meticulously from spring through fall. With a reputation that has attracted presidents and royalty, The Greenbrier provides a level of elegant service and comfort that ensures an unforgettable vacation. It is open year-round.

Accommodations: With rooms and suites in the hotel as well as guest houses and cottages, you have a wide choice of accommodations. The rooms are large and bright, with comfortable, elegant furnishings. Based on a Modified American Plan, daily rates for a standard room are $219 to $300 (depending on the season) per person, double occupancy; larger rooms and prime locations command slightly higher rates, up to $390 for a junior suite. There is no charge for children 17 and under occupying the same room as their parents. The guest cottages include one to four bedrooms, a living room, and a porch or patio; many have fireplaces. The daily per person, per bedroom rate, based on an occupancy of two to eight people, is $259 to

$475, Modified American Plan. The Creekside Cottages are available to guests visiting for a minimum of one week. Golf, tennis, and family package plans are offered. Cribs are provided at no extra charge. With the Family Package, children seventeen and under may stay free (taxes and service charges apply) in the room or may have their own room at a special per room rate. Breakfast and dinner are always included for everyone. April 1 to October 31 is high season; rates are $255 mid-week and $335 on weekends. These rates are per person for the adults, and per room for the children. Accommodations for single parents are well priced in spring and fall ($248), but rates rise sharply ($475 to $639) in summer.

Dining: The Greenbrier boasts exciting culinary experiences. Regional Southern specialties, such as spoon bread and fresh trout from the nearby mountain streams, as well as Continental dishes, make dining a special part of a visit here. The sumptuous breakfasts, featuring homemade biscuits and country ham, are a real treat. A Modified American Plan is required for all guests. A coat and tie are standard attire for gentlemen at dinner in the main dining room; live piano and violin music is featured daily. Chef Peter Timmins is one of only fifty-nine certified master chefs in the world, so prepare your palate!

The main dining room serves breakfast and six-course dinners; for a la carte dining April through October, the Tavern Room provides a sophisticated setting and gourmet dining, along with a wine bar. Sam Snead's at the Golf Club is a casual dining option to the elegant main dining room, showcasing panoramic golf course views and an open kitchen, where you can watch the food being prepared. It is included on the meal plan for dinner; lunch is a la carte. Slammin'

Sammy's is a sports lounge (with ultra-large TV and pocket billiards) and good-time entertainment spot with a daytime a la carte menu. Both are open only in summer. The Rhododendron Spa Cafe, located adjacent to the indoor pool, offers a light, spa cuisine lunch menu, smoothies, fresh juices, and snacks. Drapers Cafe—especially popular for its homemade ice cream—is convenient for light meals, snacks, and pastries throughout the day. Complimentary afternoon tea is served daily with musical accompaniment. In the elegant and warm Old White Lounge, guests gather at 5:00 P.M. for cocktails and complimentary hors d'oeuvres and later for music and dancing until closing.

Children's World: From Memorial Day through Labor Day and at the holiday times of Thanksgiving, Christmas, and Easter, the Greenbrier Adventure Zone more than fills the days of three- to twelve-year-olds. During the summer elementary-school teachers and child-development specialists supervise full-day and evening programs for Discoverers (ages three to five), Explorers (ages six to eight), and Expeditioners (ages nine to twelve), combining intellectual enrichment with outdoor activities. Creative Classrooms, an innovative series of hands-on workshops designed with Carnegie Hall, West Virginia, include mask magic, puppet making, basketry, art history, and more; drama and stagecraft classes are taught by staff and performers of the Greenbrier Valley Theatre. Along with the usual swimming, tennis, golf, nature hikes, and fishing, children can experience falconry, carriage rides, or visits to the stables and fire station. Full-day programs run from 9:00 A.M. to 4:00 P.M. Children's Cooking Classes, limited to eight students, are offered every Wednesday, Friday, and Saturday in summer for $55 per child. The fee is $50 a day (9:00 A.M. to 4:00 P.M.) for your first child and $40 a day for each additional child.

From 6:30 to 10:00 P.M. for $35, children ages six to twelve years old can join their counselors for dinner and an evening of bowling, board games, or movies. Baby-sitting services for younger children are also available at an average hourly rate of $6.00. So it's possible for grown-ups to arrange an evening or two for wining and dining.

Recreation: Avid golf and tennis players are well served at The Greenbrier. The Allegheny hills provide the beauty and the challenge of three eighteen-hole championship golf courses, one of which was redesigned in 1979 by Jack Nicklaus. The Greenbrier Sam Snead Golf Academy provides golfers of all skill levels the opportunity to improve their game. The academy provides professional teaching staff and state-of-the-art equipment and services.

The staff at the tennis pro shop can assist in finding partners on one of the five outdoor or five indoor courts. You may also confront the idiosyncrasies of your swing during instructional videotaped replays of your performance.

Kate's Mountain is the picturesque site of the Gun Club, with its four trap and skeet fields. Group tournaments can be organized, or perhaps you'll take in the action from the sidelines in the Clubhouse lounge. The Falconry Academy allows guests to interact with this exciting sport.

Fishing enthusiasts head for the well-stocked streams and lakes, while swimmers can work out in the indoor or outdoor pool or relax poolside. An exercise room is adjacent to the indoor swimming pool. The bowling center (eight lanes), table tennis, horseback riding, shuffleboard, horseshoes, croquet, bicycling, carriage rides, and movies offer additional diversions. The five hiking trails are graded by length and rise in elevation. One of the two jogging trails features twelve exercise stations. Winter brings snow hiking and sleigh rides. Downhill skiing is ninety minutes away at the Snowshoe Ski Resort.

And when the body wearies and the spirits droop, the only respectable place to be is the Spa, which pampers guests with mineral baths, massage, steam, and sauna facilities.

It was the sulfur water with its medicinal and recuperative powers that first attracted visitors to this region. For shoppers, a fine selection of fashions, jewelry, handcrafts, and gifts is presented in the Gallery of Shops.

THE GREENBRIER

300 West Main Street
White Sulphur Springs, West Virginia
24986
(304) 536–1110, (800) 624–6070
www.greenbrier.com

THE GROVE PARK INN RESORT AND SPA
Asheville, North Carolina

The scenery and climate of the Blue Ridge Mountains have long attracted visitors to Asheville. The Grove Park Inn, located on the western slope of Sunset Mountain, opened its doors to guests in 1913 and gives a feeling of pure country in the midst of the city, with grand vistas of mountains and green golf courses. Built of granite from the nearby mountains and dedicated to preserving a gracious early-twentieth-century atmosphere, the inn was added to the National Register of Historic Places in 1973. Its guest list over the years reads somewhat like a who's who: Thomas Edison, Henry Ford, Woodrow Wilson, Enrico Caruso, Béla Bartók, and President and Mrs. Franklin Roosevelt. History buffs will have a fine time wondering which room General Pershing slept in or if F. Scott Fitzgerald sat by the fireplace in the Great Hall sipping an after-dinner brandy. A fireplace there, by the way, is so huge that an adult can walk into it!

The resort's country club (originally the Swannanoa Hunt Club that began in 1893) and the inn were renovated in the late 1980s. Two wings, which complement the architectural style and materials of the main building, were added. The four-diamond, three-star Grove Park Inn is open year-round.

Accommodations: Both the historic main inn and the wings house 510 guest rooms; those offering panoramic mountain views enchant many a guest. There are twelve suites and an exclusive club floor if your entourage warrants the space or additional amenities. In the historic inn rooms a small refrigerator keeps children's drinks and snacks chilled and close at hand. Panorama Corner rooms are more spacious, with superb views, and are ideal for families. All rooms were refurbished in 2001. Rates range from $119 to $389 for a double room; a one-bedroom suite is $389 to $709. Value season is January through March, while June through October is peak season, with the highest rates. Rates are EP, although meal plans are available if desired. Various packages are also available; ask about rates. Children under sixteen stay free in their parents' room; cribs and rollaway beds are available at no cost.

Dining: A full range of refreshments, from snacks and sandwiches to full-course meals, is offered. Enjoy breakfast, lunch, and dinner in the glass-enclosed terrace of the Blue Ridge Dining Room. Casual during the day, collared shirts and long pants are requested in the evening. One of the South's most famous and popular outdoor dining verandahs, the Sunset Terrace offers majestic views and sunsets over the city skyline and mountains. Chops serves prime rib and fresh seafood for lunch and dinner; in the evening dinner music and dancing are added. In the winter months, Chops moves into the Carolina Café, also with lovely views. Sample the award-winning gourmet cuisine at Horizons, a four-diamond-rated restaurant; jackets required. In the evening you can enjoy your favorite beverage in the old-world charm of the Great Hall Bar, along with hot hors d'oeuvres and live music nightly.

Children's World: Monday through Friday from Memorial Day through Labor Day, and on Saturdays year-round, the inn organizes children ages four to twelve in Cubs Adventure Camp, a fully supervised program. Full days are 9:00 A.M. to 4:00 P.M. ($35 including lunch); half-day camps run from 9:00 A.M. to noon or 1:00 to 4:00 P.M. ($22 with snack or $27 with lunch). Usual activities include theme days, swimming, nature hikes, and arts and crafts. "Kid's Night Out" ($25) provides a "night out" for kids and parents alike from 6:00 to 9:00 P.M. on Monday through Thursday during summer. Available Fridays and Saturdays year-round, activities include dinner, night swimming (there's an indoor pool), organized games, face-painting, campfires, and movies for $30. If you prefer, the concierge desk will provide a list of individual baby-sitters, with varying fees.

Recreation: An eighteen-hole Donald Ross championship golf course meanders down the gentle mountain slope. Practice your backhand on one of the six tennis courts (three outdoor, three indoor). The staff in the tennis and golf pro shops can assist you with your playing and fashion needs. An indoor Sports Complex has racquetball and tennis courts, weight and exercise rooms, and a fully

equipped aerobics room with professionally taught classes. There are also indoor and outdoor pools available for hotel guests. And remember to make time for a walk down the garden paths and nature trails, also suitable when the urge to jog hits you. The Grove Park Inn was created as an idyllic retreat, a place for total relaxation; the addition of the Spa in 1998 simply enhanced that lofty goal. Beautifully designed, it is open to the sun, yet protected, while waterfalls and pools add to the serenity. Allow yourself to just stop—and enjoy. The access fee of $50 can be applied 100 percent toward services.

Nearby you can explore the lake or try your hand at fishing, horseback riding, cycling, mountain biking, white-water rafting, ballooning, or llama trekking. In the winter a day of skiing (cross-country or downhill) is a popular excursion. For souvenirs, you'll discover unique items at the resort's six gift shops as well as many crafts shops and potteries in the area. The Biltmore Estate is only 8 miles from the inn; an afternoon can be well spent discovering the art, antiques, winery, and formal gardens of this magnificent old estate. Strolling the streets and shops of Asheville provides hours of diversion.

THE GROVE PARK INN RESORT AND SPA

290 Macon Avenue
Asheville, North Carolina 28804
(828) 252–2711, (800) 438–5800
www.groveparkinn.com

HIGH HAMPTON INN
& COUNTRY CLUB
Cashiers, North Carolina

The verdant Blue Ridge Mountains provide a beautiful setting, and High Hampton Inn, located in the Cashiers Valley at an altitude of 3,600 feet, allows its guests an escape to clean, crisp air, clear mountain lakes, and tall pine trees. Some people like the ambience of a country inn—quiet, friendly, with rustic accommodations and good home-style cooking. Others like the atmosphere of a resort, with lots of activities and events and busy days and nights. Happily, High Hampton has managed to blend the best of both these worlds. Roam over the 1,400 acres and explore the beauties of nature in the southwest corner of North Carolina. Dating from the mid-nineteenth century, High Hampton was once the summer home of Confederate General Wade Hampton and remained in the Hampton family until the 1920s. The inn is on the National Register of Historic Places.

For more than seventy-eight years, under the continuing ownership of the McKee family, the inn has welcomed guests to an informal atmosphere for golf, tennis, swimming, fishing, and simple relaxing. The architecture of the inn is charming and rustic, blending with the natural surroundings. The wide porches filled with plants and the lobby's stone chimney with four fireplaces hint at the warmth and friendly spirit within. The inn is open only from mid-April to mid-November, with a famous Thanksgiving Houseparty to close the season.

Accommodations: The 117 rooms at the inn (some of which are suites) are simple, warm, and rustic; the knotty pine walls and mountain-style furniture echo the landscape and the crafts of the region. Many of the rooms have very pleasant views of the grounds and there are no telephones or television in the rooms. What a way to relax! Several cottages are nestled into the mountain landscape. Based on a Full American Plan, daily rates are $95 to $116 per person midweek, $101 to $126 on Friday and Saturday; children under six are $41 to $52, while older children are $68 to $71. Cribs are available for infants and toddlers at no charge. A number of privately owned homes are also available; these are fully equipped, with fireplace, deck, laundry, and kitchen. Choose from two to four bedrooms with no meals, but with daily maid service, for $262 to $484 a day. If you choose not to cook, a Full American Plan is available for $43 per person per day, or $22 for children under six years. Golf and tennis plans are offered as well.

Dining: The one dining room at the inn specializes in regional Southern cooking, and service is buffet style. Imagine down-home favorites like country ham, fresh local trout, cream of peanut soup, homemade biscuits, and vegetables fresh from the garden. The Overlook Cafe, next to the Pro Shop, serves light lunches, continental breakfast for early birds, and everyone's favorite—ice cream and sweets. Coats and ties are standard attire for men in the evening, as High Hampton clings to traditional ways. Afternoon tea is served daily in the lobby with cakes and socializing.

Wine and beer only are served in the dining room, but mixed drinks are served at the Rock Mountain Tavern, a popular spot to gather, listen to music, meet other guests, and line up partners for bridge or tennis. Movies, lobby games, bridge, and mountain hayrides fill the evening. Small groups of guests may gather on porches to compare notes, sip their own drinks, and talk about the day.

Children's World: Kids have their own building at High Hampton, called Noah's Ark, where youngsters ages three to twelve meet with counselors for daily activities such as arts and crafts, games, tennis, nature studies, and hiking. Offered from June 1 through Labor Day, the program runs from 9:00 A.M. to 2:00 P.M. and includes lunch. After a free afternoon children can rejoin their group at 6:00 P.M. for dinner (sometimes a hayride and cookout!) and games, movies, and stories until 9:00 P.M. The fee is $3.00 an hour per child. Baby-sitters are available for wee ones and for nights after 9:00 P.M.

While there's no swimming pool, a restricted, shallow area of the lake with a sandy beach is especially designed for young children. The area includes a toddlers' play-house, swings, seesaw, and jungle gym, keeping the little ones amused for hours.

Rather than a teen club, High Hampton has the Gathering Place. Here, the next generation can gather to socialize and enjoy the pool table, table tennis, and video games. Outdoor activities such as volleyball, boating excursions, and picnics or mountain hikes are planned and enjoyed by all.

Recreation: The mountain terrain and picturesque scenery make golf a challenge and a pleasure. The eighteen-hole course, designed by George Cobb, is carved on a gently rolling plateau, skirting lakes and weaving through white pine and hemlock. There are two putting greens and a practice range; lessons are available.

The tennis center encompasses six outdoor clay courts, a pro shop, and a practice area; clinics and private lessons are offered. You pay court fees and greens fees unless you are on a four- or seven-day golf or tennis package.

There are three mountain lakes, but the thirty-five-acre Hampton Lake is the center of activity, where paddleboats, canoes, rowboats, and sailboats can be rented. Blissfully, motor-boats are not allowed. These clear waters are not just for invigorating swims and peaceful excursions. When the fishing mood strikes, you'll be happy to know that one of the lakes has rainbow and brook trout; bass and bream can also be lured from the waters.

Discover the rich natural beauty of these surroundings on one of the eight major hiking trails. Or take to the mountain trails—in one and a half hours you can climb to the 4,618-foot summit of Chimney Rock for absolutely spectacular views. Take the ten-station Fitness Trail to the base of Rock Mountain. Weekly guided half-day hikes with picnic lunch and walking sticks provide yet another diversion. In a more leisurely manner, lawn sports such as badminton, croquet, shuffleboard, and archery may attract you, or maybe you'll be drawn to the gardens for a stroll among the dahlias, mountain laurel, rhododendron, and azaleas.

The inn occasionally holds workshops in such diverse areas as bridge, fly-fishing, quilting, watercolor painting, and investments—what a pleasant way to glean helpful hints on a variety of topics! While proud of its facilities, the High Hampton Inn mostly boasts of its friendly atmosphere, its low-key pace, and the serenity and beauty of its natural setting. It is also proud that High Hampton "is not for everyone." But those who stay return year after year, and their children bring their own children. It's that kind of place.

HIGH HAMPTON INN & COUNTRY CLUB

P.O. Box 338, Highway 107
Cashiers, North Carolina 28717
(828) 743–2411, (800) 334–2551
www.highhamptoninn.com

THE HOMESTEAD
Hot Springs, Virginia

Few classic institutions in the United States have captured the attention of vacationers for many years. With all its charm and grace, The Homestead ranks as one of these. Its fascinating history has roots in the 1700s, yet The Homestead has moved into this century with style, preserving an atmosphere of friendly elegance. As with several fine old resorts in this country, the medicinal quality of mineral springs first attracted people to the site of The Homestead. While The Spa is still a captivating diversion for guests, many recreational facilities have been developed over the years, with golf being the premier sport here.

The current hotel was built in 1902, with additions continuing into the late 1920s. Despite almost three decades of construction, The Homestead is a cohesive, majestic structure of red brick and white columns in Georgian style. At an elevation of 2,300 feet, the estate sprawls over 15,000 acres (yes—15,000!) of the Allegheny Mountains in western Virginia. It is open year-round.

Accommodations: The Homestead boasts more than 500 bright and spacious rooms, all recently renovated. Each wing of this National Historic Monument has its own theme. Sizes vary from traditional rooms to parlor rooms and suites; the rate is determined by the size of the room and its location. Based on a Modified American Plan, the rate for a standard double room from May through July is $198 to $236 per person per day; weekend rates are the highest. The rates are slightly lower November through March ($118 to $160), except during the Thanksgiving and Christmas holiday seasons. There is no charge for children under five and no additional charge for cribs and rollaways. Children ages five to twelve pay $47 each for meals and ages thirteen and over pay $67.

The Modified American Plan rates include the room, two meals a day, valet parking, swimming, afternoon tea, evening movies, and use of the supervised children's playground. Separate fees are charged for all other activities, and family packages are available.

Dining: Dining at The Homestead is special. Executive chef for 37 years, Albert Schnarwyler ensures that every meal is a memorable experience. Imagine baked apples and kippered herring for breakfast; consider lunches and dinners that feature local favorites such as Smithfield ham, rainbow trout from nearby mountain streams, and fresh turnip greens, as well as fine international cuisine. A selection that includes bluepoint oysters, grilled Dover sole with almonds, roast baby pheasant, and tournedos Rossini makes for difficult decisions; it's almost necessary to spend extended time at The Homestead just to sample the specialties. The sublime creations of pastries, sorbets, and fresh fruit tarts should not be missed.

The Dining Room is open year-round and requests jackets and ties for gentlemen in the evenings. During the April through October season, the 1766 Grille features fine dinner dining with French and American cuisine in an intimate atmosphere. Jackets required, and a $20 per person surcharge applies. Four miles south of The Homestead, the seasonal Cascades Club Restaurant offers a casual lunch dining atmosphere for golfers just finishing their round. The Casino Club Restaurant, also seasonal, features a hearty lunch menu in a casual setting overlooking the swimming pool, tennis courts, and lawn game area. During the summer the Casino is also open on Friday and Saturday evenings for dinner. Sam Snead's Tavern serves history along with tavern favorites for lunch or dinner. Located across the street from the resort in a late nineteenth century building, it provides a bit of local color. In winter the Mountain Lodge Restaurant is a cozy getaway for skiers and nonskiers alike. Choose the elegant Presidents Lounge for pre- and post-dinner cocktails or The Players Pub for tuning in to all the sports action, darts, billiards, and dancing to Top 40 music while drinks and snacks are served continually. Or do both! Picnic lunches can also be prepared if you choose to spend the day outdoors in the wooded mountains.

A time-honored custom at The Homestead is Afternoon Tea, served daily at 4:00 P.M. in the Great Hall. In an elegant setting graced by chandeliers and Corinthian columns, you can relax to soft piano music while sipping tea.

Children's World: Headquartered in their own Clubhouse on Cottage Row, The Homestead offers excellent daily year-round supervised activities for ages three to twelve. The Kids Club runs from 9:00 A.M. to 4:00 P.M. daily (only to 12:30 P.M. on winter Sundays); it is licensed through the Commonwealth of Virginia Department of Social Services and is a member of the National Association of the Education for Young Children and the Virginia Fine Arts Museum. "Learning through Fun" is the program's goal—kids love the "fun" aspect of the program, and parents (and kids!) like the "learning" part. Activities follow three areas, children's literary and storytelling, science and biology, and art and design. These themes weave through both indoor and outdoor activities and provide a seamless experience for kids.

The outdoor playground has been completely renovated, and children have their own fishing pond—great for kids of all ages. Other activities include tennis on special mini-courts, bowling, swimming, hiking and mountain biking, hand-led horseback rides, and exotic falconry demonstrations. In the winter, kids learn to ski at the Bunny School, and enjoy winter sports such as ice-skating, snowboarding, and snow tubing. Costs are $60 for a full day ($40 for additional children in the same family); $40 for a half day with lunch or $30 for half day with no lunch. On Friday and Saturday evenings in the summer (Saturday evenings only in the winter), Children's Dinner Programs are held from 6:30 to 10:30 P.M.; the cost is $20 per child on MAP plans, and $35 per child with no meal plan. Baby-sitting requires a two-hour minimum and is $12 an hour for the first child and $2.00 for each additional child in the immediate family.

Recreation: Even golf and tennis have hundred-year-old histories at The Homestead. There are three eighteen-hole golf courses, and the fact that native son Sam Snead started his golfing career here adds a certain panache to the atmosphere and lends credence to the caliber of play. The Old Course was opened in 1892 and revamped in the 1920s when a second course, the Cascades, was added. Robert Trent Jones designed the third course, the Lower Cascades, which opened in 1963. All three courses weave through a picturesque wooded landscape. With a putting green, a practice fairway, a pro shop, and lessons available, you have all the necessary ingredients to improve your game.

Tennis also got under way here in 1892. Today The Homestead has six courts, including two Har-Tru courts and four clay courts. Two tiers of courts are laid out to give your game privacy plus a spectacular view of The Homestead tower and the mountain valley. Tennis lessons can be scheduled, and the tennis shop is well equipped.

The facilities at The Spa include massage, aromatherapy, mineral baths, aerobics classes, and indoor and outdoor swimming pools. The beautiful indoor pool, built in 1903, is fed by the naturally warm mineral water of the nearby hot springs. There may be no proven miraculous powers in the famous mineral waters, but the benefits of a spa regimen to both body and spirit are not to be questioned.

For fans of trap and skeet, there are four fields; instruction is offered so that even novices can try this sport. Other outdoor sports include horseback riding in the wooded countryside, canoeing and kayaking, trout fishing in the Cascades Stream, and hiking or biking on the 100 miles of mountain trails. A guided hike through the Cascades Gorge is very popular. Or you may prefer to enjoy the scenery during a carriage ride in an old-fashioned buckboard or a surrey with fringe. The tractor-driven hayride to a secluded bonfire is a great family activity.

Some more-unique activities are paintball games for ages twelve and up, on a special course; mountain boarding; extreme golf; touring the unique caves in the area; a challenge course (see how much you trust your family members!); and falconry, with a history stretching back nearly 4,000 years. Lessons are available, and you even get a photograph with the hunting bird. Or opt for bowling, table tennis, billiards, or card and board games. In the evenings go dancing or take in a movie.

Winter sports are limited, but The Homestead does have nine downhill ski runs, open mid-December through March. With a vertical drop of just 700 feet, it cannot offer the diversity and challenge that a good skier seeks, but it may be a fun place for kids to learn, and it does provide an added dimension to a winter vacation. Near the lodge, which houses a restaurant, the ski school, and ski shops, is an Olympic-size skating rink; skating lessons are offered. Cross-country skiers can explore acres of mountain meadows and trails, weather permitting, of course.

THE HOMESTEAD

U.S. Route 220 Main Street
Hot Springs, Virginia 24445
(540) 839–1766, (800) 838–1766
www.thehomestead.com

HYATT REGENCY CHESAPEAKE BAY

Cambridge, Maryland

Hyatt's Golf Resort, Spa and Marina fit beautifully on the Choptank River on Maryland's eastern shore. The perfect spot for visiting wildlife refuges; two are nearby, and the Heron Point Wildlife Refuge is on the resort property. Cambridge is Maryland's second-largest deepwater port, and 1,700 miles of shoreline wind around the area. It's only an hour from urban Baltimore, but the 342 landscaped acres and the river make it feel like the country.

Accommodations: Four hundred luxurious rooms, including sixteen suites, all with balcony or patio area and minirefrigerators, and the style and amenities one expects from Hyatt. Winter is low season, when rates begin at $130; June to September rates range from $225 to $300. Packages are available; for example Sunshine on Sale, starting at $300 per night, includes a complimentary Camp Hyatt session, the fourth night free, 50 percent off the second room, and kids under twelve eat free from the children's menu.

Dining: Feasting on the local specialties is practically a requirement of your visit. Soft-shell crab, Maryland blue crab, Blue Pointe oysters, and rockfish are popular menu items, creatively prepared and presented. At Water's Edge Grill, enjoy breakfast, lunch, and dinner while watching it happen at the display kitchen. Outdoor dining may be enjoyed seasonally on the screened porch overlooking the crescent pool. At the far end of the resort overlooking the marina, sunsets and seafood specialties are equally famous at Blue Pointe Provisions, a freestanding restaurant almost on the banks of the Choptank River. The Eagle's Nest Bar and Grille, also on River Marsh Marina, is by the Golf Club, with scenic views of the greens. Perfect for sandwiches, wraps, and salads as well as nineteenth-hole libations. Dock's poolside bar personally serves you refreshments at any of the four pools, the beach, or even the hot tub. Stock up on snacks and provisions at either the Bay Country Market or the Quarterdeck Marina Store. Mitchener's Library, in the lobby, would do the famous author of *Chesapeake* proud. Stone fireplaces border a two-story glass wall with spectacular views, and outside benches invite you to tarry amid fountains or warm yourself at the fire pit. Little nooks, named after people connected to Cambridge history, like Harriet Tubman, King Ababaco, and Annie Oakley, provide cozy spots for reading, billiards, or just curling up next to the fireplace.

Children's World: Camp Hyatt at Pirate's Cove offers fully supervised fun for kids ages four to twelve daily from Memorial Day to Labor Day and on holidays and weekends year-round. Kids have their own reception desk, activity room, a multimedia room, and even an enclosed outdoor playground adjacent to the center. A long list of activities includes crabbing (of course, this is Maryland!), building sand castles, treasure hunts, kite contests, tennis, golf and nature hikes. Indoors, kids color, play board games, and participate in arts and crafts, shell art, and storytelling, just to mention a few activities. The split-level pool is always an attraction, and is partially indoors for inclement

weather. A full day with lunch, from 9:00 A.M. to 4:00 P.M., is $52.00; half-day morning or afternoon is $28.00 per child and $5.00 for lunch. Evening sessions run from 6:00 to 9:00 P.M. for $35 per child, so parents are able to have their own "night out."

Recreation: The Golf Club at River Marsh, an eighteen-hole championship course designed by Keith Foster, has an elaborate driving range, chipping and putting greens, and a pro shop. Don't know where to park your boat? The 150-slip marina should solve that problem. Relax by any of the four pools, both indoors or outdoors and on several levels. The Wintergarden pool is glass-enclosed, providing year-round enjoyment and views of the river. The volleyball court on the beach is fenced, so you don't have to chase those missed balls too far. The Stilwater European Health Spa offers twelve treatment rooms with unique indigenous spa treatments, and you can get or stay in shape at the fitness and aerobic center. Four lighted tennis courts also give a good workout, and jogging and walking trails wend through the eighteen-acre Heron Point Wildlife Refuge, where you might see an American bald eagle or a blue heron. Nearby visit Taylor's Island Wildlife Refuge, Blackwater Wildlife Refuge, or the Harriet Tubman Museum for a bit of local history.

HYATT REGENCY CHESAPEAKE BAY

100 Heron Boulevard
Cambridge, Maryland 21613
(410) 901–1234, (800) 233–1234
www.chesapeakebay.hyatt.com

KIAWAH ISLAND GOLF RESORT

Kiawah Island, South Carolina

In climate and scenery, the islands off the coast of the Carolinas offer some of the finest resort living. Set amid 10,000 acres, at Kiawah Island Resorts the beauty of the natural setting has been carefully respected, while man-made amenities have been added to provide visitors with the best in comfort, relaxation, recreation, and fun. The name Kiawah (KEE-a-wah) comes from the Indians who lived, hunted, and fished here prior to the 1600s when Charles Town was settled. An island with 10 miles of beach on the Atlantic Ocean, Kiawah is actually two resort villages, each with its own lodging and recreational facilities; a shuttle bus connects the villages. It is the only resort/development on the island.

West Beach Village (which dates from 1976) consists of the Kiawah Island Inn, condominiums, restaurants, a racquet club, shops, pools, and a golf course. At East Beach Village (the younger by five years), there are condominiums, restaurants, shops, a golf course, a tennis club, and Night Heron Park, a twenty-one-acre recreation area that encompasses pools, a lake, playgrounds, and picnic sites.

In spring 2004, Kiawah will add the Sanctuary, a 255-room ultraluxury hotel and spa.

All these conveniences and amenities, and yet you still have the opportunity to feel close to nature. The sound ecological planning at Kiawah has preserved the lagoons and marshes and ensured homes for deer, raccoon, egrets, and brown pelicans; you might even get to see a loggerhead sea turtle, alligators, dolphins, or an eagle. The drive from the Charleston Airport is about forty-five minutes. As you enter the main gates to Kiawah, you'll be given a car registration pass that reads "Please respect the wildlife that inhabits Kiawah Island. Alligators are potentially dangerous and extremely fast. They should never be fed or teased in any way." When you see alligators plying the lagoon waters, you'll understand this warning.

Accommodations: The Kiawah Island Inn, located in West Beach Village, is the right choice for those who want to be pampered. The 150 rooms, distributed among four lodges, all have private balconies overlooking the ocean, pools, lagoons, or picturesque wooded areas; the services and conveniences are typical of a fine resort hotel.

The condominium villas, cedar-shingled or natural-wood frame structures, are dispersed throughout the island in different settings appealing to all different interests. You may choose one with an ocean view or one next door to the tennis courts, one alongside the lush green fairways of a golf course, one on a lake, or one nestled among oaks and hickories and sweet gum trees. These one- to four-bedroom units have well-equipped kitchens, and most of them have sundecks or screened porches—terrific spots for having breakfast or just taking in the views. Both inn and villas have AAA Four Diamond ratings. One- to seven-bedroom luxury homes are also available.

Rates vary depending on the season and location; the inn and villas range from $109 to $299 nightly. Weekly rates for villas are $579 to $2,099. Be sure to ask about any special packages, especially golf. Cribs are free at the inn, $20 per day or $100 per week in the villas; rollaways are $25 at the inn.

Dining: You'll never have a problem here; there are enough restaurants to meet varied moods and tastes. Enjoy a spectacular view of the ocean at the elegant Atlantic Room, located at the inn. The menu features a wide variety of deep-ocean fish and shellfish caught daily. Free breakfast buffet, Sunday champagne brunch, and dinner are available.

The West Beach Café and Bar is a casual dining spot in the Shops at the Kiawah Island Inn that caters to families; it's open for lunch and dinner and features tempting focaccia-crust pizzas and sandwiches to please any palate. Nearby is Scooper's, where the ice cream and pastries are hard to resist (who can pass up an ice-cream flavor called Mississippi Mud?). Beside the inn's pool, Sundancer's serves salads, burgers, and other light fare for lunch and supper. The Turtle Point, Ocean Course, and Osprey Point clubhouses are also home to excellent restaurants. The dining room at Osprey Point carries AAA's four-diamond rating.

On Monday and most Wednesday evenings, families head to Mingo Point on the Kiawah River for an outdoor barbecue and oyster roast, followed by the down-home music of a bluegrass band. Another favorite is the weekly Family Cookout at Night Heron Park. For evening cocktails and musical entertainment, try the Charleston Bar at the Inn or Sundancer's, popular places to sip an old favorite or an exotic tropical drink. The Market at Town Center, a casual market, is located in East Beach, offering a variety of quick meals, grocery items, newspapers, apparel, wine, and even take-out pizza.

Children's World: From early May through September and at Thanksgiving, Christmas, New Year's, and Easter, children and parents alike find Kiawah Island the perfect destination for a family vacation.

Energetic college students with training in sports and recreation supervise young visitors in four different age groups in activities designed to ensure happy, fun-filled days. In fact, there's much more to do than we have room to outline. In summer Kamp Kiawah is in swing from 9:00 A.M. to 4:30 P.M. Monday through Friday. The cost is $55 for a full day with lunch included, $35 for the morning program, and $30 for the afternoon only. Divided into three groups—three to four years, five to seven years, and eight to eleven years—kids enjoy swimming, treasure hunts, crabbing, storytime, and crafts. Special nature programs with a staff naturalist allow children, teens, and even adults to have a hands-on, fun experience with nature. Ocean seining with a huge 40-foot net, canoe trips through the marshes, pond exploration, night walks on the beach, bird watching—with more than 10,000 acres of marshland and five staff naturalists, the possibilities go on and on. Costs range from $3.00 to $15.00.

Discovery Series, a free weekly program, features speakers accompanied by live snakes or alligators, storytellers, and more. Kiawah has found a successful blend of activities that includes teenagers' favorite things: sports, music, food, and loose structure. Volleyball and basketball tournaments, "teen splash" (pool time only for them), T-shirt graffiti, and a Friday-night dance with DJ are just a sample of the options.

Children also enjoy the playgrounds filled with wooden climbing equipment, swings, and slides; the largest one at Night Heron Park is built in and among the trees, hardly disturbing the natural vegetation. The Night Heron Park Center features video games, live animals, and nature wear and gear, as well as a recreation concierge.

When you want to be together and join other families, afternoon and evening hours are filled with bingo, games, nature films, family movies, and cookouts; most of these activities are free. Particularly fun is the "dive-in movie"—movies shown at the pool, with swimming allowed. Baby-sitters are available when you want to indulge in a strictly grown-up evening.

Recreation: With five excellent eighteen-hole championship golf courses and a twelve-month golfing season, golfers think they've discovered a little bit of paradise at Kiawah. Host site of the 1991 Ryder Cup and 1997 World Cup of Golf, the Ocean Course, designed by Pete Dye, is known worldwide. The Cougar Point Golf Course was designed by Gary Player, the Turtle Point Golf Course by Jack Nicklaus, the Osprey Point Golf Course by Tom Fazio, and Oak Point by Clyde Johnston; talent like this ensures challenge in a beautiful natural setting. You can enroll in group or private lessons or in a clinic, then practice newly acquired skills on the driving ranges and putting greens. The pro shops are well stocked with equipment, apparel, and accessories to enhance your game.

For tennis enthusiasts, the West Beach Tennis Club offers sixteen courts; the East Beach Tennis Club has twelve courts and a ball machine. Combined, Kiawah boasts twenty-three clay courts and five hard courts. Add a practice alley, resident pros, clinics, and group and private lessons and you have every opportunity to improve your game. Kiawah has been rated the sixth-best tennis resort in the nation by *Tennis* magazine. It offers free tennis clinics and one hour of free tennis daily to guests.

Swimmers take to the ocean from April through October or dip into one of the three pools at the inn (one for adults only, one for the family, and one a children's pool). Two 25-meter pools are located in Night Heron Park and East Beach Tennis Club. You can sign up for swimming lessons for yourself or your child (even an infant). Other water sports, such as sailing, canoeing, and sailboarding, are also popular.

Bicyclists have more than 10 miles of hard-packed beach and 30 miles of paved trails to explore (rentals, many with baby seats, are available). Joggers find a good workout on the 1.1-mile parcourse fitness trail with twenty exercise stations. Try your luck fishing in the lake or creek and surf casting in the ocean, or introduce your child to the fun of crabbing, where an old chicken neck can net beautiful blue-legged crabs. Adult exercise classes (aerobics and water exercise) are offered weekdays during the summer.

Nature lovers can participate in numerous expeditions into wilderness areas and river tours for a close look at the low-country wildlife and vegetation. The Nature Excursion Programs are unique to a barrier island, and more extensive than most resorts. Naturalists conduct marsh creek canoe trips, sea kayaking, birding walks, night beach walks, loggerhead turtle crawls, and even bird tours on bikes.

For unstructured fun, the twenty-one-acre Night Heron Park features basketball courts, a soccer field, swimming pools, a pavilion area, and a bicycle rental shop. Night Heron Park also serves as a popular gathering spot for special events, such as symphony concerts, family park cookouts, and beach music parties.

If shopping entices you, the Shops at the Kiawah Island Inn and the Town Center at East Beach Village have stores offering clothing, books, stationery, games, toys, jewelry, and gifts. And nearby Charleston (only 21 miles away) can charm you with historic houses and antiques shopping. With all it places at your disposal, Kiawah may tempt you back for many return visits.

KIAWAH ISLAND GOLF RESORT

12 Kiawah Beach Drive
Kiawah Island, South Carolina 29455
(843) 768–2121, (800) 654–2924; (800) 845–2471 (South Carolina)
www.kiawahresort.com

KINGSMILL RESORT
Williamsburg, Virginia

In 1736, Richard Kingsmill was granted land along the James River near the new town of Williamsburg, Virginia. Centuries later, much remains the same—deer and waterfowl still live in the unspoiled forest, some of the original plantation buildings still exist near prehistoric Native American sites, and nearby Colonial Williamsburg remains as a unique example of eighteenth-century America. Some things, however, have changed. Developed by Anheuser-Busch Companies, the Kingsmill of today shares its natural beauty and sense of history with both a modern-day resort and a separate thriving community of 5,000 people. The 3,900-acre site was originally selected for a new brewery, and part of the agreement was the construction of a theme park, Busch Gardens. Development has been well planned, and none of this impinges on the resort itself.

Environmental awareness is also a priority as 40 percent of the area remains green space, and future expansion of one area currently depends on a bald eagle nesting in the treetops of fifty-two prime acres near the river, which Kingsmill is preserving. No wonder it has the Audubon International Certification!

Accommodations: Kingsmill offers 400 accommodations, including hotel rooms and villa-style one- to four-bedroom suites. Organized into villa-style clusters around the Resort Center, all are within walking distance of resort facilities. Each suite contains a complete kitchen and living room; many feature fireplace and balcony. Guest-room rates begin at $139 in winter, $199 to $279 in spring and fall, and are highest in July and August at $219 to $299. Weekend rates are slightly higher. One-bedroom suites range from $219 to $399; two-bedroom suites are $358 to $698. Special lower rates are available when you purchase certain services, such as tickets to Busch Gardens or Colonial Williamsburg, a round of golf, or spa services. Be sure to check, as these are things you'll probably be doing anyway. Children under 18 stay free in the room; rollaways are not available. MAP rates with breakfast and dinner are also available. A shuttle operates throughout the property, as well as to the local attractions of Busch Gardens, Water World, and Colonial Williamsburg.

Dining: Six restaurants and lounges offer a variety of styles and menus. Eagles features exclusive beechwood-smoked cooking and hearty meals for breakfast, lunch, and dinner, along with panoramic views of the beautifully landscaped grounds and the river. The Bray Bistro brings past and present together in a unique cuisine served with generous views of the James River. The most casual venue is Regatta's Café and Market, with its open kitchen and fun foods; it also has a deli, to-go selections, and convenience items. The Deck at the Marina is right on the river, with a seafood bar, sandwiches, drinks, and live entertainment. Bray Landing is the spot to relax for coffee or a drink, while Moody's Tavern is the nighttime gathering place.

Children's World: Make your first stop the concierge desk for Junior Guest Registration. Kids receive a special Fun Map, Fun Plans, and a Kid's Fun Pack; plus everything you need to know about kids at Kingsmill.

Kingsmill Kamp uses the entire resort as a playground for five- to twelve-year-olds. Beach fun, limbo, and tug of war at the Marina; sports of all kinds; tennis and golf (including one-half hour instruction); carnival games; picnics; hiking; and crabbing; even building a bird feeder are some of the activities kids enjoy. Operating Monday through Saturday from mid-June to Labor Day, all programs include lunch and snacks. A full day costs $45; a half day is $30. As a special treat, Spa Camp is a half day of magic manicures, terrific toes, yoga, glamour shots, and lotion-potion making; at $35, it's sure to attract the young females of the species. Kids Night Out is offered Wednesday through Saturday in summer and on select Saturday nights throughout the year. It starts with pizza, is filled with fun, and ends on a tired but happy note at bedtime; for ages five to twelve, $35 per child.

Recreation: Golfers are happy with three eighteen-hole championship courses and a nine-hole par-3 course. Awards are numerous, including *Golf Magazine's* Silver Medal, *Condé Nast's Top 50 Golf Resorts,* and *Golf for Women's* Top 50 Fairways. Pete Dye designed the River Course to challenge professionals but be enjoyable to the average golfer as well; it's characterized by rolling hills, thick woods, and water everywhere. The Plantation Course by Arnold Palmer and Ed Seay is a little more forgiving, but no pushover. The Woods Course, by Curtis Strange and Tom Clark, is a parkland-style course stashed in its own private corner of the resort. The Golf Academy has an extensive program of instruction with a maximum 1:5 teacher-student ratio.

Voted one of the World's Top 75 Tennis Resorts by *Tennis Resorts Online,* Kingsmill Tennis Club offers instruction academies, events, and packages. Thirteen clay courts (including two lighted stadium courts), two Deco-Turf all-weather courts, and six hydro courts allow lots of choices, and court time is complimentary to guests.

The fifteen-slip Marina boasts a store, the Deck for dining, a small beach area, and the possibility of meeting visiting boat owners. The Sports Club is where you'll find the indoor and outdoor swimming pools, exercise classes, and fully equipped fitness room, whirlpool, steam and sauna, and 4-mile jogging course. Arrange a personal training session, work out, or simply play in the Game Room with billiards, table tennis, and video games. Stop by the concierge desk for the self-guided walking tour that includes all the plants and flowers. The Spa at Kingsmill is a welcoming place for massage, body treatments and wraps, facials, and even a special golfer's manicure.

And, of course, you'll need time for Busch Gardens, Water Country USA, and Colonial Williamsburg. Kingsmill runs frequent shuttles to all of these destinations. All different and all fun for families, you'll find more information on their Web sites. And remember to search for packages that include these attractions, which may be a value for your particular family needs.

KINGSMILL RESORT

1010 Kingsmill Road
Williamsburg, Virginia 23185
(757) 253–1703, (800) 832–5665
www.kingsmill.com

THE RESORT AT SEABROOK ISLAND

Seabrook Island, South Carolina

Sunshine and sandy beaches; lazy strolls under moss-draped oaks, palmettos waving in the breeze; enough fresh crabs, shrimp, and oysters to make your mouth water; golf, tennis, horseback riding, marina, fitness center, and water sports—is this a little bit of paradise? Visitors to this unique, private island believe so. Seabrook has the feel of a country club—no neon, no high-rises, not even any hotels! Share nature in harmony with eagles, dolphins, and bobcats, in a place where the beach is private and nothing is higher than two stories. All this is only about thirty minutes from beautiful, historic Charleston; it almost seems as though you can have your cake and eat it too. Activities and events for every member of the family support Seabrook's "something for everyone" philosophy. The resort is open year-round.

Accommodations: The one- to three-bedroom villas—all with fully equipped kitchens, many with sundecks or balconies—are distributed throughout the 2,200 acres of Seabrook Island property. Some are oceanside, with expansive views of the Atlantic, and close to the Beach Club, some line the scenic fairways of the golf courses, and some overlook the racquet club, marshlands, and tidal creeks. Some villa clusters have their own swimming pools. Rates depend on size, location, and time of year. During low season, December to mid-February, villa rates are $115 to $275. The weeks around Easter and early June through early September are high season, at $185 to $525, and the shoulder season ranges from $125 to $440. Rates are for villa accommodations only; most recreational activities have separate charges. Weekly rates (for six to seven nights) provide a savings, as do tennis, golf, honeymoon, or getaway packages. A family recreation package during June, July, and August is a good

value, with 20 percent discounts on most things, including golf.

Dining: With three restaurants, you'll surely find the cuisine and atmosphere to satisfy your taste and whim. The Island House Restaurant is elegant and offers traditional Southern cuisine and tempting seafood specialties; jackets are preferred for men at dinner. Here you might choose a sweet-potato soufflé or prawns stuffed with crabmeat. Bohickets Lounge has equally good food in a more casual atmosphere overlooking the golf course—you can watch the greens and eat them at the same time! For steak and seafood and an ocean view, head to the Seaview Restaurant, more informal than the Island House and more family oriented. Poolside cookouts are offered daily during the weeks surrounding Easter and throughout the summer season. A friendly atmosphere in which to sip a drink and discuss the day's events is provided at the outdoor Pelicans Nest, Half Shell Lounge, and Bohickets Lounge. Island House or Bohickets are open year-round; the others are seasonal.

Children's World: From Memorial Day to Labor Day, children ages four to ten have their own Monday-to-Friday Kids Club recreation program. Meeting from 9:00 A.M. to 4:00 P.M. in the Kids Club, supervised activities include golf and tennis clinics, pony rides, crabbing adventures, swimming, treasure hunts, nature hikes, puppet shows, storytelling, and arts and crafts. The cost is $42 for a full day, or $25 per half day. Lunch is available for $3.00 on the full-day program. A children's playground offers lots of equipment for the younger set.

Older children from twelve to nineteen are invited to the Recreation Pavilion every night from 8:30 to 11:00 P.M. This is their own time for video games, pool, table tennis, Foosball, air hockey, and socializing. Special theme parties, teen casino night, and even teen cruises are planned. Special nights are also planned for the entire family at a small cost.

The fun keeps on rolling at holiday times like Christmas, Thanksgiving, and Easter. Added to the regular activities may be Christmas caroling and a visit from Santa, The Little Pilgrims Program, or an Easter decorations crafts class and an Easter egg hunt. A day of adventures will give your child fond memories for years to come. With all of this, normal baby-sitters may seem a bit of a letdown, but they are available.

Recreation: With an average mid-day temperature of sixty degrees in January and eighty-nine degrees in August, golfing's fine in the Carolinas. Seabrook has two vastly different eighteen-hole courses; Crooked Oaks was designed by Robert Trent Jones Sr. and meanders through majestic oaks and dips along the sea marshes. Ocean Winds, designed by Willard Byrd, catches some of the tricky ocean breezes that make the play challenging and interesting. A fine teaching staff can help you smooth out the rough spots of your game, and the pro shop can fill in the gaps for clothing, equipment, and accessories.

Enjoy one of fifteen clay tennis courts at the Raquet Club. The Raquet Club offers a pro shop and a staff of pros who can do wonders for your backhand in individual or group lessons, camps, and clinics.

With 3½ miles of glorious private ocean beach, you might suspect that water sports tempt many visitors here. There are sunbathing, swimming, ocean fishing, and shelling. Canter along the beach at the edge of the surf or take a leisurely ride through the forests—both are possible at Seabrook, one of the few resorts with an on-site Equestrian Center. The center offers trained instructors who can give you tips to improve your technique. A junior Olympic pool, a heated pool, and a wading pool for children more than accommodate both serious swimmers and sun lovers. With their palm trees, gardens, and lovely surroundings, they also charm serious loungers in for just a quick splash. Perhaps you don't want to sing for your supper, but if you want to *catch* your supper, try fishing (in the ocean or the creeks) or crabbing and shrimping in the tidal marshes. Bicycle along the island's 10 miles of roads—many rental bikes come equipped with baby seats— or join the current craze for in-line skating.

The Recreation Pavilion takes care of a lot of your needs (rental beach chairs, in-line skates, bikes, and fishing and crabbing equipment) and is the focus of the Family Fun Program—activities that all the family members can enjoy together, like nature walks, family games, cookouts, bingo, and water volleyball. You may even challenge your child to an evening of video games.

Within 1 mile of Seabrook's gate, stroll the Bohicket Marina for chartered deep-sea fishing, creek fishing, and three family-style restaurants and shops. For the essentials and the fun of shopping, Seabrook has several stores: the Village Market for groceries; the Seabrook Shoppe for gifts, clothing, souvenirs, and sundries; and the golf and tennis shops for the latest fashions and equipment.

THE RESORT AT SEABROOK ISLAND

1002 Landfall Way
Seabrook Island, South Carolina 29455
(843) 768–1000, (800) 341–4248
www.discoverseabrook.com

THE TIDES INN

Irvington, Virginia

In eastern Virginia, peninsulas of land reach out like fingers between the many rivers heading into the Chesapeake. It is a region steeped in history, from the early-seventeenth-century settlements of Jamestown and Yorktown to the family homestead of Robert E. Lee. Its people have always had close ties to the water, originally for commerce and travel and today for recreation.

The northernmost of these peninsulas, bounded by the Potomac River and the Rappahannock River, is known as the Northern Neck. On its southern shore, on a bluff overlooking Carters Creek, sits the Tides Inn. The hotel is surrounded by water, and yachts literally dock in the front yard. A member of the Leading Small Hotels of the World, the Tides emphasizes uncrowded luxury and informal elegance in a leisurely atmosphere. Originally a stop for the steamboat lines between Baltimore and Norfolk in the late 1800s, the nearby small community of Irvington remains a quaint, picture-perfect town with friendly smiles for everyone.

Accommodations: All 106 rooms and suites are newly renovated; many have balconies or terraces and almost all have great views of Carters Creek. Rooms are located in the Main Building, the Garden House, the Windsor House, and the Lancaster House. Choose from deluxe rooms ($295), premium rooms ($295 to $325), or Vista Suites ($350 to $495). Four luxury suites ($450 to $850) are also available. Children are free in the room with parents if beds are adequate; cots are $25; cribs are complimentary. A meal plan (breakfast and dinner) is available for $99 per person for guests over ten years old; children under ten eat free. The high season at the Tides is May to October; the inn is closed from January to April.

Dining: Breakfast and dinner are served in the Dining Room. Breakfast is from 6:30 to 10:30 A.M., with an "early bird" continental breakfast or a "sleepyhead" breakfast later in the morning. At dinner jackets are required after 5:30 P.M. Just off the main lobby, the Chesapeake Club is open from 11:00 A.M. until 11:00 P.M., serving lunch, dinner, lounge food, and cocktails. Sit inside or out and enjoy the casual setting with nightly entertainment. Creekside, Commodore's is a casual seasonal restaurant for enjoying lunch and sunset drinks overlooking the pool and beach; late dinners are served on weekends. Also seasonal, Cap'n B's on the Golden Eagle Golf Course is open from lunch to sunset. It's a popular spot even with nongolfers, as the 400 rolling acres with lovely lakes and unspoiled woodlands add an extra dimension of pleasure to the New Orleans–style dining. On Saturdays in summer, splurge on a dinner cruise on the Rapphannock River on the historic yacht *Miss Ann*. And finally, if it fits your schedule or your mood, room service or picnic lunches are always options.

Children's World: In addition to the beach and swimming pool, a grassy playground with slides, swings, climbing bars, and the Chesapeake Bay Lighthouse attract young guests. From Memorial Day to Labor Day, the Crab Net Kids children's program is in session Monday through Sunday from 9:30 A.M. to 3:30 P.M., with lunch at the pool and swimming twice a day. All activities are covered for $45 per child per day. Morning sessions with lunch and snack are $30; afternoon sessions with snack only are $25. Crafts and games, scavenger hunts, sand sculpting, tennis, pitch and putt golf, bicycling, boating, and of course, crabbing keep youngsters from four to twelve years old busy. On Friday and Saturday evenings from 5:00 to 9:00 P.M., children meet as a group for dinner and evening activities, such as a "coketails and pizza party," followed by a movie. Baby-sitting is available at $10 an hour for one child with a three-hour minimum; add $1.00 an hour for each additional child.

Recreation: With water on practically all sides of the inn, boating is a natural sport here. The Premier Sailing School offers classes for all ages and experience levels. You can take off in a small craft like a sailboat, canoe, or paddleboat, or check out the yacht program and cruise the creek, the river, and the bay. The weekly routine schedules varied yachts for luncheon cruises, cove cruises, and bay-shore picnics. No additional fees are charged for use of the sailboats, paddleboats, and canoes, or for some of the yacht programs. In fact, rates include almost all activities—tennis, nine-hole par-3 golf course, bicycles to explore scenic Irvington, evening music and dancing, and the fitness and health facility.

Golf is also available, with twenty-seven holes that skirt the waterways and dip back into the trees. A nine-hole executive course is on the inn's property. A challenging course with more hilly terrain is the championship

Golden Eagle, 2½ miles from the inn.

Many of the ponds along the golf courses are well stocked for the fisherman who may also, in search of a saltwater catch, line up a trip with the dockmaster. A saltwater pool overlooks a small sandy beach, and table tennis, a pool table, video arcade, croquet, basketball, and shuffleboard are available in the activities cottage. For your evening entertainment, enjoy dancing, movies, bingo, or a pleasant stroll.

For history buffs, nearby sight-seeing excursions lead to Stratford Hall Plantation (the birthplace of Robert E. Lee), Christ Church, and Epping Forest, where George Washington's mother lived. Colonial Williamsburg is just an hour and fifteen minutes away and makes a nice day excursion.

THE TIDES INN

480 King Carter Drive
Irvington, Virginia 22480
(804) 438–5000, (800) 843–3746
www.tidesinn.com

WILD DUNES RESORT
Isle of Palms, South Carolina

Have you ever seen a three-year-old scamper across a sandy beach to the ocean? A biker pedal down paths through the marshes? A fishing boat return to harbor after a successful day's mission? A sailboat catch the sun and the wind in one skillful motion? An ace serve zing across the net? Or a golf ball soar over the fairway and over grand oaks on its way to a perfectly manicured green? Award-winning Wild Dunes can package all of these images

into quite a family vacation for you.

Wild Dunes has garnered some of the best features of the Carolina coastal islands and wrapped them up into a fine year-round resort. It is recognized by *Better Homes and Gardens* as one of thirty "Favorite Family Resorts." This relaxed and gracious community occupies 1,600 acres of the northern tip of the Isle of Palms, just thirty minutes from historic Charleston. Bounded by the Atlantic

Ocean on the east and the Intracoastal Waterway on the west, Wild Dunes delights in mild temperatures, soft ocean breezes, and fresh salt air. Relax and rejuvenate your spirits here in South Carolina's low country.

Accommodations: Wild Dunes offers Four Diamond accommodations with the new Boardwalk Inn. The ninety-three-room inn is located in the heart of the resort. A Victorian-style boardwalk leads from the inn to the villas and the Grand Pavilion with its open-air gazebo, two oceanfront pools, and 2 miles of sandy beach. These luxurious accommodations provide amenities of the finest full-service hotels and access to world-class recreational facilities. From early June until mid-August, daily rates are $179 to $339. Winter and spring nightly rates are $109 to $339. Rates are based on double occupancy. The one-, two-, and three-bedroom villas are grouped in two- to five-story buildings. Many are arranged along the beach, some border the tennis center, others look out on the fairways of the golf course, and still more enjoy the seclusion of the woods and marshland scenery. Inside decor ranges from dramatic, bold interiors to soft pastel furnishings that reflect nature's seaside colors; a fully equipped kitchen is standard in every unit. Cribs can be provided for infants and toddlers.

Spring and winter rates for a one-bedroom villa range from $88 to $312; two-bedroom villas range from $120 to $369. Early June to mid-August is high season; rates are $156 to $365 for a one-bedroom and $234 to $482 for a two-bedroom.

Private homes are also available. Category and location of a rental property will also determine the price; an oceanfront location commands the highest rate. Included with all rentals are one hour of tennis court time per bedroom per day, guaranteed golf tee times, complimentary one-hour daily family program, access to the Fitness Center, Grand Pavilion, and the Sports Pavilion Swim Center, local phone calls, and on-property transportation. Golf, Town and Country, and Winter Extended Stay packages are available.

Dining: It is not surprising that seafood is highlighted on the menus of Wild Dunes's restaurants; gumbo and she-crab soup are favorite low-country dishes. But beef eaters can find tasty, tender selections here too. With the opening of the Boardwalk Inn, Wild Dunes gained a luxurious restaurant. The Sea Island Grill, serving breakfast, lunch, and dinner, features the freshest seafood available, prepared in myriad ways. Guests may dine in the casually elegant dining room or alfresco on the piazza overlooking a lush tropical environment. Casual dining for breakfast, lunch, and dinner is found at Edgar's in the Links Clubhouse. Edgar's offers unique low-country cuisine and welcomes families. Both restaurants have children's menus. Entertainment is offered in Edgar's Bar five nights a week, and Mondays and Thursdays are Family Nights, when kids are supervised on the patio for dinner, allowing parents to enjoy quiet dining inside. The Grand Pavilion, open only in summer, has early-twentieth-century architecture, an old-fashioned boardwalk, Coney Island–style food, and an airy gazebo. If you have a hunger attack on either golf course, you're in luck. Hot dogs, sandwiches, and drinks are to be found at the Half-Way House, on the Links. The Dunes Deli & Pizzeria features light fare for breakfast and lunch, as well as limited grocery items, on the Harbor Course. Both are open year-round. At least twelve restaurants offer a variety of dining on nearby Sullivan's Island and the Isle of Palms.

Children's World: Ranked one of the top five by *Tennis* magazine for having the "Best Kids' Program," Wild Dunes knows just how to make your little ones' vacation special. Using college students majoring in recreation and child development, the scheduled activities are both impressive and nonstop. Wild Dunes's summer program for kids runs from the end of May through Labor Day and at holidays and family vacation times. Duneys Discovery Club for ages three to five provides structured sessions with two full-time staff members. Parents are welcome to drop in as kids enjoy tumbling, storytime, and arts and crafts. Operating from 9:00 A.M. to noon Monday through Friday, the cost is $25; $20 each additional child. Older children, from six to twelve years, are part of the Wild Adventure Club, held Monday through Friday from 9:00 A.M. to 4:00 P.M. Kids enjoy beach games, swimming, crabbing, scavenger hunts, putt-putt golf, and other "wild" adventures. The full-day session costs $50, with lunch and frequently an afternoon excursion to a nearby water splash park, or bowling or a movie on a rainy day. Half-day sessions are available from 9:00 A.M. to noon, not including lunch, for $25.

Li'l Dune Bug Club allows kids (ages six to twelve) to leave their parents at home for a night out to play games, watch movies, and munch goodies. These sessions are held two days a week (Tuesday and Friday) from 6:00 to 10:00 P.M.; the cost is $35 for the first child, $30 for the second, and kids get a T-shirt to wear and keep. Space is limited, so reserve in advance.

Teens gather on the beach for volleyball or at the Grand Pavilion. Tuesdays are "Movie Night" ($30) and Thursdays bring an off-site trip for dinner, bowling, and putt-putt ($35). Plans are in the works for a teen club on the beach with, among other things, black-light beach volleyball. Video movies and special pool games allow teens to socialize and hang out.

Recreation: A day of golf can begin on one of the two eighteen-hole golf courses designed by Tom Fazio. The older course, the Wild Dunes Links, is on the resort's ocean side and provides interesting play, with its many water hazards. Two holes edge by the sand dunes of the beach and are dramatically beautiful as well as challenging. The newer Harbor Course is across the island, surrounding the marina and harbor, and has its own fair share of demanding water hazards. A practice range, professional instruction, and a pro shop can help you over the hurdles with improved style and equipment.

In addition to golf, Wild Dunes offers ten-nis facilities, which have been ranked in the "Top 10 Greatest U.S. Tennis Resorts" by *Tennis* magazine. Guests receive one hour of free court time per day per bedroom. With a total of seventeen Har-Tru courts, including five lighted for night play and one stadium court, tennis players might not want to go home. Tennis instruction can take the form of private or group lessons, clinics, and camps for a week, a weekend, or an intensive one-day session. Along with its well-stocked pro shop, this tennis facility leaves you very few excuses for not improving your game.

The Isle of Palms Marina has 200 boat slips. Here you can dock your own vessel or rent a boat for fishing in the Gulf Stream. Join a charter if you need an experienced captain's guidance in snagging the big ones, or finish off a day with a cruise in Charleston's harbor. Besides taking deep-sea excursions, fishermen can cast their lines in the ocean's surf, the creek, and the lagoons.

Swimmers have pools at most of the villa complexes, the main pool at the Swim Center, two oceanfront pools on the Grand Pavilion, the pool at the Boardwalk Inn, and, of course, the beautiful Atlantic Ocean. Joggers and bikers share the nature trails, where pine, oak, and magnolia trees grow; the hard-packed sand beach is also suitable for running and biking. Along the 2-mile stretch of beach, you'll find sunbathers, strollers, and seashell collectors, and just offshore, sailors and sailboarders. At the beachfront picnic area, the kids' playground consists of natural-wood climbing equipment under the trees. For a close look at the egrets, herons, and pelicans of Wild Dunes, take a canoe trip through the creeks and marshes.

Many family events, such as a sailing class, bingo, and an afternoon ice-cream party, are planned each week. Be aware, however, that there are charges for most of the activities. And when you decide to take a break from the fun and recreation, don't forget how close Charleston is. In a day of sight-seeing, you can enjoy a historic Charleston tour of antebellum houses, fine restaurants, and shopping for antiques or at more modern boutiques.

Nighttime comes alive at Wild Dunes. Featured entertainer Ronnie Johnson heats it up at Edgar's Bar five nights a week with his style mix of rock, country, and Jimmy Buffett. From mid-June to mid-August the resort features a Sunday welcome party, "Shaggin' at the Beach" on Tuesday and Friday (with Shag lessons!), karaoke on Wednesday, and steel calypso music Saturday and Sunday afternoons.

WILD DUNES RESORT

5757 Palm Boulevard
Isle of Palms, South Carolina 29451
(843) 886–6000, (800) 845–8880,
(888) 845–8926
E-mail: reservations@wilddunes.com
Web site: www.wilddunes.com

SOUTHEAST

Alabama

Florida

Georgia

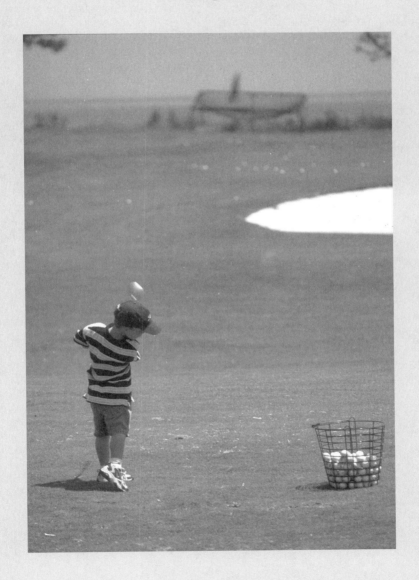

AMELIA ISLAND PLANTATION
Amelia Island, Florida

Like many of its counterparts along the coasts of the Carolinas and Georgia, Amelia Island Plantation is a well-planned and carefully executed development that combines resort living with an appreciation for natural beauty. Similarity to its sisters is no surprise, for this land was purchased in the late 1960s by Charles Fraser of Sea Pines in Hilton Head, one of the first resorts to blend nature's beauties with gracious amenities, setting the standard for resort communities that followed.

Amelia Island Plantation, which opened in 1974, occupies 1,350 acres of the southernmost island in the Golden Isle chain along the eastern seaboard of the United States. Open year-round, it is on the coast of northeast Florida, about a forty-five-minute drive from Jacksonville. Besides palmettos and oak trees, a 4-mile sandy beach, marshlands, and lagoons, this corner of paradise is blessed with mild temperatures year-round and balmy ocean breezes. Amelia Island Resort is a two-time winner of *Family Circle* magazine's "Best Family Beach Resort" award, AAA Four Diamonds, and *Southern Living's* Reader's Choice award for "Best Resort."

Accommodations: You can lodge in one of 249 oceanfront hotel rooms at the Amelia Inn and Beach Club—all with private balconies —or in a villa or hotel room overlooking the ocean or a lagoon, bordering the tennis complex or one of the fairways of three golf courses. The one- to three-bedroom villas have complete kitchens; many have private patios, balconies, or screened porches. Architecturally, the multilevel accommodation buildings arranged throughout the property are of various contemporary styles, with stucco or natural-wood facades.

Rates vary according to size, location, and category; for the villas, some rates are per person, others are per unit. Packages are plentiful and suit every need imaginable. Be sure to ask when you call for reservations, as Amelia Island practices yield control—if your dates fit a time when they have vacancies, the price will be even better. Some all-inclusive packages that feature recreation and the children's program can be very cost-effective. For example, daily rates in the Amelia Inn range from $178 to $338, double occupancy. Children under age sixteen stay free in the room; cribs are available. And daily rates for a one-bedroom resort villa range from $188 to $328, while an ocean villa costs from $198 to $408.

Dining: When cooking in your villa seems just too strenuous after a day of sunbathing, gather the family at the Verandah in Racquet Park. Located in a building tucked among old oak trees, the dining room has large windows overlooking the tennis courts. Sample such fresh seafood from the Atlantic as sea bass, flounder, shrimp, and crab in the family-style atmosphere.

More elegant dining is available in the Amelia Inn dining room. With expansive views of the ocean, this restaurant features seafood, quail, and roast duck and desserts like Southern pecan pie. In addition to dinner, breakfast and a sumptuous brunch on Sundays are offered.

Stop by the Marche Burette, an old-fashioned fresh-food market, for fruits, vegetables, meats, and fresh-baked breads. You may be tempted by the delicious aroma to stay for a sandwich and coffee. Also appropriate for breakfast and lunch is the Golf Shop Restaurant at Amelia Links or the Longpoint Clubhouse. At the Beach Club Grille, burgers, wings, and ribs are served; TVs add action to a meal. Seaside Sweets, at poolside (seasonally), will satisfy your sweet tooth, while the Dunes Club Bar serves light lunches and tropical drinks poolside (seasonally) between Sea and Turtle Dunes. Roberto's will deliver pizza to your door, and Cooper's has scrumptious homemade ice cream. Falcon's Nest for happy hour and evening entertainment is the place to see and be seen on Amelia Island.

Children's World: Kids Camp Amelia children's program entertains kids three to ten years old daily, year-round. Activities include swimming, crabbing, sports, and arts and crafts. Take nature walks and enjoy many activities with the resident naturalist for a small fee. June through August, golf and tennis clinics and field trips are offered at special rates.

The cost for the full day kids' program (8:30 A.M. to 4:00 P.M.) with lunch is $45, the morning session (8:30 A.M. to 1:00 P.M.) with lunch is $35, and the afternoon session (12:45 to 4:00 P.M.) is $25.

Teen Explorers has just the kind of loosely structured activities that older children (eleven and up) prefer. It provides a chance to socialize while participating in fun activities. Programs and costs vary (from free to $70), so check with the recreation department for details and to register.

Just for Kids presents themed dinner parties just for kids ages three to ten. Hours are from 6:00 until 9:30 P.M. Wednesday through Saturday from March 1 to Labor Day, when a buffet dinner is served; it drops to Thursday through Saturday (room service menu) for the rest of the year. The cost is $30, but it's half price ($15) if parents are dining at the Amelia Inn or Verandah Restaurant.

At Aury Island, a tree house and a dock for fishing and crabbing are reserved just for the twelve-and-under set. At the Beach Club little ones have their own wading pool and a playground filled with wooden climbing equipment. To find a baby-sitter, you can pick up a list of names and numbers at the main registration desk; rates begin at $12.50 per hour, with a four-hour minimum.

Recreation: The Amelia Links, thirty-six holes of golf designed by Pete Dye and Bobby

Weed, offer variety in play, as each course has its own personality. Oak Marsh weaves through groves of oak, palmetto trees, and marshlands, while Ocean Links skirts the Atlantic Ocean, with five holes along the sand dunes and sea oats of the beach. The eighteen-hole Long Point Golf Course was designed by Tom Fazio. Lessons can be arranged through the pro shop, where you will also find equipment and fashions.

Racquet Park is well situated among beautiful live oaks, a lovely setting for twenty-two Har-Tru courts. Some are lighted for evening play. The site of the Bausch and Lomb Women's Championships, this tennis complex offers adult and junior clinics, ball machines for solo practice, and a pro shop for equipment and apparel.

Also part of Racquet Park is the Health and Fitness Center. Complete with racquetball, indoor heated lap pool, exercise equipment, steam room, sauna and whirlpool facilities, and aerobics classes, it fills the bill for a good workout. For relaxing rejuvenation, visit the spa, with full services and delightful treats like a Watsu massage, performed in warm, thermal mineral water.

Swimmers can choose the ocean or pools for their hours of fun in the sun. In addition to the Olympic-size pool at the Beach Club, each of the groups of villas (except the Lagoon Villas) has a swimming pool—twenty-three pools in all.

Along the 4-mile beach, you can collect shells, sunbathe, play volleyball, ride horseback (the Seashore Stables are just 2 miles away), and fish in the surf for whiting, sea trout, and bluefish. Surrounding the island in bays and sounds and the Gulf Stream are tarpon, flounder, trout, redfish, red snapper, and king mackerel. The waters in this area give up some beautiful prizes, and for advice, insider's hints, tackle, and information on charters, head to the Amelia Angler.

Bicycle along 7 miles of trails (rental bikes with baby seats and children's bikes are available), jog along the wooded paths and down the beach, or maybe even challenge the kids to a half hour of video games at the Beach Club Game Room.

For an outing of a different sort, browse through the Shops at Amelia Island Plantation, or discover the Victorian district of Fernandina Beach at the north end of the island. The Amelia Island Plantation Resort Guide is worth checking upon your arrival; here you'll learn of classes, movies, hayrides, and cookouts.

AMELIA ISLAND PLANTATION

6800 First Coast Highway
Amelia Island, Florida 32034
(904) 261–6161, (800) 874–6878,
(888) 261–6161
www.aipfl.com

THE BREAKERS
Palm Beach, Florida

In the 1880s Henry Flagler, a railroad magnate and cofounder of Standard Oil, was advised to spend time in Florida for his health. From this happenstance evolved a world-class luxury resort. Flagler discovered the warm climate of the Atlantic Coast, was captivated by the scenery, expanded railroad lines down the eastern seaboard, and set into motion the development of Palm Beach as a winter playground of the wealthy.

The original Palm Beach Inn, built in 1896, was destroyed by fire in 1903. A second hotel, The Breakers, also succumbed to fire in 1925. Efforts to rebuild were begun immediately, and the new facility was opened at the end of 1926. The project was inspired by buildings of the Italian Renaissance; the era's artistic influence is evident in the loggias, courtyards, and hand-painted vaulted ceilings that adorn The Breakers. Open year-round, the hotel has completed a $100 million renovation and maintains its status as a Mobil five-star and AAA five-diamond resort. Listed on the National Register of Historic Places, The Breakers is also a member of the Leading Hotels of the World. The grand beauty of this sparkling structure is perhaps met only by its natural setting on 140

acres of lush semitropical landscape bordering the blue-green waters of the Atlantic Ocean.

Accommodations: The 560 well-appointed guest rooms, including 58 suites, have views of the ocean, the well-tended formal gardens, or the golf course. During the summer (low season), from mid-May to October 31, rates for a single/double room are $275 to $495 per day; there is no charge for children sixteen and under sharing a room with parents. Cribs and rollaways are provided at no charge but must be requested prior to arrival. During the high season, from November to mid-May, rates range from $435 to $895 per day. Holiday and vacation packages are also available. Suites range from $495 to $4,000.

For those who enjoy more privacy, choose the Flagler Club, The Breakers' concierge level located on the top two floors, with restricted access and additional guest services and amenities. Rates here are $485 to $960 (varies by season).

Room rates are European Plan, without meals, however options for meal plans exist. Breakfast only is $25 per person; MAP (breakfast and dinner) is $100 per person; children two to twelve are $30. Tax is not included, and a $25 surcharge applies to L'Escalier, The Breakers's French restaurant.

Dining: Dining at The Breakers can be as formal or as casual as one desires, with five restaurants and four bars to choose from. An array of hot and cold breakfast items, as well as an a la carte menu, is available in the Circle Dining Room. Lunch is available at The Reef Bar, Palm Beach's only bar on the beach, offering refreshing libations and light snacks, and at the new Beach Club Restaurant, the heart of The Breakers's new spa, featuring classic luncheon fare and selections of spa cuisine. Lunch and dinner are served in The Seafood Bar, an upscale oceanfront raw bar reminiscent of the plantation homes of old Florida; or The Flagler Steakhouse, featuring oversize steaks and chops. For dinner only, try L'Escalier, with its French ambience; jackets are required and reservations are recommended. To say L'Escalier's wine list is exceptional is an understatement; it has consistently earned *Wine Spectator*'s "Grand Award" every year since 1981. More than 500 vintages are represented in the display wine cellar.

At The Breakers restaurants, the under-elevens have their own menus. Children under three eat free, and everyone gets a special coloring book. A new family-friendly dining facility, located in the new Family Entertainment Center and called simply the Italian Restaurant, serves lunch and dinner daily.

Children's World: With its broad spectrum of amenities, creative recreational programs and activities, and family-friendly mind-set, The Breakers formed a Kids' Advisory Board, composed of young people ages five to twelve, to advise the resort on children's wants and needs. In response to this advice, there is now a year-round children's program called Coconut Crew Camp.

Children ages three through twelve enjoy Coconut Crew Camp's year-round supervised activities, including active sports, contests, pool and beach games, arts and crafts, in-door games, seashell hunts, nature walks, lawn games, swimming, croquet, and more. Offered from 9:00 A.M. to 3:00 P.M. as a full-day experience ($70, lunch included) or a half-day ($40, morning or afternoon; lunch is $5.00 extra).

The agenda for all programs is relaxed and flexible, so your child has the freedom to choose only specific events or to stay with the group for longer periods. Baby-sitting is available around the clock.

The new Family Entertainment Center houses an arcade, movie, huge TV, computers, crafts, playroom, and pizza available right next door at the Italian restaurant. Children ten years and older are welcome on their own; younger children may be accompanied by parents, or supervised by on-site staff for a $10 hourly fee.

Recreation: Allow yourself to be pampered; a staff of 2,000 people is dedicated to making a stay here memorable. Stroll through the beautiful gardens or the half mile of private beach, linger under the palm trees, relax on a patio surrounding a fountain, or indulge at the new Oceanfront Spa and Beach Club.

The award-winning Breakers Palm Beach features a vintage golf experience, resulting from the recent renovation of its historic 18-hole Ocean Course and the creation of a golf and tennis clubhouse designed in the grand "Old Florida" style. Another 18-hole course, Breakers West, is located 10 miles away.

On par with the revitalized golf facilities are ten newly constructed tennis courts, all of which are surrounded by lush gardens, lighted at night. Tennis fans will enjoy the spaciousness of the easily accessible clubhouse.

The Mediterranean-style Beach Club offers four pools, including a lap pool and children's pool, a Jacuzzi, and ten cabanas overlooking one-half mile of private beach. The Spa at The Breakers features seventeen private treatment rooms, steam and sauna rooms, men's and ladies' lounges, a beauty salon, and an ocean-view fitness center.

Sunbathe beside the majestic Atlantic, or

sip a tall, cool cocktail on the patio or at the Reef Bar. Bicycle or jog on the paths through the gardens, join a deep-sea fishing or fly-fishing excursion for an offshore adventure, go snorkeling, or sign up for scuba instruction. For periods when you are not feeling so energetic, play a game of shuffleboard, croquet, horseshoes, boccie ball, bridge, or backgammon. Other events throughout the week include exercise classes such as water aerobics, yoga, and Tai Chi; family movies; shopping at any of the resort's twelve boutiques; and historical tours. Add lectures, crafts, garden tours, concerts,

shopping on the famous Worth Avenue, and cooking demonstrations and you'll have to stretch your vacation to fit it all in.

THE BREAKERS

One South County Road
Palm Beach, Florida 33480
(561) 655–6611, (888) BREAKERS
www.thebreakers.com

CALLAWAY GARDENS

Pine Mountain, Georgia

Cason Callaway was a textile industrialist in Georgia. In the 1930s he became so enamored of the countryside around Pine Mountain that his life began to change. He turned from industry, first to farming and then to gardening. He learned that the plumleaf azalea was peculiar to this area of Georgia, and he was determined to nurture it and share its beauty with others. He established the Ida Cason Callaway Foundation, in honor of his mother, and opened his gardens to the public in 1952. While the gardens remain the focal point of the setting, the resort has grown to include gracious lodging, pleasant restaurants, and sports activities such as golf, tennis, swimming, and fishing. This naturally wooded and carefully cultivated land—14,000 acres of lakes, woodlands, and gardens—is located 70 miles south of Atlanta, in the Appalachian Mountain foothills of west Georgia. Callaway's stated purpose is to provide a wholesome family environment where all may find beauty, relaxation, inspiration, and a better understanding of the living world. A public, educational, horticultural, and charitable or-

ganization, it is owned and operated by the nonprofit Ida Cason Callaway Foundation. Its wholly owned subsidiary, Callaway Gardens Resort, Inc., a regular business corporation, operates the recreational, lodging, and retail facilities at Callaway. After-tax proceeds go to the foundation to support its efforts. And it shows. Highway 27 bisects Callaway Gardens and makes it seem very spread out; having a car is helpful, if not essential, and it's easier to find your way once you get oriented to the layout.

Accommodations: The Mountain Creek Inn, near the entrance to the gardens, is a 349-room hotel, which also houses restaurants, lounges, and the Fitness Center. From mid-March through December a double room starts at $124 a night. During the winter months rates start at $103; suites are $150 to $309 a night.

Next door to the inn is the Tennis and Racquetball Club; next to that are the luxurious Mountain Creek Villas: one- to four-bedroom units with fireplace, screened porch or patio, and fully equipped kitchen.

Nightly rates for a two-bedroom villa are $300 to $366, depending on the season.

Many families opt for one of the Southern Pine Cottages, which are arranged in small clusters amid tall trees near Robin Lake. All have well-equipped kitchens; some have fireplace, screened porch, deck, or outdoor grill. Daily rates for a two-bedroom cottage range from $270 to $317. A $15 Resort Services Fee will be added per room, per night, and includes admission to the gardens, use of the Callaway Fitness Center, in-room coffee and daily newspaper, and admission to Robin Lake Beach (open seasonally).

Summer Family Adventure, a tradition for forty-three years, has now been expanded to include four-day packages beginning on Wednesdays, as well as the weekly Saturday to Saturday packages. Monday through Friday, from 9:00 A.M. until 3:00 P.M., guests participate in "day camp." Mom and Dad can participate in planned activities for adults or have time to enjoy their own activities while the children are at camp. Evening events focus on the entire family. Four-day rates are $1,599 for cottages, $1,799 for villas. Seven-day rates are $2,331 (cottage) and $2,962 (villa); rates are for two-bedroom units. Many other packages are offered; inquire about weekend, recreation, or extended stays. Cribs are provided at no charge; rollaway beds are $15 per day in the inn only.

Dining: Located in the inn is the Plantation Room, known for its buffets—particularly the Friday-night seafood buffet and the Sunday brunch—open for breakfast, lunch, and dinner. The Piedmont Dining Room, in the Conference Center, is open daily for all three meals, and offers both a la carte and buffet service.

With red-checked tablecloths supporting the atmosphere that its name connotes, the Country Kitchen, located in the Country Store on Highway 27, serves breakfast, lunch, and dinner in a friendly, family-style setting. It's famous for its muscadine bread and country bacon. Sandwiches and snacks are available in the Champions Restaurant at the golf pro shop and the Flower Mill Deli, a soda-shop/diner near the cottages (open seasonally). At the Beach Pavilion, grab a snack and sit at one of the picnic tables overlooking Robin Lake. The Fine Cone is perfect for ice cream on a summer day. A welcome addition to Callaway dining is the Discovery Cafe, where the view is as enjoyable as the food. It offers indoor/outdoor eating overlooking mountain and lake.

At the end of the day, stop at the cozy Lobby Bar & Grill in the Mountain Creek Inn for a drink and a light meal.

Children's World: For forty-one summers Florida State University's Flying High Circus has performed at Callaway Gardens. With the big top pitched at Robin Lake Beach, this area becomes the focus of the Summer Family Adventure Program from June through mid-August. If daily (except Wednesday) circus performances are not enough to charm youngsters, the performers also act as counselors, directing kids in games and sports and teaching them a few juggling tricks and circus acts too. In addition, kids go sailing, swimming, waterskiing, roller skating, and biking. They attend golf and tennis instruction and grow imaginative in crafts classes. Kids ages three to eighteen can participate. The Summer Discovery Program provides an informal look at the animals, plants, and ecology at Callaway Gardens. Family events, such as barbecues, square dances, and movies, are also planned.

If you cannot schedule the Summer Family Adventure and are staying a couple of days at the inn, you can enroll your child on a daily basis for $50 a day. Besides the program, there are children's playgrounds at the inn and at the cottage area.

Recreation: The Virginia Hand Discovery Center, nestled in the woods on the edge of Mountain Creek Lake, should be your first stop. It's several facilities in one, all devoted to enhancing the harmony between man and earth. A staffed information desk and interactive kiosks provide guests an overview of all there is to see and do in the Callaway's 14,000 acres. Inside an orientation theater, the film *Time & the Gardens* plays continuously, depicting the evolution of the Gardens at Callaway. The center also houses an education wing, lecture hall, museum/exhibit hall, the Discovery Gift Shop, and Discovery Café. Outside, a transportation court provides guests with alternate means of getting around.

The gardens are a continuous source of beauty, pleasure, peace, and serenity. This is a place to enjoy, to reflect, and to learn. The colorful, changing displays of begonias, snapdragons, geraniums, zinnias, pansies, tulips, marigolds, chrysanthemums—the list seems endless—are presented in the outdoor garden of the John A. Sibley Horticultural Center. Depending on the season, visitors who explore the walking trails are treated to mountain laurel, hydrangeas, narcissus, magnolias, dogwoods, crabapples, hollies, wildflowers, and 700 varieties of azaleas (the famous plumleaf blooms during the summer). At Mr. Cason's Vegetable Garden, you can wander through row after row of more than 400 different types of fruits and vegetables. Workshops on topics like flower arranging and bonsai techniques are available year-round. The John A. Sibley Horticultural Center, a five-acre, innovative greenhouse design, is an architectural as well as a horticultural feat. The Cecil B. Day Butterfly Center houses up to 1,000 butterflies (representing more than fifty species) in a lush tropical setting. Learn about eagles, hawks, and owls as they swoop over your head in the Birds of Prey show.

In 1999 Callaway Gardens added the world's largest azalea garden. The Callaway Brothers Azalea Bowl features more than 5,000 specimens of both hybrid and native azaleas in a forty-acre landscape.

Besides its magnificent gardens, the resort also offers more traditional diversions. Four golf courses (three eighteen-hole courses and one nine-hole course) unroll past forests and lakes. The names of the courses are descriptive of their surroundings—Mountain View (the most challenging and home to the PGA tour's Burch Challenge), Gardens View, Lake View (the most picturesque), and Sky View. A driving range, two pro shops, and a year-round instructional program complete the golfing facilities.

The Pete Sampras in your party has ten lighted tennis courts from which to choose. Eight clay and two Plexipave courts are at the Tennis and Racquetball Club, which also houses two racquetball courts and the pro shop. The instructional program includes private or group lessons, or you can practice on your own with a ball machine.

Robin Lake is the center of lots of summer fun, from paddleboat rides and circus performances to swimming and sunbathing along the mile-long sandy beach. Besides the lake, overnight guests can enjoy the pools at the inn, at the Mountain Creek Villas, and at the cottage area.

On the shores of Mountain Creek Lake is a boathouse where you can rent a motorboat and fishing tackle—the lake is stocked with bass and bream—or a Sunfish sailboat, paddleboat, or canoe. You can also discover the lakes from their shores as you bicycle along the trails and paths.

You may want to spend an afternoon at an organ concert (daily during the summer) in the chapel on Falls Creek Lake. For indoor exercise the Fitness Center offers equipment for unwinding. For an afternoon of history, you can take the 15-mile trip to Warm Springs and Franklin Roosevelt's Little White House.

CALLAWAY GARDENS

U.S. Highway 27, P.O. Box 2000
Pine Mountain, Georgia 31822
(706) 663–2281, (800) 225–5292
www.callawaygardens.com

CHEECA LODGE AND SPA

Islamorada, Florida

Stretching more than 150 miles south from Miami, the Florida Keys enjoy a subtropical climate and a friendly, laid-back philosophy. Just getting there is an adventure. As you travel along U.S. Highway 1, you get the feeling that you're the string connecting a necklace of islands. And sometimes there are no islands—just a narrow ribbon of concrete in the middle of a very wide ocean—or two! The Atlantic Ocean and the Gulf of Mexico both border this strip of islands. Islamorada is just 75 miles from Miami, but really it is another world.

Accommodations: Cheeca Lodge and Spa is a twenty-seven-acre luxury oceanfront resort (AAA four diamond, Small Luxury Hotel of the World), with more than 1,000 feet of palm-lined beach, not often found in the Keys. A variety of accommodations—154 villa rooms or suites and 49 rooms in the main lodge—are spread throughout the landscaped grounds. Generous in size, all guest rooms are air-conditioned and also have ceiling fans, and most have a private balcony. Sixty-four villa suites feature kitchen, screened-in porch, living room, and one or two bedrooms. Mid-December to April rates are the highest, when standard rooms range from $159 to $425; oceanfront rooms are $209 to $675; and one-bedroom suites are $229 to $1,000. In summer the rates drop to $139 to $465 for rooms, $199 to $825 for one-bedroom suites. Children under sixteen stay free in their parents' room. Specials and packages are offered year-round. A daily $15 per room resort fee covers amenities.

Dining: Savor fine dinners at the Atlantic's Edge, a plantation-style restaurant with lovely panoramic views of the ocean. Dine inside or outside next to the free-form swimming pool at the Ocean Terrace Grill, sampling the local specialty, stone-crab claws, or soups and sandwiches; there is a special children's menu. An-

other indoor/outdoor dining option is the Curt Gowdy Lounge, great for snacks, cocktails, and piano entertainment in the evenings.

Children's World: Award-winning Camp Cheeca has a mission: learning about the environment while having fun. Children ages four to twelve are busy from 9:00 A.M. to 4:00 P.M. in the summer, weekends year-round, and for special holiday weeks. Little campers (ages four to six) go from 9:00 A.M. to noon, allowing a more challenging afternoon schedule for older campers (ages six to twelve). There is a morning session only on Sunday. A full day costs $38; a half day is $25. Box lunches are available for $7.50 per child. If they're only interested in a specific activity, children may participate on an hourly basis for $10 per hour, and parents are always welcome to join children in the camp. Learning to snorkel and fish, creating nature art or sand sculpture, feeding the fish or exploring the beach—everything has an ecological approach that kids really respond to. There's a good mix of activities, with field trips, scavenger hunts, arts and crafts, and Saturday Sundae (everyone's favorite). "Kids Night Out," Fridays and Saturdays from 7:00 to 9:00 P.M., costs $25 and includes entertainment, snacks, and games. When fewer than four children are present, camp will be open only for the morning session. Families with three or more children receive a reduced rate. Baby-sitting rates vary according to season.

Recreation: You can be on the go from dawn to dusk, or make the most strenuous activity of the day deciding between a hammock, chaise longue, or tiki hut on the beach. Consider renting a paddleboat, catamaran, kayak, or beach cruiser bicycle, or try parasailing. Maybe just a pool float is more your speed. The three pools are all very different; a free-form swimming pool, a lap pool, and a saltwater lagoon keep boredom at bay. Play tennis on one of the six lighted courts, or try the Jack Nicklaus–designed nine-hole executive golf course. Take a self-guided walk along Cheeca's Nature Trail, or watch the sunrise from the pier—or maybe the sunset.

The Avanyu Spa is Cheeca's newest amenity. This newly constructed, state-of-the-art health spa and fitness center offers the latest in massage therapy, facials, aromatherapy, body wraps, spacious fitness room, men's and women's steamrooms, and a spa boutique.

It's a fisherman's paradise here, with more than 600 species of marine life and a calendar of what's running each month that fills a page. No wonder Islamorada is known as the sport-fishing capital of the world. A nice touch is that the chef will, on request, prepare your hard-won catch. Cheeca has its own dive center, with equipment and instruction. The *Cheeca View* doubles as a dive boat twice a day, then does sunset and moonlight cruises. The biggest problem is trying to fit all the options in.

Theater of the Sea, the world's second-oldest marine park, is a natural lagoon where humans and marine animals interact (kids love getting kissed by a sea lion!). They've gone beyond a glass-bottom boat—here they have a bottomless boat. Hmm, neat trick. If you want to range farther afield, the concierge can help arrange a swim with the dolphins, or a trip to either Key West, the southernmost U.S. city, or Pennekamp State Park, the first underwater state park. Combine a visit to Miccosukee Indian Reservation with an airboat ride through the Everglades.

CHEECA LODGE AND SPA

Islamorada, Florida 33036
(305) 664–4651, (800) 327–2888
Web site: www.cheeca.com

THE CLOISTER
Sea Island, Georgia

Charming, gracious, and oh, so civilized —The Cloister is in the heart of the "Golden Isles," one of the most historic areas of the old Spanish Main. Family holidays at this fine old resort are fun-filled, and the elegance of a bygone era prevails. The Cloister boasts that here children learn manners as well as golf, tennis, and swimming. The dress-for-dinner standard and the children's weekly dances (seasonally) reinforce this philosophy.

Sea Island's rich history dates back to the antebellum days of the Old South, when a large cotton plantation was active on what is now the Sea Island Golf Club. The ruins of a slave hospital standing near the Clubhouse recall this period. In the early 1900s the property was acquired by Howard Coffin, an automobile engineer who had visions of creating a resort on this lovely 900-acre island, with its temperate climate and ocean breezes. His dreams were realized in the construction of The Cloister. Designed by Addison Mizner, who is known primarily for his work in Palm Beach, this "friendly little hotel" (as Coffin described it) opened its doors in October 1928. It successfully weathered the Depression and over the years has warmly greeted guests from the rich and famous to the mere plebeian with good taste. Ivy-covered walls, gently swaying palm trees, impeccable gardens, and wide verandahs set the stage for a memorable vacation. The resort is open year-round.

A two-phase, five-year project to completely rebuild The Cloister and expand residential options will begin in late 2003. The company is committing $200 million to the project, and promises to retain the gracious hospitality and attributes that have made the hotel special for the past seventy-five years.

Accommodations: Two hundred seventy rooms and suites are located in the main building (the original hotel), set back a couple of hundred yards from the beach; Guest Houses, which are all on the beach; and Terrace Houses, located on neighborhood streets between the beach and tennis center. The original structure has a Mediterranean style with red-tile roofs and courtyards. The architecture of the newer buildings and the gardens complement this style and maintain the flavor of a gracious island retreat. Rooms range from traditional, tastefully decorated bedrooms and baths to deluxe rooms and oceanfront suites. Also available are privately owned "cottages" (two to eight bedrooms) ranging from modest to grand. View them at www.seaislandcottages.com.

Room rates (double occupancy, not including meals) begin at $300 per night, depending on the type of room and time of year. Rates do include many recreational activities although golf, tennis, spa treatments, shooting school, and horseback riding require additional fees.

Children fifteen and under stay free when sharing a room with parents. In addition, this age group is also exempt from golf and tennis fees, although some restrictions apply.

Dining: Dining is elegant as well as very appetizing and sumptuous. In the main dining room of The Cloister, gentlemen and boys over twelve wear coats and ties for evening dinners. On Wednesday and Saturday evenings formal attire is preferred but optional, so ladies frequently choose to wear cocktail dresses, while men wear dinner jackets or suits. More casual attire is appropriate at the Beach Club (open for breakfast, lunch, and seafood dinner buffets) and at the golf clubhouses for luncheon and dinner. Casual means collared shirts and slacks, with jackets

optional. No tank tops, blue jeans, or cutoffs, please. Reservations are required.

American and Continental cuisines are featured. Given the ocean-side location of the resort, it's no surprise that fresh seafood specialties are prominent on the menus. Whether you choose the gracious setting of the dining rooms, with fresh flowers on the tables and lovely views of the gardens, or the more casual atmosphere of the clubhouses, you'll find that the careful attention to preparation makes meals a visual delight as well as a culinary treat.

For light refreshments during spring and summer, there's a snack bar near the swimming pools at the Beach Club. High tea is served afternoons during cooler months in the Spanish Lounge, and afternoon juice and cookies in the Davis Love Grill are a favorite pastime. Special evenings are frequently scheduled, such as a supper at Rainbow Island.

Children's World: The junior staff will charm your child with active days. During the summer, from June through Labor Day, and during Easter, Thanksgiving, and Christmas holidays, energetic, friendly counselors provide daily supervised play for youngsters ages three (no pull-ups or diapers, please) through eleven, from 9:30 A.M. to 3:00 P.M. (9:00 A.M. to 1:00 P.M. for three- and four-year-olds) at no charge. Activities include swimming, fishing, crabbing, art sessions, games, and nature walks, just to mention a few.

During the summer months children ages four through eleven can even join their counselors for dinner from 6:00 to 9:00 P.M. (Sunday and Family Beach Supper nights excluded), allowing parents to dine at their leisure. For younger children, baby-sitters are available.

Juniors and teens (ages twelve to nineteen) also have access to excursions and activities, including shopping trips to the Village of St. Simons Island, "dive-in" movies in the pool, kayaking, and socials. Some excursions do require small fees. It's essential to check the weekly calendar for additional events, because the junior staff also plans various activities for different age groups.

Teen dances and pool parties, table tennis tournaments, swimming and hamburger parties, and crabbing parties frequently appear on the agenda. A daily Family Activity Hour features fun for all ages.

Recreation: Whether you choose a leisurely stroll along the 5 miles of private beach, a rigorous game of tennis, a round of golf, or a refreshing dip in the pool, your vacation stay can be as relaxing or active as you wish.

The Cloister offers twenty-five well-maintained Har-Tru clay courts, an automated practice court, and instruction by a professional teaching staff. Even a little criticism of your backhand is easy to take in a setting graced by oak trees and azaleas. At the pro shop you can pick up equipment and new tennis togs and sign up for a tournament or partner matching.

The Sea Island Golf Club, located on neighboring St. Simons Island, is just a short drive over the small bridge spanning the Black Banks River. Once you arrive you'll be charmed by the Avenue of Oaks—majestic moss-draped oak trees leading up to the Lodge at Sea Island Golf Club. There are thirty-six championship holes. The Seaside Course, redesigned in 1999 by Tom Fazio and listed on numerous top courses lists, is a par-70 links course. The Plantation Course, redesigned by Rees Jones in 1998, is a par-72 parkland-style course. A third course, Retreat, was redesigned by Davis Love III and reopened in August 2001. The Golf Learning Center, a joint venture of Sea Island and *Golf Digest,* offers state-of-the-art practice and learning facilities with a video analysis system. There's a driving range at each club, and back on Sea Island you'll find a putting green and a chip 'n' putt area for some extra practice time. And if you're a real devotee, rest assured that golfing interests do not fade with the setting sun; join the discussions with the pros at golf seminars two evenings a week.

The Beach Club overlooks the Atlantic, so you can choose an ocean swim or a few laps in one of the two pools. Besides a dining room and a snack bar, the Beach Club offers table tennis, volleyball, shuffleboard, and a terrific soak-up-the-sun atmosphere. Other water sports include sailboarding and sailing in the ocean, snorkeling and scuba diving, and boating and fishing in the river. After excursions through the waterways, you might try exploring the grounds as you jog, bike, or ride horseback. Many folks enjoy a horseback ride along the beach or through the marshes, or you may contact the stables about moonlight supper rides. At the Shooting School you'll find instruction in sporting clays, trap, and skeet shooting as well as all the equipment necessary to learn these sports. And after golf, tennis, swimming, sailing, and skeet-shooting lessons, if you're still dying to try something new or to brush up on dusty skills, sign up for dance instruction. After a couple of sessions, you'll no doubt be a hit dancing nightly to the hotel's Sea Island Orchestra.

The Sea Island Spa offers a full range of services. You can join an exercise class, develop an individualized program, consult a nutritionist, have a massage, or relax with a facial.

Special programs are planned throughout the year; they may be just the thing to schedule a family vacation around. Food and wine seminars, bridge festivals, and a personal financial-planning seminar are standard events at The Cloister.

At any time of the year, be sure to check the weekly calendar. You might want to see a movie, play bingo, listen to a classical piano concert, head to an exercise workout, join a nature walk, or take in a lecture on the local wildlife. But don't crowd your schedule too much, for one of the nicest pleasures at The Cloister is simply strolling through the gardens and discovering the camellias, gardenias, wisteria, geraniums, and petunias.

THE CLOISTER

100 First Street
Sea Island, Georgia 31561
(912) 638–3611, (800) SEA–ISLAND
www.seaisland.com

CLUB MED/SANDPIPER
Port St. Lucie, Florida

Club Med is practically synonymous with a carefree, fun-in-the-sun holiday, a tradition going back more than forty years. In fact, they opened the first Mini-Club for children in 1967. The only warm-weather village that Club Med operates in the United States is Sandpiper, and it has not only a Mini-Club but a Baby Club as well. Located in Port St. Lucie, Florida, about an hour's drive north of Palm Beach, the Club Med village covers more than 400 beautifully landscaped acres along the St. Lucie River. The verdant green landscape and the clear blue waters make an attractive setting for a fun-filled, sun-filled vacation.

Accommodations: Sandpiper is one of the most luxurious Club Med properties, termed the "finest." It seems more like a deluxe hotel, boasting brick-colored tile floors covered with kilim carpet, original artwork by local artists, and a separate dressing area, with large closets. Unlike most Club Med villages, the rooms here have telephone, TV, and minifridge. Each room has a private balcony or terrace and is located in one of several three-story buildings near the river. Renovated in 2000, it now features a Florida Country Club look.

Club Med pioneered the concept of all-inclusive vacations—rates here include everything except scuba, ATP tennis, and some golf. And that's everything! Accommodations, all meals, children's programs, sports and instruction—even all-day snacks, drinks, and an open bar. Rates are complex and changing—it's best to inquire for your specific dates. Oddly, summer rates are the highest. In January weekly rates per adult begin at $881; $585 for children ages two through fifteen. July and August rates are $1,055 for adults and $625 for children. Babies under two years old are always free. During certain weeks in spring and fall, kids under twelve (one per adult) stay free. Club med rates often include air flights—ask for specifics. Three-night packages and

day passes are also available. A Club Med annual membership is required; $55 per adult, $25 per child, plus a one-time fee of $30 per family.

Dining: The main dining room is informal, serving breakfast, lunch, and dinner buffets. Dining at Club Med is a bountiful experience, with selections of American, French, and Continental delicacies. It's also a good chance to meet people and socialize. The Club has its own baker and pastry maker—yum. No fewer than twelve different fresh-baked breads are served at every meal. But not to worry, there are enough activities daily to work off any calories from overindulging. A special kid-friendly menu is served to children early at lunch and dinner. Parents may join their children while they eat, and the G.O.s (*gentils organisateurs*—French for "gracious organizers") supervise as well. High chairs and booster seats make life easier for the little ones. After their early dinner, kids return to the Mini-Club. Mom and Dad, meanwhile, savor a superb and blissfully quiet dinner, perhaps in the Riverside specialty restaurant—beautifully decorated, smaller, and more intimate, table service is the order of the day here. Complimentary wine is served with lunch and dinner, thanks to the French heritage of the Club. A new policy at the Club Med is a completely open bar, so that drinks and snacks are now available all day long, whenever you desire. No more pop beads!

Children's World: Kids are thoroughly entertained at Club Med. In fact, you may almost have to make an appointment to see your little one. The Baby Club is available for infants ages four to twenty-three months. Strollers, baby monitors, bassinets—all the necessary equipment can be borrowed; and a pediatrician is either in the village or on call, plus one registered nurse. Each baby gets her own crib, and there's even a special Baby Chef, who prepares food using only natural ingredients. Lunch is handled by the G.O.s, but parents are on duty for dinner. Need juice or milk in the middle of the night? No problem; just go to the twenty-four-hour convenience room. Depending on their ages, babies are changed, fed, napped, and played with in the adjacent garden, with swings and toys. The more mobile go on walks or play on the beach.

Babies may be brought back to the Baby Club in the evening, in their pajamas, and can sleep there while parents take in a show or stroll along the river. The Siesta Club is provided from 8:00 P.M. to 1:00 A.M. at a cost of $20 per child per night.

The Petit Club is for two- to three-year-olds, the Mini-Club is for four- to ten-year-olds, and the Junior Club entertains eleven- to seventeen-year-olds. Each has its own area with club house, its own G.O.s, and an unbelievable number of age-appropriate activities.

In addition to all the usual activities of children's programs, Club Med also offers circus workshops, with real trampolines, trapeze and low-wire work, juggling, trick bikes, and clowns. At the end of the week, the entire group puts on a show under the Big Top for adoring parents. It's really terrific, and the kids are so proud of themselves. There's intensive tennis for kids eight and older, and soccer, softball, in-line skating, sailing, waterskiing, and much more—all included in the one price. A new program is called Mini-Scientist, making science fun and engaging (and educational, although no one notices). Evening fun continues with "disco," pajama parties, and games. During certain holiday times, special programs are devised for the teens to meet and interact.

Recreation: The sun is warm, the water inviting. You have four swimming pools to choose from and a little sandy beach where you can splash in the river. A shuttle leaves hourly for the twenty-minute ride to the Atlantic for ocean swimming. In the calm water of the river, you can glide along on a sailboat and later have a go at waterskiing. Tennis clin-

ics are held daily on the eighteen courts; after intensive sessions, you will surely find improvement in your game. A program with one-hour daily lessons at all levels is another option. Aerobics classes, calisthenics, and volleyball games always pop up on the agenda. Perhaps you prefer a routine in the fitness center or biking and jogging along the paths through the property. Maybe you can sneak in a trial swing on the trapeze—it's scary, but very safe.

Speaking of swings, unique to Sandpiper is a concentrated golf program with free lessons at all levels. On-site golf includes an eighteen-hole championship golf course, Sinners, designed by Mark Mahannah, a driving range, a free nine-hole par-3, two putting greens, a chipping green, and a practice sand trap. For serious golfers, the Golf Academy provides two and a half hours daily instruction and course play at an additional cost. You may want to bring your own golf balls (or purchase them there); clubs may be rented. Greens fees are quite reasonable ($40 for two days or $60 for three days) and include a golf cart.

The Mini-Clubs run from 9:00 A.M. to 9:00 P.M. Afterward the whole family can enjoy the evening entertainment, usually a show or participatory fun. After the kids finally fall into bed, the nightclub continues into the night.

If you have time, which we doubt, Club Med offers a mind-boggling array of excursions. You may not want to mention it to the kids, but Disney World is only two hours away. Also nearby are the Kennedy Space Center, hot-air ballooning, and deep-sea fishing. Palm Beach shopping is also within close striking distance.

CLUB MED/SANDPIPER

3500 SE Morningside Boulevard
Port St. Lucie, Florida 34952
(772) 398–5100, (800) CLUB–MED
www.clubmed.com

HAWK'S CAY RESORT

Duck Key, Florida

Located in the heart of the Florida Keys is Hawk's Cay Resort, on a tropical sixty-acre island. The resort, built in the late 1950s, has hosted numerous presidents and film stars. The rambling Caribbean-style hotel sets the tone for the relaxed, elegant atmosphere that you'll find here. Ceiling fans, indoor plants, wicker furniture, and French doors in the lobbies and lounges echo the easygoing pace. The temperatures are mild, averaging in the low eighties in summer and the low seventies in winter, and the water stays warm and comfortable year-round. Water sports, from deep-sea fishing, fly-fishing, sailing, diving, and snorkeling to swimming, sunset sails, ecotours, and water-skiing, are, naturally, the main focus of this island resort. The only living coral reef in the continental United States is just offshore, and Hawk's Cay has seven resident dolphins.

Accommodations: This comfortable inn has the ambience and style of a Caribbean resort. Most of the 160 rooms and 16 suites are wrapped around a saltwater lagoon and several freshwater pools, with views of the Atlantic Ocean or the Gulf of Mexico. Each has a private balcony, separate dressing area, and a small refrigerator. During the high season, January through April, room rates range from $250 to $400; suite rates, including the presidential suite, range from $455 to $1,200. Low-season rates, May through mid-December, are $210 to $355 and $375 to $1,100, respectively. The resort has added 269 two- and three-bedroom villas, modeled after Key West conch houses, that offer water settings and a full kitchen. They are the perfect home away from home for families and range from $375 to $1,100. A daily resort activities fee of $10 per unit for the inn and $20 per villa covers unlimited tennis, daily access to Indies Club and fitness center, use of the boat ramp, chaise lounges, towels, and more.

Dining: If you like fresh seafood, you'll find dining here a treat. There are four tempting restaurants to choose from, each with its own distinctive style and menu selections.

Start the day with a fabulous breakfast buffet presented in the Palm Terrace. Breakfast hours begin as early as 7:00 A.M. and continue until 11:00 A.M. For casual lunches and dinners, the Cantina at poolside offers a variety of Mexican or Caribbean fare, as well as rum concoctions that recall the island's history as a stopover for Prohibition rumrunners. Also enjoy casual outdoor dining at the Indies Grille, featuring sandwiches, salons, snacks, and a kids' menu.

The WatersEdge, dockside at the marina, is open for dinner, specializing in steak and fresh-off-the-boat seafood. Porto Cayo features a blend of Caribbean and Italian specialties in an elegant indoor setting or outdoor cafe ambiance. Truman's Bar brings back the nostalgia of when President Harry Truman vacationed here.

Children's World: Hawk's Cay is going all out to please the kids, and the program is growing and changing as their returning families change. Operating daily year-round, the schedules are flexible and geared to the needs of guests. The Indies Club is the new area dedicated to kids. Here you'll find two pools, one with pirate ship/water cannon playground in the center and a new tree house that presents the opportunity for hours of climbing fun with slides, a bridge, tire swings, and lots more. Treasures is the area for kids eleven and under, while teens have the Shanty, their own recreation room filled with all that's dear to teenage hearts. There's a teen spa (ages eight to fifteen) with mini-treatments and a fitness center.

Hawk's Cay is experimenting with some new concepts. When the resort is filled, the more traditional program will be in effect. Daily full- and half-day Kids Club programs will keep children happily occupied with swimming, tiki-boat races, scavenger hunts, fishing, and ecology tours. Little Pirates is for children ages three to five years, while the Islands Adventure Club entertains ages six to twelve years with sports and nature-oriented games. Cost for either program is $50 for the full day (9:30 A.M. to 4:30 P.M.), including lunch; $25 for half days. Lunch is $5.00 for half-day sessions, and hours vary according to whether or not lunch is served.

A more flexible plan designates one room, staffed with counselors, where kids can come and go on a sign-in/sign-out basis, participating only in activities that interest them. Charges will vary. Additionally, every day there are at least two free planned activities—volleyball, limbo contest, face painting, and the like.

Kids Night Out, for ages six to twelve, includes dinner, a movie, and a make-and-take craft. It's available on Friday and Saturday evenings from 7:00 until 10:00 P.M. for $35 per child. Individual baby-sitting can also be arranged.

Recreation: Hawk's Cay guests have playing privileges at the eighteen-hole Sombrero Country Club championship course, approximately 10 miles away. For tennis buffs, two Har-Tru courts (lit for night play) and six Laykold courts beckon. Get instructions from on-site pros, participate in a variety of scheduled clinics, tournaments, and round robins, or sharpen your skills with a ball machine.

But truly, the water tempts, entices, and captures the heart of visitors. It establishes the mood and is the setting for most of the recreation. Swim in one of the many pools or the saltwater lagoon, or stretch out beneath the tropical sun, but don't forget the sunscreen!

Discover the mysteries and wonder of undersea life. The coral reef offshore is home to a colorful array of tropical fish and is one of the best spots in the country for snorkeling and scuba diving.

Fishing here puts you in the big league, and it's exciting. Just offshore you'll find red snapper and mackerel; farther out in Gulf Stream waters are marlin, dolphin, and tuna; and tarpon ply the waters in Florida Bay. Charter a vessel at the marina for an excursion. The Marina at Hawk's Cay offers eighty-five slips and can dock yachts more than 100 feet long.

Explore the island by bicycle—child-, teen-, and adult-sized bikes are available for $5.00 per hour, with helmet. Or take a self-guided walking tour to learn about the indigenous vegetation and tropical birds such as the brown pelican and the blue heron.

Unique to Hawk's Cay is the Dolphin Connection, a program designed to study, protect, and increase public interest in dolphin biology and ecosystems. Training sessions and interactive programs are offered daily. Sign up for a once-in-a-lifetime memory-making swim with the dolphins.

HAWK'S CAY RESORT

Mile Marker 61
Duck Key, Florida 33050
(305) 743–7000, (800) 432–2242,
(888) 443–6393
www.hawkscay.com

Jekyll Island, Georgia

Jekyll Island, midway between Savannah, Georgia, and Jacksonville, Florida, and just 6 miles off the Georgia coast, is truly a gem. A barrier island, it's only a 1½ miles wide and 9 miles long. Part of the state park system, a state law limits development on Jekyll to 35 percent of land above mean high water. Therefore, only one-third of the island can be developed, leaving wonderful beaches, ancient oaks, and dense maritime forests untouched and in their natural state. Of the approximately 5,000 acres, 65 percent will remain a nature preserve for future generations to enjoy.

Jekyll has an illustrious history that began in 1886 when it became a huge private club for some of America's wealthiest tycoons. The Rockefellers, Vanderbilts, and Morgans were the first families to vacation here, so you're keeping good company when you vacation on Jekyll Island. Their "cottages" (only 8,000 feet or so, not the size of the Newport mansions) are now part of the Historic District, with museums, tram, and carriage tours.

Because it's such a small island, and much of the recreation is provided by Jekyll Island itself, we're listing two hotels: both with summer children's programs; one on the ocean side and one on the intercoastal waterway. Take your pick!

JEKYLL INN OCEANFRONT RESORT

Jekyll Island, Georgia

Accommodations: Set on fifteen ocean side acres, the Jekyll Inn is the island's largest oceanfront resort. The entire facility is nonsmoking, and 263 guest rooms and villas offer a choice of lodging styles. Children under seventeen stay for free; cribs and rollaways are available for $10 nightly. Midseason rates apply mid-February to late May, while high season is late May through August. Rates for a standard guest room are $69 to $99, oceanfront rooms are $109 to $159, and one-bedroom villas are $149 to $219. Weekly rates during high season range from $520 to $940. Winter rates are even better. Soak up the mild winter weather in a villa at monthly rates (prorated for shorter stays); villa rates range from $900 to $1,200 from October through January, and double that February through April. Some winter guests have been coming to the Jekyll Inn for over twenty-five years!

Dining: The Italian Fisherman serves breakfast, lunch, and dinner in a casual atmosphere. Local seafood dishes highlight the menu, and the breakfast buffet claims to be "the best on the island." In winter the Tea Cottage South features special tea menus each month; in summer enjoy drinks and live music at the open-air Tiki Bar. For evening entertainment, stop by the Pelican's Roost for live music.

Children's World: As one of the Meri-Star properties, the Jekyll Inn participates in Fun Factory programs for children. While there's a somewhat standard formula for success, with supervision by "funologists" and innovative educational programs, sports, activities, and creative projects, each resort customizes the program to their unique attractions. Kids become members, with regular newsletter and Web site fun available after returning home. The program runs from Memorial Day to Labor Day, Tuesday through Saturday from 9:00 A.M. to 5:00 P.M. Morning sessions run from 9:00 A.M. to 12:00 P.M.; afternoon sessions are from 1:00 to 5:00 P.M.; lunch is from 1:00 to 2:00 P.M. The cost is $5.00 per session plus $5.00 for lunch. Counselors tell kids to wear their bathing suits and bring sunscreen, a towel, and a smile. Kids love to spend time in the playground and the outdoor pool overlooking the ocean; the beach is accessible, but only at low tide. In the evenings family activities are planned each day: movie nights, karaoke, a bonfire with s'mores, or bingo. On Fridays and Saturdays the Fun Factory offers dinner and evening fun from 5:00 to 8:30 P.M. for $10 per child.

Recreation: Families have the entire island as their playground. The island is actually a state park, so much of the recreation is leased or run by the state of Georgia. See the entry at the end of the Jekyll Island Club Hotel for details.

JEKYLL INN OCEANFRONT RESORT

975 North Beachview Drive
Jekyll Island, Georgia 31527
(912) 635–2531, (800) 431–5190
www.jekyllinn.com

JEKYLL ISLAND CLUB HOTEL
Jekyll Island, Georgia

Remember that clubhouse we mentioned that Rockefeller and friends built so long ago? Well, it's been restored to its original splendor, completely modernized, and is now enjoying a new life as the Jekyll Island Club Hotel. The hotel complex is the focal point of the historic district, and their goal is much the same as one hundred years ago—to provide relaxation and recreation in an exclusive setting. The four-diamond, four-star resort is part of the National Trust for Historic Preservation, and a registered National Historic Landmark. *Travel and Leisure* ranks the club one of the 500 best hotels in the world, and its elegant architecture, proud heritage, and excellent service explain why.

Accommodations: Guest rooms and suites tastefully blend century-old mahogany furnishings and Victorian fireplaces with marble bathrooms with whirlpools and telephones with data ports. Lodging prices listed are in the Clubhouse, the annex, or Sans Souci, originally built in 1896 as a six-unit apartment building—perhaps the first ever condominium? High season is early March to mid-August; rates range from $159 for a Clubhouse Double to $349 for the Presidential Suite; from December 1 to early March rates range from $109 to $289 for the same accommodations; children eighteen and under stay free in their parents' room. Crane and Cherokee Cottages have comparable rates—talk with the resort for the best selection for your family. The Summer Family Getaway package offers a traditional room with two double beds and the children's program (no meals) for $499 for three nights, or $699 for five nights. Meal plans, per person, are $76 for Full American Plan, and $58 for Modified American Plan (breakfast and dinner); children thirteen and under pay $38 and $29 respectively.

Dining: The Grand Dining Room is open daily for breakfast, lunch, and dinner, and boasts a scrumptious Sunday brunch. Emphasis is on seafood and gourmet Continental cuisine. The new Courtyard at Crane, open for lunch daily and dinner Sunday through Thursday, offers alfresco dining with Northern California cuisine. Café Solterra bakes their own yummy pastries and breads, along with New York deli offerings, and will pack a picnic lunch for you to take on your travels. Grab a light snack at the Beach Pavilion or the Poolside Bar and Grill and never have to leave your lounge chair. At the end of the day, Vincent's Pub encourages conversation and cocktails.

Children's World: Memorial Day to mid-August, Club Juniors is available Monday through Friday from 9:00 A.M. to 4:00 P.M. Cost is only $18 per day per child, with lunch included. Half days are $9.50, or the weekly rate is $75. There may be additional fees for some activities. Days are filled with bicycle safaris, sand casting, treasure hunts, a dolphin cruise, tennis, canoeing, crafts, and crabbing at Clam Creek. And, of course, swimming, including trips to the nearby water park, is high on the favorites list. Kids will be delighted, and should certainly sleep well after all of this activity!

Recreation: Choose between the outdoor swimming pool or the Beach Pavilion, 1 mile away on the Atlantic Ocean. Of course, the club has a regulation size croquet lawn, so do bring the proper white clothing—you know, long flowing dresses for women, white duck for the men, short pants for boys, and hair ribbons for the girls. Complimentary transportation is provided for guests to points throughout the island.

Jekyll Island Recreation: Families have the entire island as their playground. The island is actually a state park, so much of the recreation is leased or run by the state. In fact, Jekyll Island has Georgia's largest public golf resort. Sixty-three holes (three eighteen-hole and one nine-hole course), with professional instruction and a clubhouse with proshop, rental clubs, restaurant, and lounge meet your every golfing need. Picturesque but demanding, Dick Wilson's Oleander is consistently ranked among the best courses in the state. A driving range, putting greens, and practice bunker complete the golf scene. And for the budding Tiger Woods in your family, start at the two miniature golf courses or try some junior instruction. A first-class tennis center with twelve courts (one indoors); Summer Waves Water Park; and boating, from paddleboats on the lake to sea kayaking; are all here. There's a wonderful new playground for children, with areas for both toddlers and older children. Fishing from the wharf or a relaxed sunset horseback ride along the beach promotes mind and body relaxation. And the beach stretches the length of the island, calling for nice long walks. Twenty miles of bicycle trails and jogging paths provide the perfect way to enjoy this island. Treat all your senses as you watch for deer, marsh hares, and beautiful shorebirds; smell the wonderful pinewoods and salt air; listen to the sound of the ocean and feel the wind on your skin. The Tidelands Nature Center educates and explains about barrier islands, and encourages kids to "please touch" the flora and fauna. Tours of the Historic District via tram or horse-drawn carriage or a stroll through the village are entertaining pastimes. Many restaurants and shops will beckon. It's easy to adjust to this lifestyle.

JEKYLL ISLAND CLUB HOTEL

371 Riverview Drive
Jekyll Island, Georgia 31527
(912) 635–2600, (800) 535–9547
www.jekyllclub.com

MARCO ISLAND MARRIOTT RESORT

Marco Island, Florida

An island oasis drifting off the southernmost tip of the Florida Gulf and nearly lost in the Ten Thousand Islands, Marco Island Marriott Resort blends a tempting twist of tropical and sun-splashed excitement into an unforgettable island escape. The resort's guests get lost in the intriguing contrasts: Waves of sun-drenched beaches, always-warm Gulf waters, and passionate sunsets present a tame, pampered complement to the tangled wildness and sweeping sawgrass prairies of Florida's famous nearby Everglades.

Not just your typical high-rise-on-a- Florida-beach, the three-star, four-diamond Marco Island Marriott has just completed a $60-million renovation and expansion. All deluxe guest rooms have been redesigned and renovated, plus there are new restaurants, a Fantasy Tiki pool with water slides and water features, and the Balinese Health Spa. A new beachside terrace is also planned.

Accommodations: All of Marco Island Marriott Resort's 727 guest rooms and 54 suites have private balconies. Poolside or beachfront lanais—each with a private balcony entrance—and a secluded cluster of seaside villas complete the resort's accommodations. Daily rates, depending on size, are $130 to $230 in the low season (May through September) and $280 to $350 in the high season (December through April). Packages are available.

Dining: Shimmering turquoise-flecked waters, sweeping pearlescent sands, and lush, cascading gardens create a tropical backdrop for four distinct restaurants at the resort. The two new restaurants are Tropiks, providing great family dining for breakfast, lunch, and dinner; and Kurrents, with an upscale and trendy ambience for fine seafood and steak dinners. Quinn's on the Beach cooks up a treasure trove of savory sandwiches and Caribbean appetizers from almost dawn until after dusk, while the Calypso Grill at Quinn's serves unique seafood dinners. Check out Scoozie's for pizza and sandwiches, or have a light lunch and drinks at the Tiki Bar and Grill. For coffee and pastries, try Fidalgo Bay.

Children's World: The Tiki Tribe at Marco Island Marriott Resort—the first resort in North America to be awarded the National Parenting Center Seal of Approval—is a pinnacle of pint-size fun, occupying youngsters ages five through twelve with cool water play, sand-castle creations, coconut bowling, arts and crafts, and zany relay races. The program operates daily year-round, from 10:00 A.M. to 3:00 P.M. The cost is $30 for a full day, including lunch and an ice-cream snack. A second child is $25. A unique Rainy Day program offers hours of indoor entertainment for the whole family on those rare days without sunshine.

Recreation: Choreographed by a team of fun-in-the-sun experts, daily activities include aquaslimnastics, tennis aerobics, island bike and trolley tours, beach volleyball, table tennis, and step aerobics. Sun worshippers and soul searchers relax under thatch-topped tiki huts, play beach volleyball, or scour the shore for seashells. Endless Gulf activities include sailing, kayaking, windsurfing, water-skiing, bumper tubing, Wave Runners, and parasailing. Three sparkling pools and a children's wading pool are available. Golfers can enjoy the off-site, newly refurbished eighteen-hole championship golf course called the Rookery. The clubhouse facility includes an elaborate pro shop, complete locker room facilities, the Clubhouse Grill for breakfast or lunch, and Nick Faldo's School of Golf. For tennis enthusiasts, there are thirteen Har-Tru and three hard-surface courts (four lighted for night play), a tennis shop, daily clinics, private lessons, round-robins, match mate services, and special instruction for young learners. Fabulous fishing is accessible, or you can work out with Florida-style aerobics and fitness programs. Be sure, though, to save time for ecotour adventures or some on-site shopping. Briggs Nature Center is only 8 miles away, or you can visit Everglades National Park (30 miles).

MARCO ISLAND MARRIOTT RESORT

400 South Collier Boulevard
Marco Island, Florida 34145
(239) 394–2511, (800) 438–4373
www.marcomarriottresort.com

MARRIOTT'S GRAND HOTEL RESORT, GOLF CLUB & SPA

Point Clear, Alabama

The charm and graciousness of the Old South has not faded in southern Alabama. Marriott's Grand Hotel has preserved its rich tradition of elegant service as a premier resort for more than 150 years. Known as the Queen of Southern Resorts, the four-diamond hotel is set on 550 acres in Point Clear, on a peninsula in Mobile Bay. In this secluded location, the quiet lagoons, majestic oak trees draped in Spanish moss, and beautiful gardens can make you forget the worries and concerns of the workaday world. Leave your troubles and anxieties on the doorstep and enter this vacation retreat, where your biggest dilemma will be whether to play a round of golf, ride horseback in the peaceful landscape, stroll along the sandy beach, or sip a mint julep while watching the sun set over the bay.

The fascinating legacy of the Grand Hotel captures the heart of many a history buff. First discovered as an ideal location for a resort retreat in 1847, the hotel was the site of lively antebellum social events in its early years. Then, during the days of the Civil War (or as some folks down here still call it, the War of Northern Aggression), it served as a hospital for Confederate soldiers. After the war the hotel resumed its original function and once again became the center for leisure activities. A fire in 1869 and a hurricane in 1893 destroyed some of the old facilities, but rebuilding efforts and expansion were frequently undertaken in order to maintain accommodations for guests. Today's main hotel building was constructed in 1941. In 1967 the Bay House was added, and 1983 brought the addition of two buildings—the North Bay House and the Marina House. The most recent renovation and addition of a European-style spa was completed in early 2003.

Accommodations: The main building has been described as rustic, but don't be deceived; this is rustic in a grand old manner. The lobby here is a charming octagonal structure that focuses on a massive fireplace. From its wide planks of pine flooring to its cypress-beamed ceiling, visitors immediately sense a warm, hospitable atmosphere. There are a total of 400 guest rooms in the different buildings and the cottages. Many rooms are decorated with white cypress paneling and ceiling fans (maintained primarily for ambience, but also to capture the bay breezes; air-conditioning relieves the sultriness of summer days). Open year-round, the hotel has two rate structures. In the winter season (November through February), daily room-only rates range from $129 to $169 midweek. Special rates that include breakfast for two are just $10 more, and children under five can dine from the special children's buffet. Summer rates (March through October) are higher: $169 to $209 weekdays or $189 to $229 weekends. There is no charge for cribs and rollaways.

Dining: The Grand Dining Room offers an elegant but casual atmosphere for breakfast, lunch, and dinner. An orchestra performs nightly here during dinner and afterward for dancing. Since the hotel is located on Mobile Bay and so close to the gulf, many of the house specialties rely on the fresh local seafood. Oysters, red snapper stuffed with crabmeat, and seafood gumbo are a few of the selections. The hearty-meat-and-potatoes fan will find excellent prime rib of beef. The gourmet will be enticed by the elegant Bayview Room for intimate and scenic dining.

For a sumptuous buffet breakfast, try the Grand Buffet in the Grand Dining Room, where you may sit in a gazebo area with beautiful bay views. Lunch is served not only in the Grand Dining Room but also at the Lakewood Golf Club, which is set in a wooded landscape. While soaking up the sunshine, you may choose snacks, sandwiches, and grilled favorites poolside at either the Pelican's Nest or the Marlin Bar. The Birdcage Lounge also serves light snacks and delightful cocktails with spectacular views, and live entertainment nightly.

Children's World: The Grand Fun Camp is in operation daily from Memorial Day to Labor Day, on all major holidays, and on weekends year-round. Every day a group of friendly counselors coordinates fun-filled activities. Five- to twelve-year-olds frolic from 10:00 A.M. to 2:00 P.M. and from 6:00 until 10:00 P.M. The cost is $20 per session including lunch or dinner. Swimming, shuffleboard, putt-putt golf, arts and crafts, video games, fishing, and sand-castle building entertain children, who will no doubt entertain their parents as they recount a day's adventures. Special events include movies and puppet shows. A new swimming pool on Mobile Bay with waterfalls and slides also has a children's area with playground and tree house that kids love. Individual babysitters are also available on an hourly basis.

Recreation: In the old days of the resort, two favorite spots were the wharves—one for men and one for women, because sunbathing and swimming in mixed company were unacceptable. Having come a long way since then, the Grand now offers innumerable popular activities for its guests. Given this prime location and mild climate, water sports attract many visitors. After a little warm-up fishing in the bay, you might take on the challenges of deep-sea fishing. Your catch may be your evening's dinner, prepared

especially for you by the hotel chefs. Reserve a sailboat or paddleboat for an afternoon's outing, or bring your own boat to the forty-slip marina. Splash in the waters of the bay along the sandy beach, or take a dip in the beautiful pool, the largest on the Gulf Coast. There's also a family pool, as well as a new indoor pool.

If you're more of a landlubber, the championship thirty-six holes of golf are a suitable diversion. Regardless of their level of play, all golfers appreciate the rolling, wooded setting of oak and pine. The facilities of the club include—instructors, carts, putting greens, and locker room. The eight rubico tennis courts (four lighted) lure many ace players, and novices can enroll for lessons with one of the pros. Head to the stables for horseback riding around the picturesque lakes and lagoons, or jog or bicycle (rentals available) through the gardens and along the boardwalk.

Slower-paced activities include croquet, putting green, and video games. You may want to wind up the day in the hot tub or with a treat from the full-service spa. In the 1930s the Grand Hotel advertised itself as the place of "Every Creature Comfort." Many visitors today feel that reputation has withstood the test of time.

THE RESORT AT LONGBOAT KEY CLUB

Longboat Key, Florida

An island retreat, the Resort at Longboat Key Club specializes in relaxation and recreation for golfers and tennis players. Located on a barrier island in the Gulf of Mexico just west of Sarasota, it doesn't shortchange swimmers and sun worshippers either. The resort enjoys a lush, tropical setting between the gulf and Sarasota Bay that seems worlds away from your regular routine, yet is only fifteen minutes away from the Sarasota Airport.

Accommodations: Seven modern buildings, four to ten stories high, are arranged throughout the property to afford guests magnificent views of the gulf, the bay, and the golf course fairways. Of the 232 accommodations, each with its own balcony, the majority (220) are suites, each with a king-size bed, a sleeper sofa, and a fully equipped kitchen. Summer is the low season, when guest rooms range from $180 to $255 a night and club suites start at $220 a night; the deluxe two-bedroom suites command $430 to $565 a night. During the high season (Christmas through late April), a guest room is $295 to $435 a night, while suites cost $350 to $1,120 a night. During the rest of the year, prices fall between these parameters. Up to two children (seventeen and younger) can stay in a suite with their parents at no additional charge. A Family Stay and Play package for two adults and two children includes four nights' suite accommodation, daily breakfast, two days at the Kid's Club, daily Fitness Centre, tennis, bicycles, and one beach lounger. Summer rates begin at $960.

Dining: Dining can be as elegant or as casual as you choose. On the sophisticated side is Sands Pointe, the signature restaurant. Tempting fresh seafood dishes are frequently featured on its menus. For more casual dining, drop by Spike 'n' Tees, and for truly relaxed mealtimes, saunter over to Barefoots, at poolside. Enjoy lunch and dinner at the nearby Grill at Harborside, open Wednesday through Sunday.

Children's World: The Kids' Klub operates year-round, Tuesday through Saturday. Experienced counselors direct youngsters ages five to twelve in a full 9:30 A.M. to 3:00 P.M. program. Swimming, beach fun, volleyball, basketball, field trips, and arts and crafts are all part of the schedule. The program is $25 per child per day, and includes lunch and admission to attractions. Regularly visited attractions and things to do include the Mote Marine Laboratory, Sarasota Jungle Gardens, Gulf Coast World of Science, Planet Fun, movies, bowling, skating, and miniature golf at Pirate's Cove. The average cost of individual baby-sitting is $15 an hour, with a three-hour minimum.

Recreation: The Islandside Golf Course has eighteen holes, and the Harborside Course has twenty-seven holes. Recipient of *Golf Magazine*'s Silver Medal, with palm trees and quiet lagoons throughout these courses, who can have a bad game? Two complete pro shops, a golf school, and professionals to guide players in private lessons and tournaments round out the picture for golfers.

Thirty-eight Har-Tru tennis courts await your ace serves and graceful lobs. Six of these are lighted for night play. Two tennis shops, ball machines, a videotaped game analysis, and a professional staff will urge you on to better play. Recognized as a "Top 50 Tennis Resort" by *Tennis* magazine, tennis play is complimentary here.

Swimming in the outdoor pool or the gentle waters of the gulf may top off your day. Bicycle along the nature trails, stroll on the snow-white beach, or spend an afternoon snorkeling or sailing. You can even organize a deep-sea fishing expedition through the concierge.

The resort's newest recreational amenity is a 4,000-square-foot fitness center, which features weight-training and cardiovascular equipment as well as instructor-led aerobics classes. Fitness-center equipment is available to guests on a complimentary basis. For soothing life's daily stress and the ultimate in personal pampering, neuromuscular, sports, and Swedish massage are also available.

SOUTH SEAS RESORT

Captiva Island, Florida

Located at the northern tip of Captiva Island on the Gulf of Mexico, 3 miles off Florida's southwest coast, Captiva Island is connected to the mainland via Sanibel Island and the Sanibel Causeway. It has a fascinating history going back at least 5,000 years and involving Colusa Indians, pirates, homesteaders, and a prosperous key-lime plantation. South Seas Resort is approximately 30 miles from the Southwest Florida International Airport in Fort Myers.

Dubbed "Florida's Tahiti" for its subtropical climate and lush foliage indigenous to the Southern Hemisphere, Captiva Island—famous for its shell-covered beaches—has been rated one of America's most romantic beaches. South Seas Resort is a 330-acre island resort with 2½ miles of beach, a full-service yacht harbor and marina, recreational options from golf and tennis to island excursion cruises and water sports, fine restaurants, shopping, children's programs, and a complimentary open-air trolley transportation system.

Accommodations: The South Seas Resort boasts more than 600 luxurious units, ranging from deluxe hotel rooms and villa suites to three-bedroom beach homes and cottages. Rate ranges from May to mid-December are $209 to $689 and January through April are

$269 to $1,249, reflecting accommodation type, location, and view. Children sixteen and under stay free, and four-day Family Fun packages can provide good value.

Dining: The resort's legendary King's Crown Restaurant features exquisite architecture and an award-winning culinary team. Discover fine dining in an elegant waterfront setting where New American cuisine is graciously served, traditions of yesterday are preserved, and new traditions are created. *Florida Living* magazine readers have honored King's Crown with the distinction of "Best Restaurant with a View." Chadwick's Restaurant features casual dining in a tropical setting. It is open for breakfast seasonally, and lunch and dinner menus feature daily breakfast and lunch buffets, a Sunday champagne brunch, and evening theme buffets, including Caribbean Celebration Buffet, Bourbon Street Bash, Key West Clambake, and Seafood Extravaganza. The mahogany and leather Porter House is the place for steaks and wine.

Dine indoors or in the open air at Cap'n Al's Dockside Grille overlooking the Yacht Harbour. Cap'n Al's serves breakfast, lunch, and dinner daily with a childrens menu. Enjoy Mama Rosa's Pizzeria, offering eat-in or take-out dining; the convenience of delivery is provided after 5:00

P.M. Choose from mouthwatering pizza, garden-fresh salads, and delicious subs. Fresh dough is made daily on the premises. Uncle Bob's Ice Cream Emporium serves delicious, old-fashioned soda fountain and ice-cream treats and tempting candies, and sells educational toys and kites. Pelican Pete's Pool Bar and Grill is a full-service bar specializing in tropical libations; poolside dining at the north end features grilled sandwiches, snacks, and more.

For dining entertainment, the King's Crown Lounge, located in the King's Crown Restaurant, offers cocktails and live, easy-listening entertainment. Chadwick's Lounge has a full bar and live entertainment nightly. A steel-drum band is featured Tuesday evening and a jazz quartet during dinner on Thursday evening.

Children's World: Activities for all ages are available. A professional staff organizes daily itineraries of recreational and educational activities, where kids dress up like pirates or mail coconuts to their friends. Fun Factory™, for children ages four to eleven, includes activities such as Nature Camp, Pirate Mania, Circus at South Seas, and Dinner Theatre. Fun Factory is a program offered by Meri-star resorts at eleven properties, with supervision by "funologists" and innovative educational programs, sports, activities, and creative projects. While there's a somewhat standard formula for success, each resort customizes the program, and kids become members, with newsletter and Web site fun available after returning home. Two age groups, four- to six-year-olds and seven- to twelve-year-olds may combine if groups are small. Each day is centered on a theme unique to the individual resort—for Captiva, it's often pirates and shells. The program runs year-round, Monday through Saturday from 9:00 A.M. to 1:00 P.M. Evening sessions from 5:00 to 8:00 P.M. on Monday, Thursday, and Saturday give Mom and Dad an opportunity for a quiet dinner or a solitary seaside stroll under the stars. Each session costs $35.

Teens are well looked after, in the style they like. Sunday kayak excursions ($15) or a Tues-day rally ($20) get them acquainted with each other, easily. Monday Murder Mystery evenings ($10), a pizza "jam party" on Thursday, and a wild game of Capture the Flag on Saturday night round out the offerings.

Supervised social events for teens, such as parasailing, waterskiing, volleyball tournaments, pool parties, canoeing, kayaking, and golf are sure to provide hours of enjoyment.

Recreation: Dozens of recreational activities are available to guests of South Seas Plantation, including a par-36, regulation nine-hole golf course; tennis on eighteen courts; biking; and water sports, including game fishing, sailboarding, snorkeling, sailing, and excursion cruises to nearby islands. Paddle a kayak into a mangrove forest or zoom around on a WaveRunner; or just watch the manatees play around the marina.

Workshops feature yoga, professional fitness training, aerobic exercise classes, canoe excursions, sailing clinics, guided shelling excursions, family fishing, shell art, and more. Family activities include log rolling contests, bingo, alligator races, or hydrocycles. A variety of nature activities for the whole family include Dolphin and Manatee Awareness, Shells of Captiva, Wildlife Refuge Trips, and Birds of Captiva. The Nature Center celebrates the biodiversity of these barrier islands with a "please touch" approach. *The Explorer Bulletin,* a current schedule of activities, is given to guests upon check-in. Preregistration is required for all activities.

Shopping at South Seas includes quality boutiques, gift shops, pro shops, grocery store and gourmet deli, ship's store, and full-service beauty salon.

SOUTH SEAS RESORT

P.O. Box 194
5400 Plantation Road
Captiva Island, Florida 33924
(239) 472–5111, (800) 965–7772
www.south-seas-resort.com

SUNDIAL BEACH RESORT

Sanibel Island, Florida

Sanibel is a barrier island off the south-west coast of Florida that has some of the best shelling in the world. Two-thirds of the island remains a nature preserve—it also preserves a taste of Florida as it once was. No neon and high-rises here; in fact, locals call it Nature's Theme Park. The Sundial is the island's only full-service resort, set on thirty-three lush, tropical acres along the Gulf of Mexico.

Accommodations: Two hundred seventy condominium units provide a home-away-from-home atmosphere; choose a one- or two-bedroom and revel in full kitchens, com-fortable and roomy bedrooms, and living areas, most with screened balconies. Select a garden view, partial gulf view, or gulf-front unit; rates vary according to season and loca-tion. A one-bedroom unit is $189 to $299 May to mid-December; $395 to $519 be-tween January and late April. Children sixteen and under stay free with existing bedding. A three-night/four-day Family Fun Plan treats you to dinners, a day at the Explorer Club or free sports rentals, unlimited videos, and a disposable camera to capture all the fun. Cost is $817 to $1,366 for a one-bedroom and $1,022 to $1,784 for two bedrooms.

Dining: Hunger is easily satisfied at Sun-dial. Windows on the Water boasts unique gulf-shore cuisine garnished with spectacular beach views. Open for breakfast, lunch, and dinner, it's noted for the Sunday champagne brunch. Teppanyaki tables at Noopie's put you in the midst of the cooking action—perform-ance cuisine at its best. Open nightly from 5:30 P.M.; check the times for one of the seven shows. Crocodial's Poolside Bar & Grill has sandwiches, salads, cold drinks, sunset happy hour, and afternoon entertainment on weekends. Beaches Bar & Grill serves up views, happy-hour specials, and nightly "is-land style" entertainment Tuesday through

Sunday until 11:00 P.M.

A five-minute drive brings you to the Dunes Clubhouse, a good choice for lunch or dinner. Dine indoors or on the patio. Lunches of salad, homemade soups, and sandwiches are offered Monday through Sat-urday; open for dinner Wednesday through Saturday with Mexican or Italian themes. You've an entire island of dining choices as well. In fact, two islands, as a bridge connects Sanibel to nearby Captiva Island and its associ-ated property, South Seas Resort. Stock your larder or buy goodies to take home at local grocery stores and shopping centers.

Children's World: The concept behind Kid's Explorer Club is that if kids don't have a good time on vacation, you won't either. They're dedicated to helping you achieve that goal. Programs for children ages four to eleven are extensive and flexible—a few hours, a day, or a week. Part of the Fun Fac-tory program, it's by no means an assembly-line production, as each resort puts its own personal touch on activities and themes. Aquacize, hermit crab races, and shell crafts are on the agenda. The program blends games, sports, and learning, and all with equal parts of fun and action. The morning session is from 9:00 A.M. to 1:00 P.M., and costs $22. In addition, six activities are planned daily between 10:00 A.M. and 4:00 P.M.; some are age specific (four and up, or seven and up) and some are for all ages; kids may participate as they like. Fees range from complimentary to $9.00 for materials or ex-cursions. Wacky Sunglasses, Coconut Paint-ing, Dolphin Discovery, Oceans Alive, and even a worm-eating contest are just some samples. When you check in at the front desk, make sure you're a member of Explorers so you'll receive a discount. Kid's Night Out from 5:30 to 8:30 P.M. on Friday and Saturday

($22) has a weekly theme, such as Luau, and gives parents a chance to kick up their heels.

Sun-Dial-a-Story line provides a two-minute bedtime story or nursery rhyme for your child. Different every day, it may become a habit.

Recreation: A professional recreation staff plans myriad daily activities for all ages. In addition to the Kid's Explorer Camp, teens and 'tweens are enticed into participation with beach volleyball, bicycles, or boogie boards. Family activities bring everyone together for squirt gun painting, shell symposiums and crafts, crazy sand bottles, or candy bar bingo. Some activities are complimentary; others may have a small fee for supplies.

The Dunes Golf and Tennis Club offers a championship course, an aqua driving range, and two practice greens. Better practice your swing before hitting the course, as the back nine is part of a wildlife preserve and plenty of critters are watching. It's equal parts sports and nature experience. Are you a tennis family? Sundial's got something for everyone: free clinics for the Tiny Tots (ages four to seven), junior, and adult clinics for $15. Between the club and the resort there are nineteen courts for practice and play. Courts are complimentary for guests and two of the hard courts are lighted for night play. Golf and tennis pro shops have all the latest gear and game advice.

Fish from beach, pier, bridge, or boat—gulf waters have more than 1,000 species of marine life. Or stay on top of the water with kayaks and catamarans. Swim in one of the five heated pools or work out in the fitness room.

Environmental Discovery Programs schedule both lectures and hands-on experiences. The ECO (Environmental Coastal Observatory) Center was the first to be situated in a resort. Spend fascinating hours with the aquarium, the touch tank, and a hermit crab petting zoo learning about all that surrounds you on this beautiful island.

SUNDIAL BEACH RESORT

1451 Middle Gulf Drive
Sanibel Island, Florida 33957
(800) 965–7772, (239) 481–3636
www.sundialresort.com

TRADEWINDS ISLAND RESORTS/ISLAND GRAND
St. Pete Beach, Florida

Hugging the sugary white sands of the Gulf of Mexico, three stellar beach resorts, the Island Grand, Sandpiper, and Sirata, are making history as the largest resort complex on Florida's Gulf Coast. Known collectively as the TradeWinds Island Resorts, these properties occupy thirty-five of the most desirable acres on St. Pete Beach. With limitless beachfront recreation, sumptuous dining, and exclusive golf privileges at one of the area's private country clubs, the TradeWinds Island Resorts offer guests access to three resorts in one.

The Island Grand resort is a classic four-diamond, family-friendly beach resort. Canals with white swans meander through the property, awaiting your visit via gondola or paddle-boat. The Grand Palm Colonnade, a garden atrium lined with two-story palm trees, provides a shady welcome. The children's program is headquartered here, so it's most convenient for families. An eighteen-acre island hideaway, TradeWinds Island Grand offers endless diversions, award-winning service, and classic Florida charm.

Accommodations: The 378 guest rooms and 207 suites are all newly renovated (2002/2003) with bright, colorful tropical furnishings and clean white accents. Every room features a microwave, refrigerator, toaster, and dishware. Suites have separate bedrooms, kitchenette, and living area, most with balconies. February, March, and April are high season; May through mid-December rates are lower. Hotel room rates range from $189 to $359; one-bedroom suites are $249 to $449. No charge for children twelve and under sharing the room. A daily Explorer Value Pass ($12 per room; $17 per suite) is required; this covers parking, telephone, tennis courts, fitness center, beach cabanas, and other services. Summer family packages are well priced and offer many extras; inquire about "Beach Blanket Bingo," with a 1950s theme, or "Swashbuckling by the Sea," with pirates and a yo-heave-ho! Contact the resort for information on the many packages offered with a price range that is sure to fit your family quite nicely.

Dining: Feast on the specialties of the house: island medleys of Gulf Coast cuisine, tall tropical coolers, and barefoot beach bars. Enjoy breakfast buffets, poolside lunches, and sunset dinners. Savor aged steaks and fresh native seafood, or experience the intimate elegance and excellent fare at Palm Court. Indulge in room service, deli specialties, an ice-cream shop, and even a Pizza Hut. Unwind at the waterside piano bar or enjoy evening entertainment at the lounge. At TradeWinds Island Resorts, seventeen dining and entertainment venues, with options to charge them to your room account, await your pleasure.

At the Island Grand Resort, choose from the Palm Court, an elegant bistro where you may dine indoors or on the patio under the stars; Bermudas, open for breakfast (try the buffet) and dinner, offers seafood, regional specialties, and steaks, with a children's menu; or the Flying Bridge, an authentic floating Florida "cracker cottage" docked over the main canal—probably one of the only restaurants you can boat under! Fare and dress are casual; appetizers, salads, and sandwiches are served. Step back into the 1940s in the Old Florida Shrimp Shack for shrimp and cold beer, or catch the big game at B.R.Cuda's Sports Bar. Enjoy seasonal live entertainment at B.R.Cuda's, the Flying Bridge, the Shrimp Shack, or Salty's Beach Bar.

Children's World: All day, every day, the enthusiastic recreation counselors (known as T.A.Z. Team members) of TradeWinds Action Zone offer activities from A to Z, with recreational options for every member of the family. T.A.Z. Team members supervise tons of planned fun stuff from aerobics to zany, wacky wordies, family swim meets, sun catcher creations, or a hunt for sharks' teeth.

The KONK Club, short for "Kids Only, No Kidding!" is specially designed for children four to eleven years old. Each day's program is themed a little differently, lasts from 9:00 A.M. to 1:00 P.M. and includes a meal ($25). KONK Club activities are scheduled at the Island Grand. KONK kids even have their own special nighttime programs from 6:00 to 9:00 P.M. (Tuesday through Saturday; cost is $20 with dinner), providing a great way to make friends with other kids, and giving Mom and Dad a little time alone. Monday evening is reserved for the "dive-in" movie.

Be sure to look for Beaker, the TradeWinds huggable purple toucan mascot. You're likely to spot Beaker at KONK Club activities or making rounds at each of the resorts. Or call Activities to schedule a bedtime tuck-in: Beaker will come to your room to make sure all kids are tucked in toucan-style.

Teens will enjoy the variety of activities and attractions at the three resorts and in the surrounding area. With tennis, golf, swimming, snorkeling, Wave Runners, Shell Island and Dolphin Watch Cruises, minigolf, parasailing, and numerous other activities, teens can be as active as they choose. If there's enough interest, the T.A.Z. Team will schedule excursions or special events. What a great opportunity to meet young people from all three resorts. Pre-registration is required for off-site trips.

Recreation: Escape to the magic of the TradeWinds Island Resorts and discover a place where you can do "everything under the sun"—or absolutely nothing at all. The Golf Concierge Desk will arrange tee times at any of the public courses in the Tampa Bay area; guests also enjoy privileges at the private Pasadena Yacht and Country Club, just ten minutes away. Four Har-Tru clay courts serve all resort guests, so reserve early. The Action Zone Activities Center coordinates all the recreation activity for every member of the family—and it's extensive. Whether aqua aerobics, tie-dye towels, glow-in-the-dark volleyball, or Hunt for Redbeard's Buried Treasure, the T.A.Z. staff has you covered.

Kidscape at the Sirata Beach Resort calls to video buffs of all ages, with games and high-tech entertainment. The swirl of whirlpools, the heat of sauna, the refreshing depths of ten pools entice. Dip into the shimmering surface of the sea. Comb miles of sandy beach for shells. Curl up with a book in a tropical courtyard or a beach cabana. Toast the sunset. Explore the resorts' meandering waterway, complete with swans, ducks, and egrets. Pamper yourself at Body Works salon with massage, aromatherapy, and body wraps. Relax. You're a million miles away . . . from everything. You're now on island time.

TRADEWINDS ISLAND RESORTS/ ISLAND GRAND

5500 Gulf Boulevard
St. Pete Beach, Florida 33706
(727) 367–6461, (800) 237–0707
www.tradewindsresort.com

MIDWEST

Illinois
Indiana
Michigan
Minnesota
Missouri
Wisconsin

EAGLE RIDGE INN AND RESORT

Galena, Illinois

With 6,800 acres of rolling, wooded terrain and sixty-three challenging holes of golf, Eagle Ridge is a major Midwest golf resort, awarded *Golf Magazine*'s "Silver Medal" for excellence eight times. When you're not on the links, you'll find that 220-acre Lake Galena is a focus of resort activity. Located in northwest Illinois, just minutes from historic Galena with its well-preserved nineteenth-century architecture, Eagle Ridge is only 150 miles from Chicago.

Accommodations: The Eagle Ridge Inn, with its eighty rooms, sits in the center of the resort, on a bluff overlooking the lake. In addition, resort homes and villas are scattered throughout the hills and consist of one- to eight-bedroom accommodations; choose from views of the fairway, the lake, or secluded woods. During peak season, from May 23 to late October, inn rooms are $199 to $289 a night (children under eighteen sharing a room with parents are free); a one-bedroom villa is $209 to $269; the resort homes are $399 to $999 a night. The resort homes are also available for weekly rental, and many different packages are offered.

Dining: An elegant dining spot in the inn is the Woodlands Restaurant, where you'll enjoy steaks, pastas, and seafood along with beautiful views of the lake. Next door is the Woodlands Lounge, for cocktails and more casual dining. Each golf course has its own snack bar and nineteenth hole. Spike's Bar and Grill offers great views of Eagle Ridge's newest golf course, the General, and a casual-dining menu of appetizers, soups, salads, sandwiches, and barbecue favorites. Children's menus are available. Paisano's, offering a casual cafe and take-out, satisfies your (or your child's) passion for pizza and pasta, and offers Italian desserts and coffees as well. When stocking up on provisions, stop by the General Store for deli selections and freshly baked pastries.

Children's World: The Camp Eagle Youth Program is in operation from Memorial Day through Labor Day as well as weekends and holiday times throughout the year; it is designed for four- to twelve-year-olds. Monday through Saturday the 9:00 A.M. to 4:00 P.M. day is filled with swimming, hiking, boating, games, and arts and crafts; the fee of $30 a day includes lunch. A half day with lunch is $25 (9:00 A.M. to 1:00 P.M.); from 1:00 to 4:00 P.M. without lunch is the same cost. On Friday and Saturday nights, dinner, movies, and games entertain children from 7:00 to 10:00 P.M. ($25 an evening). Teens can enjoy a Saturday-evening excursion ($25) that might include a volleyball game, cosmic bowling, movie outing, or Alpine slide—all with dinner at a local pizza parlor (requires at least eight participants). Individual baby-sitting is available at $10 an hour.

Recreation: The North and South Courses each provide eighteen holes of championship golf set in rolling hills and wooded countryside. The nine-hole East Course, characterized by elevated tees, is an excellent test of accuracy. The latest addition, the General (1997), is a challenging layout. For serious instruction, the professionals of the Troon Golf Institute at Eagle Ridge can guide you in everything from the basics to business golf. One-, two-, and three-day programs are offered.

On Lake Galena, fishermen go in search of bass, walleye, and crappie, and fly-fishing school improves their catches. Boaters head out in paddleboats, canoes, and pontoons. Swimmers can take a dip at the indoor pool adjacent to the fitness center in the inn; or pamper yourself at the spa. Horseback riding along 40 miles of trails begins at the Shenandoah Riding Center. Rent a mountain bike, or hike the trails to seek out native plants and wildlife. For a solitary excursion, the fitness trail has twenty-one exercise stations, or round up the whole family for a volleyball game (two courts) or a tennis match (four courts). Special events happen all the time at Eagle Ridge. In June the Great Galena Balloon Race fills the sky with over twenty hot-air balloons. All season you can discover the thrill of ballooning with a daily dawn or dusk flight ($150 per person). Fourth of July brings a rodeo and carnival; and in August the Civil War returns with battle reenactments, Lincoln's Gettysburg Address, and a Victory Ball. In October the annual Galena Country Fair, in nearby Galena, of course, showcases artists and their work, with games, raffles, and prizes. From the end of July to mid-August, you can combine an Eagle Ridge holiday with watching the Chicago Bears in summer practice at nearby Platteville.

In the winter, sports lovers turn to tobogganing, sledding, and ice-skating. Forty miles of cross-country ski trails are carefully groomed. Nearby Chestnut Mountain offers downhill skiing on seventeen runs.

EAGLE RIDGE INN AND RESORT

44 Eagle Ridge Drive
Box 777
Galena, Illinois 61036
(815) 777–2444, (800) 892–2269
www.eagleridge.com

FRENCH LICK SPRINGS RESORT
French Lick, Indiana

French Lick Springs is a curious name with an interesting history behind it. This area of southwest Indiana was settled by French traders more than 200 years ago. Subsequently, mineral springs were discovered and, because animals lapped the waters from the wet rocks, locals dubbed it "The Lick." The British moved in during the early nineteenth century; by the 1830s the first hotel was built on this site as visitors were attracted to the healing powers of the mineral waters.

At the end of the century, fire destroyed the original buildings, but the property was purchased and the facilities reconstructed and expanded by Thomas Taggert, then mayor of Indianapolis. Under Taggert's guidance French Lick Springs developed into a first-class resort, with restaurants, golf courses, and a spa. The early-twentieth-century elegance and the devotion to health and recreation were hallmarks of the resort. Today French Lick Springs encompasses 2,600 acres of rolling foothills of the Cumberland Mountain range and is dedicated to making the "Golden Days" of the Taggert era an ongoing reality. Today, just as in the 1800s, it's all about the mineral water. Pluto Mineral Spring is housed in a gazebo set in the midst of beautiful flower gardens that change with the season. The resort is open year-round, and the spa still offers hot mineral baths. As with many hotels recently, French Lick Springs schedules more meetings and groups during the week, leaving the weekends for vacationers. For this reason, organized children's activities are scheduled only on weekends, generally between Memorial Day and Labor Day.

Accommodations: The rambling main building and its adjacent wings house almost 500 rooms and suites. The large and gracious front porch hints at the relaxed pace that prevails here, and the colorful flower gardens create a serene vista. Rates for accommodations vary depending on the size, location, and view of a room and range from $89 to $179 per day, based on double occupancy. Children under age eighteen stay free; cribs are $10 a day. Package plans are available for golf, tennis, holiday weekends, and the spa's health and fitness programs.

A Modified American Plan is available (breakfast and dinner). The cost is $35 per day per adult, $15 per day for ages five to twelve years, and free for children under five. The plan is valid only for Le Bistro; a $20 surcharge applies to Jack's Steak House.

Dining: French Lick Springs lays claim to the "invention" of tomato juice. Legend has it that one morning in 1917, the chef ran out of oranges. Not wanting to disappoint the guests, he pureed tomatoes, added water, and the rest is hotel history.

Jack's Steak House, open every Thursday, Friday, and Saturday for dinner, serves choice beef and select seafood specialties in a historical setting. Open Friday and Saturday only after Labor Day, with resort casual attire requested.

Le Bistro is a casual steak-and-sandwich restaurant open for lunch and dinner. Combine pizza and bowling at the family-oriented Pizzeria in the Recreation Center on weekends, and don't forget to stop at Double Scoops for ice cream. The Country Club Restaurant overlooks the golf course, and the Hoosier Dining Room serves Sunday brunch and international buffet dinners. Sip cocktails in the Derby Bar, the Country Club Lounge, or Le Bistro Bar.

Children's World: The Kid's Club, for ages five to twelve, is not a regularly scheduled program. Rather, on weekends from Memorial Day to Labor Day and on holidays, it is offered on demand. A sign-up sheet is at the desk, and if enough children (five to six) are interested, activities will be scheduled. It may be a surrey ride, putt-putt golf, swimming, games, or other similar activities.

The cost is $25 per half-day session including lunch; $40 for the entire day includes lunch and a snack. A Saturday evening "Pizza Party" entertains children from 5:30 to 9:00 P.M. while parents enjoy a leisurely evening ($25). A list of baby-sitters is available; average cost is $6.00 per hour.

Thursday afternoons find children ages five through twelve at the Equestrian Center for "Horse Sense," basic techniques for building confidence ($15). On Tuesday afternoons, teens can "just head on down there, pardner" for a round-up ($16). Children's tennis clinics are also available on request.

The unsupervised outdoor playground—filled with swings, slides, monkey bars, teeter-totters, a merry-go-round, and a sandbox—is a big hit with youngsters.

Teen events such as mini-golf tournaments, horseback rides, and scavenger hunts may be organized by the Social Staff but are not supervised.

While the children's program is limited, French Lick Springs tries to offer what they feel their family guests want. Weekend activities include such family activities as bingo, a hotel "history" tour, treasure hunts, lawn sports, hayrides and cookouts, surrey rides, or a 20-mile, off-site trolley tour. Live theater on Saturday afternoons showcases favorites like *Willy Wonka and the Chocolate Factory.*

Recreation: You may not be able to shine in sports quite like Boston Celtic whiz Larry Bird, a native son of French Lick, but at least you have the facilities here where you can focus on improvement. On the gentle, wooded hills, through stands of butternut and oak trees, you can play golf from mid-March to mid-November on two eighteen-hole courses. The Hill Course was designed by Donald Ross. The golf clinics offered April through September put you through the paces in improving your swing, grip, and stance and provide guidance in scrutinizing a course with a bit of strategy.

The tennis complex includes eight indoor courts and ten outdoor lighted courts. Tennis players, too, can have workouts in clinics that cover analyzing a stroke and planning a strategic performance in doubles. Junior camps are also available. One of the largest tennis facilities in the Midwest, *Tennis* magazine ranks French Lick one of the top fifty tennis destinations.

The Equestrian Center has a variety of activities for adults and children alike: guided trail rides on over 30 scenic miles of trails, special lessons for children and teens, haywagon rides to the campsite, or a romantic jaunt in a lantern-lit surrey.

Take to the hilly terrain on foot, hiking along the many paths; or go for a warm lazy swim in the indoor or outdoor pool. Stroll through the gardens and challenge other guests to lawn games like shuffleboard, volleyball, croquet, badminton, and horseshoes. Rent a bicycle, go bowling (six lanes), play pool, or hit the video games in the Recreation Center. During the winter, enjoy cross-country skiing, horse-drawn sleigh rides, and ice-skating at nearby Paoli Peaks.

Don't forget the tradition of the magical quality of the mineral waters. At the Spa you can have mineral baths and massages. Work out in the exercise room, soak in the whirlpool, and block out the rest of the world while sitting in the sauna.

Nearby activities include the restored Pioneer Village at Spring Mill Park, Marengo Caves, skating at the Roller Dome, and a train ride at the Railway Museum.

FRENCH LICK SPRINGS RESORT

8670 West State Road 56
French Lick, Indiana 47432
(812) 936–9300, (800) 457–4042,
(800) 960–3577
www.frenchlick.com

GRAND GENEVA RESORT
Lake Geneva, Wisconsin

Tucked into the southeastern corner of Wisconsin, between Milwaukee and Chicago, are Lake Geneva and the four-diamond Grand Geneva Resort and Spa. Less than a day's drive from nine states and sixty million people, the resort sits in the midst of 1,300 acres of pristine Wisconsin countryside and has as its stated goal "to be a destination for relaxation and pleasure." Built in the 1960s as a Playboy Club, it has undergone extensive renovations, overcome its past, and reopened in 1994 with a brand-new image. The town of Lake Geneva has been called "the Newport of the Midwest," and that flavor is cultivated here.

Accommodations: A total of 355 newly renovated guest rooms, including forty-one suites, overlook the rolling green hills and private clear blue lake (some also overlook a courtyard parking area, so specify view desired when you book). Decor is that of an elegant and comfortable vacation home. In summer, rooms are $249 to $319 and in winter $149 to $239. Suites range from $229 to $339 in winter and from $339 to $489 in summer. Timber Ridge Lodge provides 225 one- and two-bedroom all-suite accommodations. Located near the water park, it's spacious and convenient for families. Rates begin at $289. Children stay free in the room with parents; a daily resort fee of $10 per person covers transportation within the resort, telephone, spa and sports center, newspaper, and in-room coffee.

Dining: Almost everyone likes Italian food,

so the bistro-style Ristorante Brissago is sure to please. Open for dinner only, the restaurant features wood-roasted pizza and homemade pastas; the atmosphere is special without being stuffy. Another restaurant choice, the Newport Grill, puts the kitchen right on display, so you get the full effect of sight and aroma as well as the taste of typical Midwestern dishes such as grilled steak, chops, and fresh seafood. The Grill is open for dinner only but serves a bountiful Sunday brunch. The Grand Cafe offers American cuisine and buffets; it's open for breakfast, lunch, dinner, and a special Sunday brunch. From 6:00 A.M. till dusk, snacks and sandwiches are available in the Links Bar and Grill at the golf pro shop. At Timber Ridge Lodge, Smokey's Barbeque House serves dinner (and lunches in summer season), or grab a bite at the Hungry Moose Snack Bar throughout the day. All of these restaurants have a children's menu. For evening cocktails or live entertainment, stop by the Newport Lounge or the Lobby Lounge.

Children's World: Located in the Spa and Sport Center, Kids Are Grand is a comprehensive child-care program designed to be flexible. Children are accepted from ages eight weeks to ten years, and age-appropriate activities are planned. Scheduled year round on Friday and Saturday from 7:30 A.M. until 9:30 P.M., it's available Sunday through Thursday on request. Fees are $8.00 per hour ($6.00 each additional sibling), and there's a five-hour limit per day. Meals are ordered from the children's menu at an additional fee.

Kids Are Grand summer sessions run Monday through Saturday, from mid-June to late August, for ages five to twelve. Children under five are welcome at the drop-off child care. Each week is themed, and activities are central to that theme: Carnival; Wild, Wild West; Art of Culinary; the Great Outdoors; Turn Back the Clock (to the '50s); and more. Swimming, pony rides, paddleboating, and hiking are regular activities. Monday through Thursday, morning sessions are from 9:00 A.M. to 1:00 P.M.; afternoon sessions are from 3:00

to 7:00 P.M. Friday and Saturday times are 9:00 A.M. to 2:00 P.M. and 4:00 to 9:00 P.M. The cost is $40 on weekdays and $50 on weekends; session fees include snacks and lunch, or dinner, and any activities cost.

Recreation: All the amenities for a resort vacation are here. Two PGA tour-quality golf courses lure golfers. The Highlands, one of the first Scottish-design courses in the United States, was designed by Jack Nicklaus and Pete Dye. The other course, the Brute, designed by Robert Bruce Harris, is one of the longest courses in the Midwest, measuring over 7,000 yards. Putting greens, driving ranges, and scrupulous attention to grooming keep golfers coming back. *Golf for Women* recently placed Grand Geneva on its list of "Top 100 Women-Friendly Fairways." So much for "the Brute"! Other awards include *Golf Magazine*'s Silver Medal, and its reader survey for being one of the top three courses in value and in the top four for speed of play. Pick up a tennis game on one of the two indoor or five outdoor courts, or work out at the Sport Center, which features a variety of cardio and weight-resistance equipment and indoor volleyball, basketball, and a climbing wall. The Spa and Sport Facility is an adult facility, and an adult must accompany children and teens at all times. Age restrictions also apply; ages sixteen and up may use the basketball court; ages ten and up may use the climbing wall by appointment ($20 for three climbs); and ages vary for spa treatments. Facials, massages, and herbal body wraps are guaranteed to make you feel like a new person. A private lake provides paddleboating or hydrobiking opportunities. Exercise your arms with a rowboat or your legs with a paddleboat, or just relax and cruise beautiful Lake Geneva on one of the excursion boats, like the *Lady of the Lake,* a modern reproduction of a Mississippi paddle-wheel steamer. More water opportunities present themselves at the indoor and outdoor 50,000-square-foot water park, Moose Mountain Faces, at Timber Ridge Lodge. Slides, pools, a lazy river, and two activity pools make this a very popular spot (admission $21/day). For serious swimming, try the lap pool. Jogging, biking, and fitness trails wind through the property, taking advantage of the natural beauty. Finish the day with a quiet carriage ride under the stars.

In the wintertime Grand Geneva has its own skiing. Even if there is no snow elsewhere in Wisconsin, with snowmaking there will be snow at the resort. Fifteen slopes descend from the top elevation of 1,086 feet, with a 211-foot vertical drop. Night skiing, 10 kilometers of cross-country skiing, and a special area for snowboards ensure winter fun for everyone. The Ski School uses Station Teach-ing to allow individuals to progress at their own rate, mastering each "station," then moving on. Enjoy sleigh rides, hot chocolate, and ice-skating when the pond freezes over.

GRAND GENEVA RESORT

Highway 50 East at Route 12
7036 Grand Geneva Way
Lake Geneva, Wisconsin 53147
(414) 248–8811, (800) 558–3417
www.grandgeneva.com

GRAND TRAVERSE RESORT AND SPA
Acme, Michigan

Long known as the Cherry Capital, this area of northwest lower Michigan has a lot more to offer visitors than just its beautiful orchards and fine fruit. Besides providing memories of Ernest Hemingway, who spent many summers here and used this area as the setting for several short stories, Grand Traverse Resort and Spa offers guests golf, swimming, sailing, cross-country skiing, and a complete sports complex and spa. Set on 950 acres of forests and orchards with ½ mile of shoreline on East Grand Traverse Bay, the year-round resort boasts fine golf courses designed by Jack Nicklaus and Gary Player.

Accommodations: The six-story resort hotel and even taller Tower, which house 424 rooms, are adjacent to the Plaza, the site of summertime barbecues and wintertime ice-skating. With four distinct seasons, hotel room rates range from $115 in winter to $255 in summer, midweek; weekends are slightly more expensive. The deluxe Tower encompasses 186 suites, 2 lounges, a restaurant, and boutiques. Rates range from $145 to $285 for luxury with a view and your own private whirlpool. The 236 condominium units are spread throughout eight clusters of buildings. Some overlook the bay, and some skirt the golf courses; many have a fireplace. A shuttle service connects the condominiums with the other resort facilities. Rates for a one-bedroom unit range from $125 to $295; about $30 more with valley view. Studio, two-, and three-bedrooms are also available. Children under eighteen sleep free when sharing a room with their parents. Be sure to inquire about the many package plans. Cribs are available at no charge; rollaway beds are provided at a daily charge of $15.

Dining: Sweetwater Cafe features an open kitchen in the center of the restaurant and offers casual family dining with a children's menu and local in-season specialties such as cedar planked whitefish and cherry cobbler. It is open seven days a week for breakfast, lunch, and dinner. The Trillium Restaurant, located on the sixteenth and seventeenth floors of the Tower, serves panoramic views of the bay and golf greens along with a fine dining experience of northern Michigan regional specialties. Open for dinner daily, and an a la carte Sunday brunch; reservations are recommended. A children's menu is available in most restaurants. The Grille, in the resort's Clubhouse, also provides an informal setting for dining and cocktails. Other choices include Jack's Lounge, the Trillium Lounge, and the Shores Beach Club, on the bay.

Children's World: Grand Traverse provides grand care for children ages six months to eight years, Monday through Saturday, year-round; in the summer, mid-June through August, Camp Traverse entertains six- to twelve-year-olds. For younger children, six months to eight years, state-licensed day care is available in the Cub House, a 2,000-square-foot children's center. Rates are hourly; $7.50 per hour for children under two and a half, and $6.50 for older children. The ratio is one caregiver for up to three infants and toddlers. Hours are Monday through Thursday from 7:30 A.M. until 9:00 P.M.; until 10:00 P.M. on Friday and Saturday. From June to mid-September, the Cub House is also open on Sundays. Diapers and snacks are provided for a small fee, or you may bring your own. Each event through the day is geared to a specific age group; you must register in advance.

Camp Traverse operates mid-June through August for ages six to twelve, and offers a full or half-day program with a weekly theme and field trip, plus sports, crafts, cook-outs, swimming, and hiking. Generally the camp is divided into two groups for more age-appropriate activities. Full-day (9:00 A.M. to 4:00 P.M.) cost is $40; 9:00 A.M. to noon is $25; and noon to 4:00 P.M. is $30. Lunch is $3.00 extra. A full-week camp is $145 plus lunches. Kids may arrive early (7:00 to 9:00 A.M.) or stay late (4:00 to 6:00 P.M.), having a pre- or post-camp adventure, for $8.00 per child. In addition, Friday night is Junior Night Out, when kids gather for pizza, tennis, and a swim from 7:00 to 10:00 P.M. for $25. On Saturday, Kid's Club offers dinner, crafts, and games and maybe a bonfire, for $28 from 6:00 to 10:00 P.M. or $33 to stretch it another hour, until 11:00 P.M.

An adventure playground near the Spa Complex also keeps youngsters well entertained, and the electronic-game room may mesmerize them. Also somewhat mesmerizing is Bogey Bear, an amiable 6-foot tall teddy bear, who makes an appearance at 11:00 A.M. on weekends. Usually dressed as a golfer or a surfer, he shares cookies and milk with the youngsters, and parents get a complimentary photo. Individual nannies can be scheduled with the assistance of the spa staff.

Recreation: The pride of Grand Traverse Resort and Spa is the Bear. Designed by Jack Nicklaus, this golf course meanders through cherry and apple orchards, with plenty of hardwood forest areas for contrast; it is quite scenic as well as challenging. The older course, Spruce Run, also offers championship play. The resort's third course is the Wolverine, a championship course designed by Gary Player in 1999, complete with a state-of-the-art clubhouse. Located within walking distance of the main resort, the clubhouse serves all three courses. The Jim McLean Golf School program provides sessions from May through September. For your comfort and refreshment, beverage carts tour the greens and there's a halfway house, the After Nine, on the Bear.

The Spa Complex is a championship setup too. With four outdoor and five indoor tennis courts (instruction available), indoor and outdoor swimming pools, and an exercise/weight room, you'll get quite a workout. Afterward you'll probably head straight to the saunas. A full-service spa provides all the pampering you need with signature services such as massage and exfoliation featuring the area's famous cherries.

If water sports capture your interest, Grand Traverse has just about every type of boat imaginable: power boats, ski boats, sailboats, sailboards, jet skis, parasailing, catamarans with special breakfast cruises for children, sunset cruises, canoes, kayaks, fishing boats, and even tall ships. River floating is an adventure for the whole family, from knee-deep streams to more challenging rivers. Swim or sun at the private Beach Club, with its own pool and poolside bar, where lazing away the afternoon is a worthwhile activity in itself. Fishermen seek out the many lakes and streams for trout and salmon; farm fishing or a charter trip on the bay are also options. Hike or jog through the hills and past the orchards; the scenery is so good for the soul that you may not notice you're also helping your body. Bikes are complimentary, so enjoy some of the child-friendly trails. Or rent horses from a nearby stable and let them do the work! Also complimentary is croquet, basketball, and volleyball, so challenge the kids, if you dare. Picking fruit at one of the nearby orchards allows you to truly savor the results of your work—cherries, apricots, peaches, apples, or blueberries, depending on the season. And speaking of savoring something, at Moomer's you can sit on the porch eating homemade cherry ice cream while watching the cows in the pasture. Yum. Part of this area belongs to the Ottawa-Chippewa Nation, and several nearby casinos provide evening entertainment.

But don't be deceived; Grand Traverse is not just a summertime resort. In the fall trees burst into autumn colors and make a beautiful backdrop for horse-drawn hayrides and trips to nearby wineries for sampling and festivals. In the winter cross-country skiing takes over; on-site, the golf course transforms into a ski trail (up to 2 kilometers) with woods and gently rolling hills, covered only with natural snow. More dedicated skiers can do cross-country at the Vasa Pathway, less than 1 mile away; and three downhill ski/snowboard areas are less than an hour away. Take a sleigh ride through the woods; or try the complimentary sleds, tubing, or ice-skating in the Plaza. And remember, while working out at the Spa Complex, you'll never know how low the temperature dips outside.

In the spring, when the weather is warm enough for you to want to pick up a golf club, the cherry orchards come to life. The white blossoms of the trees blanket the hillsides for more than half the month of May.

GRAND TRAVERSE RESORT AND SPA

100 Grand Traverse Village Boulevard
Acme, Michigan 49610
(231) 938–2100, (800) 748–0303, (800) 236–1577
www.grandtraverseresort.com

GRAND VIEW LODGE

Nisswa, Minnesota

Nestled among the Norway pines on the north shore of Gull Lake is Grand View Lodge, the focal point of this 900-acre resort. Built in 1918 of native cedar logs and now a National Historic Site, the lodge welcomes guests year-round. If charm and friendly service, style, and attention to detail are important to you, this is your place. Awards are common to the Grand View, but well deserved. *Midwest Living* rates them one of the "Top 40 Best of the Midwest"; *Golf Digest* gives it a five-star rating, one of only twelve such courses in the United States, as well as ranking it the only "Silver Medal Resort" in Minnesota in 2002. Located 142 miles northwest of Minneapolis, the lodge is within a fifteen-minute drive of seven golf courses, Paul Bunyan Center, and animal parks.

Accommodations: In addition to the lodge, sixty-five cottages border the lake. Deluxe suites and town homes are also nearby. The twelve rooms in the lodge are comfortable for couples, while a cottage is the right choice for a family. Since these range in size from one to eight bedrooms, owner Fred Boos explains that they "try to fit the cabin to the family." Some cabins feature a kitchenette and living room; all have decks as well as large picture windows and views of the lake. Suites and town houses overlooking the Pines golf course also are available. Daily maid service is provided for both the lodge and the cabins. Reservations are accepted on a daily as well as weekly basis. Rates from $325 (double occupancy, per day) include two meals a day, golf at the Garden Course, discounted golf rates at the Pines, the Preserve, and Deacon's Lodge championship courses, tennis, and the children's program. For children, the charge is $10 to $65 a night, American Plan, depending on the age of the child.

Dining: There are several restaurants: the main dining room in the historic lodge, Freddy's in the Pines Clubhouse, the Preserve Steak House in the Preserve Clubhouse, Sherwood Forest (also a historic building, nestled in the woods), and the Italian Garden, a magical little cottage really in a garden. Dress is casual. Barbecues on the beach are often planned. Children may dine with their parents or their counselors when on the kids' program. A special menu for children features fresh fish, steaks, chicken, and ribs. Cocktails are served on the large, three-level redwood deck or in the North Woods Lounge, where you'll hear live music nightly. The smorgasbord is a traditional Sunday event—great fun and all you can eat.

Children's World: From Memorial Day weekend to Labor Day weekend, Grand View has two well-organized programs, for children ages three to six and seven to twelve. There is a wonderful wooden playhouse in the woods with slides and climbing equipment, a well-stocked play area, the beach along Gull Lake, and a swimming pool that your kids probably won't want to leave—ever. This pool has jets, geysers, waves, and slides. Oh, my! The programs run from 9:00 A.M. to 3:00 P.M. and from 6:00 to 8:00 P.M., Monday through Saturday. The schedule includes arts, games, storytime, movement activities, exercise, and swimming.

The staff is college age and generally has past experience with children. The program is included in many of the packages; otherwise the cost is $18.00 for a full day, $9.00 for half-day sessions, and $15.00 for the evening program. Rates include meals when appropriate. For those under age three, the front desk can arrange baby-sitting with either an off-duty staff member or selected local persons.

Recreation: The lake attracts swimmers, fishermen, sailors, and sunbathers. Here you can also venture out in a pontoon or kayak or practice some waterskiing. A twenty-seven-hole championship golf course is aptly named, given its setting: The Pines. The nine-hole Garden Course is perfect for the entire family. The Preserve, an eighteen-hole championship course, is located just 10 miles north of Grand View Lodge. Arnold Palmer's Deacon's Lodge, rated one of the "Top ten new public courses in the nation" by *Golf Magazine,* is the newest addition to Grand View's golf family.

A tennis complex with seven Laykold courts is set among tall trees. Court time is free. The tennis pro teaches private lessons, organizes tournaments, and conducts free group lessons for children eight to nineteen years old. Two hitting walls and an automatic ball machine allow for extra practice before a good match. For a change of pace, take a yoga or cooking class, visit the fitness center and hot tubs, or enjoy the new indoor pool. Rent a bike, or go for a horseback ride through the wooded trails. Celebrate the new Glacial Waters Spa, an Aveda Concept Resort Spa with full services. In winter the north woods become a wonderland of snow. Enjoy ice-skating, build a snowman or snow-woman (or snowchild!), or go for walks in the snow. Then jump in the Jacuzzi, cozy up to the fireplace, and just enjoy.

GRAND VIEW LODGE

23521 Nokomis Avenue
Nisswa, Minnesota 56468
(218) 963–2234, (800) 432–3788
www.grandviewlodge.com

THE HOMESTEAD
Glen Arbor, Michigan

The Great Lakes are truly great—and not just in size. While Lake Michigan's 22,400-square-mile area is indeed impressive, imagine the possibilities it affords in recreation and relaxation: swimming, boating, and fishing in the water, and on land, hiking and biking the wooded trails beyond the lake's sandy beach. At The Homestead all this great potential is realized, and that may be why it's called America's "freshwater resort."

Voted "The #1 Nature Escape in the Midwest" by readers of *Family Fun* magazine. The Homestead is a waterfront resort community located on the northwest shore of lower Lake Michigan. Its 500 acres embrace gently rolling land covered with pine trees, aspens, and oaks; 1 mile of sandy beach on Lake Michigan; and 6 miles of shoreline along the banks of Crystal River. Surrounding the resort is the Sleeping Bear Dunes National Lakeshore; besides ensuring The Homestead's secluded position, this national preserve opens up additional opportunities for nature explorers. The resort is closed in April and November.

Accommodations: The Village is the center of most activities; accommodations, restaurants, shops, and a heated swimming pool are located here. Fiddler's Pond and Little Belle in the Village offer guest rooms and suites overlooking the pond. Fiddler's Pond underwent a $1.2-million upgrade and renovation in 2002, harking back to the traditional decor of decades of wooded lakeshore summer cottages—the kind one remembers from childhood. One- to four-bedroom condominiums, each with a full kitchen, are located on the beach, along Crystal River, on a ridge overlooking the shoreline, and in the Village. Crystal River cuts through the hills and runs more or less parallel to the lakeshore a short way before emptying into the lake. Where the river and the lake merge is another center of activity, the Beach Club.

Fiddler's Pond rooms are $79 to $225 a night; Little Belle's rates are $116 to $270 a night. A one-bedroom condominium unit ranges between $126 and $426 a night depending on the location you choose; lakefront and lake-view units are the most expensive. The rates for larger units graduate to $720 a night for a four-bedroom home/condominium. Rates vary with season, location, and view; from May through October, a "Family Fun" package offers a family of four two nights accommodation, four meals per person, and a half-day or evening session at Camp Tam-A-Rack. A summer weekend at Fiddler's Pond ranges from $267 to $325; at Stony Brook Lodge rates are $413 to $539. Cribs are provided at no charge; children are free when staying in their parents' room. An on-property shuttle service is available to guests.

Dining: At the Beach Club the Cafe Manitou draws diners to its ideal location on the beach; open daily in the summer only, its setting and attire are casual, and you can dine indoors or out.

Around the bend in the Village, Nonna's boasts a bountiful breakfast and northern Italian dinners, and Whiskers attracts pizza and burger fans. Also in the Village, at Cavanaugh's you can pick up groceries, deli sandwiches, a ready-to-serve meal, or snacks all day long. In the winter skiers gather in CQ's Cabin for its cozy atmosphere and friendly conversation.

Children's World: Camp Tam-A-Rack was built especially for children and is the center of the summer program. Indoors, there's space for art, cooking, music, stories, film, and napping. Extensive outside play areas include a tepee, a multilevel fort, water cannons, woods, creeks, lawns, and two gyms. Sentries is for ages two months to four years; Scouts is geared toward five- to ten-year-olds. Sessions are from 9:00

A.M. to noon, 1:00 to 4:00 P.M., and 5:00 to 8:00 P.M.; cost is $32 to $45 for half-day or evening sessions and $55 to $75 for the full day. It's available from June through late August and on select weekends throughout the year.

Teenagers enjoy meeting other teens at the game room or during canoe races, volleyball games, tennis matches, and pizza parties. Like the events for the younger group, some are free, while others require a fee. Private swimming lessons can be arranged; junior tennis and golf clinics are offered for young adults ages twelve to seventeen and juniors ages six to eleven.

In the winter the children's program teaches five- to twelve-year-olds fun-in-the-snow activities with ski lessons. It is offered for two and a half hours twice a day, Friday through Sunday, and on holidays from mid-December through March. Costs are comparable to the summer program.

Any time of year, individual baby-sitters can be hired, at approximately $7.00 per hour. The resort staff assists in making the arrangements.

Recreation: The clear waters of Lake Michigan are fine for sailing, boating (rentals available), fishing, and swimming. Maybe still a little nippy in June, the lake's temperature averages sixty-five to seventy degrees by July and August, and its sandy bottom is particularly attractive to young swimmers. The river waters tend to be warmer, and both the Beach Club and the Village have a heated pool and a hot tub, so guests have their pick of swimming conditions. Fishing is good sport in the river as well as in the lake, and canoeing up the river allows you to investigate the local wildlife. Sailing and windsurfing in the river can be a challenge, but tubing, kayaking, and canoeing are very manageable. And Lake Michigan is always an option. The 1 mile of beach along the shore is a real luxury.

Hike, jog, and bicycle (children's bikes and bikes with children's seats are available for rent) on the 24 miles of wooded trails; a self-guided nature tour can introduce you to the area's flora and fauna.

Being surrounded by the Sleeping Bear Dunes National Park is a real treat. The largest fresh water sand dunes in the world, some reach up to 450 feet and forty degrees of steepness. The Dune Climb is a thrill for everyone; you may climb and play on the land-side of the dune or sit at the picnic tables and laugh at others. It's a memorable experience either way. Take a ferryboat ride to the islands in Lake Michigan, sample the wines of local vineyards, or just take a relaxing stroll along the beach at sunset.

For tennis players, the Beach Club, with its five clay courts, is the site of many exciting matches. Here you can join a clinic, take private lessons, and watch real talent during professional exhibitions. If you're still looking for things to do, drop by the aerobics exercise class; work out on the fitness trail, with twenty exercise stations; head to the playground at River Park; or throw your hat into a volleyball tournament. Now here's ingenuity in utilizing space: A nine-hole par-3 golf course is built in part on the downhill ski slopes!

When the weather cools, the swimmers give way to skiers and snowboarders, who discover nature's wintertime beauty. Take a brisk hike on the beach or boardwalks. Try cross-country skiing or snowshoe the wooded hills. The frozen ponds are ideal for ice-skating. Downhill skiing is modest, with fifteen runs and 350 vertical feet, but the view down a snowy slope to whitecaps on the lake is an uncommon juxtaposition you'll long remember. All runs benefit from artificial snowmaking, and those lighted for nighttime skiing add another dimension to a winter holiday.

THE HOMESTEAD

Wood Ridge Road
Glen Arbor, Michigan 49636
(231) 334–5000
www.thehomesteadresort.com

THE LODGE OF FOUR SEASONS
Lake Ozark, Missouri

Lake of the Ozarks, a man-made lake developed in the 1930s, has provided scenic and recreational diversions for the residents of central Missouri for more than sixty years. Overlooking the lake, in the wooded gentle hills of the Ozarks, is the Lodge of Four Seasons. Opened in 1964, the family-owned Lodge has grown over the years into a major year-round resort. Today it is a convenient escape from city cares for St. Louis and Kansas City residents and is a vacation spot for visitors from farther afield as well. Native limestone decorates the entrance, and the warmth of a Midwest welcome is balanced by the beauty and serenity of the Japanese gardens.

Accommodations: Guests choose from 303 newly renovated guest rooms or two- and three-bedroom condominiums—lodging is spread throughout the 3,500-acre resort community. Connecting rooms are available and most feature balconies. Choose from standard, deluxe, or premier rooms or VIP suites. Lodge Condos (starting at $245) are located in a landscaped, semi-secluded community; Charleston Condos starting at $275, the newest, are set on a cove overlooking the Lake of the Ozarks. Room rates for fall, winter, and spring range from $89 to $129 weekdays; summer rates are $149; weekends are $20 to $30 more year-round. Children under eighteen share their parents' room at no extra charge; complimentary cribs are available.

Dining: HK's Steakhouse, winner of the Beefpacker Award, even has steak soup! Order Angus beef from a custom grill or try the signature favorite, turkey steak. Have breakfast, lunch, or dinner, inside or outdoors, at Breezes; and be sure to be there Friday evenings for the Pasta Bar. The atrium windows of Toledo's Room encompass garden and lake view—Sunday brunch is served the first Sunday of each month. Have breakfast or lunch with warm freshly baked bread and pastries while enjoying the "sidewalk waterfall" at Soleil. It only feels like it's outside. Seasons Ridge Sports Bar & Grill is found on the nineteenth hole; in summer, the poolside Parrot Bar is great for a sandwich and drink and sunning; and Breezes Sports Bar has the requisite wide-screen TV for your favorite game. Start the evening with cocktails and friends at the Lobby Bar, and wrap it up with dancing and easy listening music at the Blue Moon Jazz Club and Martini Bar.

Children's World: The Adventure Club provides a fun-filled day of activities for children ages four to twelve. The Adventure Club is open every day Memorial Day to Labor Day, from 9:00 A.M. to 5:00 P.M. The cost is $35 for a day (including lunch), $25 for a half day (morning or afternoon). And everyone gets a free Club T-shirt. Kids enjoy swimming, nature walks, fishing, games, movies, arts and crafts, theme days, and cookouts. Kids Night Out operates from 6:00 to 9:00 P.M. on Friday and Saturday during the summer and includes dinner, games, movies, and time well spent with peers. The cost is $28. Many resort activities encourage quality time for families to enjoy together, such as ice-cream socials, crafts, and demonstrations. The Adventure Club's staff is certified in Red Cross first aid and water safety training.

Recreation: The sports enthusiast will be well satisfied at the Lodge of Four Seasons, named one of the "Top 50 Golf Resorts" by *Condé Nast Traveler*. Witch's Cove, a championship eighteen-hole golf course designed by

Robert Trent Jones Sr., interests players with its narrow, undulating fairways and glimpses of the lake's blue waters. A second eighteen-hole championship golf course, Seasons Ridge, is carved into the rolling Ozark terrain, where multiple tee boxes accommodate golfers of all skill levels. Golf instruction is offered at both of these courses. In addition, golfers can turn to the nine-hole executive course to sharpen their skills. Equipment and attire can be purchased at the pro shop, if you've forgotten anything. If water sports are your life's love, you certainly won't feel slighted with both indoor and outdoor pools to enjoy. Swimmers can also venture out into the lake or sunbathe on the private beach. The lake is a favorite of boaters; the full-service marina can handle more than 200 boats and is the base for lake activities, from boat rentals and waterskiing to fishing guide services and parasailing. The Lodge of Four Seasons also offers a scenic excursion boat that takes guests on a smooth journey around the lake.

Guests can truly unwind at Spa Shiki. Try a full body massage or other services at the full-service spa. Browse through on-site shops, catch a movie in the lodge's cinema, or simply take a stroll through beautifully landscaped Japanese gardens. If you have any energy left, hike along wooded paths or try your hand at trapshooting. Volleyball, basketball, and tennis are even more options to fit into a busy schedule. At the end of a very full day, you may choose to stop and have a drink at the Lobby Bar, dance at Blue Moon, or retire early for a well-deserved repose.

THE LODGE OF FOUR SEASONS

Championship Golf Resort and Spa
Horseshoe Bend Parkway
Lake Ozark, Missouri 65049
(573) 365–3000, (800) THE–LAKE
www.4seasonsresort.com

LUDLOW'S ISLAND LODGE

Cook, Minnesota

Minnesota has a reputation as the land of 10,000 lakes (ever wonder who counted them all?), and Ludlow's Island Lodge is well situated on one of these—picturesque Lake Vermilion. The resort facilities are located on Ludlow's Island and on the north and south shores of the lake. A boat shuttle connects the three areas. Water-related activities are the primary recreation at this three-star, three-diamond wooded resort. Fishing, swimming, sailing, and exploring any of the 365 islands provide wonderful experiences. The seclusion among the pines and birches, with the lake practically at your front door, makes this retreat a real back-to-nature experience. The resort is open May through September, and is a member of the "Distinctive Lodges." The resort is run by the Ludlow family—for families—and has been for sixty-three years.

Accommodations: Twenty cabins with enchanting names like Stardust, Evergreen, and Twilite are located on the island and the shores. Designed with knotty pine or cedar interiors, all have a fireplace and outdoor deck; most have a screened porch. They range from one to five bedrooms, with a fully equipped kitchen (yes, even a dishwasher and microwave). Spring (May) and fall (September), daily rates start at $200 for two adults and $30 for each child under seventeen. Early June through September, the most common rentals are weekly. Rates for two adults range from $2,000 to $3,150 for a four-story "treehouse"; ages eighteen and over are $175 per week; ages six to seventeen are $100; and ages five and under are $40. Daily summer rates are calculated at one-sixth the weekly rate. And packages are available—some out of the ordinary, such as "Breakfast with the Bears," "Visit the Wolves," or Family Fishing Camps.

Dining: You may dine in your cabin, and do your own cooking. Or you may dine in your cabin and have meals delivered by a local restaurant. Full menu choices are posted in the cabins; burgers and pizzas are also available. Place your order by 5:00 P.M. and dine by 7:00 P.M. Or, if you're getting cabin fever, try one of the several local restaurants, where dining is casual and family-oriented and someone else does the dishes!

Children's World: One planned activity (an hour or so) just for children is scheduled every day Monday through Friday. Boat rides, nature hikes, and fishing derbies introduce kids to the surrounding woods and waters. Pontoon tours give an opportunity for viewing beaver lodges and eagles' nests; and planting a white pine with your name on it is a great introduction to ecology. Water-skiing, tubing, basketball, and picnics keep kids active, and seaplane and Friday afternoon amphibious car rides in the lake are exciting for the whole family. Unique is the only word for a 1954 Chris-Craft Constellation converted to a "playhouse," and kids love it for picnics and fantasy voyages to faraway places.

The island is not open to the public and no cars or traffic are allowed, so children have the security and freedom to roam—with an entire island to explore, Ludlow's keeps structured activity to a minimum. Movies are shown in the afternoons, and one lodge has a goodly supply of books and games. Teens like to gather at the video-game room or in the evening for more "grown-up" movies. The two-story tree house and a small camping island for overnight trips are among the biggest attractions for the younger set, but the swings, the lake (with a section roped off for children's safety), and the sandy beach are good play areas, too. Kids also enjoy exploring the trails in the forest, just like Paul Bunyan of

Minnesota lore. The recreation complex on the south shore has a children's play area. The management will arrange baby-sitters; cost is $6.00 per hour.

Recreation: Fishing buffs relish this bit of paradise on the south shores of Lake Vermilion. Walleye, bass, and crappie lure fishermen to these waters. There's no excuse for not landing the big one; a fishing clinic is held every week, and a guide is available for private excursions. The staff at the lodge will fillet and freeze your catch. Besides fishing boats, the lodge has canoes, kayaks, paddleboats, old-fashioned rowboats, and a sailboat for guests' use. Waterskiing and hydrobikes add a new dimension of fun to water sports.

The recreation center houses an indoor racquetball court, two Tru-Flex tennis courts, and a fitness center. After a good workout there,

you may enjoy a leisurely swim or a relaxing sauna. Along the north shore you can take a stroll down the 1½-mile hiking trail. There are many additional miles of hiking and biking trails in the area. Half a dozen or more golf courses are within an hour of Ludlow's, including the Legends, *Golf Digest*'s pick for the number-one public golf course in the country.

LUDLOW'S ISLAND LODGE

P.O. Box 1146
Cook, Minnesota 55723
(218) 666–5407, (877) LUDLOWS
(583–5697)
www.ludlowsresort.com

Mackinac Island, Michigan

Step off the ferry into a Victorian village—another time, not just another place. A place out of time, where cars are not permitted and quaint streets are lined with galleries, fudge shops, restaurants, and boutiques. The pace is leisurely and friendly, and adventures await discovery. Permanent residents barely outnumber horses (600 of the former, 500 of the latter) and almost 80 percent of Mackinac Island is a state park, so it's all about outdoor fun. Sailing, fishing charters, and six championship golf courses are just the beginning. Stroll or bike the quiet streets and enjoy the clean air; ride horseback or hike the nature trails and forest preserve. Take a tour, or win a free pizza from Freighters Deli when you complete the Discover Mackinac Island self-guided tour. Get a $5.00 savings card from www.mackinac.com and go to town!

Lots of limestone formations and caves, particularly Skull Cave, provide hours of entertainment for youngsters and adults alike. History is abundant here as well; Benjamin Blacksmith Shop; the Astor Warehouse where mink, otter, and beaver pelts were stored and counted; Colonial Michilimackinac (easy for you to say!); the Woodland Indian Museum; and historic Mill Creek just for starters. At Fort Mackinac (ca. 1780), the restored British and American outpost, you'll see colonial reenactments, period characters, and cannon firings. Visit the Tahquamenon River with its magnificent waterfalls; with a drop of nearly 50 feet, the Upper Falls is one of the largest east of the Mississippi. A fun way to get there is via an old-style train, the Toonerville Trolley, and riverboat.

Winter brings its own magic to Mackinac with horse-drawn sleighs, cross-country skiing (*Condé Nast* votes it one of the top-ten destinations for this sport), and ice-skating. Christmas and February winter festivals light up the season.

Two lovely hotels offer special programs for families, so we'll let you decide!

GRAND HOTEL

Mackinac Island, Michigan

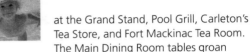

The world's largest summer hotel since 1887 is also the grande dame of Mackinac Island. Afternoon tea, croquet on the green lawn, seemingly endless white columns stretching to the blue sky, and flowers everywhere reflect the best of the Gilded Age. Relax on the front porch, the longest in the world, and visible even from Lake Michigan. Offering gracious hospitality, the serenity of age and privilege permeates the Grand Hotel, open from May through October.

Accommodations: Past the red-carpeted entry and beyond the impressive Victorian Parlor and public rooms lie almost 300 guest rooms and suites, no two of which are alike. Each has its own unique character, and the suites are filled with antiques and furnishings from around the world. They are also named: after presidents, first ladies, and famous people and places. Take some time choosing, as a wide variety of room sizes, locations, and rates are available. When the hotel opened in 1887, the rates were $3.00 to $5.00. Today's rates in the peak Social Season (mid-June to late August) are per person, MAP (breakfast and dinner) and range from $199 for a small inside room to $314 for a named suite. Shoulder season rates are approximately $20 lower. Children to age eleven are complimentary, twelve to seventeen are $49, and eighteen and older are $99. A $5.00 per person baggage transfer fee is automatic.

Dining: In all public areas of the hotel, the dress code is casual resort wear during the day and formal attire after 6:00 P.M.; jackets and ties for men, ladies in their finest. Start the day with breakfast in the Main Dining Room with a wide selection of choices. Dinner at the Grand is everything you'd expect, right up to demitasse in the Parlor and nightly orchestra music. Lunch choices include the Jockey Club at the Grand Stand, Pool Grill, Carleton's Tea Store, and Fort Mackinac Tea Room. The Main Dining Room tables groan under the weight of the Grand Luncheon Buffet, a tradition here.

Children's World: From Memorial Day to Labor Day, children age five years and up are welcome to join the complimentary daily activities from 11:30 A.M. to 2:30 P.M. and again from 6:00 to 9:00 P.M. Different things are planned each day, for example a hike, picnic lunch, and duck-pin bowling; a trip to Fort Mackinac; or dinner and a movie. Older children (twelve to teens) are welcome if the program interests them; they often come with friends or younger siblings. Babysitting is available at $15 per hour.

Recreation: The Jewel is the Grand's golf course; comprised of Grand nine and Woods nine. Although you arrive at the course by horse-drawn carriage, there are gas-powered carts on the course. The tennis pro will help you with your game on the clay courts, and you can stay in shape on the jogging trail, or the ½-mile Vita exercise course. Exercise machines and masseuse are in the cedar grove by the swimming pool, and bicycles are available to rent. The serpentine-shaped Esther Williams swimming pool is a popular gathering spot— *The Time for Keeps* with Esther Williams and Jimmy Durante was filmed here in 1949. The hotel is happy to arrange any off-site excursions you desire.

GRAND HOTEL

Mackinac Island, Michigan 49757
(906) 847–3331, (800) 33-GRAND
www.grandhotel.com

MISSION POINT RESORT
Mackinac Island, Michigan

Northern Michigan is known for its glorious outdoors; add to this the quaintness of a historical island, subtract automobiles, and you have the perfect equation for a family resort. Mission Point nestles gracefully on its eighteen acres overlooking Lake Huron, just minutes from the village. It's summer Victorian, but substantial, and quite pleasing to the eye.

Taking advantage of existing architecture, Mission Point has renovated the Observation Tower, offering island visitors extraordinary views of Lake Huron and the Straits of Mackinac. This all-glass structure on the resort's property serves as the perfect spot to watch sailboats approach the southeast coast during the island's annual yacht races.

Accommodations: In the recently renovated 242 guest rooms and 92 suites, casual and comfortable elegance is reflected in three styles: Nautical, Lodge, and Northern Michigan. Views of the island are superb, and some rooms offer fireplaces and Jacuzzis. Shoulder season rates range from $119 (Carriage room) to $339 (Lodge Suite); weekends cost more. Peak season (June through August) rates are $194 to $414, respectively. Rates are based on double occupancy, and children eighteen and under stay free with parents. Family packages are available from $329 per night and include lodging, some meals, ferry transportation, and activities. Regular season is May through October. Check with the hotel in October for winter dates (generally Christmas to March if they open).

Dining: Here's the great thing about dining at Mission Point: Not only is it delicious, it's free for ages twelve and under when ordering from the children's menu and accompanied by parents. Well, a $1.50 service charge is added for each child, but really! Who could complain? And all the restaurants have children's menus. At the Great Straits Seafood Company, world-renowned Chef Ernst Ackermann adds his flair to a culinary palette of fresh fish and steaks. For the casual side of island dining, try the Round Island Bar and Grill, where guests can watch passing freighters while enjoying appetizers, sandwiches, and spirits in an alfresco setting. Freighters Deli and Outdoor Cafe offers sandwiches and salads for guests on the go as well as indoor and outdoor dining with spectacular views of Lake Huron and the Straits of Mackinac. The Euro Garden Cafe, an open-air dining experience, serves a tempting array of European dishes from the chef's own personal recipes. It's worth noting that the resort has gourmet picnic baskets to go, a great addition to a day of island exploration. The Straits Lodge opens mid-December to mid-March for hearty winter fare.

Children's World: The Discovery Club is Mission Point's answer to that age-old question, "What can I do now, Mom?" Near the Activity Center, the Discovery Club offers indoor space plus activities throughout the resort and field trips for older children. Little Ones, ages two to four years, have circle time, balloons, and bubbles, or a teddy bear picnic. Ages four to ten enjoy themed days, such as Wild Kingdom or Space Day, with outdoor games, arts and crafts, storytelling, and nature hikes. 'Tweeners, from eleven to fifteen, are not too cool to enjoy pool and pizza parties and back-to-the-'60s tie-dye sessions. Discovery Club sessions run from 9:00 A.M. to 10:00 P.M. throughout the week from Memorial Day to Labor Day, and on weekends only to the end of the season. The program is flexible and activities vary depending on the average age of the group. Each counselor accepts only six children, so it's a good idea to sign up early. The cost is $10 per half-day session, *but*—a half-day session is either 9:00 A.M. to 4:00 P.M. or 4:00 to 10:00 P.M.! And it's $16 for a full day (both sessions). Meals are extra.

With a 3,000-square-foot area in which kids spark their imagination with a variety of interesting activities, Discovery Club includes a Parent and Toddler Room, Gross Motor Skills Rooms, and a Kreative Korner Room, as well as some of the kids' traditional favorites like the 12-foot tepee. The active atmosphere of the resort is complemented by Mackinac Island itself, a natural adventure park offering outdoor explorations and historic sites.

At Discovery Club kids enjoy a variety of supervised opportunities including arts and crafts, learning ancient Indian lore, plus field trips to the Island's Butterfly House, the 150-year-old British Fort, or along the Island's bluff for bald-eagle spotting. Parents are encouraged to sign children up one day in advance, allowing the counselors to plan appropriate activities and guarantee its one-to-six counselor/child ratio. As an added convenience, pagers are available for parents of young guests.

Recreation: The Greens, an executive eighteen-hole putting green, is identified as "a short course in relaxation." With picturesque views and restaurants within walking distance,

it's a fun course. If you're a tennis buff, register early for the one court. The Activity Center is the heart of the resort's recreation, sheltering the Health Club and Spa, with Discovery Club adjacent. Tennis, bicycle, and in-line skate rentals, and the indoor game room are here, along with exercise equipment and massages—marvelous at the end of an active day. Relax by the outdoor heated pool with a cool drink or take a leisurely stroll drinking in the view. Step back in time at the early-twentieth-century theater that presents the latest movie releases. Diversions for the whole family include picnic games, bingo, sundae building, lawn games, and a hayride through Mackinac Island.

MISSION POINT RESORT

One Lakeshore Drive
Mackinac Island, Michigan 49757
(800) 833–7711, (906) 847–3312
www.missionpoint.com

MARRIOTT'S TAN-TAR-A RESORT AND GOLF CLUB

Osage Beach, Missouri

Located in central Missouri, Marriott's Tan-Tar-A Resort rests comfortably in the foothills of the Ozark Mountains. The resort complex covers 420 acres and stretches along the shores of the scenic Lake of the Ozarks. The hilly terrain and lakeside exposure provide a lovely backdrop for many recreational activities. Tan-Tar-A is only a three-hour drive from either St. Louis or Kansas City.

Accommodations: The 989 guest rooms and suites are in the main resort buildings and

in smaller two-story accommodations bordering the lake and the golf course. Some have a fireplace and a deck or patio. The high season is mid-May to mid-September, when rates are $99 to $195 a night. During the low season (November to mid-March) prices drop to $90 to $120 a night. In the remaining months the rates are $89 to $180 a night.

Dining: If you have to start your day with a latte, Java Lakes is the spot for you. For casual family meals, the Black Bear Lounge serves breakfast, lunch, and dinner, and has a deck for summer dining. Children four years and younger eat free from the buffet. For a fancier evening, try Windrose on the Water, where you'll enjoy luscious steaks and fresh seafood. If all you want is a quick bite, the Food Court has Burger King, Sbarro, and Eskimo Pie ice-cream shop. At the golf course, the Oaks serves lunch overlooking the course. For liquid refreshment and snacks the Jetty Bar is adjacent to the Arrowhead Pool, and Tradewinds is near the Tradewinds Pool. Mr. D's Lounge serves cocktails at days' end.

Children's World: Camp Tan-Tar-A, for children ages four to ten years, is in session Monday through Saturday, from early June through mid-August. The fee for the 10:00 A.M. to 4:00 P.M. schedule is $25 for the first day and $20 for each additional day and includes lunch and a T-shirt. Half-day sessions are $15. Activities include swimming, beach games, races, treasure hunts, and crafts. Kids ages seven to thirteen can join a guided fishing tour for two hours ($30 per child).

A less structured routine is found at the Kids Kabin—a cabin filled with games, toys, dress-up, Legos and more. In summer the Kabin is open in the evenings only, Monday through Saturday, from 6:00 to 10:00 P.M. Dinner at Burger King, a movie, and play is $9.00 per hour for one child; $1.00 per hour each additional child. Fall, winter, and spring, the program operates on Saturdays only, from 9:00 A.M. to 12:30 P.M. and again from 6:00 to 9:00 P.M. The cost is the same as summertime. Children under age four are welcome to the Kabin on Friday and Saturday evenings, but must be supervised by a parent. These rates also apply to in-room baby-sitting, available on a limited basis, with a three-hour minimum.

Recreation: The lake is the venue for boating fun for everyone. You can rent ski boats (waterskiing instruction available), sailboats, paddleboats, kayaks, fishing boats, and Wave Runners. You can even try parasailing. Though there's a small sandy beach that's nice for sunbathing, the lake is primarily the domain of boaters and fishermen. Swimmers usually opt for time at one of the five pools (four outdoors, one indoors).

Golfers can take on the challenges of the Oaks (an eighteen-hole course) or Hidden Lakes (nine holes). Liquid refreshments from the on-course "jigger joggers" may or may not improve your game. The Racquet Club houses indoor tennis and racquetball courts as well as billiards. Outdoors and adjacent to the club are basketball and volleyball courts. Tennis buffs can also try the complimentary outdoor tennis courts near the Racquet Club.

At the fitness center you can use the exercise room as well as the indoor pool, and you can indulge in the many programs at the Windjammer Spa. Facials, massages, aromatherapy, and detoxification treatments are just some of the pleasures from which to choose.

Back in the great outdoors, find a good horse at the stables for a nice trail ride, rent a mountain bike, jog along the paths around the property, test your skill at the trap range, or challenge the kids to a round of miniature golf. If you still have time and energy, try bowling, shuffleboard, horseshoes, and table tennis. Even the shoppers in your family will have plenty of fun in the dozen shops, featuring jewelry, toys, fashions, and country crafts. And be sure to take an evening cruise on the lake; the *Ozark Princess* sails four nights a week during the summer season.

In the winter ice-skating is available for both adults and children.

MARRIOTT'S TAN-TAR-A RESORT AND GOLF CLUB

State Road KK
Osage Beach, Missouri 65065
(573) 348–3131, (800) 826–8272
www.tan-tar-a.com

RUTTGER'S BAY LAKE LODGE

Deerwood, Minnesota

If you have ever entertained thoughts of owning your own lakefront cottage in the land of 10,000 lakes, Ruttger's Bay Lake Lodge may satisfy your yearning. Set on 400 acres directly on Bay Lake, in north-central Minnesota, the Lodge emphasizes relaxed outdoor recreation in surroundings of clear lake waters, tall trees, and pine-scented air. Open May through September, it is family run and family oriented. With its old-fashioned hospitality, a family tradition since 1898, the lodge allows you a well-deserved escape to the peace and serenity of the North Woods.

Accommodations: For years the lakefront cottages and the lodge rooms have been favorites among vacationers. To these have been added condominiums and villas. Many have views of the lake, and all include a refrigerator, cable television, and air-conditioning. Ruttger's has both EP and MAP rates. The Modified American Plan includes not only breakfast and dinner daily, but complimentary golf and Kids Kamp, plus many other resort activities; the same rate applies to a variety of accommodations, and is mandatory for the lakeside cottages. Children under three years old stay at no charge; ages four to eight are $60; ages nine to fifteen are $80 in high season; rates drop to $40 per child over three at other times. On the European Plan, rates vary according to season, weekends, and size and location of accomodations; children under the age of eighteen are free. Early July to mid-August is the high season and weekend rates are the most expensive. As an example, the MAP plan ranges from $84 to $183 per adult; on the EP plan (lodging only, use of pools, tennis, and beach) per room rates vary from $87 to $202 in the lodge or villas, $114 to $291 in a one-bedroom, and $206 to $447 in a two-bedroom golf course condo. One week in July

is designated Family Value Days, when kids stay and eat free (one per adult), adults pay only $145 per person and daily special family events are planned. Cribs and rollaways are $10 each.

Dining: The Modified American Plan is mandatory for cottage guests, and the homemade pastries are practically a requirement. The Log Dining Room is an inviting setting, with natural logs, an open-beamed ceiling, and a stone fireplace. Service is a la carte or buffet. For casual dining and drinks, lunch and dinner are also served at Zig's, which overlooks Bass Lake and the eighteenth hole of the Lakes golf course. Auntie M's Kaffeehaus offers specialty coffees, panini sandwiches, pastry, and ice cream. The main lodge and Zig's both have picture windows that are great for viewing the North Woods while sipping a cool drink. The Bear Pine Bar is a full-service bar with appetizers and sandwiches, which can be enjoyed on the deck or around the pool with a spectacular view of Bay Lake.

Children's World: Kid's Kamp is a supervised program for ages four to twelve that runs Monday through Saturday, from mid-June to Labor Day. Planned by a certified teacher and kept in motion by energetic young counselors, from 9:00 A.M. to 3:00 P.M. kids are occupied with swimming, boating, fishing, and nature hikes. Indoors the fun continues with music, crafts, and games; or time at the playground near the cottage. Tuesday and Friday evening sessions from 5:00 to 8:00 P.M. allow parents to have a relaxing dinner and moonlight stroll by the lake. Teens are neither ignored nor overstructured; golf mixers, or water-skiing and wave-boarding clinics suit them just fine. Kids Kamp is complimentary on the MAP program; for EP guests, the charge is $21 for the day session, $13 for the evening session, or $32 for both. Baby-sitting can be arranged by the staff.

Recreation: With such a beautiful lake, you might find yourself drawn to the water almost continuously through the day—for sunning, swimming, waterskiing, fishing, and boating, and for building sand castles along the beach. Swimmers also enjoy the indoor and outdoor pools, and tennis fans turn to the two Omni-turf and three Laykold courts. Round up a game of volleyball, basketball, or horseshoes; play table tennis and shuffleboard; or go walking through the woods. Practice on the putting green, and plan a round of golf on the Lakes, the eighteen-hole championship course, or Alec's Nine. And treat yourself to pure relaxation in the lounge or TV lobby, the whirlpool or sauna, or just pull up a lawn chair and kick back. The staff naturalist directs programs introducing visitors to the

loon, osprey, and bald eagle. Waterskiing, sailboats, motorboats, pontoon boats, and fishing boats are available. Families can partake of bonfires and cookouts, pontoon cruises, stargazing, talent shows, and family movie nights. Evenings come alive with adult pleasures such as wine tasting, bridge socials, or karaoke.

RUTTGER'S BAY LAKE LODGE

Box 400
Deerwood, Minnesota 56444
(218) 678–2885, (800) 450–4545
www.ruttgers.com

SHANTY CREEK
Bellaire, Michigan

Shanty Creek, located in northern Michigan, is actually three resorts in one, which translates into a bit of variety for guests. Summit Village is elegant and contemporary, with stunning 360-degree views encompassing Lake Bellaire; Schuss Village has the European charm of an Alpine village; and Cedar River Village sits amidst the gentle hills and hardwoods and is home to the Lodge, a collection of eighty-five modern luxury suite condominiums. Together they encompass 4,500 acres of rolling woodlands on the shores of Lake Bellaire. In the summertime golfing is the favorite activity; in winter skiing is the preferred sport.

Accommodations: Lodging choices are innumerable: guest rooms, studios, condominiums, and chalets. Some are equipped with a fireplace or whirlpool; others have a deck. You

might have a view of the lake, the forests, a fairway, or the Alpine village. Rates start at $90 a night for a guest room and rise to $420 a night for a deluxe two-bedroom condominium. Children ages seventeen and under stay free when occupying a room with their parents. Cribs can be added to your accommodation for a fee of $10 a day. The many package plans available offer good savings.

Dining: The Lakeview Dining Room is an elegant restaurant at Summit Village. Open for breakfast, lunch, and dinner, it's hard to decide which is better, the food or the view. Lakeview draws its menu from the fields, forest, orchards, and lakes of northern Michigan and has a children's menu. La Vigna Italian Bistro at Cedar Ridge Village is the newest addition to the dining scene and serves dinner nightly overlooking the eighteenth green. The specialty of the house at Ivan's is fun, especially in summer when the Schussycats entertain; this energetic troup of college students is always popular. Ivan's menu includes favorites like steak, fish-and-chips, big salads, pizzas, and sandwiches and a kid's menu. Other dining choices are Arnies, in the Clubhouse at the Summit, serving sandwiches and soups at lunch and dinner; and light fare and hearty breakfasts at the Weiskopf Grill in the Lodge at Cedar River, or the Schuss Golf Deck at the Schuss Mountain Golf Club. Choose your preferred style of evening entertainment: Schussycats at the Village, cool jazz at Cedar River, or American favorites at the Lakeview.

Children's World: We may have become accustomed to purple dinosaurs, but a purple goose? That would be Gandy, Shanty Creek's mascot, with his own Web site fun page so kids can meet him before they actually meet him! Shanty Creek programs serve children from two months to twelve years old during most of the year. The programs are planned and supervised by a recreation specialist and an experienced childhood educator, so there's expertise combined with enthusiasm, which in this case equals innovation.

The Shanty Creek Child Care Center is open every day from 9:00 A.M. to 4:30 P.M. for children two months through age three, mid-June through Labor Day, and late November to mid-March. It's a nurturing, playful, and safe environment, with a separate area for naps. Full-day rates are $36 with lunch; a half day is $21 morning or afternoon; or try the golfer's special, $29 for a five-hour block of time, including lunch.

Camp Gandy, operating daily from mid-June through Labor Day, has hiking, swimming, music, and arts and crafts and is specially designed to meet the needs of younger children, ages four to eight years. Camp is open from 9:00 A.M. to 4:30 P.M. at the Family Activity Center in Schuss Village. Rates are the same as the Child Care Center. Adventure Camp for ages eight to twelve has

the same hours, rates, and location, but the activities are more challenging and age-appropriate and include sports, disc golf, and longer hikes. Schussycats, the college performance group, also does workshops with kids, who sometimes get to perform in the evening show at the resort.

When the ski season starts, the daily Child Care Center program accepts infants to six-year-olds. In addition to stories and indoor play, the older children discover the excitement of outdoor play in a winter wonderland. The same fees as above are charged for this program.

Young skiers to be, ages three to five, combine indoor play with sledding and ski instruction in their 10:00 A.M. to 4:00 P.M. schedule. Snow Stars, for ages three to five years, helps kids learn to ski and have fun doing it. Cost is $50 for a full day, $40 for a half-day session, and includes lunch, lift tickets, and snacks; equipment rentals are $10 to $14 additional. Snow Angels is a similar program for the same age group, but is more individualized, with smaller groups. It's the "fast track" and is generally available on weekends. Cost is $90 for the full day and covers everything, even a pager for parents.

Kid's Academy, for older children (ages five to eleven), runs from 10:00 A.M. to 4:00 P.M. daily. This is more serious instruction but still doesn't lose sight of the fun of skiing. The fee is $40 full day, $30 half day with lunch. Ski rentals are not included in these fees. Smart Riders, for budding snowboarders, is available most weekends and holidays for ages six to twelve years. Sessions are at 10:00 A.M. and 1:30 P.M. and the cost is $30.

Just for You is another child-care service that matches caregivers with your child's age and needs. Cost is $8.00 per hour, with a two-hour minimum. With parents' permission, children may use the resort facilities under this individual supervision. Shanty Creek also will do their best to accommodate children with special needs—call them.

Recreation: Golfers experience a bit of a dream come true here. The resort's original course is the eighteen-hole Summit Golf Course. Another championship eighteen holes make up the beautiful Schuss Mountain Course. And the crowning gem is the Legend, an exciting eighteen-hole course designed by Arnold Palmer. With the carefully maintained courses complemented by an experienced teaching staff, all golfers will surely improve their games here. The new Cedar River Golf Club, designed by Tom Weiskopf, is another winner. Awards are numerous: *Golf Magazine* rates Cedar River among the "Top Ten in the U.S. You Can Play;" the Legend as one of the top four courses; and Shanty Creek in the "Top 5 in Quality of Main Course." *Golf for Women* calls Shanty Creek "one of the most women-friendly." PGA professionals at the Golf Academy can give you all you need to really enjoy the game.

Other summertime activities include tennis, with eight courts; biking on the mountain trails; horseback riding; and boating. At the Fitness Center work out on the Nautilus equipment, head to the racquetball courts, hit the steam room or sauna, and wind up the day with a massage. Schedule time at the Wellness Spa for a real treat. With indoor swimming pools and a heated pool outdoors, swimmers are satisfied whatever the season.

On-site diversions are too numerous to list, but start with basketball, croquet, disc golf, volleyball, board games, and shopping. The state's only solar-lighted disc golf is here at Shanty Creek, and evening family clinics are fun for all. Add evening entertainment and nightly family activities such as bardic story-telling at the campfire, and you may not have time for a sunset sail aboard a tall ship, or a visit to the Turtle Creek Casino or nearby Traverse City.

The ski season starts in November and continues through late March or early April, depending on how generous Mother Nature has been. There are forty-six runs for downhill skiers, almost 20 miles of groomed trails for cross-country skiers, and two terrain parks for snowboarders. When you're not on skis, pile the whole family into a horse-drawn sleigh for an old-fashioned ride in the woods. Or if you're brave enough, take a dip in the heated outdoor pool. Après-ski at any of the three villages is easy with the free resort shuttle service that operates year-round.

SHANTY CREEK

One Shanty Creek Road
Bellaire, Michigan 49615
(231) 533–8621, (800) 678–4111
www.shantycreek.com

SOUTHWEST

Arizona
New Mexico
Texas

ANGEL FIRE RESORT

Angel Fire, New Mexico

Impressed by the pink glow on the mountains, Indians named this area "the land of Angel Fire." This year-round resort in the ancient Sangre de Cristo Mountain range of northern New Mexico allows for escape, renewal, and rejuvenation. Angel Fire encompasses 20,000 acres of scenic mountain beauty and seems to sit at the top of the world. The air is clear, and the vistas stretch for miles in all directions. The Village of Angel Fire, actually a small incorporated township, is also rather spread out; so when we refer to "the village," think driving or taking the Magic Bus (50 cents) that goes just about everywhere.

Accommodations: Angel Fire can accommodate approximately 4,000 guests in a variety of lodges and condominiums scattered through the village area. At first glance, this number of guests conjures up images of crowds, but remember that this still leaves approximately five acres of land per person! The Angel Fire Resort Hotel offers 129 rooms located at the base of the ski mountain. Prices range from $80 to $209 for a room. Mountain condominiums, within walking distance of lifts, restaurants, and shops, include studio to three-bedroom units; price range for a two-bedroom is $125 to $364 (holidays). Cribs are provided at $15 per night.

Dining: Hungry? Choose from a variety of foods including Italian, Mexican, and steak house specialties. Dress is casual, and many restaurants have special menus for children. At the resort have breakfast or dinner at the Branding Iron; Jasper's Bar serves drinks and a bar menu; while Alder's Italian Bistro is a favorite with kids and adults alike. In the village have your favorite pizza at the Pizza Stop, try the barbecue at Rocky Mountain, or enjoy good old-fashioned family fare at Zebbediah's. For a splurge, with older kids or even without kids, sample the Roasted Clove. The Angel Fire Country Club matches up spectacular mountain views with tasty lunches and dinners in summer only. Live entertainment enlivens weekends at Angel Fire Village House.

Children's World: During winter, from Thanksgiving to the end of March, the focus is on snow sports, skiing, and snowboarding. Young skiers ages four to twelve can join the Children's Ski and Snowboard Center, which runs from 9:00 A.M. to 3:30 P.M.; a $65 to $78 daily fee covers lessons, lift tickets, rentals, and lunch.

Very young or nonskiing children can participate in daily activities at the newly built (2003) and state-licensed Angel Fire Resort Day Care. Children six weeks to six years old can join the fun, even on an hourly basis, from 8:00 A.M. to 5:00 P.M. daily in winter; Monday through Friday in summer. These sessions are a combination of indoor play—such as games, treasure hunts, and crafts—and outdoor play that emphasizes winter fun in the snow, such as "snowercise" and snow sculpture. The fee is $6.00 per hour, $50 to $60 for a full day, or $35 to $40 for a half day. Parents must provide diapers, bottles, formula, and other supplies.

In summertime the Angel Fire community sponsors children's supervised activities in June and July. Monday through Thursday, for three hours in the morning, ages six to twelve can join local children to experience various weekly themed programs, such as a science fair, sports, cooking, children's theater, even dog training, where dogs can be "borrowed." It's very much a work-in-progress; call (505) 377–2544 for details and cost.

Recreation: While the primary diversion in winter is skiing or snowboarding, Angel Fire considers itself a "snow sports" resort. Sample

22 kilometers of cross-country skiing at the summit of the mountain, plus snowmobiles, snowshoes, snow biking, snow skating, snow blades, and snow tubing. If it has to do with snow, you can do it here! In February 2004 Angel Fire will host the thirtieth annual World Championship Shovel Races. Yup, two categories (for all ages): sitting on the shovel, or building a race car on the shovel. You've got to see it to believe it! For more ordinary ways of getting down the mountain, adults get a free ski/board lesson with purchase of lift tickets, and children under six ski free. More than two-thirds of the trails are for beginners and intermediates. The vertical drop is 2,077 feet, and the longest trail is a cruising 3½ miles long. Six chairlifts cover 30 miles of trails, two ski shops are ready to rent or sell equipment and accessories, and lessons are available.

Once the snow melts, these same trails offer fantastic opportunities for mountain biking, hiking, backpacking, and horseback riding. Catching a trout from the annually stocked lake can be an exhilarating experience, but if fishing is not your sport, you can canoe or paddle in these waters. Have a swim in the pool, play tennis, or bicycle on the paths around the resort. At an elevation of 8,600 feet, the eighteen-hole golf course weaves through a wooded terrain of aspen, spruce, and ponderosa pine. Practice on the driving range and putting green, or enlist the expert advice of the golf pro. A good summer option for the entire family (if parents have the stamina!) is the High Adventure Passport. A two-night stay garners two coupons for any activity; upgrade the passport with extra activities for $4.00 per coupon and indulge in fishing, the human maze, mini or disc golf, paddle or row boats, mountain biking, chairlift rides, tennis or golf range, or game room tokens. Nearby, raft on the Rio Grande or visit Eagle Nest, a little town where Old West–style gunfights may erupt on the street at high noon. In August enjoy Music from Angel Fire, a twenty-year tradition of classical music concerts performed by professional musicians from across the country. Whatever your activity, the crisp mountain air and clear azure sky enhance it.

ANGEL FIRE RESORT

P.O. Drawer B
Angel Fire, New Mexico 87710
(505) 377–6401, (800) 633–7463
E-mail: reserve@angelfireresort.com
Web site: www.angelfireresort.com

THE ARIZONA BILTMORE
Phoenix, Arizona

A classic hotel, the Arizona Biltmore is often referred to as the "jewel of the desert." At the entrance to the grounds, Main Drive is lined with lovely private homes and landscaped with citrus trees and flowering oleander, petunias, and pansies. The main structure at the end of this drive is an architectural masterpiece. Inspired by Frank Lloyd Wright and constructed of Biltmore blocktile, the buildings reflect the gracious charm and innovative spirit of the 1920s. Exploring the thirty-nine acres of this fine establishment is an adventure in architectural history and a delightful experience in imaginative landscaping. Stroll along the beautifully manicured lawns and gardens for visual delights in carefully tended beds of yellow pansies or pink petunias or multicolored snapdragons. In dining, shopping, and recreational activities, the Biltmore has consistently maintained its reputation as a world-class resort and it is open year-round.

As at many resorts now, the Biltmore's primary clientele during the week is business groups or conventions, with families visiting more often on weekends. One result of this pattern is that activities for children and families tend to cluster around weekends and holidays only, although they are presented year-round.

Accommodations: Of the 734 well-appointed rooms and suites, approximately 100 are located in the main building; others are arrayed in several buildings and cottages bordering flower beds. Many rooms have mountain or garden views, and all rooms have been recently remodeled. Rooms rates range from $195 to $885 mid-May through September, when temperatures of over 100 degrees Fahrenheit are not uncommon; $325 to $1,425 October through December; and $375 to $1,675 in the more temperate winter months, January to mid-May. Summer specials from $135 with the third night free exist, so do inquire about packages and specials. Children under eighteen can stay free in the same room with their parents. Cribs are provided at no extra charge.

Dining: Enjoy regional and American cuisine for breakfast, lunch, and dinner in the casual atmosphere of the Biltmore Grill, featuring an exhibition kitchen and outdoor patio overlooking the gardens. The Café, with its outdoor terrace and terrific views of the Squaw Peak Mountain, is open daily for "deli-style" breakfast and lunch. Both have menus for children and teens. Have dinner at Wright's, the award-winning signature restaurant, where the striking architecture enhances the enjoyment of the food. As if Maine lobster with truffles and fennel or filet mignon Roquefort with caramelized shallots and pomegranate syrup needed enhancing! Private wine tastings can be arranged—the Biltmore has one of the most extensive wine lists in the re-

gion. If you're near the water slide and new pool, try the Cabana Club Restaurant and Bar for sandwiches and cool drinks during the day and cocktails and entertainment in the evening. The only thing watery about the drinks is the setting, at the swim-up bar. Being right next to the water slide makes it a good place for lunch with the kids, and they have their own menu favorites such as macaroni and cheese and hot dogs. The grand atmosphere of the lobby also provides several grand options for the tummy. Traditional tea is served from 2:30 to 5:30 P.M. The Squaw Peak Lounge allows you to sit either indoors or outdoors, listen to music, and savor the view of the mountain along with your drinks and hors d'oeuvres. Here you also have room service with a twist; guest room dining allows you to order multicourse meals and have them delivered separately, so your entree doesn't get cold while you savor the appetizer. And, if you have a patio grill, a chef will come and do the cooking. Sweet.

Children's World: Kids Korral offers a structured program only on weekends, for ages five to twelve years; however, it is presented year-round. During summer and holidays, the program is on Friday, Saturday, and Sunday, from 9:00 A.M. to 5:00 P.M. Swimming, hikes, cooking classes, yoga, golf, and tennis are on the menu for children ages five to twelve years old. Water Balloon Launch is one of the most popular "sports"—as fifty-plus kids line up around the swimming pool with slingshots and water balloons—best observed from a safe distance. Full-day ($65 with lunch) and half-day ($35) sessions are an option.

Kids Korral is also a canopy-draped area with rubberized floor to provide shade and fun things to keep kids happy and out of the sun. Playground equipment is extensive and includes a track ride, snake pole, triple slide, chain net climber, arched bridge, a bowed ladder—the list goes on and on. Picnic tables and chairs give a place in the shade for parents to sit and supervise. While there's no evening supervised program for children, families can enjoy dive-in movies, s'mores and bonfires, pottery painting, the putting course, and the game room with table tennis, pool, air hockey, and music.

Recreation: The setting of the Biltmore alone could charm you for days on end, but once the inner spirit is renewed, try your hand at some of the many recreational activities. Seven lighted tennis courts attract tennis enthusiasts; schedule yourself for a tennis clinic or private lessons.

The avid golfer can take on one of the two eighteen-hole PGA courses or refine a technique on the putting greens and driving ranges. At the pro shop you can seek out the guidance of the teaching staff, pick up some vital accessories, or rent equipment.

The eight swimming pools can mean either invigorating laps or a relaxing dip. One of the fifteen cabanas will protect you from the desert sun, and the 92-foot water slide is guaranteed to get a "wow!" To check out the scenery and still test your athletic abilities, rent a bicycle or jog along the trails flanking the Salt River Canal. Indulge at the Biltmore Spa, which offers more than eighty European body and skin treatments, fitness center, steam room, saunas, and whirlpool. Or perhaps you

will alternate rigorous athletics with less demanding games of croquet or lawn chess.

If shopping is your interest, discover a varied and extensive line of merchandise in the hotel shops: jewelry, silver, regionally crafted products, both Southwest and Native American artists; and tennis, golf, and swimming clothes and accessories. Adjacent to the grounds is the Biltmore Fashion Park, filled with more shops and restaurants and reached by a shuttle bus.

Venturing further a field, take an excursion to the Grand Canyon, visit the spectacular red rocks of Sedona, or float aloft in a hot-air balloon. Horseback riding or Jeep tours give an up-close view of the desert. And, of course, the delights of metropolitan Phoenix are at your doorstep.

THE ARIZONA BILTMORE

2400 East Missouri
Phoenix, Arizona 85016
(602) 955–6600, (800) 950–0086
Web site: www.arizonabiltmore.com

THE BISHOP'S LODGE RESORT AND SPA
Santa Fe, New Mexico

Just a ten-minute drive north of Old Santa Fe, 1,000 acres of the foothills of the Sangre de Cristo Mountains comprise the range of the Bishop's Lodge. At an elevation of 7,200 feet, this area of north-central New Mexico shares its warm sunny days with cool crisp nights. The clean mountain air, the setting, and the atmosphere

of the lodge combine to emit the flavor and tradition of the old Southwest. The adobe architecture, a reminder of the area's Spanish and Native American heritage, and the friendly spirit of the staff give the Bishop's Lodge its true Western flair.

In the nineteenth century the ranch was the home of Archbishop Jean Baptiste Lamy, a pioneering French cleric who became the Southwest's first Catholic bishop. His life was the inspiration for Willa Cather's novel *Death Comes for the Archbishop* (good background reading for an introduction to the history and topography of the region). The private chapel built by the archbishop still stands, a sentinel to the lodge's history. The property was purchased by the newspaper publisher Joseph Pulitzer and then acquired in 1918 by James Thorpe. A National Historic Hotel, the lodge is currently managed by Lendlease. The facilities have undergone expansion and renovation, with a strong emphasis placed on customer service and satisfaction. The lodge is open year-round, and many families return year after year; three generations of family visitors are not uncommon.

Accommodations: The lodge's one hundred-plus rooms and suites are grouped in several adobe buildings nestled among fruit trees and flower beds. The North and South lodges are the oldest, both having been grand summer homes before World War I. All of the rooms are decorated in warm earth colors with a Southwestern flair; deluxe rooms include fireplaces and many have outdoor sitting areas. The beds are simply delicious, firm mattresses with soft, feathery inserts. Rates are based on double occupancy; children under age four stay at no charge, others pay $15 per day. Cribs and rollaways are available on request. January through May, historic rooms range from $149 to $219; deluxe rooms from $279 to $389. Summer rates are $259 to $339 and $449 to $579, respectively. September through November, rates are $139 to $219 and $289 to $389. Holidays and weekends are more expensive, as are suites.

A resort fee of $9.00 per day per person (thirteen and older) allows use of the facilities (pool, tennis, fitness center); activities such as yoga, tai chi, aerobics, and hiking; fishing, with all the equipment; and shuttles to Santa Fe and the nearby ski area in winter. Also included is the daily gratuity for housekeeping, in-room coffee and tea, daily newspaper, parking, and local and long-distance telephone access.

Dining: Las Fuentes (The Fountains) reflects a new concept in cuisine, Nuevo Latino, bringing together the color, taste, and music of Puerto Rico, Cuba, Argentina, Salvador, Columbia, the Caribbean, and other Central and South American countries, for your dining pleasure. It's open for breakfast, lunch, and dinner, with a children's menu in summer. The decor is classic Santa Fe: beamed ceilings, Navajo rugs, Spanish chandeliers, and four life-size murals done in the 1920s by W. E. Rollins. For cocktails and lighter fare, stop by El Rincon, a cozy corner bar opening onto the Terrace, with al fresco dining for all meals. Sunsets, stars, and soft summer breezes accompany the nightly entertainment.

Children's World: During the summer months, kids four to twelve years old gather down by the corral, at Camp Apaloosa. Different activities every day and a ratio of one counselor to seven children keep it interesting and interactive. Full-day programs (8:00 A.M. to 4:00 P.M. and 6:00 to 9:00 P.M.) include a daily afternoon swim and a mix of activities: nature hikes, pony rides, archery, tennis, a "Kid's Rodeo," and Frisbee golf on the active side; sand art, plaster sculpture, murals, and animal masks for artistic expression. In addition a pond stocked with trout and an outdoor play area with swings, a slide, jungle gym, and a sandbox translate into active fun for kids.

Evening sessions feature Native American stories and crafts, movies, pajama parties, and skits. The day program includes breakfast and lunch for $52; the evening program is $39, including dinner. Children may have meals with their counselors in their own dining room or at picnics, pool parties, and cookouts.

While Bishop's Lodge doesn't have a winter program for kids, Ski Santa Fe, fifteen minutes from the lodge, offers day care from 8:30 A.M. to 4:30 P.M. for ages three months to three years. Rates are $58 for a full day, $42 for a half day, or select hourly care at $12 per hour. Only full-day packages are available during holidays. Snacks and lunch are provided, and children are divided by age. Snowplay, which has the same hours, is a fun introduction to the skiing environment for ages three and four, with indoor and outdoor play, games, and activities. Full-day rates are $64; half day is $48.

The Little Chips Ski Program for four year olds provides a full day ($64) that includes a two-hour lesson in the morning with lunch and snacks provided. The afternoon continues with Snowplay (outdoor and indoor ski play), activities, and games. The half-day session ($48) is a two-hour lesson only, with snacks and lunch included. Children may be transferred to Snowplay at their instructor's discretion. Chipmunk Corner, for ages five to nine, places children into classes according to their age (five to six and seven to nine) and abilities. All children are tested to determine accurate levels. The same rates apply: $64 for a full day, 8:30 A.M. to 4:30 P.M.; and $48 for a half day, 8:30 A.M. to 1:00 P.M. or noon to 4:30 P.M. Equipment rental is $12 for either program.

Recreation: Except on Tuesdays, the horses' day of rest, recreation at the Bishop's Lodge begins with horseback riding on scenic mountain trails. Experienced wranglers match you and your ability with the appropriate steed from a stable of thirty horses. Children must be over eight years old and four feet tall (free pony rides are offered for the little ones), and the maximum weight is 225 pounds. Choose from a group ride (more sedate) or schedule private rides if you want to canter and gallop through the mesa. A memorable experience is a sunrise or sunset ride through the canyons and foothills of the Sangre de Cristo Mountains; once a week in summer you can enjoy a hearty "cooked on the range" breakfast or an evening barbecue. The Santa Fe National Forest is adjacent to the grounds of the lodge and provides more opportunities to explore the gorgeous scenery on horseback. If you're a little skittish about mounting a horse, there are many hiking trails both on the resort grounds and nearby, ranging from moderate to strenuous, with the same great views.

Lots of other recreational fun can easily fill your days. Fish the mountain streams for trout, swim in the pool, or just bask in the glorious New Mexico sunshine. The nearby country clubs of Santa Fe, Cochiti Lake, and Towa Golf Resort grant lodge guests golfing privileges on their eighteen-hole courses. At the Tennis Center, you can play on one of the two courts, have a lesson with the resident pro, and purchase some new accessories at the pro shop. At 7,000 feet, you'll need stamina, lots of water, and perhaps special tennis balls. On the skeet and trap-shooting ranges, experts offer instruction, and rental equipment is provided. Play a game of table tennis or treat your sore muscles to a relaxing hour in the whirlpool.

ShaNah is a native word meaning vitality and wisdom, and the highly acclaimed ShaNah Spa & Wellness Center is more than a place to be pampered; it's also about healing, nurturing, and ancient native wisdom. You can experience a facial, massage, body polish, native hot stone massage, or Ayurvedic treatment. All sessions begin with an optional (but highly recommended) Native American Blessing Ceremony to open the heart and set the intention—it may change your whole outlook on life.

Be sure to reserve at least a day to discover the narrow streets, interesting adobe architecture, quaint shops, and art galleries of Old Santa Fe. Open-air performances of the Santa Fe Summer Opera Festival are a special attraction, and dance and music performances abound. Pueblo Indians show their jewelry and pottery on blankets around the Palace of the Governors or at the famous Tesuque Indian Market, and visitors are welcome to attend the colorful ceremonies at nearby pueblos.

Fall brings crisp days with dazzling colors. The horses are energized and the ski lift opens for spectacular views from the top of the mountains. In winter, Santa Fe's cultural events are still in full swing, entertainers are showcased at the reservation casinos, and the big fireplace at the lodge is a welcome gathering spot. The lodge offers a "Ski and Spa" package in winter: Monday through Thursday two adults ski free at the nearby Ski Santa Fe slopes, then return to enjoy a rejuvenating spa visit. The 12,053-foot summit at Ski Santa Fe boasts 1,703 vertical feet of skiing and forty-four runs winding through stunning terrain with the perfect powder typical of New Mexico.

THE BISHOP'S LODGE RESORT AND SPA

P.O. Box 2367
Bishop's Lodge Road
Santa Fe, New Mexico 87501
(505) 983–6377, (800) 732–2240
www.bishopslodge.com

ENCHANTMENT RESORT
Sedona, Arizona

Nature was about 350 million years creating the incredible landscape surrounding this area, but it's well worth the wait. Reputed to have special magnetic energies, Sedona has become a focal point for metaphysical healing and "New Age" spirituality, as well as an international art scene. Whatever it is, there is indeed something magical in the air, in spite of encroaching commercialism. Enchantment Resort is very well named. Nestled within the walls of Boynton Canyon, 5 miles northwest of town, it is surrounded by the Coconino National Forest, and is a welcome escape from touring and town. The land surrounding the resort is sacred to the Yavapai-Apache as the birthplace of their tribe; in fact, the resort has a Native American ambassador on staff to explain the land and share tribal stories and tradition. This four-star, four-diamond resort has awards too numerous to list that include being one of the Top 10 Family Resorts in America according to *Parents* magazine; one of the Top Five Family Resorts in Arizona by *FamilyTravel*; one of *Conde Nast*'s Top 30 North American Resorts; one of *Travel & Leisure*'s Top 100 Hotels of the United States and Canada; and one of the Top Ten Hotels & Resorts in the United States in the 2003 *ZagatSurvey*.

Accommodations: Pueblo-style architecture blends in with the landscape, and the 220 rooms can be arranged in various combinations of guest rooms, studios, and junior suites; when connected, these create one- or two-bedroom casitas or haciendas. This also creates many rates. Basically rates begin at $195; hacienda studios and casita junior suites range from $245 to $525; and one-bedroom suites range from $375 to $855. Suites feature Southwestern decor with beehive fireplaces, high ceilings, native crafts, and patios with dramatic views. High season is mid-February to mid-June, and the end of August through December.

Dining: People drive up from Phoenix and down from Flagstaff just to experience the Yavapai Restaurant. With menu items such as cold smoked buffalo tenderloin; Anaheim chile relleno, stuffed with duck and rolled in blue corn; and Rocky Point shrimp, served with a vanilla bean beurre blanc and mango habanero salsa, it's no wonder! Huge windows reveal a 180-degree vista of the stunning red rocks of Boynton Canyon; dinner, lunch, and a breakfast brunch are served daily, while a Sunday Jazz Brunch is very popular. Tii Gavo, a more casual restaurant serving lunch and dinner, has a children's menu and entertainment on weekends. Mii amo Café is part of the self-contained spa, offering eclectic and healthy cuisine. In summer, guests may dine on their terraces or poolside as well.

Children's World: Daily year-round, trained counselors at Camp Coyote keep children ages four to twelve active and engaged at the colorful Camp Center. Kids enjoy treasure hunts, swimming, tennis and golf, outdoor crafts, and games, all with a daily theme: Desert Dweller, Canyon Fun, Wild West, Southwestern, or Native American days. Often, a Park Ranger or a Native American storyteller will drop in for a surprise visit. A full day, including lunch, is from 9:00 A.M. to 3:30 P.M. and costs $70; half-day morning ($35) or afternoon with lunch ($40) is another option. On Friday and Saturday, the dinner and evening program operates from 5:00 to 9:00 P.M. ($45). The Resort Concierge can arrange baby-sitting for $15 per hour, with a three-hour minimum, for one child. Additional children in the same family are $2.00 extra per hour per child. Payment in cash is requested directly to the party providing the sitting services; there is no charge from the resort.

Recreation: If you can tear yourself away from just staring at the landscape, lots of activities await. Walk leisurely along the trails with your sketchbook or take a more strenuous hike. Mountain bikes are here for the adventurous, or championship croquet, bocce ball, and table tennis for a slower pace; swimming, of course, under an unimaginably blue sky; or combine the two with a rousing water volleyball game. A Cayman-style pitch-and-putt golf course and a putting green will whet the golfer's appetite for the two championship courses nearby in Sedona. Tennis players are well served by a variety of clinics and mixers on the seven courts. U.S. Park Rangers are stationed at the resort, and give lectures and guided walks three times weekly. Enchantment Resort and the U.S. Forest Service have jointly established the Boynton Canyon Preservation Fund, a privately funded effort to create programs to improve and preserve the tranquil beauty of the canyon. It's a stellar spot for stargazing through the resort's telescope, especially with an expert to explain what you're seeing. Curious about what a vortex really is? Come to the lobby on Tuesday at 5:00 P.M. and understand the mystery. Enchantment Marketplace is not the usual resort retail shop; here you'll find local art, photography, music, and jewelry.

Mii amo is a full-service destination spa located within the resort—the name is a Yuman word for "journey, or moving forward; a passage." Actually a boutique hotel within the resort, it offers seventeen rooms and suites, with three- to seven-day packages. It has its own fitness room, indoor and outdoor pools, and a restaurant, along with twenty-four treatment areas where magic is created with blue corn body polish or Sedona-clay wraps. Mii Amo blends spa services with Native American healing and spirituality, and takes full advantage of an exquisite natural setting. Enchantment guests over age sixteen have access to spa facilities and treatments for an $18 fee.

In other venues, music and nature blend at the 5,000-seat amphitheater in the Sedona Culture Park, Oak Creek Canyon beckons you with gorgeous winding drives and picnics along the creek, and Slide Rock is a natural combination of smooth rocks and splashing water that kids love. The Grand Canyon is only two hours away.

ENCHANTMENT RESORT

525 Boynton Canyon Road
Sedona, Arizona 86336
(928) 282–2900, (800) 826–4180
www.enchantmentresort.com

FLYING L GUEST RANCH

Bandera, Texas

Bandera, 40 miles northwest of San Antonio, claims to have invented dude ranching during the Depression when an enterprising rancher decided to take in "dudes" for extra money. So now, with true Texan style, they have laid claim to being the "Cowboy Capital of the World." Seven rodeo world champions have hailed from here, however, so there may be something to it. Set in the midst of the beautiful Texas Hill Country, this is not the dry, barren Texas of the movies. Here there are verdant green hills, oak and maple trees, wildflowers and flowing rivers, not sagebrush and sand.

The Flying L Ranch was first settled in 1874. It became a dude ranch in 1946 when Jack Lapham, a retired Air Corps colonel, started to realize his dream of a place where "a modern person can go and find himself in the midst of yesterday." (OK, who can figure out the name of the ranch based on this story? You already did? Good!) The ranch became a favorite "watering hole" for celebrities, including John Wayne, Tex Ritter, Buck Owens, Chill Wills, Slim Pickens, and Willie Nelson; the television program *The Cisco Kid* was filmed here. The motto of this award-winning ranch is "Whoever says you can't have it all has never been to the Flying L."

Accommodations: You can bunk in style here—all forty-four suites offer real Texas-style lodging with room to spread out. The villas are geared toward comfort; all include a refrigerator, microwave, coffeepot, cable TV; daily maid service, and a real wood-burning fireplace. Daily rates in low season are $80 to $99 per adult; high season (summer and holidays) rates are $98 to $118 per adult. Children twelve to seventeen are two-thirds of the adult rate, and ages three to eleven are half the adult rate. Children under three stay free. Family packages include villa accommodations, breakfast and dinner buffets daily, horseback riding and use of the ranch amenities, nightly Western entertainment, and the supervised children's program. Discount rates are given for five nights or more.

Dining: Breakfast and dinner are included in the rate and are hearty examples of fine Texas Hill Country cuisine. Seven days a week, from 7:30 to 9:30 A.M., start your day with a delicious breakfast buffet in the Main House dining room. Breakfast here was rated "#1 in Texas" by the tourism council. Lunch is on your own, with burgers and fries at the pro shop or an afternoon picnic from your refrigerator. Dinner is from 5:30 to 7:30 P.M., either in the Main House dining room or creekside. During summer and holidays, the buffet menu is loaded with favorites that "kids hanker for." Always popular are the cookouts by the creek, under the open sky and old live oaks. Especially when you arrive by hay wagon and horseback.

At 5:00 P.M. the Branding Iron Saloon opens, and there's family entertainment every night—cowboy music, dancing, gun slinging, or a rodeo, usually topped off with a marshmallow roast and s'mores making. Do the kids love that!

Children's World: Children are divided into two groups, ages three through five and six to twelve. Programs run from 8:30 A.M. to noon and from 1:00 to 4:30 P.M. Activities include feeding animals, nature walks, scavenger hunts, sports, fishing, and crafts, such as making leather bracelets and vests. Golf and tennis clinics are included for the older children along with trail rides with the grown-ups, while the little ones can take pony rides at the Kids Korral every day. The program runs Monday through Saturday during summer, spring break (March through April), and holidays. The supervised children's activities program is included in the rates.

Recreation: The only activity not included in your price is golf. Drive, chip, and putt on the popular par-72, fully irrigated course. A driving range lets you perfect your skills if you don't get distracted by the beautiful view; private lessons are also available. Try the outdoor heated swimming pool or venture off the ranch to the Medina River for a little inner tubing or canoeing. Tennis, bikes, sand volleyball, horseshoes, hayrides, rodeo events, a playground, and a seasonal petting corral add to the fun. And after all that exercise, a good soak in the outdoor Jacuzzi may be just what the old bones need.

In the Bandera area, fish in the crystal waters of Medina Lake, tour a working Longhorn ranch, visit the Cowboy Artists Museum in Kerrville, tour the World War II Nimitz Museum, or enjoy antiquing in the German town of Fredericksburg. On Bandera's Main Street there's a working blacksmith shop. Nearby excursions include San Antonio (the Alamo, Market Square, and the River Walk) and various theme parks such as SeaWorld, Fiesta Texas, and Splashtown. Visit natural wonders such as the caverns. All in all, the ranch promises "a rootin', tootin' time."

FLYING L GUEST RANCH

P.O. Box 1959
Bandera, Texas 78003
(830) 460–3001, (800) 292–5134
www.flyingl.com

HYATT REGENCY HILL COUNTRY RESORT
San Antonio, Texas

The Texas Hill Country is as much a state of mind as it is a region. It certainly doesn't look like Texas—its green rolling hills, abundance of water, wildflowers, and variety of trees surprise the first-time visitor. San Antonio calls itself "a big city with small-town charm," and, as the number one tourist destination in Texas, has a multitude of attractions for families to enjoy—including the famous Alamo, centerpiece of Texas history, and the River Walk, lined with shops and restaurants along the tree-shaded banks of the San Antonio River.

Twenty minutes from downtown, a scenic drive meanders through the landscape, culminating at the Hill Country Hyatt lobby entrance, reminiscent of a Texas ranch house and complete with fireplaces, antler chandeliers, and overstuffed furniture—even a shady back porch. In fact, the resort's 200 acres are a part of the Rogers–Wiseman Ranch, honored for being in continuous agricultural production at the hands of one family for one hundred years or more. Hyatt has successfully adapted a full-scale destination resort into this casual, laid-back lifestyle; the results are downright pleasurable. Especially the Ramblin' River—the centerpiece of the property and the greatest place to get into an inner tube, kick back, and just relax.

Accommodations: Traditional German-style Hill Country architecture with native limestone and decorative wood exterior, the two- and four-story hotel has nine guest-room wings, housing 500 rooms. A stand-alone two-story luxurious guest house styled after a ranch house is in the courtyard—there's even an authentic windmill! As usual with Hyatt, the rooms are large and well decorated, ranging from standard to Regency Club level, with no-smoking rooms and suites available. Room rates are from $210 to $315; suites from $295 to $2,250. Children under eighteen are free in the same room as parents. Packages are a good value and may include golf, the children's program, or other family excursions. At most Hyatt Resorts, Family Plans allow an opportunity to reserve a second room for children at half price, based on availability—be sure to ask.

Dining: The flavor is definitely Tex-Mex, so expect tortillas even for breakfast, but you have lots of options here. The Springhouse Cafe features regional specialties, a large buffet and salad bar, and Sunday brunch. A wood-burning oven makes great pizzas. In the clubhouse, the Antlers Lodge has the ambience of a country lodge and puts the accent on regional Southwestern cuisine of steak, chicken, and seafood. Many entrees are mesquite-grilled and accompanied by a spicy Tex-Mex sauce. Golfers will find sandwiches and light snacks in the Cactus Oak Tavern at the halfway point on the golf course. The General Store offers hamburgers, deli sandwiches, and home-baked cookies as well as licorice sticks, wine, sodas, fresh coffee, and muffins. Papa Ed's Pool House serves up sandwiches and grilled food by the pool. In the evening relax at Aunt Mary's Porch, an open-air bar just off the lobby, or kick up your heels at Charlie's Long Bar, an old-fashioned Texas saloon complete with tin ceiling and a 56-foot copper-top bar. Yes, they have the tequila with the worm. Pool, shuffleboard, backgammon, and chess enhance the bar area.

Children's World: Camp Hyatt, only at select Hyatt resorts, offers not only supervised programs but also children's menus and

an opportunity to buy a second room for the kids at half price. Custom tailored for ages three to twelve, Rowdy's Camp Hyatt operates year-round during holidays and weekends, and daily throughout the summer. The program runs from 8:00 A.M. to 5:00 P.M. and keeps the kids busy with games and activities. Activities have a decided Western flavor, with a cowboys-and-Indians theme predominating: searching for arrowheads, watching for coyotes on the golf course at sunset (yes, they are sometimes there), totem poles, Wild West collages, and rodeo round-up games join the nature hikes and sand-castle building. A special Camp Hyatt room serves as a meeting place and for indoor activities; a different schedule is posted for every day of the week. Full- and half-day sessions may be arranged; cost for half-day sessions is $35, lunch is $10 extra. If you want to have an evening for grown-up pursuits, the evening session runs from 6:00 to 10:00 P.M. daily in summer, on Friday and Saturdays year-round, and costs $40 with dinner.

The perfect "spot" for youth may be the new *SPAhhht,* a first-class spa experience for today's youth—bright and colorful, with the accent on vibrant energy, not serene calm. Air-brushed nail art, hair weaving and up-do's, henna tattoos, and massage are what's happening here.

Recreation: Golfers enjoy the Arthur Hills–designed course with its 170 acres of rolling, scenic terrain. It truly blends into the countryside and has been recognized as one of the premier courses in the United States. Tennis is available on three courts, with a pro on hand. Walking, jogging, and biking paths crisscross the property, and the health club features aerobics classes and all the latest equipment—and, of course, a massage to help you recover from your workout. Windflower, the Hill Country Spa, has twenty-one treatment rooms to pamper you. Using all natural, mostly local ingredients in the services, try a peach pecan body scrub and what else? Yellow rose facials, of course.

By far the most popular spot, though, is the Ramblin' River, modeled after all those Hill Country river experiences. Pick up an inner tube, drop your cares, and let the lazy current carry you away. The journey varies from brisk to slow and allows riders to swim, walk, or take detours into two swimming pools, a cascading waterfall, or even a little sand beach.

Day excursions to SeaWorld, Six Flags, Fiesta Texas, Splashtown water park, or many of the nearby Hill towns, each with its own personality and charm, can pleasurably fill your days or evenings. Visit the Natural Bridge Caverns, with active formations more than 140 million years old, or stroll through Bandera, the self-proclaimed "cowboy capital." The Alamo is a must, and missions, museums, and Market Square, which feels like shopping in Mexico, are all nearby.

HYATT REGENCY HILL COUNTRY RESORT

9800 Resort Drive
San Antonio, Texas 78251
(210) 647–1234, (800) 233–1234
www.hillcountry.hyatt.com

HYATT REGENCY SCOTTSDALE RESORT AT GAINEY RANCH

Scottsdale, Arizona

Entering the private road that leads to this resort does not prepare you for the beauty of this lush and luxurious oasis in the midst of the Arizona desert. Water surrounds, cascades, falls, bubbles, flows, even sprays from the air; water and flowers are everywhere. You feel as though you are part of the landscape, not separated from it. Twenty-eight fountains, forty-seven waterfalls, and hundreds of palms, fir trees, and flowers create a 27-acre garden, part of the 560-acre Gainey Ranch, a planned residential complex that includes golf, parks and lakes, private homes, and businesses. Ecologically, this is a fragile area; fortunately the Hyatt has an admirable environmental program that focuses on reducing energy consumption and landfill; a waste-water reclamation plant irrigates the golf course.

Accommodations: The double "H" shape of the four-story resort provides five courtyards and four glass-enclosed atriums, with a movable 820-square-foot glass wall at the center of the lobby that allows a panoramic view of the McDowell Mountains and Sonoran Desert. The main building, inspired by the desert work of Frank Lloyd Wright, houses 493 rooms and suites; on either side are seven two- and four-bedroom freestanding casitas with fireplaces and terraced balconies overlooking the lake. The decor blends with the desert setting, using natural textures and artifacts. Children under eighteen stay free in existing bed space of parents' rooms, and every room has the Disney channel. Rates vary according to season and range from $160 to $510. Rates are higher in the Regency Club, which offers VIP service, complimentary breakfast, beverages, and evening hors d'oeuvres. Casitas range from $690 to $3,000 per night.

Dining: The Golden Swan is the hotel's specialty restaurant, named one of the best in the world by *Travel/Holiday* magazine and one of the top five in the Southwest by *Condé Nast Traveler.* One can dine indoors or out, in a charming gazebo nestled inside a lagoon. A special Sunday buffet called Chef's Brunch is served right in the kitchen, where you can watch and talk with the chefs, making sure your food is hot and fresh. The Squash Blossom restaurant is open for breakfast, lunch, and dinner, with a warm Southwestern ambience and regional specialties (try the Arizona toast or a wide variety of salads and sandwiches or fajitas). Ristorante Sandolo is a casual Italian bistro, overlooking the pool, where the servers serenade you. After you dine, enjoy a Venice-style gondola ride on the resort's waterways. Again, a *sandolier* will sing to you. (You can enjoy the gondola ride for $8.00 even if you don't eat.) Both restaurants have a children's menu and indoor/outdoor seating with very clever "air-conditioning." A very fine, invisible mist cools and moisturizes the air above you, making it comfortable year-round. Poolside, the Waterfall Juice Bar and the Water Garden Grill serve snacks, lunch, yogurt, and fruit drinks. The Coffee Bar features gourmet blends complemented by homemade Italian biscotti. In the evening watch the cascading fountains and listen to classical flamenco guitar or perhaps a marimba band as you relax in the Lobby Bar.

Children's World: Camp Hyatt Kachina, designed in 1989, is the prototype children's program for all Hyatt resorts. It operates daily year-round and offers three- to twelve-year-olds a well-balanced program of activities focusing on the flora, fauna, culture, and geography of the area. A specially appointed Camp room has all the crafts and games children like best. And don't forget the ten swimming pools, one complete with a white-sand beach and a three-story water slide. Each day has a different theme, related to the geographic area. Making tribal clay beads or arrowhead necklaces, designing sand pictures in the Salt River, listening to a Hopi storyteller, or planting a cactus garden put children firmly in

their environment while having fun. Campers enjoy a desert scavenger hunt, puppet theater, Mexican bark painting, Native American dancing, and much more.

Age groups are three to five and six to twelve. The morning session, from 9:00 A.M. to noon, is $30, and the afternoon session, from 1:00 to 5:00 P.M., is $40. Lunch, from noon to 1:00 P.M., can be added to either session for $10. The full day costs $80, including lunch. Friday and Saturday only Camp Kachina continues with an evening session from 5:00 to 9:00 P.M. The cost is $50, including dinner. During holidays the resort offers activities designed for the entire family, from cowboy roping, cowboy guitarists, and Native American dancing to family fun sing-alongs round the campfire and "dive-in" movies. Another pursuit that families enjoy is the Lost Dutchman Mine, a hands-on "dig" for jewels. A poster helps identify your find, and you get to take your treasures home.

Recreation: Where do we start? With the twenty-seven-hole championship golf course at Gainey Ranch Golf Club? Actually, it's composed of three separate, individually designed courses—the Dunes; the Lakes, with five lakes and lots of water hazards; and the Arroyo, the most difficult. Or with the eight tennis courts or 3 miles of jogging and cycling trails? Or the Sonwai Spa, with facials, massage, and body treatments incorporating ancient Hopi and Sonoran Desert traditions?

Let's start with the two-and-a-half-acre water playground—most impressive in this dry, desert area. The design is a combination of Roman, Greek, and Art Deco and is truly spectacular. Zip down the 30-foot water slide, stroll over an aqueduct connecting six of the ten pools, swim around (or through!) the "Big Gun," a 5-foot-wide waterfall, or "thunderfall" as the hotel terms it, at the end of the aqueduct. Relax in the Grecian temple with 16-foot hot tub and four "cold plunges" in each corner. Water comes from all directions—from fountains, trailing down tall glass columns, and from waterspouts along the roof. Build sand castles on the beach at one end or play volleyball at the other. Kids may never want to leave this watery fantasyland.

As part of the Native American and Environmental Learning Center, the Native American Sculpture Garden features the bronze and marble works of Apache artist Craig Dan Goseyun. The award-winning Native Heritage Seed Garden, with over thirty indigenous plants, has been carefully researched and developed and represents early agricultural practices of the natives of the area. And it's practical as well—plans are to eventually use the produce in the resort's signature cuisines.

Phoenix attractions include a zoo, a desert botanical garden, and stately old homes; in Scottsdale, find an IMAX theater, the world's highest fountain, and shopping on Fifth Avenue. View large cats in the wild at Out of Africa; experience a re-creation of the Old West at WestWorld or Rawhide, Arizona's

largest Western-themed attraction. Pick up a copy of *GUEST* for lots more ideas. If you have time to venture farther, the concierge will help you plan excursions to the Grand Canyon (five hours away) or Montezuma Castle, a 600-year-old Pueblo Indian cliff dwelling only ninety minutes away. Who knew the desert could be like this?

HYATT REGENCY SCOTTSDALE RESORT AT GAINEY RANCH

7500 East Doubletree Ranch Road
Scottsdale, Arizona 85258
(480) 991–3388, (800) 233–1234
www.scottsdale.hyatt.com

HYATT REGENCY TAMAYA RESORT AND SPA
Santa Ana Pueblo, New Mexico

Not many families can boast a vacation on a Native American reservation. Set on over 500 acres of protected land along the Rio Grande between Albuquerque and Santa Fe, in an area steeped in history that goes back over 1,000 years, the Hyatt Tamaya is unique. Owned by the Santa Ana Pueblo tribe, it is actually on the reservation. The architecture is reminiscent of a Southwestern pueblo, and artwork and cultural treasures are displayed throughout. Every effort has been made to honor the culture, history, and people of the area, and the natural beauty of the Sandia Mountains and the Bosque surrounds you with tranquillity. You're invited to experience

this very special place and step into the traditions and sanctity of another culture.

Accommodations: Open-air courtyards and patios or balconies overlooking the scenic mountains abound throughout the resort's 350 pueblo-style guest rooms and suites. Traditional designs used in Santa Ana pottery and blankets decorate the rooms, along with textures of natural stone, wood, and adobe and the colors of maize, pumpkin, and turquoise. Coffeemakers and refrigerators add convenience, and suites offer a small separate parlor. Rates during the low season (November through April) are $275 to $350; $355 to $400 during the May to

October high season. Children seventeen and under stay for free in the room with parents, or a second room for children may be reserved at 50 percent discount. There is also a $10 per room daily resort fee.

Dining: The Corn Maiden, the signature restaurant, serves dinner only, Tuesday through Saturday. Tapas, grilled specialties, and perfect sunsets are the order of the day. The Santa Ana Café has unusual regional cuisine, such as wild-mushroom and duck enchiladas, in an indoor or outdoor setting for breakfast, lunch, and dinner casual dining, with a children's menu. Expect red and green chilies, they're found in most dishes, even breakfast eggs, but are generally mild. The atush bar and grill on the Twin Warriors Golf Course attracts nongolfers as well as golfers for lunch and cocktails, while the Plaza Pool Bar and Grill satisfies your hunger without having to leave the pool. The Trading Post Deli and General Store can supply morning coffee and pastries along with sandwiches and snacks—and the requisite jar of salsa to take home. Turquoise margaritas and live entertainment are enjoyed from the porch of the Rio Grande Lounge—the sunset is on the house.

Children's World: Camp Hyatt activities are steeped in the history and lore of the Santa Ana people, the Tamaya; but it's so much fun the kids barely realize they're learning. Tribal storytellers and traditional dances both entertain and educate; learning about the Rio Grande, the local vegetation, and native wildlife, such as reptiles and coyotes, occupy the nature hikes; and baking bread in traditional ovens gives a tangible reward for effort. Camp Hyatt operates year-round, daily from 9:00 A.M. to 9:00 P.M. with an option for lunch ($10 extra) with the morning session ($25). Afternoon or evening sessions include meals; cost is $35.

Recreation: Golf fans will like the eighteen-hole, 72-par Twin Warriors Golf Course designed by Gary Panks, with cascading waterfalls, arroyos, and juniper and pinon trees. The nearby stables are reached by wagon ride,

and you'll find horses to suit every taste. Hay-wagon rides and complimentary pony rides for the younger set, and guests from eight to eighty can enjoy a calm trail ride through the back country of the Santa Ana reservation's cottonwood forests, ancient ruins, and 1,200-year-old Indian petroglyphs. The three-hour Chuckwagon Experience promises to work up an appetite for the ribs, baked beans, and apple pie that wait for you at trail's end. A wonderful (and comfortable) way to enjoy the sunset is on a carriage ride.

A huge circular swimming pool dominates the courtyard, looking very much like a *kiva* (the sacred place in the pueblo, generally underground). Two other pools and a two-story water slide provide plenty of water time. Two tennis courts, bike riding, and nature trails along the Rio Grande, plus a fitness center, keep you active. Ashtanga yoga and meditation areas contribute to a feeling of relaxed yet energized well-being. The Tamaya Mist Spa full-service luxury spa uses distinctive treatments with native herbs and natural ingredients of the earth to soothe your inner self. Shop at the Galleria Tamaya, take a hot-air balloon flight—the sky's the limit here.

Srai-Wi is the new family program with unique and unforgettable shared experiences—in fact, the word means "to gather children together and share with them" in the Tamayan language. Cooking, stargazing, nature hikes, and storytelling, adobe-making lessons, lassos and horse care, and much, much more—all with the distinctive Native American perspective and tradition.

HYATT REGENCY TAMAYA RESORT AND SPA

1300 Tuyuna Trail
Santa Ana Pueblo, New Mexico 87004
(505) 867–1234, (800) 233–1234
www.tamaya.hyatt.com

LOS ABRIGADOS
RESORT AND SPA

Sedona, Arizona

Close to the Grand Canyon and just two hours from Phoenix, Sedona is noted for its spectacular red rock formations and scenic canyons. For centuries it has been a sacred place to the People, the earliest inhabitants, and legend holds that the Grandmother Spirit of the World still lives here. There is a magic quality in the air that many attribute to the energy points that converge here. At the least, the light, color, and awe-inspiring red rocks combine with the many artisans living here to create something special.

Accommodations: Los Abrigados, Portuguese for "the shelters," is in the heart of the small town of Sedona but stands in the midst of twenty-two acres of private ranchland/park and feels secluded. All 175 guest suites have oversize living rooms and separate bedrooms plus a balcony or private patio. Many feature a private whirlpool and fireplace. The plazas, walkways, and bridges connect the suites and main hotel area. Suites range from $225 to $425 (two bedrooms); $240 reserves one with spectacular views of the red rocks. Children fifteen and under stay free in the same room with parents. Cribs are available at no charge. The Los Abrigados Lodge, a sister property located a short mile away, provides optional lodging. A two-story motel-like structure in the heart of "uptowne," it's literally in the middle of the action. Steps away are restaurants, galleries, shops, and tours; the rooms are pleasant, with balconies, gas fireplaces, and limited views. A concierge in the well-appointed lobby is helpful in planning your stay, and guests here enjoy privileges at the Los Abrigados Resort. Joey Pizza, adjacent to the lobby, is a branch of the main lodge restaurant known for inventive Italian cuisine—kids love the breakfast pizza with

bacon and egg. Rates range from $119 to $169 nightly.

Dining: Steaks and Sticks, for casual dining with a Southwestern flavor, also provides diversion in the billiards room (hence the "sticks"). An open copper and brass kitchen and library-style lounge with fireplace add to the coziness. More intimate dining is found in the Celebrity Room, lined with caricatures of famous guests. Serving breakfast, lunch, and dinner, imaginative dishes with an accent on indigenous ingredients make dining an adventure. The restaurant offers a children's menu and also features a "spa cuisine menu," lighter versions of many favorites. On the Rocks Bar & Grill serves lunch, snacks, and dinner in a casual atmosphere. You'll always know the score, as the television with the area's largest screen is here. Frequently kids eat free when accompanied by an adult diner—be sure to ask. Forty "Joes" from literature, sports, and entertainment line the walls of Joey Bistro. Think you know Italian food? The imaginative dishes here may challenge you. Imagine marsala sauce mozarella, roasted eggplant pesto, or gorgonzola and mascarpone cheeses in crisp pasta shells—it's not just spaghetti and meatballs! A variety of restaurants can be found right next door at Tlaquepaque Village, a re-created Mexican village/plaza with tiled courtyards, fountains, and many craft shops.

Children's World: Leapin' Lizards! No, you won't find Little Orphan Annie here, for kids are far too well looked-after. But that is the name of the children's program at Los Abrigados. Children entering kindergarten through age twelve can spend the day (9:00 A.M. to 4 P.M.) or pick and choose from a different list of a la carte activities every day. Monday through Saturday, from early June until mid-August, kids are entertained by such things as wacky water relays; sand castles and sculptures; tie-dye shirts; Creature Feature Play in the mushroom waterfall, where kids get a "beach ball creature"; and games galore. Any kind of ball game—tennis, miniature golf, volley, giant beach ball, and more; swimming, playing at the creek, or a water rodeo Wet Wild West. Kids can even bead their own leapin' lizard. Tuesday and Friday, activities are scheduled at 5:00 P.M.: Kids' Kamp Out Campfires, flashlight tag, burgers, hot dogs, s'mores; and a powwow, with dinner at the firepit and tepee making. A la carte activities last from one to three hours, and prices range from $6.00 to $16.00 when purchased individually. Cost for the full day with lunch is $30; supervised free play occupies the time between organized activities. Preregistration is not required.

The Teens Program is just what this age group wants. A happy hour at the pool with soda and pizza and movies at a local theater are offered twice a week; selected activities that enable them to socialize with their peers, but casually, with a lot of space, and in a cool way, dude.

Baby-sitting can be arranged. For a nice touch, you can order "Teddy Bear Turn Down Service"; a cookie, teddy bear, and signed card at bedtime and a close to the fun-filled day ($10).

Recreation: Roll over Beethoven, Tchaikovsky is playing through! Next to Oak Creek, among tall sycamore trees and colorful flowers, the new eighteen-hole family miniature golf course not only offers fun for golfers of all ages and skills, but it's done to classical music!

After a game of tennis or volleyball, relax at the heated outdoor pool and chat with other guests. Enjoy the jogging and walking trails or just sit by the creek and dream. It may be difficult to choose between the family pool with water features and the adult pool with Jacuzzi, but you can do both. The Sedona Spa—10,000 square feet of state-of-the-art equipment and professional services provides a combination of fitness and relaxation. Massage, full body treatments and masks, facials and fitness classes/personal training contribute to physical and mental well-being. Weekly classes in watercolor painting, Native American medicine wheel, cooking, or astronomy are both educative and fun.

Nearby are two championship golf courses, designed by Robert Trent Jones and Gary Panks. Hiking, fishing streams, horseback riding, and jeep tours can also be arranged. The Grand Canyon is a two-hour drive away; and closer is Oak Creek Canyon, with Slide Rock State Park, aptly named for the stretch of slippery creek bottom that forms a natural slide. For Southwestern art at its best, Tlaquepaque Village, next door to the resort, demands a visit.

Red Rock Fantasy is the West's largest holiday light display, with more than one million lights. From late November until mid-January it transforms Los Abrigados into a spectacular holiday light show.

LOS ABRIGADOS RESORT AND SPA

160 Portal Lane
Sedona, Arizona 86336
(928) 282–1777, (800) 521–3131
www.ilxresorts.com

TANQUE VERDE RANCH

Tucson, Arizona

In the Arizona desert, 2,800 feet high in the foothills of three mountain ranges, Tanque Verde Ranch has been serving travelers for more than one hundred years. Once merely a stagecoach stop, today it is a year-round resort, voted one of the top ten Family Fun Resorts of North America by the Travel Channel. The owners live on the property, adding to the feeling of a "family place." The area is rich in the history of Native Americans and Spanish settlers who dubbed the area Tanque Verde—immortalizing the deep pools of artesian water found here. Located 12 miles outside Tucson, it borders Saguaro National Park. The saguaro cacti are immediately recognizable to anyone who has seen a Western movie or a picture of the desert. They stand quite tall, with "arms" curving up toward the sky.

Accommodations: The seventy-four guest rooms and suites are scattered throughout the grounds in individual cottages called "casitas"; most of the casitas have patios, corner fireplaces, and a feeling of privacy. The decorative motif is Native American, and antiques and original art are carefully arranged to lend warmth. Cribs are available, and there are refrigerators in the rooms. Room rates range from $280 (summer) to $480 (winter) per day based on double occupancy. Children three and under are $15 per day; ages four and up pay $90 to $110. Based on a Full American Plan, room, three meals a day, and all ranch activities (including the fully supervised children's program for ages four through eleven) are included in the rate.

Dining: Most meals are served in the Main Dining Room, with beautiful views of the pool and the Rincon Mountains. A variety of tables, seating from two to ten people, make shared dining easy and encourages an informal, friendly atmosphere. Dress is casual and appetites are generally big due to the desert air and the exercise. American and Continental dishes are standard fare and, as expected, Spanish and Mexican specialties also appear on the menu. A separate children's dining room is reserved for youngsters and their counselors, who can take all meals together. Children are also welcome to dine with their parents. The food is delicious and plentiful. Breakfast combines a buffet and a la carte ordering; lunch is a lavish buffet with the famous "sweet talk" table. Early morning rides with a cowboy breakfast on the trail and a twice-weekly outdoor barbeque around the campfire in the cottonwood grove with rootin', tootin' live Western entertainment are popular meal options.

Children's World: The ranch offers a year-round, seven-day-per-week, fully supervised program for four- to eleven-year-olds; twelve-year-olds may participate if they like. This is an active program that provides a fantastic ranch experience. Horseback riding forms the core of the program and is adjusted to fit the abilities and interests of the youngsters. Buckaroos (ages four to six) generally ride in the corral, starting at 7:00 A.M. in the summer (8:00 A.M. in winter). Riding lessons, swimming, hikes, nature lessons, playtime, and Western crafts are nonstop until 3:00 P.M. If that's too strenuous for your child, pick up a weekly schedule at the front desk and pick and choose. The Wrangler Kids (ages six to twelve) have the same hours, but a more active, individualized riding program geared to their skills. Again, it's go, go, go all day, but the kids love it. Parents may ride with their children if they wish. In the winter months the fun continues with an evening program from 6:00 to 8:00 P.M. The children's programs are included in the rate. Baby-sitting can be arranged for infants and toddlers at an additional cost.

Recreation: Active relaxation is the by-word at Tanque Verde. The clear desert air and low humidity, coupled with abundant sunshine, make all the activities pleasant. Horseback riding is the major part of the program. Whether you're interested in a slow-moving trail ride or a spirited sprint, the right mount can be found from a string of 150 horses, the largest in Arizona.

Early morning and late afternoon are perfect times for strenuous outdoor activities such as tennis on one of the five courts. In the middle of the day, seek out one of the two swimming pools or the children's wading pool for a cool dip. Numerous guided nature walks introducing visitors to the Sonoran Desert ecology are conducted along trails throughout the 25,000 acres. Some 200 species of birds have been identified in the area, making the ranch very popular with avid bird-watchers. It's not uncommon to see wildlife such as rabbits, coyotes, and snakes on trail rides. Fishing is also a popular pastime. If you prefer wheels to hooves, take a mountain bike for a spin. The final touch to the active relaxation concept is the El Sonora Spa, well equipped with its swimming pool, sauna, whirlpool, exercise room (although who would really need it?!), and lounge. In nearby Tucson, six championship golf courses grant playing privileges to ranch guests. From here visitors can take side trips to Tucson, to old Spanish missions, and to Mexico, which is about a ninety-minute drive away.

TANQUE VERDE RANCH

14301 East Speedway Boulevard
Tucson, Arizona 85748
(520) 296–6275, (800) 234–3833
www.tanqueverderanch.com

Taos Valley, Taos, New Mexico

Whether you want to experience great outdoor mountain adventures such as skiing, rafting, hiking, and biking or whether you prefer elegant art galleries, gourmet dining, shopping, and a taste of exotic cultures, Taos Valley will satisfy you. A passion for the outdoors permeates the air and stunning mountain vistas, sophisticated shops, cultural events provide opportunities to pursue your pleasures.

Taos is a place where the present is enjoyed and history is honored. It is a place where different cultures have both clashed and blended over time. The earliest visitors to the area came some six thousand years ago, when nomadic hunter-gatherers passed through the Taos Valley. Ruins from as early as 900 A.D. have been discovered. The Pueblo Indians settled in Taos Valley about 1000 A.D. They were followed in the mid-1500s by the Spanish Conquistadors, some of whom stayed and established over 500 missions. In the 1700s the French traders and fur trappers arrived, and land grants were given to sixty-three Spanish families. By the 1800s gold was discovered, and the area became a favorite with guides and mountain men such as Kit Carson, who called Taos home. In 1898, two artists stopped to have a wheel repaired, became enchanted, and simply stayed. They invited all their friends and this was the beginning of Taos's love affair with art and artists. Some of the visiting luminaries of the early twentieth century included D.H. Lawrence, Thornton Wilder, Thomas Wolf, and Georgia O'Keefe. In the 1960s, with the filming of *Easy Rider*, Taos was again transformed, this time by a peaceful invasion of "hippies." Today, several close-knit but varied communities coexist amicably, and Taos remains a vibrant center for the arts.

Taos Ski Valley and the town of Taos complement each other; one can enjoy both while staying at either place. Along with the Taos Ski Valley area, we've included El Monte Sagrado, a family-friendly resort in town just in case you don't want to commute!

TAOS SKI VALLEY

Taos Ski Valley, New Mexico

In the early 1950s, Ernie Blake searched carefully for just the right spot for a ski resort and rediscovered this bit of northern New Mexico. Since then, skiers have been coming to Taos Ski Valley for the incredible powder snow and the glorious sunshine. Several ski magazines are calling Taos one of the hottest places to ski, citing the steep, challenging terrain and trails for all abilities so all levels may ski together. Once again, Taos has the number one ski school in North America, featuring the Ski-Better-Week. Grouped according to ability, each group remains with the same instructor, developing new, close friendships and improving skills.

Two hours from Santa Fe, or a three-hour drive from Albuquerque, Taos Ski Valley combines lodging, restaurants, shops, and a beautiful mountain. The town of Taos is only 18 miles away and, with its Indian and Spanish heritage, is an interesting alternative for dining, shopping, and entertainment (see end of listing). The Taos Valley operates during the ski season only, which generally runs from Thanksgiving through mid-April, and provides good value for families.

Accommodations: Every skier's dream is to be on the mountain. The Taos Valley Resort Association (800–776–1111) represents more than 95 percent of all lodging in and around Taos. For lodges right near the slopes—such as Hotel St. Bernard and the Thunderbird Lodge—rates for a one-week package run $1,490 to $1,790 per person double occupancy; besides the room, this package includes meals, lifts, and morning lessons. A one-bedroom condominium right at the slopes charges $1,135 to $1,635 per person for a one-week package; this fee covers lodging, lifts, and morning lessons. One-bedroom condos further away from the slopes (2 to 4 miles) cost $895 per person for the weekly package.

All facilities offer a nightly rate, but the week package, known as a Ski-Better-Week, is good value for your money.

Dining: On the mountain there are quick and easy stops like the Phoenix Restaurant; the Whistlestop Cafe, serving hamburgers, sandwiches, and pizza; and the Bavarian. At the base, you can go really casual at the Snack Bar or delightfully international at the restaurant in the Thunderbird Lodge or family-style at the nearby Hotel St. Bernard. On the way to Taos, you'll find the Old Blinking Light, a fun Mexican restaurant; or try the Steak Out, on the mountainside with beautiful views overlooking the Rio Grande Gorge. In the town of Taos, a wide selection of restaurants awaits you. And, of course, there's always your own fine cooking in your condominium!

Children's World: The Kinderkäfig is Taos Ski Valley's children's center and site of the ski school and day-care facility. It's the hub of activities for children ages six weeks to twelve years; a safe and creative learning environment with its own lifts, terrain, and qualified instructors. It's totally for the kids and there are areas where the NO PARENTS ALLOWED sign is up. You'll find kids-only bathrooms, snacks, and shops. The Kinderkare (six weeks to three years old) full-day program includes two snacks, lunch, and nap time. The half-day program includes snack and either snow play or nap time. Reservations are required. Walk-ins are accepted on a space-available basis. Children are divided into age groups of six weeks to one year and one to three years old. The cost for this program is $68 for a full day, $40 for a half day, or $20 per hour. The Junior Elite program (three to twelve years old) is also divided by age groups and includes all-day lesson, lift ticket, lunch, and rentals. Junior Elite I is for children ages three to first grade, while Junior Elite II covers second grade up to fifteen, with further breakdown of ages. The programs run from 8:00 A.M. to 4:30 P.M.; older children are on the slopes from 9:45 A.M. to 2:30 P.M. Full-day cost, with lunch, is $85; a half day is $75. Five- and six-day packages are $400 and $480.

Also for kids, there's tubing on the bunny hill on Wednesday, Friday, and Saturday nights between 4:00 and 7:00 P.M. The cost is $7.00 and parents need to supervise. There is no snowboarding at Taos Ski Valley. When not on the program, kids under six years old ski free with a ticketed adult.

Recreation: Partially located in the Carson National Forest, the Taos ski area is in the Sangre de Cristo Mountains, the southernmost part of the Rockies. The base village sits at 9,207 feet, and the peak towers above at 12,481 feet, affording skiers more than 2,600 feet of vertical drop down 110 different slopes. This is a challenging mountain with just over 50 percent of its runs classified as expert; however, even the novice can feel that classic mountaintop high, since some beginners' runs descend directly from the highest lift at 11,819 feet. In a ski season that lasts from about Thanksgiving to Easter, the average annual snowfall is over 305 inches,

plus there's snowmaking on more than 98 percent of beginner and intermediate terrain.

When you can pull yourself away from the open bowls, dramatic chutes, and lazy meandering-down trails lined with spruce and aspen, you might consider cross-country skiing, a sleigh ride, or an evening skier's seminar on such topics as avalanches and adjusting to the altitude. Skiers in January experience the added pleasures of Taos's jazz festival. Also in January is the two-week Winter Wine Festival, when the grape takes over the Ski Valley. Scores of vintners come from faraway places bringing their wares; seminars and wine tastings warm the winter cold. Several restaurants in Taos build special menus around a particular vineyard, and your dinner is accompanied by a lesson in wines and food.

TAOS SKI VALLEY

P.O. Box 90
Taos Ski Valley, New Mexico 87525
(505) 776–2291, (800) 776–1111,
(800) 347–7414
www.visitnewmexico.com

EL MONTE SAGRADO
Taos, New Mexico

Winter's not all there is in the valley, as the pleasures of the town of Taos are to be had throughout the year. Late spring and summer bring great white-water rafting, trout fishing, mountain bikes and hikes, horseback riding, and golf. Add museums, art galleries, and music festivals and it's a whirl of activity in a gorgeous setting. Special events include a Kite Festival in June, the Taos Pueblo Pow-Wow in July, a storytelling festival in September, and the Hot Air Bal-

loon Rally in the fall, when the trees are gloriously adorned in color.

El Monte Sagrado means the sacred mountain; it is an exciting and unusual new resort (2003) right in the heart of Taos, .5 mile from the Plaza. The concept and underlying philosophy of the resort is based on sound environmental development and water conservation, geared to demonstrate that you needn't give up comfort and even luxury to protect our natural resources. Guests, as well as the public, may take an ecotour to see environmental responsibility in action; the resort utilizes the most current concepts in ecopreservation and sustainability.

Accommodations: On site, find eighteen hotel-style rooms, each with a Native American cultural theme; and twenty suites, each with a global theme—Japanese, Egyptian, Balinese, or Mayan and Moroccan are samples. Rates begin at $450 nightly for a room, $1,200 for a suite.

An interesting option, especially for families, is the El Monte Casitas. Eleven off-site private homes in and around Taos Plaza provide historical adobe-style lodging with kitchens, fireplaces, and patios, even yards (that you don't have to mow!). The resort will gladly stock the pantry with your favorite foods. Guests have open access to resort facilities. Rates are $150 to $550 nightly, and weekly rates are even less.

Dining: *De La Tierra* means "of the earth," and that's precisely the focus of the resort's main restaurant. New Mexico flavors and foods and artistic presentation are highlighted. Open for breakfast, lunch, and dinner. The Anaconda Bar opens at noon, closes at midnight, and is a lively gathering spot. And we don't even need to mention that you are in the heart of Taos, with over fifty fine choices for dining and entertainment.

Children's World: While there is no organized program for children, there is a definite interest in family activities. The resort owners, Dharma Living, also own the adjacent Yaxche School, an alternative learning experience for children in kindergarten through eighth grade. Plans are to incorporate the school into family programs such as stargazing, with one of the best telescopes in New Mexico, or cooking school with the Taos School of Cooking. The concept is one of open interchange and benefit. Other family activities include horseback riding, river rafting, and even a llama trek into the mountains. Baby-sitting is available on request.

Recreation: An all-natural swimming pool without chlorine is a wonderful experience. You can also swim in the outdoor pond that's part of the water reclamation project—the resort will explain how it all works. Visit Detlevs, the full-service spa showcasing soaring glass ceilings, waterfalls, and tropical plants or lounge in the Jacuzzi under the stars. For true relaxation, sit in the large grassy "sacred circle," where food and drink are not allowed and a peaceful atmosphere prevails. So sit back, relax, and savor the experience of Taos.

EL MONTE SAGRADO

125 La Posta Road
Taos, New Mexico 87571
(505) 758–3502, (800) 828–TAOS
www.elmontesagrado.com

ROCKIES

Colorado
Montana
Utah

ASPEN/SNOWMASS VILLAGE

Aspen, Colorado

Say "a small mountain town in Colorado with a very cosmopolitan feel" to anyone, and the response will be "Aspen." Aspen is synonymous with chic, the playground of the rich and famous; Snowmass is devoted to its motto "A Mountain of Family Fun." Each has its niche, and who splits hairs when the best of both worlds is all within a 10-mile radius in one resort area? When talking Aspen skiing, you've actually got four mountains to consider: Aspen Mountain (sometimes called Ajax), Snowmass, and Aspen Highlands and Buttermilk in between. A combined skiable terrain that totals more than 4,000 acres provides more runs and variety than you could possibly test in a two-week ski vacation. Lift passes are valid for all four mountains. Though best known for skiing, both resort areas are open year-round.

Aspen's origins are rooted in the silver boom of the early 1880s. Many of the charming Victorian structures have been preserved and renovated; today they house boutiques, art galleries, hotels, and restaurants. Aspen is just waiting to tempt you. Folks here boast that 75 percent of their visitors return every year and more than 90 percent come back sooner or later. So if you give it a shot, you may just have to plan on being hooked.

Accommodations: Whatever your preference in lodging, you should have no problem finding the perfect place to hang your hat in the Aspen and Snowmass area. From moderate to expensive, from quaint to modern, all the possibilities seem to be here. For the most part, lodgings in Aspen are in the village; at Snowmass they're slope-side with immediate access to trails. This is not, however, a hard-and-fast rule, and because shuttle buses always cruise the roads, there's no problem getting to the lifts and from one mountain to another.

With close to one hundred hotels, lodges, inns, and condominiums in the Aspen area, it is indeed fortunate that the resort associations publish descriptive lists to help you sort through the possibilities. You'll discover everything from a cozy cabin to a five-star deluxe hotel. Just have your priorities straight and decide what's important to you—space, location, a hot tub, spa shower, or fireplace and bear rug? And contrary to the image, costs range from $79 for a room up to $5,000 for a presidential suite. If you're adventurous and a last-minute type, you may find great deals at the Virtual Hostel, which features last-minute specials on lodging and lifts within the upcoming two-week period, winter and summer. Central Reservations (www.stayaspensnowmass.com or (888) 649–5982) has all the details and can help you plan what's exactly right for your family, as far in advance as you want.

Dining: As with lodging arrangements, the dining possibilities seem almost limitless. Whether you've got a hankering for pizza, quiche, fresh veggies and salads, a juicy steak, spicy Szechuan, or northern Italian cuisine, you'll find the right spot among the more than one hundred restaurants in and around Aspen. Seventy-five are listed under "family oriented atmosphere." Particularly family-friendly restaurants are Boogie's Diner, Brothers' Grill, Little Annie's Eating House, and S'no Beach Café and Bar. And, of course, restaurants and refreshment stops are at the mountain bases and on the mountains. For sweets, stop by the Paradise Bakery or Cafe Ink.

Children's World: At Snowmass, even the youngest traveling companion will not keep you from days on the slopes. From 8:30 A.M. to 4:00 P.M., Snow Cubs caters to infants and toddlers, eight weeks to three and a half years old, in a play program filled with puppet shows, stories, arts and crafts, snowman building, and sledding.

Children are grouped by age, with dedicated rooms for each group; lunch is included. Three-year-old Cubs can learn to ski on a contoured slope with magic carpet. The Bear Den is the indoor center for Big Burn Bears, kids three and a half to four years old; preschoolers learn to ski in their own area; ski time varies by individual child. Grizzlies, for ages five to six, spend their day on the mountain with their own beginner area and direct lift; classes range from beginners to accomplished. A full day is $94; half day is $62 for all programs; equipment is not included. Powder Pandas is Buttermilk Mountain's ski school for three- to six-year-olds, with the same hours and rates; it's convenient for parents skiing Aspen Mountain or Aspen Highlands.

Bears and Pandas on Boards are the popular snowboard programs for ages five to seven. Groups of three children learn safety and skills; the full-day cost of $164 includes equipment, five-hour lesson, and lunch. Bears are at Snowmass, Pandas gather at Buttermilk. Night Hawks is a winter evening camp program for ages three to ten available from 6:00 to 10:00 P.M. at $12 per hour; late-afternoon and evening baby-sitters are also available through Snowmass Ski School.

Older kids and teens are also well treated at Aspen/Snowmass. Kids First Turn introduces seven- to twelve-year-olds to skiing and snowboarding; Kid's Group Lessons divides into small groups by ability. From 9:30 A.M. to 3:15 P.M. with instruction, lift tickets, equipment, and lunch is $79; both programs are offered at Buttermilk and Snowmass. The teens "Too Cool for School" skiing and snowboarding program operates every day of the season at Snowmass. First Turn Teen Group lessons and Extreme Camps are organized by age (thirteen to seventeen) and skill, and taught by the most experienced instructors. Hours are 9:30 A.M. to 3:15 P.M. and cost is $64, lift ticket not included. Optional evening activities with other teens include ice-skating and pizza parties.

Operating a summer program (June through August), Camp Snowmass emphasizes a healthy, active outdoor schedule of fishing, hiking, swimming, nature walks, visits to the nature preserve, and picnics. Camp Snowmass is located slope-side at the end of the Snowmass Mall and is divided into Cubs, for three-year-olds, Junior Base Camp for ages four to five, and Base Camp for ages six to ten. For a day's events from 8:00 A.M. to 4:00 P.M. Monday through Friday, the cost is $70; multiple days cost less. Kids can bring their own lunch or it's provided for $6.00. Adventure Series, for eight- to thirteen-year-olds, has a variable cost and Explorers have weekly adventures such as hiking, overnight camping, kayaking, and rafting or mountain boarding. In addition to daily activities, other special activities are regularly planned; a camp ticket plus an extra charge will apply. Horseback riding programs on Wednesdays for the Cubs ($5.00); and Thursdays ($25.00 to $35.00) for older kids; Friday is special-activities day, with such events as rafting, go-carts, climbing wall, miniature golf, swimming, and the fairy caves. Rocket Days, where budding scientists build their own rockets, and Nights on the Mountain are also planned.

Just for Kids, on Aspen Mountain, has free activities and entertainment for kids of all ages and families from mid-June to Labor Day. A different two- to three-hour activity every day might include arts and crafts, cooking classes, yoga for kids, adventure hikes, or carnival games. ARC, the Aspen Recreation Center, is 83,000 square feet of fun, with an NHL-size ice rink, climbing wall, and Aquatic Center with pools, beach, river currents—the works. And Aspen boasts one of the top five skateboard parks in the country. Whew, almost too much fun!

Recreation: From the end of November to mid-April, skiing is on everyone's mind, and regardless of your skiing ability, you'll have plenty of runs to schuss down. Aspen's reputation as a mecca for advanced skiers is well earned, with 26 percent of the runs down Ajax ranked as expert, 26 percent most difficult, and the remaining 48 percent more difficult. But beginners and intermediates should not grow faint in the face of overwhelming ventures, for the other mountains accommodate the not quite so adept. Aspen Highlands is 30 percent intermediate and 18 percent each in advanced and beginner categories; the total vertical drop is 3,635 feet. The vertical rise at Snowmass is almost 4,400 feet, and 55 percent of the runs are intermediate. Buttermilk with 2,000 vertical feet is known as the best place to learn, with almost half of its runs designated for beginners. A teaching staff that totals more than 1,000 ski professionals can introduce a beginner to the slopes (except at Aspen Mountain) as well as help an expert perfect techniques in mogul skiing, snowboarding, and telemarking. At Buttermilk and Snowmass, look for special three-day, first-time-on-skis or -snowboard packages. But each mountain has its secrets: Parks and pipes are popping up at Buttermilk, and it was home to the 2003 X Games, the world's largest alternative sports championships; although Aspen Highlands is famous for black and double black runs, there's actually more green and blue; Snowmass is a haven for snowboarders, and offers everyone easy, uncrowded access to the mountains; and who knew that Aspen Mountain has groomed, intermediate cruising runs?

On-mountain family adventures are waiting everywhere. The Family Zone at Snowmass has adventurous kids' trails, a children's race arena, Trenchtown terrain park, and interactive tree trails. On Buttermilk, Max the Moose hosts Fort Frog, an adventure center with Western fort and Native American village. Twilight snowcat rides to dine in a rustic cabin, magic shows in Snowmass, sledding, tubing—no wonder *Child Magazine* calls this the number one family resort.

Wintertime fun continues with ice-skating at the Aspen Ice Gardens and the Silver Circle,

dogsled rides at Krabloonik Kennels, snowshoe tours, cross-country skiing, sleigh rides at Snowmass Stables and T Lazy 7 Ranch, snowmobiling, and hot-air ballooning (yes, even in winter!). Many of the lodging complexes have swimming pools and exercise equipment. The tennis and athletic clubs also provide opportunities for indoor workouts. Evening entertainment includes films, concerts, plays at the Wheeler Opera House, and classical music at Harris Hall.

Though skiing is practically synonymous with Aspen, this place does not turn into a ghost town when the snow melts. During the summer, the hills are alive with cultural events. The Aspen Music Festival, nearly fifty years old, runs from the end of June to the end of August and is complemented by the Aspen Community Theater and the Jazz Aspen Snowmass Music Festivals. The Anderson Ranch Arts Center in Snowmass has a summer program of classes in photography, ceramics, painting, and printmaking.

You can just about have your pick of outdoor activities: horseback riding, hiking, jogging, rafting, kayaking, fishing, hot-air ballooning, and jeep tours. There is also lift-served mountain biking at Snowmass Ski Area. An eighteen-hole golf course is located on the west perimeter of Aspen; another is in Snowmass. Tennis courts at condominiums and racquet clubs dot the valley. But even in summer you have to take at least one gondola ride—to the top of Aspen Mountain for a spectacular view of this bit of the Rockies.

ASPEN/SNOWMASS VILLAGE

425 Rio Grande Plaza
Aspen, Colorado 81611
(800) 598–2004, (888) 649–5985
www.aspensnowmass.com

BIG SKY OF MONTANA
Big Sky, Montana

The sky isn't really bigger in Montana—not by scientific measurements, that is. But don't tell the folks around here that. These die-hard Westerners believe they've got the market cornered on the best, biggest, bluest sky ever; and if you don't watch out, by the end of a visit here, you'll be a believer too.

In the wintertime, skiing Lone Mountain (summit elevation 11,166 feet) can make you feel that it's almost possible to touch that beautiful, clear sky. Lone Mountain and adjacent Andesite and Flat Iron Mountains are carved with more than 150 named runs covering 85 miles on three mountains; a terrain park, and a half pipe add up to fine skiing at Big Sky.

During the summer, these mountains and their evergreens, the sunshine, and clean mountain air make the perfect setting for hiking, horseback riding, mountain biking, scenic gondola rides, white-water rafting, and fishing, as well as golf and tennis.

Open late November through mid-April and early June through early October, Big Sky is located in southwestern Montana just north of Yellowstone and is surrounded by rivers and national forests.

Accommodations: Two tall structures, the Shoshone/Huntley/Yellowstone Center and the luxurious new Summit at Big Sky, mark the Village. Combined, they total nearly 500 hotel rooms, suites, and condominiums. Many more accommodations are in the vicinity, with different sizes and access to lifts. The Meadow Village, near the golf course, and the Canyon area along the highway complete the area's lodging choices. Big Sky Resort was the vision of the late NBC newscaster, Chet Huntley, who built it in 1973 and owned it until 1976. In 2001, Boyne USA announced a ten-year plan to include $400 million in improvements at Big Sky.

Recently remodeled, The Huntley Lodge is at the base of Lone Mountain; the Explorer chairlift is right out the back door.

The lodge has 200 rooms, some with views straight up the mountain, and an outdoor heated swimming pool, sauna, and Jacuzzi. In the complex you'll find a dining room, lounge, shops, and ski storage.

Attached to the Huntley is the Shoshone Condominium Hotel, with ninety-five suites; it's also ski-in, ski-out. The newest property, the ten-story Summit, combines the best of a hotel and condominium stay. Ski-in, ski-out convenience, dining, lounge, and fitness center, and flexible lock-offs allow a variety of accommodations.

Children ten years and under stay free with existing bedding; $15 for cribs and rollaways. Hotel rates are based on season and number of people in the room; winter has four seasons. At the Huntley, based on two people, rates range from $134 to $226 nightly. The Summit begins at $139 and goes to a high of $462 during the Christmas holiday season.

At the area's condominiums, the studios and one- to four-bedroom units have kitchens and fireplaces. While all the complexes (Stillwater, Skycrest, Lake Big Horn, Powder Ridge Cabins, Saddle Ridge Town Homes, Arrowhead, Beaverhead, Shoshone, Snowcrest Lodge) are in close proximity to the slopes, Snowcrest is closest to the lifts. Some complexes feature heated swimming pools, saunas, and Jacuzzis. Winter condominium rates have a wide range; from $146 for a one-bedroom in budget season to $1,229 at the Summit for a three-bedroom sleeping ten in holiday season.

Summer rates begin at $147 for a deluxe room at the Huntley Lodge and go up to $426 for a three-bedroom unit at the Summit. With dozens of choices for accommodations and several seasons from which to choose, you are sure to find amenities that meet both your expectations and your budget.

Dining: If you are staying in the Huntley Lodge or just cannot face cooking after a busy day, you can dine at the Huntley Dining Room. Chet's Bar and Grill is popular for its warm atmosphere, nightly entertainment, and regular poker games. The Summit features the Peaks Restaurant and the Carabiner Lounge. In winter take the sleigh ride up into the mountains for dinner, and in summer join an outdoor Western barbecue. Next door to the Huntley Lodge is a collection of shops, restaurants, and bars in the Mountain Mall. Here you'll find casual spots for pizzas, deli sandwiches, and burgers; in winter, the Lone Peak Café offers hearty meals at breakfast, lunch, and dinner. On-mountain dining during ski season offers delis and coffee carts at the Mountain Village, the Dug Out, MR Hummers, Dante's Inferno, Sun Dog Café, and the new Timbers restaurant. In summer the Bunker Bar and Grill is a good stop after a round of golf. Expanding out to the Big Sky area, restaurants and nightspots offer live music, dancing, and family fun nights.

Children's World: During the ski season, Handprints Daycare Center is open daily from 8:30 A.M. to 4:30 P.M. for children six months to eight years old. Located at the Snowcrest Lodge, across from the ski school, the facility is a state-licensed day-care center with experienced teachers. Lunch and two snacks are served daily, and two nap rooms provide a spot to rest. Little ones enjoy a combination of indoor and outdoor play: sledding, snow play, stories, songs, and arts and crafts. Open daily from Thanksgiving to mid-April; reservations and immunization records are required. Rates vary by age and activities and do not include ski equipment and lessons. Infants six months to two years are $80 for a full day; two to eight years are $70 full day, $50 half day (lunch included in morning session). Primarily for younger children, the center does offer skiing options (additional cost) for those children three and over who may not wish to ski all day. Lessons last forty-five minutes for age

three, and two hours for ages four to eight. Day-care rates are $95 for a full day, $65 for half-day sessions.

The Snowsports School programs are for children ages three to seventeen. The Small Fry Try for ages three and four is forty-five minutes and the perfect introduction to skiing—of course, it takes almost that long to get them ready! The cost is $31, not including day care and equipment. Mini Camp, for ages four to six and Ski Camp, for ages six to fourteen, have flexible schedules that allow for early drop-offs, afternoon activities, and morning or afternoon ski lessons with or without lunch. The complete package, 8:30 A.M. to 4:00 P.M., is $99 for Mini Camp and $94 for Ski Camp; a la carte prices are in place for various options. Prices do not include equipment and lift tickets for children eleven and over. Kids ten and under always ski free.

The Teen Mountain Experience is in operation during Christmas week and Presidents' week in February. Teens explore the mountain with similar-age-and-skill group while refining techniques. Full day is $75; half-day cost is $42.

The game room in the Huntley Lodge, open from 10:00 A.M. to 10:00 P.M., offers video games and television. No special activities are organized for children during the summer, but baby-sitting arrangements can be made any time of the year through the activities desk at the lodge. The average rate is $8.00 per hour. There are free family activities organized daily throughout the winter.

Recreation: The 4,350-foot vertical drop takes you through open bowls and tree-lined trails. The average annual snowfall is an amazing 400-plus inches. Skiing starts mid-November (an opening guaranteed by snowmaking if Mother Nature is skimpy with her supply) and continues into April. Whatever your level of skiing, you can join lessons at the ski school. Cross-country skiers enjoy treks over broad meadows and through stands of pine trees. Just 5 miles from the resort, the Lone Mountain Guest Ranch maintains 65 kilometers of cross-country trails. When you're not on skis, swim in one of the heated pools or take a trip to Yellowstone for snow-mobiling, snowshoeing, and sight-seeing with free ranger-guided wildlife tours. Dog sled-ding is fun and Cat skiing gives you access to over 1,000 acres of terrain that averages up to 10,000 vertical feet of skiing and snow-boarding. For the hardy, backcountry skiing gets updated avalanche forecasts with the maps and rental equipment. Or take a sleigh ride combined with hearty food, live enter-tainment, and songs and stories.

When the weather warms up, the moun-tains are terrific for hiking and backpacking. For horseback riding, you can link up with Big Sky Stables through the resort concierge. You may prefer adventures in white-water rafting or the quiet solitude of fishing for prize-winning trout in the mountain streams.

The eighteen-hole golf course was de-signed by Arnold Palmer and is well situated in the mountain meadows. Play tennis (six courts, two of which are at the resort) and volleyball, or relax with a Swedish massage or a leisurely guided nature walk, learning about the wildflowers of Big Sky.

BIG SKY OF MONTANA

P.O. Box 160001
1 Lone Mountain Trail
Big Sky, Montana 59716
(406) 995–5000, (800) 548–4486
www.bigskyresort.com

BRECKENRIDGE SKI RESORT
Breckenridge, Colorado

The town of Breckenridge likes to say it was born in the rowdy gold rush of the 1860s, spent its childhood in Prohibi-tion, its teen years in the 1960s, and reached maturity at the turn of this last century. It's a town that doesn't stand still, a town where there's action-plus, all the time. An old gold and silver mining camp proud of its history, Breckenridge is a charming town with care-fully restored buildings that attest to its Victo-rian-era heyday. And the years of skiing have resulted in the development of 2,208 acres of skiing territory on four beautiful mountain peaks. All this skiing in a historic setting is a one-and-a-half-hour drive west of Denver—not so close that it is inundated by locals, yet close enough that once you land at Denver In-ternational Airport, your ski holiday begins with a scenic tour through the Arapahoe Na-tional Forest on your way to Breckenridge.

Like every other Western mining town turned ski resort, Breckenridge has numerous hotels, vacation homes, and condominiums that can be investigated through Breckenridge Central Reservations (800–221–1091). Best known as a winter recreation area, Breckenridge is in fact open year-round. Beaver Run Resort (800–525–2253, www.beaverrun.com) and the Village at Breckenridge (877–428–7829, www.breckresort.com) warrant special atten-tion because of their locations and amenities. With lifts just steps away from either one, these self-contained resorts make life just a little bit easier for families. Besides their own restaurants and shops, the resorts share a child-care center.

Accommodations: Beaver Run is an at-tractive complex of granite and wood build-ings just skirted by the Country Boy trail and is home to the Beaver Run Superchair. The 500 hotel rooms are spacious, and condominiums vary from suites with in-room spas to four-bedroom units. Fireplaces and private balconies are features of all the condominium units; they also have fully equipped kitchens. Children stay for free when staying with their parents, and cribs for infants and toddlers are provided without charge.

During the high ski season, February 1 through the first week of April, a double hotel room is $165 to $305 and a one-bedroom/one-bath condominium that sleeps four is $300 to $545 a night. During the rest of the ski season, rates are lower, with the exception of the holiday period at the end of December when higher rates are in effect. Spring and fall rates are $90 to $100 per night for a double room and $110 to $125 a night for a one-bedroom/one-bath condominium. Summer rates are $135 for a hotel room and $170 for a one-bedroom suite. Two-, three-, and even four-bedroom suites are available. Packages and special offers include third night free, 30 percent discount for early booking, and ski, golf, and spa packages.

The Village at Breckenridge is a Western-style resort with 357 bedrooms in 270 guest accommodations, ranging from hotel rooms to condos; the Liftside Inn building features studio apartments; and Plazas I, II, and III house one- to three-bedroom condominium units. Most of the condo accommodations have kitchens, fireplaces, and balconies with views of the mountains or Maggie Pond, the ice-skating center. Children twelve and younger sharing a room with their parents stay for free; crib rental is available upon request.

The Village defines the ski season as early November through late April; during this time a double hotel room is $120 to $195, studios are $125 to $210, and a one-bedroom/one-bath condominium is $160 to $290. Rates are lower during early and late weeks of the season and higher at holiday time. During the summer a double room is $85 to $120 a night, and a one-bedroom/one-bath condominium is $115 to $160 a night.

Dining: Elegant dining at Beaver Run takes place at Spencer's Steaks and Spirits Restaurant in a warm setting enhanced by oak and cane furnishings. Menu offerings include a selection of USDA choice beef entrees, seafood favorites, and other specialties like the all-you-can-eat prime rib. The Copper Top Cafe and Lounge is open winters-only for skiers, but G.B. Watson's Deli is good for snacks year-round, and Tiffany's Sports Pub provides evening and nighttime amusement.

For elegant dining in the Village at Breckenridge, try the Breckenridge Cattle and Fish Company, which features steak, game, and prime rib. The Maggie, open winter-only for lunch and après-ski, has a ski-in, ski-out location at the bottom of the Quicksilver Super6 chairlift. A deck and outdoor grill for sunny days and the largest big-screen TV in Breckenridge make this a popular place. Café Breck, steps from the ski slope, starts your day with a hearty breakfast, and continues with lunch and dinner. All restaurants at the Village have children's menus. Relax and unwind at the Park Avenue Pub, with its own separate smoking lounge. Drinks, late-night snacks, and a varied menu have something for everyone.

In town more than five dozen restaurants and saloons (out West bars are called saloons—don't forget that!) offer atmospheres from quiet to lively and cuisines that run all over the globe—Mexican, Italian, Greek, and German. A popular spot for steak and seafood is the Whale's Tail on Main Street. The ice-cream shop, also on Main Street, makes for a nice break during an evening walk.

Children's World: Children of all ages have a plethora of riches in Breckenridge. Kinderhut, located at Beaver Run, provides for the wee ones; Beaver Run has their own nonskiing program for ages five to twelve (also in the summer); and Breckenridge's Ski and Ride School, in the Village, offers lessons for ages three to fourteen. If you want to be near your infant, toddler, or first-time young skier, it's probably best to stay at Beaver Run and use Kinderhut.

Breckenridge's Ski & Ride School helps skiers and boarders of all ages improve their skills while having fun. The Children's Centers and slope-side nurseries at Peak 8 and Peak 9 provide individualized care for infants, toddlers, and preschoolers. Rates are $75 to $80 for a full day; $60 to $65 for half-day care. The school recommends the use of helmets for children fourteen and younger; helmets are available to rent or purchase. Ages three to six go from 8:30 A.M. to 3:30 P.M. for a full-day session, including lunch and snacks. Prices are $91 to $101, without ski rental, depending on the season. As an example of the difference, for program and ski rental, the cost is $106 to $118. Half days are based on available space and run $76 to $86, and do not include lunch. Ages seven to fourteen must have a lift ticket and go from 9:30 A.M. to 3:45 P.M. Lift and lesson are $91 to $101; lift, lesson, and ski rental $106 to $118; and lift, lesson, and snowboard rental is $113 to $125. Half-day classes again are based on availability, do not include lunch, and are offered in the afternoon only. A fast-track Learn to Ride (LTR) program for ages seven to fourteen includes trampoline training, snowboard lesson, and a low student/instructor ratio. Classes are from 9:00 A.M. to 3:00 P.M., limited to six people, or even preferably four, grouped by age, and include lunch with the instructors. The cost is $180 to $193 for everything.

In the evenings, Café Breck at the Village Resort becomes a haven for kids of all ages, with KIDS B.A.S.H. (Breckenridge After Ski/Snowboard Hangout). Adults are allowed to stay, or can drop kids off from 5:30 to 8:30 P.M. for food (a kid's buffet is under $5.00) and fun with supervision ($30 for first child; $15 each sibling).

The Kids Day Off program at Beaver Run Resort is loaded with activities for kids ages five to twelve. From 9:00 A.M. to 5:00 P.M. youngsters can swim, enjoy the Alpine Super Slide, visit museums, and go sledding, ice-skating, and on treasure hunts and gold-mine tours. Cost is $70 for a full day with lunch;

$35 each sibling. Daily in the summer, it's generally three times weekly in the winter. Kids Night Out, from 6:00 to 9:00 P.M. offers dinner, indoor miniature golf, arts and crafts, and more fun activities for $30, $15 each sibling. The program is flexible, generally daily in the summer and three times weekly in the winter, and will run on request for three or more children.

Kinderhut (800–541–8779, www.khut. net) is a Colorado state-licensed day-care center and a Professional Ski Instructors of America–affiliated ski school located at Beaver Run Resort, on Peak 9. The Infant Nursery for children six weeks to one year old has a ratio of 1:3, with a maximum of seven children. Care is highly individualized.

Toddler Nursery, for ages one to two and a half years, has a minimum caregiver ratio of 1:5, with a maximum of thirteen children daily. Activities such as snow play, puppets, story time and crafts keep children happy and busy. Nursery hours are 8:15 A.M. to 4:15 P.M.; a full day is $82, while a half day is $60. Kinderhut's Ski School provides beginner ski instruction for ages two and a half to six years, with progressive instruction in balancing, stopping, and turning. Mountain lessons on the Quicksilver Chairlift are for those children who have mastered basic skills, and teacher-to-child ratios will not exceed 1:5. A full day costs $89 to $98, a half day is $60; all Ski School prices include boots, skis, lunch, and a pager for parents. Kinderhut also helps with baby-sitting ($15 per hour with a four-hour minimum) and stages a New Year's Eve party for children.

Summertime is just as busy. Kinderhut offers child care for ages one (and walking) to three years; $55 for the full day and $45 for a half day. Adventure camp is for ages three to six, Monday through Friday from 7:45 A.M. to 5:15 P.M. ($55). Mornings only are also an option ($45). The camp's goal is to provide children with the opportunity to explore new activities in a safe, nurturing environment; to build confidence through successful interactions with the world. Horseback riding, yoga, swimming, rock climbing, ice-skating (yes, even in the summer), story time at the library, or a trip to the fire station are just a taste of the fun in store. Wow! How much can one kid do?

Recreation: If you said to some skiers that you'd found 146 trails, an average annual snowfall of 300 inches, a ski season from late October to early May, and a vertical drop of more than 3,398 feet, they might think you'd died and gone to heaven. Breckenridge gives you all this on its four interconnected mountains—Peak 7 is the latest addition in skiable terrain, while Peak 10 boasts the highest elevation, at nearly 13,000 feet. It also gives outstanding views over Summit County, with 55 percent expert runs, 32 percent intermediate runs, 13 percent beginner runs, bowl skiing, above-the-timberline skiing, and lots of famous Rocky Mountain powder. You can line up a free guided tour of the mountains or plunge right away into group or private instruction.

Cross-country enthusiasts head to the Breckenridge Nordic Center for more than 40 kilometers of groomed trails. Try snowmobiling or dog sledding; ice-skating on Maggie Pond, or the indoor, year-round ice rink; and a horse-drawn sleigh ride to a steak-and-baked-potato supper on the mountain.

At both the Village at Breckenridge and Beaver Run, you can jump into the indoor/outdoor pools, relax in one of the many outdoor hot tubs, or, if your muscles weren't tested enough on the slopes, finish up in the exercise rooms. An additional Beaver Run attraction is an indoor miniature golf course, where you can count on a fun family evening in a huge indoor area for video games and active play.

During warm-weather months venture out from the resorts and go biking through town, hiking in the woods, fishing in mountain streams, sailing on Lake Dillon, horseback riding on trails bordered by wildflowers, and white-water rafting on the Arkansas and Blue Rivers. Play a round on Breckenridge's eighteen-

hole championship golf course designed by Jack Nicklaus. During July and August the mountains ring with classical and jazz music from the Breckenridge Music Institute.

The Riverwalk Center, an award-winning performing-arts facility, is the focal point for summer cultural activities, including a kids concert series.

The Breckenridge Recreation Center is a state-of-the-art facility with both indoor and outdoor pursuits. Inside you'll find tennis, racquetball, and wallyball courts, a gym with running track, two pools (lap and leisure), dance/aerobics, and rock climbing. Outdoors there are more tennis courts, a basketball court and two softball fields, rugby and soccer fields, a skateboard park, a sundeck, and a playground.

Peak 8 Fun Park has a little bit of everything: a mountain bike park with 35 miles of trails, SuperChair rides for easy access to hiking trails; a SuperPutt miniature golf course; and a climbing wall. Most popular is the SuperSlide, which gives downhill thrills while sitting down. It's a ½-mile, three-track slalom course on a small sled. Add to this a Power Jump (a modified trampoline where you go so high you have to wear a harness) and Colorado's largest human maze, two levels of labyrinth twists and turns; the price tag for all this unlimited fun is $48 for a half day and $60 for a full day; tickets for each attraction range from $4.00 to $10.00. You just may need a longer vacation.

BRECKENRIDGE SKI RESORT

Box 1058
Breckenridge, Colorado 80424
(970) 453–5000, (800) 789–SNOW
www.breckenridge.snow.com

THE BROADMOOR
Colorado Springs, Colorado

As majestic as the neighboring Rocky Mountains, The Broadmoor reigns over Cheyenne Lake and 3,000 surrounding acres. The original hotel, known today as Broadmoor Main, was built in 1918 by Spencer Penrose, an enterprising man who made his fortune in gold mining in Cripple Creek (less than 20 miles from Colorado Springs) and copper mining in Utah. He dreamed of fashioning a Colorado resort along the lines of the grand European hotels that he had seen. The Mediterranean-style structure, with its pink-stucco facade, almost glimmers in the sunshine. Inside, the Italian Renaissance trappings include wood-beamed ceilings, crystal chandeliers, gilt-framed mirrors, and hand-painted wall and ceiling decoration. Penrose's dream was realized—The Broadmoor fared well indeed when compared with its European counterparts. And the guests who followed were as impressive as the hotel, from royalty and presidents to movie stars and millionaires.

Over the years, facilities and buildings were added to the original complex. Broadmoor South stands next to Broadmoor Main and is architecturally compatible with the original, because its design utilizes light-colored stucco for the exterior walls. Across the lake is Broadmoor West. A modern structure, it nonetheless blends well within the context of the resort as a whole. In 1995 an additional 150 guest rooms were completed, and Lakeside Suites was completed in 2001. This newer twenty-one-room building hosts the most luxurious accommodations on the property. The architecture of this wing is reminiscent of Broadmoor Main. The newer structures reveal precise attention to architectural design, aesthetic decoration, and fine art. The Broadmoor has just completed a $75-million refurbishing, bringing new grandeur and elegance. The resort is open year round and is the longest running consecutive winner of both the Mobile five-star and the AAA five-diamond awards.

Accommodations: Some 700 rooms and suites are divided among the five main buildings of The Broadmoor. All are handsomely decorated and look out at either the clear blue Cheyenne Lake or the dramatic Colorado mountains; it's a tough task to find a view that's less than terrific. Broadmoor West features rooms with private balconies. During the high season, from the first of May through October, the European Plan is $325 to $470 a night. Suites begin at $540. Winter room rates are $230 to $350; suites begin at $400. Rates are for one to four people. An "incidental services" fee of $14.00 per room and $2.50 per person is added daily. Holiday family packages include extras such as complimentary meals for twelve and under, bikes and paddleboats, movies, and passes to the Cheyenne Mountain Zoo. Cribs are provided at no additional charge. For an extra $15 a night, a rollaway bed can be added to your room.

Dining: In the eighty-four-year history of the hotel, there have only been four executive chefs; current chef Sigi Eisenberger was born in Austria, continuing the European tradition begun in 1918 by the first chef, who was brought here from Italy. The Broadmoor's eleven restaurants have a tradition of excellence. On the top floor of Broadmoor South, the four-star, four-diamond Penrose Room is an elegantly formal restaurant, with traditional French menu, superb views, dinner music, dancing, and an Edwardian decor, with emphasis on elaborate styling. Jackets are required for men. Charles Court, another award-winnign restaurant, in the West building, offers fine dining without the formalities, yet still with wonderful lake views. One of the world's most extensive wine lists (more than 600 choices and 3,000 bottles, with prices ranging from $12 to $1,300 a bottle!) complement such entrees as Colorado rack of lamb and Copper River salmon.

Also at Broadmoor Main are the Tavern, exquisitely adorned with Toulouse-Lautrec lithographs, and the Lake Terrace Dining Room, opening onto the Sun Lounge, with palms, ficus trees, and a tiered Italian fountain. Sunday brunches here are an extravaganza featuring more than seventy items. Café Julie, a sidewalk cafe in Broadmoor West, offers a relaxed shirtsleeves-and-shorts atmosphere for sandwiches, salads, and burgers. Espresso is a favorite stopping place for cappuccino, pastries, quiche, sandwiches, and eclairs in Broadmoor Main. One of the merriest dining spots is the Golden Bee, an authentic nineteenth-century English pub located behind and below the International Center; it is open for lunch and dinner and until the wee hours, with live ragtime and sing-alongs. Stratta's Italian Restaurant, in the spa complex, is open for breakfast, lunch, and dinner with traditional American fare during the day and classic Italian favorites at night. The Grille at the Golf Club has all-day dining with a big-screen television, as well as take-out for sports enthusiasts. The Pool Café has two locations; seasonally outdoors with salads and grilled meats and fish plus summer drinks, and year-round at the Spa with light snacks and smoothies.

Relax in the West Lobby Bar, with dark oak and overstuffed chairs, or on the outside terrace overlooking Cheyenne Lake; for the atmosphere of a fine English library, sip port in the Penrose Lounge. For evening entertainment, stop by Star's Club and Cigar Bar, a lively nightclub with dancing.

Children's World: Memorial Day to Labor Day, daily from 9:00 A.M. to 4:00 P.M., things are buzzing with the Bee Bunch. Scheduled for ages four to twelve years, activities vary daily and include trips to the Cheyenne Mountain Zoo, bowling at Bear Creek Lanes, arts and crafts, paddleboating on Cheyenne Lake, picnics in the park, and scavenger hunts. Pony

rides are also available for younger children, while older kids can enjoy golf clinics, tennis lessons, and horseback riding at the Triple B Ranch. Separate day and evening programs are also offered to give parents maximum scheduling flexibility. However, a one-week advance reservation is requested, and a $25, twenty-four-hour cancellation policy applies.

The Bee Bunch Room in the West Building is the gathering center, and the staffing ratio is one counselor to five campers. Groups are divided into Explorer Bees (four to six years old) and Adventure Bees (seven to twelve years). Morning sessions meet from 9:00 A.M. to noon; afternoons from 1:00 to 4:00 P.M.; cost is $25 per session. Lunch can be added to either session for $15 and is served from noon to 1:00 P.M. The full-day program includes lunch and is priced at $65; family rates are available for the second child on the full-day program and evening camp.The youngsters meet again for dinner and games or a movie from 6:00 to 10:00 P.M., granting their parents opportunities to sample the gourmet creations of the Broadmoor chefs. The children's meals are planned to ensure cleaned-up plates; the pizza, fried chicken, and hamburger dinners are favorites among the younger set and are included in the program cost of $45. Baby-sitting is available, again with one-week advance registration. Contact the Children's Concierge, which also has information on family activities at the hotel and nearby.

Recreation: Golfing at The Broadmoor began when the original hotel opened in 1918. Donald Ross designed that first course and was followed by Robert Trent Jones and Ed Seay/Arnold Palmer. Two of the courses are designated Audubon Sanctuaries. Once golfers discover the challenging variety of these forty-five holes, the incredibly scenic setting, the top-quality equipment and accessories of the golf shops, and instruction with the resident pro, they may never explore the rest of The Broadmoor—and that would be a pity.

Tennis magazine named The Broadmoor the fourth greatest tennis resort in America

(2002) and has ranked the year-round tennis program under Dennis Ralston number one for the past three years. Nine landscaped Plexicushioned courts, all with Rocky Mountain views, are located at the Tennis Club. The Club includes one stadium court, and two courts are covered with a heated, illuminated bubble for play during winter months. Play a set or sign up for classes and clinics.

An afternoon can be spent swimming at one of two heated swimming pools at Broadmoor Main and the Golf Club. Part of the renovation was the creation of a spectacular new infinity edge pool at the north end of Cheyenne Lake, complete with two water slides built into Slide Mountain, a connecting swim-under bridge, a children's wading pool, two fourteen-person hot tubs, thirteen cabanas, and the Main Pool Café. Rent a paddleboat for a spin on the lake or a bicycle for a tour around the lake. Twenty minutes away, the Stables at Broadmoor give you a chance to experience wilderness beauty close-up; along with your trail ride, you may glimpse elk or buffalo. The many biking, walking, and running trails are another way to spend rewarding time in the great outdoors. Or stroll along One Lake Avenue to enjoy a variety of specialty shops and an art gallery.

The Broadmoor Spa, Golf and Tennis Club is more than 90,000 square feet of luxury: state-of-the-art fitness facility, full-service spa, full-service salon, and private locker rooms with all amenities, including fireplaces!

A nonstop itinerary of off-property activities includes white-water rafting, hot-air ballooning, fly-fishing, mountain biking, and hunting expeditions. Or perhaps you'll opt to take the famous cogwheel up to Pikes Peak. The quaint town of Cripple Creek, Garden of the Gods, the new Olympic Training Center, the Cheyenne Mountain Zoo, Manitou, and Seven Falls all make wonderful family excursions.

THE BROADMOOR

1 Lake Avenue
Colorado Springs, Colorado 80906
(719) 634–7711, (800) 634–7711
www.broadmoor.com

C LAZY U RANCH
Granby, Colorado

Ride 'em, cowboy! With a little time at C Lazy U Ranch, you could live up to this label. Experienced wranglers match you with just the right horse to call your own during a vacation stay, and guide you on trail rides through the gorgeous Colorado high country. Beautiful vistas stretch in every direction, with mountains everywhere. Expect to meet some locals on the trail rides—moose, coyotes, owls, and even mountain lions share the area. Situated two hours west of Denver, at an elevation of 8,300 feet, the ranch sprawls across more than 8,000 acres of Peaceful Valley. A lot of territory to roam combines with warm sunny days that give way to cool nights—a spectacular setting for learning Western ways. Since 1946, C Lazy U has operated as a guest ranch. That adds up to a lot of experience, not only in riding and roping, but also in welcoming and entertaining visitors. For the past twenty-five years, C Lazy U has consistently earned the Mobile five-star and AAA five-diamond ratings. Open from early June through mid-October, September is reserved for adults only. The ranch opens again from mid-December to mid-February for the winter holidays. The owners' philosophy is that C Lazy U is not just a hotel, nor is it a resort. Rather, it is a unique vacation spot, your home for the duration of your stay.

Accommodations: Forty comfortable rooms and suites are in the main lodge and the guest cottages that surround it. About seventy-five percent of these have a fireplace, stocked with wood and ready to take the chill off the evening. With no televisions or telephones in the rooms, it's a real vacation. But don't be nervous, at the Executive Corral you'll find two data ports, telephones, and a fax machine; and two public areas have televisions.

Minimum stays vary by season: Summer requires a seven-night stay (Sunday to Sunday); Holiday season (December 20 to January 3) has a five-night minimum; Winter Playtime has a two-night requirement; and September, which is reserved for adults only, requires a three-night stay. Rates are per person and vary based on season, number of people, and size of accommodation. Rates per adult, based on double occupancy, range from $2,125 to $2,650 for a week; the average is $2,225. Children from three to five years old receive a $200 discount. During the winter season, children seventeen and under receive a 20 percent discount. These rates cover virtually everything you'll want or need during your visit: upscale lodging, three meals a day, afternoon and bedtime ice cream and all day tea and lemonade, your own horse with five hours of daily trail rides or instruction, use of the recreational facilities, and the supervised children's program. The only extras are trap and skeet shooting, bar drinks, and a massage, if you choose.

Dining: At C Lazy U you'll get the hearty meals that you need to maintain an energy level consistent with the fresh air and outdoor fun. The warm, rustic dining room is located in the lodge, the main building of the ranch. Here guests sit at tables set for ten, a good way to make friends and enjoy relaxed dining. But don't expect baked beans and coffee in a

tin pot. C Lazy U's outstanding menus include Black Angus prime rib, rack of lamb, and jalapeno-stuffed mountain trout. Breakfast is the family meal, with just about anything you want to order; or try the special of the day— breakfast burritos, raspberry pancakes, or chocolate chip waffles for starters. Lunch is generally buffet-style, by the pool at the Patio House. Children and teens eat lunch and dinner with their counselors; families regroup at about 4:30 P.M. for ice cream and cool drinks and again after dinner for the evening activities. Evening cookouts are planned frequently.

The lodge also houses a comfortable living room, well-stocked with books, and a cozy bar, where drinks and hors d'oeuvres are served nightly at 6:30 P.M. Another bar is located in the Patio House, adjacent to the swimming pool, with both a television and fireplace; enjoy an evening cocktail and swap tall tales with other guests about the day's adventures. Then cap the day off at 9:00 P.M. at the Ice Cream Bar with something special for your sweet tooth.

Children's World: With C Lazy U's special attention to youngsters, the kids may turn into wranglers before you do. Starting at age three (the ranch does not provide care for younger children), kids get a good introduction to life out West. Three-year-olds are instructed in how to ride, and a little of how to feed and care for their horse; at age six they can go out on trail rides. Everyone is assigned a horse for the entire week, based on individual ability, and children are divided into three groups: three- to five-year-olds, six- to twelve-year-olds, and teenagers. Some boots are available if children (or even adults) do not have their own, and helmets are recommended but not required.

The day begins at 9:00 A.M. with horseback lessons or a ride, and maybe lunch on the trail or a swim in the reservoir along the way. Lunch with the counselors, then "cabin time" during the heat of the day, or a nap and movie in the Children's Center, a comfortable indoor place for reading, art projects, and resting. Afternoon brings another trail ride or swimming, tennis, or games—the program is very individ-ualized. Ice cream at 4:00 P.M., with a little "parent time," and then kids gather at 5:45 P.M. for dinner and evening activities until about 8:30 P.M., when families regroup for a hay ride, games, or dancing. Teens, as they much prefer, have their own separate program of riding, hayrides, and cookouts. C Lazy U is well-arranged and safe for children to roam a bit; there's little or no traffic and everything is within easy walking distance.

Recreation: The main attraction of a ranch is horseback riding, and this is one of the most comprehensive programs we've seen. From a string of more than 160 horses, you'll be as-signed a mount that suits your ability. Guided by experienced wranglers, you'll ride the high country across mountain meadows or sage-covered hills, and through tall evergreens along Willow Creek. For three hours in the morning and another two in the afternoon, the focus is on horses. The programs are flexi-ble, and participants may decide which they wish to join—it might be instruction (basic or advanced) in the outdoor or indoor arenas, or a choice of trail rides (slow and scenic, medium, or fast). On Friday mornings, family rides are scheduled.

But there's more to this ranch than just horses. Enjoy a group walk before breakfast. Between trail rides, sneak in a little fishing in the pond near the lodge or at a secluded spot along Willow Creek, then have the trout for breakfast! Ranch hands are glad to instruct you in the art of fly-fishing. Adults have a catch and release policy, while kids can catch up to two fish. Go hiking or spend an after-noon on the skeet range (trap and skeet shooting are the only activities not covered in the package rates), play tennis on one of the two Laykold courts, or swim in the heated pool. Try volleyball, basketball, shuffleboard, or horseshoes, or take the ranch's name to heart, and simply laze about in the sunshine or the shade of a tree with a cool drink.

For more activities, seek out the Patio House, the principal recreation center, with a well-equipped fitness room, locker rooms, and showers. When you fear that saddle sores or tennis elbow may set in, retire to the whirlpool or sauna. A game room features Foosball, table tennis, and billiards; a televi-sion room and a large all-purpose activity room with fireplace invite relaxing or socializ-ing, as you desire. Complimentary laundry fa-cilities are also found in this complex.

In the evenings the entire family joins in on campfire sing-a-longs, hay rides, square dancing, and rodeos—just so you don't for-get you're "out West." Nearby excursions might include Rocky Mountain National Park, with stunning scenic vistas, or the glacial snow fields and the Alpine terrain and tundra of the Continental Divide. Or visit the little town of Hot Sulfur Springs with over twenty naturally heated therapeutic pools. Off-site, white water rafting and golf can be arranged.

During the winter season guests take to skiing—cross-country on the 25 kilometers of trails maintained by the ranch and downhill at Winter Park (25 miles) and Sol Vista (10 miles) ski resorts, accessible via the ranch's complimentary shuttle service. Enjoy horse-back riding in the snow or in the indoor 12,000-square-foot heated riding arena, or take a sleigh ride on an old-fashioned cutter. Ride an inner tube down the tubing hill or across a meadow behind a snowmobile, and ice skate or play hockey or broomball on the groomed skating pond. Then snuggle in for hot drinks, the fireplace, Western dancing, and cowboy songs. Yippee-yi-ay!

C LAZY U RANCH

P.O. Box 379
Granby, Colorado 80446
(970) 887–3344

CLUB MED/CRESTED BUTTE

Crested Butte, Colorado

Crested Butte is Club Med's new ski hotel-village for families, replacing Copper Mountain. Open from mid-December to early April only, it makes the most of the short season—you'll find every imaginable snow sport here, along with all of Club Med's conveniences for families and totally all-inclusive policies. Set in southwestern Colorado, at an altitude of 9,375 feet within the Gunnison National Forest and the Elk Mountain Range, Crested Butte bills itself as "the last great ski town." From its beginning in the 1880s as a mining supply camp, now the town of Crested Butte has one of Colorado's largest National Historic Districts, with a permanent population of 1,600-plus hearty souls. The Gunnison Country is one of Colorado's most beautiful mountain regions of alpine valleys and 14,000-foot-high peaks.

Accommodations: This is Club Med's only U.S. ski village, newly opened after a $6-million renovation of a former Marriott hotel. Sitting at the base of the Crested Butte chairlift, it's designed with lodging, dining, skiing, and entertainment all right there at your ski-tip. Two hundred fifty-six rooms and suites accommodate from one to eight people; amenities include TV, telephone, and minirefrigerators. Three-, four-, and seven-night stays are options. Club Med pioneered the concept of all-inclusive vacations; currently there are more than one hundred villages in more than forty countries all over the world, and definitely an international mix of guests. Three-night land-only packages are $540 to $810 for adults and $120 to $375 for children ages three to fifteen. Seven-night packages range from $1,120 to $1,750 for adults and $280 to $875 for children. Packages include lodging, all meals and drinks, full-day ski and snowboard lessons, ski passes, complete children's programs, and all hotel amenities.

Dining: Mirabel, the main restaurant, has the traditional Club Med "bountiful buffet" and community seating, which creates a convivial atmosphere. Kids can eat lunch and dinner early in a special section of the dining room with the counselors. Junior Club Med (ages eleven to seventeen) also have their own section of the dining room. The second restaurant requires reservations and is smaller and more intimate, with a la carte service and an upscale French cuisine.

Three bars serve guests: the Main Bar, near the big restaurant; the huge Sports Bar, with pool tables, games, and the ski-in, ski-out entrance to the slopes; and the fireplace skier's bar for gathering for warmth after fun times in the snow. Club Med's new policy of including all drinks and snacks in the package means that now everything you eat and drink is free!

For an adventure on your own, you might try dinner at 10,000 feet—an unusual dining experience where you ride up the mountain in an open sleigh pulled by a snowcat, then enjoy a four-course dinner at Andiamo Italian Restaurant.

Children's World: Club Med is famous for their nonstop activities, even for kids, who are accepted here from age four. Skiing lessons begin at age four, and snowboarding lessons start at age six. Certified Club Med instructors provide full-day lessons and clinics. Eight levels, from beginner to competition, are offered based on the skier's ability. Children must wear safety helmets during downhill ski lessons, which use more than eighty trails and all ski lifts, plus the Kids Corral for younger children. The Children's Club has its own facility, and the Kids Corral provides a gentle slope and tow ropes for the littlest family members.

In addition to skiing, Mini Club (ages four to ten) activities include puppet shows, video games, and snow-sculpting contests. All children participate in the Mini Club Show, performed weekly for delighted parents. Hours are 8:00 A.M. to 5:00 P.M., and again from 6:30 to 9:00 P.M.—you may see your children for a quick hug and clothing change; otherwise, they're far too busy. Mascots Clubber and Medy delight youngsters throughout the week by joining in their activities, even skiing with them. Once a week they lead a costume parade through the village where kids enjoy showing off the costumes they've made themselves. Mini Scientist programs engage children in educational exploration that just seem like fun. And finally, Siesta Club, nighttime supervision for the little ones, is available for $20 per child between the hours of 9:00 P.M. and 1:00 A.M. During certain holidays, informal programs are set up for teens to meet and socialize easily with their peers.

Recreation: The mountain is the centerpiece of recreation, and is quite impressive with a summit elevation of 12,162 feet and vertical drop of 2,775 feet. Eighty-five trails, served by fourteen lifts, break down into 15 percent beginner; 44 percent intermediate; 10 percent advanced; and 31 percent expert (that's the double black diamonds, you know). Extreme sports have a good hold here. There's also a Terrain Park and a new Snowdeck Park, a mini-terrain park, at the base of Keystone Lift, open to snowdecks, skis, and snowboards until 8:00 P.M.

Included in the Club Med package is full-day ski and snowboard instruction at all levels, beginner to expert, for all ages, including adults; ski passes, and all the amenities of the hotel. Equipment rental is not included in the price, but is available. There's a fitness room if you just can't miss your daily routine, a heated pool and sauna, whirlpool, and massage (extra charge) if you overdo.

Other off-site activities that are not included in the package are snow mobiles, snowshoeing, cross-country skiing, dogsled tours, snowcat rides and ice-skating. If all of that sounds cold, warm up with a hot après-ski drink at the fireplace, a new movie at the cinema, or jump in the sauna or Jacuzzi. Evening entertainment is geared toward the entire family.

The little town of Crested Butte offers old-fashioned charm but up-to-date entertainment with its quaint shops and wide variety of pubs and restaurants. The village operates a free shuttle into town for exploring or dining out. Club Med Excursions (extra cost) include dogsled tours, the Black Canyon of Gunnison National Monument, and horse-drawn sleigh rides. Special events may be ski clinics by Kim Reichelm, Wayne Wong, and J.P. Auclair or other notable skiers, or special ski movies.

CLUB MED/ CRESTED BUTTE

500 Gothic Road
Crested Butte, Colorado 81225
(970) 349–8700, (800) CLUB–MED
www.clubmed.com

DEER VALLEY RESORT

Park City, Utah

Skiing for most folks means a little bit of the rugged outdoors—windburned cheeks, the raw natural beauty of mountain vistas, fresh tracks through pristine powder. Deer Valley has redefined skiing somewhat. It's all of the above but with an added twist. Instead of the Western flair you'd expect in Utah, there's a more sophisticated European atmosphere at Deer Valley. This is warm hospitality with a heavy dose of pampering—from the guest-service attendants who help you unload your skis to the quite comfortable chairlifts to the signature food items in Snow Park Lodge.

Deer Valley, less than 40 miles east of Salt Lake City, is actually four mountains: Bald Eagle Mountain, whose summit is 8,500 feet; Bald Mountain, which rises to 9,400 feet; Flagstaff Mountain, with the summit at 9,100 feet; and Empire Canyon, with a summit of 9,570 feet. The hubs of activity are Snow Park Lodge at the base of Bald Eagle Mountain and Silver Lake Lodge at midmountain. Silver Lake Village is in effect the midmountain point, for it is from here that lifts ascend to Bald Mountain's summit. With the feel of a European village, the area has three restaurants and a small ski shop. Snow Park Lodge houses a restaurant and lounge, the ski school, the ski rental shop, the children's center, and a well-stocked ski shop.

Both lodges are very tastefully designed; inside the columns are natural tree trunks at least 2 feet in diameter, and wood accoutrements abound—from the handrails to the ceiling beams, from the facial tissue dispensers to the trash cans. You'll find no plastic chairs or Formica-topped tables in the dining areas here—no indeed! Understated elegance and tasteful attention to detail are hallmarks of Deer Valley, the first country club for skiers.

Accommodations: At 8,200 feet amid the aspens and pines, the midmountain Stein Eriksen Lodge is a Norwegian-style hotel built of stone and wood. Stein Eriksen's name has been synonymous with elegant skiing since his gold-medal victory in the 1952 Olympics. It's fitting that the 2002 Winter Olympics were on his home mountain. Today, Eriksen serves both as host of the lodge and director of skiing for Deer Valley Resort. The lodge consistently garners awards and is a four-star, five-diamond property. Daily rates for the fifty-nine rooms range from $350 to $475 in winter value season; $670 to $910 at winter's peak. The 111 suites are $540 to $620 (value) and $1,070 to $1,205 at peak times. Summer season (June to mid-October) rooms range from $205 to $245 and suites are $285 to $340. Shops, two restaurants, a swimming pool, and a health club complement the lodge.

In addition, there are more than 500 units at the base of the mountain, along the trails, and near Silver Lake Lodge. The condominiums range from one- to five-bedroom units with fully equipped kitchens and living areas with fireplaces. Most have private Jacuzzis and individual decks or balconies; some include saunas and some feature ski-in/ski-out access. Daily maid service is available. One-bedrooms start at $250; two-bedrooms at $350. There are substantial savings during value seasons, typically early December and early January, while rates increase during holiday periods. During the summer months rates range from $99 a night for a one-bedroom unit to $159 a night for a two-bedroom unit, with a minimum two-night stay. All summer bookings receive two chairlift ride vouchers. Contact Deer Valley Central Reservations (800–558–DEER) for complete customized vacation planning.

Dining: Dining at Deer Valley is a gourmet experience. The four-star Glitretind at the Stein Eriksen Lodge heads the list in elegance. The

Valhalla, named after the "heavenly feasting hall" of Viking heroes is also here, with regional cuisine and a tasting menu. The Snow Park Lodge and the Silver Lake Restaurant in the Silver Lake Lodge are "cafeterias." What misnomers! Though they're self-service, the lavish lunchtime displays (homemade breads and pastries, salads, quiches, deli sandwiches) are hardly typical of the standard quick bite between ski runs. The newest day lodge in Empire Canyon offers deck dining with scenic views of the Daly Bowl and Chutes. Start with morning espresso, have lunch from the gourmet grill, and snacks are available until 3:30 P.M. The evening seafood buffet at the Snow Park Lodge is popular for fresh seafood and lots of it; while the Mariposa at Silver Lake Lodge offers traditional European fare and candle-lit dinners. In the Valley, McHenry's is a great place for lunch and family dining; Stelvio at the Goldener Hirsch Inn serves Italian/Austrian cuisine; and the Olive Barrel is always popular for northern Italian hearty dishes from the brick oven. Your taste buds can really get a workout in Park City. Try the Continental cuisine at Adolfs or the Riverhorse Café, with live entertainment; both are local favorites. Chimayo is imaginative Southwestern with a French technique, and Wahso is Asian grill cuisine with that same French influence, in a setting reminiscent of 1930s Shanghai. Mikados for sushi, Grappa for the feel of a Tuscan farmhouse, and Zoom, Robert Redford's restaurant in the train depot station are all delightful diversions. All these provide interesting alternatives to your own gourmet cooking in your condo.

Children's World: Deer Valley's Children's Center is a state-licensed facility providing indoor supervision and activities for nonskiing children. Located on the main level of the Snow Park Lodge, the center is open daily from 8:30 A.M. to 4:30 P.M. during the ski season and can accommodate infants as young as two months of age. The cost for all children is $82 for a full day with lunch; reservations are essential, especially in peak winter months. Children are divided by age into groups for

two to eight months, nine to twenty-four months, and two to twelve years old. Activities include storytelling, art, singing, toys, and lots of play time, and quiet time for the littlest ones.

The Ski School instructors are trained specifically in techniques that teach children not only how to ski, but to love skiing. A safe, fun, nurturing environment prevails; programs end at 3:45 P.M. so you may take a run with your child, and you'll get daily progress reports. The Adventure Club is divided into small groups, each with age-appropriate activities. Fawns (three to three and a half years) meet from 9:00 A.M. to 4:30 P.M. and alternates children's center activities with snow play and a one-hour private ski lesson. Children must be three and a half to participate in Bambi Club, and will have morning and afternoon lessons, along with indoor activities. Children must be willing to ski and the daily program cost is $125; ski rental is $16. Reindeer Club meets from 10:15 A.M. to 3:45 P.M. for ages four and a half to six years and costs $120 for lesson, lift ticket, and lunch. Average class size is four to six students; children's center activities are available when needed. Adventure Club ($120), for the seven- to twelve-year-olds, has an average size of seven to ten students, and all levels will have the opportunity to improve their skiing. And finally, the Teen Escape ($120) lets teens enjoy a mountain experience with their peers while being coached on the dynamics of skiing. They'll need pocket money for lunch, and the program is only offered during holiday and peak periods.

Deer Valley's Summer Adventure Camp is one of Park City's longest-running summer camps. Beginning mid-June, it operates from 9:30 A.M. to 4:00 P.M. Monday through Friday until late August. Drop-in hours are 8:00 A.M. to 5:30 P.M. Campers bring their own sack lunch and water. Programs are split into three groups, with excellent counselor to camper ratios: Adventure Camp Mountaineers for first graders through twelve years (1:8, $42);

Adventure Camp Explorers for ages four through kindergarten (1:5, $45); and Jamboree for the wee ones, ages eighteen months through three years (1:4, $50). Half days at Jamboree are $30, and based on availability; reservations are recommended. Jamboree activities include little-red-wagon rides, a walk to the duck pond, wading pool water games, and art, music, and movement.

All ages get to enjoy usual summer camp activities plus leisurely time to simply enjoy and appreciate the great outdoors and play with friends. Each week's activities revolve around a different theme and include nature studies, swimming, mountain biking and hiking, team sports, along with mini–film festivals (kids produce their own videos), karaoke, and talent shows. Weekly field trips incur an extra cost.

Recreation: There are eighty-eight downhill runs, nineteen lifts, and a vertical drop of 3,000 feet. Combine these with well-groomed trails and a restricted number of skiers on a daily basis—what more could a skier ask for? Beginners are able to ski each of the four mountains. The mountains are beautiful, and the attention to them and to the skiers is high quality. Full- and half-day private and group lessons are available. Cross-country ski lessons are also offered nearby; trails roll over broad, open expanses and through aspens and evergreens. No snowboards are allowed at Deer Valley. Other winter pleasures include snowmobiling, snowshoeing, sleigh-ride dinners, and even hot-air ballooning. Park City is alive with shopping, art galleries, theater, bars, and clubs. And of course, the Utah Olympic Park provides ski jumping, bobsledding, and luge rides.

If you don't have a sufficient workout on the slopes, maybe the exercise rooms will test your limits. Then relax your weary muscles in one of the saunas or Jacuzzis.

Though primarily a winter wonderland, Deer Valley operates year-round. In warmer weather, June to Labor Day, guests enjoy 50 miles of lift-served mountain biking/hiking and scenic chairlift rides. The Utah Symphony stages outdoor concerts, and all the summer mountain pleasures are here: golf, tennis, swimming, horseback riding, fishing, boating, rafting and kayaking, and hot-air ballooning. Stroll along Park City's Historic Main Street, which offers shops and dining options.

DEER VALLEY RESORT

P.O. Box 1525
Park City, Utah 84060
(435) 649–1000, (800) 424–3337
www.deervalley.com

FLATHEAD LAKE LODGE
Bigfork, Montana

Mix some city slickers with a few expert wranglers out in Montana horse country, toss in beautiful scenery and clear blue skies, and come up with quite a different vacation experience at Flathead Lake Lodge. On 2,000 acres in northwest Montana, just south of Glacier National Park, this dude ranch specializes in water sports and just about anything that has to do with horses, from riding them to shoeing them. The lodge is situated in a private bay on Flathead Lake; at 15 miles wide by 30 miles long, it's the largest freshwater lake in the West. The surrounding timberland stretches up into the Rocky Mountains. The ranch is open from May to October, and one- or two-week visits are standard.

Flathead Lake Lodge has been in the Averill family since 1945; son Doug took over in 1971, and he and his family now live at the ranch. Hospitality is a way of life here, and families return again and again for a memorable vacation. The lodge has been rated in the top 2 percent of best vacation spots, and acclaimed by *Better Homes and Gardens, Bon Appetit, Sunset Magazine, Travel & Leisure,* and *Good Morning America.*

Accommodations: The main lodge is the focus of activities and dining; in a warm and rustic setting, the old stone fireplace lures many guests to gather for cozy chats. There are guest rooms here and in the south lodge; the historic log lodges accommodate four people with a small sitting area. Many families find the two- and three-bedroom log cottages particularly attractive; some of the lodge rooms and the guest cottages have views of the lake. The weekly rate for an adult is $2,366; for a teenager, $1,771; for six- to twelve-year-olds, $1,596; for three- to five-year-olds, $996; and for infants and toddlers, $105. A one-week stay runs Sunday to Sunday; rates include lodging, three meals a day, and all recreation, including horseback riding, tennis, use of the boats and sports equipment, and the Kids Camp. Cribs are available at no additional charge.

Dining: Dining is a family affair, with good home cooking, and breads and desserts made fresh every day. Guests gather at the long tables in the lodge dining room or at the picnic tables out on the patio overlooking the lake. Children eat together before their parents, allowing grown-ups time to get acquainted and plan the next day's events. Kids eat at 8:00 A.M., noon, and 6:00 P.M.; adults eat half an hour later. A daily happy hour in the Saddle Sore Saloon allows tall tales to be swapped as you wet your whistle. With three hearty meals a day, you better work and play hard, although appetites are always good. An evening barbecue ride gives everyone a chance to sample buffalo, grown on the ranch.

Children's World: The children's program is for any child old enough to participate in organized group activities, and divides roughly

at age six. The friendly staff—mostly energetic college students who can keep up with excited youngsters—guide children through the day's activities. They can swim, lend a hand with the daily chores, and learn to ride horses. Children six years and older join cowboys on the horseback-riding trails in the mountains. After the trail riders depart, children under six are given special attention and supervised pony rides. All kids become "junior wranglers" and learn about grooming, barn duties, and caring for the horses. On Saturday mornings, kids show off at the Children's Rodeo, much to the delight of parents. Arts and crafts are scheduled in the morning and afternoon and projects get pretty creative. All the other pursuits dear to kids' hearts are here as well—swimming, boating, tennis, volleyball—all the ranch activities are available to them. Youngsters ages six to twelve get to spend an overnight in authentic teepees, telling ghost stories around the campfire, and a fire truck ride to the ice-cream store is a real treat. Teens are encouraged to participate in all the ranch activities; some activities such as trail rides, team penning, games, and boat cruises are planned just for them. Child care for children too young for the camp is available but not included in the weekly rates.

Recreation: The great outdoors awaits you. Horses are a way of life here; ride 'em, rope 'em, or test your nerve and verve in competition. Take an early-morning breakfast ride to work up a good appetite, then enjoy a breakfast cookout amid the tall pines. Old-fashioned Western rodeos are part of the evening activities.

Take a dip in the large swimming pool or the crystal clear waters of the lake. Sailing, canoe races, and waterskiing may fill your afternoons. Cruises on the lake are organized several times a week. Fish in the lake or the nearby streams, and add a trout to a cookout dinner or spin a good story about the one that got away.

It's easy to find partners for a game of tennis (four courts) and to organize table tennis or volleyball. Pick up a game of, what else? Horseshoes! You might take a stroll along the wooded trails and pick berries. You can schedule full- or half-day excursions for white-water rafting, river tubing, and wilderness fishing. The National Bison Range, only an hour away, attracts many visitors; seeing real live buffalo is a highlight for kids—and parents. Courtesy cars are available for trips to Glacier National Park and Kalispell, "The Best Mountain Town in Montana."

FLATHEAD LAKE LODGE

Box 248
Bigfork, Montana 59911
(406) 837–4391
www.averills.com

KEYSTONE RESORT
Keystone, Colorado

Like many fine Western ski resorts, Keystone first attracted settlers in search of the rich minerals in its mountains. Today visitors flock here seeking light powdery snow and the mountain high for which the Rockies are known. At the base of Loveland Pass, 70 miles west of Denver, Keystone has 116 runs on three interconnecting ski mountains and a vertical drop of more than 2,900 feet. The resort remains open year-round, so when summer rolls around, many folks hang up their skis and head for Keystone's golf course (designed by Robert Trent Jones Jr.), the Keystone Tennis Center, and the Keystone Music Festival.

Winter and summer there are more activities for families than you could possibly do in one vacation. There's even a special line, (800) 354-4–FUN, to help you plan it all. And at Keystone, you get more than a room. The Adventure Passport gives you access to lots of free activities, such as sleigh rides; hockey, ski, and Nordic lessons; Kids' Night Out; tennis clinics; bike rentals; wine tasting; and more.

Accommodations: Keystone spreads out over a large area, with 1,600 lodging units in seven neighborhoods; the Web site has an excellent interactive map with all the details of each area's lodging. If you want to walk or short shuttle to the slopes, Mountain House base area and River Run Village are within 200 yards of the lifts. Both areas have Children's Centers. Skier Services and the Ski and Ride School are located at Mountain House, along with mountainside dining and après-ski activities; this is the original base area of Keystone. The Inn at Keystone Hotel is an economical choice with a cozy lobby, restaurant, and nightlife—and the hot tubs are on the roof, with great views! Rates begin at $219 in winter, $69 in summer. A variety of condominiums offer more space, many only steps from the slopes or golf courses. Winter rates begin at $260; summer rates start at a low $99.

River Run Village is the newest addition to Keystone. Lone Eagle and the Timbers are ski-in, ski-out, upscale condos on the eastern slopes of Keystone Mountain, and are the closest lodging to the slopes; rates range from $399 to $785. Cross over the Snake River to River Run Village for shopping, dining, and nightlife. River Run Village is the largest ski area development project in North America; eventually over 4,500 residential units are planned. In East Keystone, deluxe and premium condos are on the outskirts of River Run Village, in the White National Forest along the Snake River, and appeal to those who want to be close to nature, and get away from it all. North Keystone, on Tenderfoot Mountain Ridge close to the conference center and Keystone Village, offers good value condominiums and town houses, and is a shuttle ride to lifts and River Run Village. West Keystone and Keystone Ranch shelter a variety of lodgings, the golf courses, and Keystone's best restaurant, the Keystone Ranch. And last, but certainly not least, is Keystone Lakeside Village. The Keystone Lodge Hotel, a rustic yet elegant four-diamond property, is in the heart of Keystone Village, a festive place of shops, galleries, and restaurants spread along the lakeside. It's the center of the action, with a playground, ice rink, and the lake. Free shuttles run throughout Keystone and connect the mountain bases.

Dining: From romantic gourmet dinners in a mountaintop restaurant more than 2 miles high to family picnic lunches carried by llamas, unique and award-winning dining choices set Keystone Resort apart from other mountain resorts. The resort features dozens of dining options that range from gourmet six-course meals to a Western family-style cookout and include Summit County's only AAA four-diamond-rated restaurants—the Alpenglow Stube and Keystone Ranch.

At the Keystone Lodge, the Garden Room features Continental cuisine and a Sunday brunch; the Edgewater is a casual restaurant open for breakfast and lunch. Among the numerous restaurants in the village, you'll find Pizza on the Plaza; Idabelle's, for Mexican fare; and Bighorn Steakhouse. At River Run, Kickapoo Tavern, Paisano's, Pizza on the Run, and the Fritz Alpine Bistro all satisfy families. Several restaurants will provide take-out if you prefer eating in your condo. In the summertime you can hop a hayride to Soda Creek Homestead—in winter a sleigh ride takes you there—for a juicy steak dinner. Take the gon-

dola to Der Fondue Cheese for a fun evening of dipping and Bavarian music.

Children's World: Keystone has not one but two children's centers, one located at Mountain House base area and a new facility at River Run. For ages two months to twelve years, both operate daily from mid-November to late April. River Run is modeled after a children's museum with bright colors, a central play area surrounded by breakout areas for different ages, and lots of hands-on, interactive play. A full day (8:00 A.M. to 5:00 P.M.) including lunch, is $77; a half day is $62, morning or afternoon. In winter, snow-play programs are designed to introduce kids to the snow. Learn-to-ski programs begin at age three with group lessons and snow play, at Mountain House only. A full day includes lesson, lunch, and snacks and costs $97 to $104; half-day programs also with lessons, snacks, and lunch, are $87 to $94.

At Mountain House and River Run, lessons for children ages four to fourteen are grouped by age and ability level. Keystone has children's on-mountain adventure areas and trails. All packages include lesson, lift ticket, equipment rental, and lunch. One-day package is $97 to $104; multiple-day packages are also available. Helmets are recommended, and can be rented for $10. You must register by 9:00 A.M.; pickup is from 2:30 outside to 4:00 P.M. inside. Special kids' adventure days, ski-cology (learn to ski while learning about the environment, native wildlife), and snow-blade days are also scheduled. Kids must be seven or older to snowboard. Mom, Dad, and Me is a one-hour private lesson for two adults and one child every day at 3:00 P.M.; cost is $50, and it's a great way to spend family time on the slopes.

Kids' Night Out provides movies, games, and crafts while parents dine at any Keystone Restaurant. It's free with the Adventure Pass, Sunday through Thursday from 6:00 to 10:00 P.M.

Keystone has temporarily suspended their summer day camp program. They are currently recommending Lake Dillon Pre-School, 6 miles away in Dillon. Ages six weeks to six years are cared for and entertained Monday through Friday, from 7:00 A.M. to 6:00 P.M. in a pleasant, state-licensed facility. Cost is $65 for the full day; mornings may possibly be arranged for $50. Call (970) 468–1606 for details. Keystone schedules family activities almost daily.

Recreation: With three interconnected mountains—Keystone Mountain, North Peak, and the Outback—Keystone offers terrain for skiers and snowboarders of all levels. Keystone Mountain offers mainly beginner and intermediate terrain, with night-skiing operations that keep the mountain open until 9:00 P.M. North Peak challenges guests with more intermediate slopes and runs that plunge down mogul-filled terrain. The Outback features only intermediate and expert runs. Some of Summit County's best tree skiing is found on the Outback. Skiers can find deep powder in open bowls adjacent to the Outback. And the twenty-acre snowboard terrain park features two half-pipes. Nighttime lighting makes Keystone's terrain garden the largest night-snowboarding operation in Colorado.

The ski season opens at Keystone in mid-October (Colorado's earliest opening date) and continues into late April. Whether you're trying to figure out what a snowplow is or you're looking for perfection in powder skiing, the more than 350 ski and snowboarding instructors can guide you through the 1,749 acres of skiable terrain.

Other winter sports at Keystone include ice-skating at the Skating Center in the village, cross-country skiing from the Keystone Cross-Country Center into Arapahoe National Forest (cross-country and telemark lessons are offered), snowmobile tours into the backcountry, sleigh rides, and indoor tennis.

Summertime at Keystone means golfing on the masterfully designed Robert Trent Jones Jr. course; eighteen holes with a Scottish flair respect the woodlands, meadows, and a nine-acre lake. The River Course, designed by Hurdzan-Fry, follows the path of the Snake River for the front nine. The back nine threads through a pine forest, bringing beauty and stunning views to the game. Courses are open from June to mid-October; golf pros offer private lessons and clinics.

Keystone is a haven for mountain-bike enthusiasts. The resort offers a special program called Dirt Camp, a series of instructional mountain bike camps that provides intense riding retreats for "mud studs" and "wannabes." Even if you're a beginner and conquering single-track, Dirt Camp helps you hone your mountain-biking skills. One-hour beginning clinics are free with the Adventure Passport.

Another important summertime attraction here is the Music Festival. Ranging from classical to pop, the National Repertory Orchestra and the Summit Brass carry the season from June through Labor Day.

At the Keystone Tennis Center, two indoor courts permit year-round play, and an additional twelve outdoor courts expand summertime possibilities. Ball machines, video analysis, and group and private lessons aid players in their game.

Fishermen take to the local haunts for rainbow trout; boaters sail on Lake Dillon (5 miles west of Keystone) or skim across Keystone Lake in a paddleboat or kayak. Bicyclists ride the paths along Snake River, and hikers plod along the trails through wildflowers and aspens into the national forest. Horseback ride from the Keystone Stables through the Snake River Valley (breakfast rides are specialties), tour the high country of the Arapahoe National Forest by four-wheel drive, go whitewater rafting down the Colorado and Arkansas Rivers, be treated to a lunch of rattlesnake meat and buffalo, or enjoy the great outdoors and mountain scenery on a gondola ride to Keystone Mountain's summit.

Family-friendly activities are scheduled almost daily in summer; kite flying and scavenger hunts on Mondays; mural painting, storytelling, and marshmallow roasts on Tuesdays; gold panning and Music with Kids on Thursdays; and a stargazing workshop on

Fridays. Pony rides and Children's Theater, guided hikes, and free mountain bike clinics augment the playground in Keystone Village and the family fun park in River Run. Miniature golf, strolling around the lake, and feeding the ducks—families don't lack for activities here.

Reservations and more information on these activities (including dining at Keystone's award-winning restaurants) can be arranged by the Keystone Activities and Dining Center well before a guest arrives, so that everything is already in place at vacation's start. The number to call is (800) 354–4-FUN.

KEYSTONE RESORT

P.O. Box 38
Keystone, Colorado 80435
(970) 496–2316, (877) 625–1556
www.keystoneresort.com

MOUNTAIN SKY GUEST RANCH
Emigrant, Montana

"Just turn me loose, let me straddle my own saddle underneath the Western sky." At Mountain Sky all guests (age seven and older) are assigned their own special horse. Careful matching of horse and rider according to the latter's age and skills ensures a compatible duo during a vacation stay. Under the guidance of experienced wranglers, you'll be swaggering like a Montana cowboy before the week is out.

Mountain Sky Guest Ranch has a rich history dating back to the mid-nineteenth century. This is no modern mock-up of Old West ranching. It was an active operation during the days of cattle empires and witnessed the excitement of the gold-mining era. With its genuine Western flavor, Mountain Sky offers visitors a combination of "wide open spaces" and upscale comforts. Located just 30 miles north of Yellowstone National Park, Mountain Sky sits in Paradise Valley, in southwestern Montana. Surrounded by national forest and wilderness areas, the wooded mountainous landscape of Montana's high country is a beautiful vacation setting.

Accommodations: Guests are lodged in thirty rustic but modern cabins; each one has a refrigerator and fresh fruit delivered daily. Some cabins date back to 1929, when guests first began arriving; others have porches or picture windows to catch the spectacular mountain views.

All rates include lodging, meals, a horse for each guest over six years old, all ranch facilities, participation in all activities, and gratuities. Spring and fall have no minimum-stay requirements and are for adults only; rates are $295 per person, per night. June, July, and August are for families, and weekly rates are $2,590 to $3,150 for adults; children seven to twelve years old are $2,135 to $2,555; and children six and under are $1,680 to $1,925. During the summer the vacation week runs from Sunday to Sunday; within a couple of days, you'll make friends not only with your horse but also with the other guests.

Dining: Meals are served in the dining room of the main lodge and at barbecue cookouts. Understanding that the atmosphere of the great outdoors can generate healthy appetites, the chefs often prepare hearty as well as gourmet meals. Buffet-style breakfasts with made-to-order omelets and pancakes start the day off right. Lunches are generally served outdoors, in a casual buffet style, with homemade soups, salads, fruit and cheese, and "world cuisine" of Mexican enchiladas, Chinese stir-fry, or Italian pizza and pasta. And evening brings hors d'oeuvres at the Mountain View Lodge and a choice of poolside barbecue hot off the grill or gourmet dinners with wine. Desserts are famous here; chocolate decadence with an Irish cream anglaise or warm Valrohna cake with huckleberry ice cream and fresh huckleberries are just the beginning. Yum. Rugged attire (jeans, boots) is standard most of the time; Tuesday- and Saturday-night dinners are a bit more formal. For good conversation and evening cocktails, drop by the Mountain View Lounge.

Children's World: In summer trained counselors guide children of all ages in a program of activities. The youth schedule includes arts and crafts, nature walks, and swimming. There's even a small fishing pond reserved for children. Children ages seven and older learn horseback-riding skills with the Children's Wrangler. With the exception of family cookouts twice a week, children can stay with their friends and counselors for evening meals. The game room for teens features table tennis, a jukebox, and a pool table. There is no additional charge for these activities; the supervised children's program is part of the weekly rate. Mountain Sky's well-trained counselors promise everything from "cuddling your infant to amusing your teenager," so parents are free to enjoy some time on their own. The younger children, even infants and toddlers, are included in those activities that are appropriate, always with close supervision and care. Teens

meet on Sunday evening to plan their week, so they can choose their own excursions.

Recreation: Horseback riding is the primary sport at the ranch. Mounting your own horse and exploring hundreds of miles of trails can be as invigorating or relaxing as you want to make it. Besides morning and afternoon excursions, guests enjoy evening dinner rides, morning rides with breakfast and cowboy coffee, and all-day treks through Paradise Valley with scrumptious picnics.

In between take a dip in the heated swimming pool, play a game of tennis, or hike in the woods. Go on your own, or join one of the twice-daily hikes or adventures to historical sites, flower-filled meadows, or the wonders of Yellowstone. You might glimpse moose, elk, or even a bear. Big Creek, right in front of your cabin door, beckons anglers; a fly-fishing instructor is ready to teach you the basics and the trout are waiting. Table tennis, volleyball, softball, and horseshoes are popular games at the ranch. After active adventures, unwind in the hot tub or sauna often under the clear, starlit sky. Capping off a fun-filled day, evening Western dances, hayrides, and campfire sing-alongs are frequently planned.

MOUNTAIN SKY GUEST RANCH

P.O. Box 1219
Emigrant, Montana 59027
(406) 333–1491, (800) 548–3392
www.mtnsky.com

SNOWBIRD SKI AND SUMMER RESORT

Snowbird, Utah

Snowbird's diverse terrain includes some of the most challenging skiing in the world. Yet surprisingly, the size of its intermediate, novice, and beginner areas is greater than the total terrain of many notable resorts. Every night more than half the slopes and trails are groomed, paving the way for beginner and intermediate skiers, while leaving the rest for those who seek the light, dry Utah powder. Whatever your proficiency and desire, Snowbird accommodates you with more than 2,500 acres of wide-open bowls, gladed tree runs, steep chutes, nightly groomed trails, and cruising boulevards. From the 500 acres of terrain on Mineral Basin to the terrific novice and intermediate terrain off the Baby Thunder Chair, you'll be amazed by the sheer excitement of skiing the "Bird."

Here are a few more facts about Snowbird: a vertical rise of 3,240 continuously skiable feet; average annual snowfall of 500 inches; yes, 500 inches, and it's that "dry" Utah powder known worldwide; the longest descent, Gad Valley, at 3½ miles; the longest designated run, Chip's Run, at 2½ miles. Snowbird enjoys one of the finest ski seasons in the world. Beginning in mid-November, the ski season regularly extends 200 days. In fact, skiers have even been known to celebrate the Fourth of July on the slopes.

Snowbird offers ideal family vacations. According to *Skiing* magazine, "Snowbird has come up with what might be the best family ski value at a major ski area." The resort has also been awarded the Family Channel's Seal of Quality. Family Travel Forum selected Snowbird as one of the Top Ten Getaways for Tiny Travelers.

Accommodations: A cozy slope-side pedestrian village, Snowbird harmonizes fittingly with the rugged, natural beauty of Little Cottonwood Canyon. And everything at the resort—accommodations, restaurants, shops, skiing, and activities—is within easy walking distance.

Snowbird has three distinctive condominium properties: the Inn, the Lodge at Snowbird, and the Iron Blosam Lodge. Each offers homelike features, such as fireplaces and kitchens; pools, saunas, exercise facilities, and other services are included or easily accessible. Snowbird's flagship accommodation, the Cliff Lodge and Cliff Club, offers easy ski-in/ski-out access along with North America's foremost Persian and Oriental rug collection. Three restaurants, two lounges, and the world-class Cliff Spa and Salon make it the perfect place to retire after an exhilarating day on the slopes.

Winter rates for a room in the lodge range from $125 to $339; summer rates drop to $69 to $179. One-bedroom condominiums with full kitchen begin at $245; two bedrooms at $380; summer rates are lower. Call Central Reservations at (800) 453–3000 to help find the best accommodations for your family.

Dining: The dining at Snowbird is diverse, with over ten restaurants and lounges to please a variety of tastes and styles. Snowbird dining offers everything from Niçoise-style striped sea bass to mountain-grilled burgers to coconut beer-battered shrimp. The Aerie Restaurant is Snowbird's flagship of fine dining. Try the Lodge Bistro for cozy dinners, the wonderful view from the Atrium, or great steaks at the Steak Pit. Casual dining is found at the Birdfeeder, Keyhole Junction, and Wildflower; and families enjoy the Forklift, and, of course, Pier 49 S.F. Pizza. Children's menus are available at all sit-down restaurants. Find après-ski at the Aerie Lounge, Keyhole Cantina, Wildflower Lounge, or Lodge Bistro Lounge; nightlife with weekly jazz at the Bird, and live music, dancing, pool, and thirteen TVs at the Tram Club.

Children's World: From family ski zones to the Mini Mining Town kids trail, Snowbird is certain to please young skiers. And remember, children under twelve ski free. Snowbird's youngest guests, six weeks to three years old, are well cared for in a safe, fun environment at Camp Snowbird, a state-licensed child-care facility where an open-door policy allows parents to drop in, with picture ID, of course. Registration is required at least two weeks in advance; the $25 fee is applied toward the final day. A full day is from 8:30 A.M. to 4:30 P.M. and costs $80. Half days cannot be reserved, but are sold daily if space is available.

Day Care Camp for ages three to twelve includes snow play, arts and crafts, table games, and free play. A full day is $70; half day, morning or afternoon, is $50. When kids also take a ski lesson, the cost is $30 to $40 per day.

Camp Snowbird's ski school has one and a half–hour sessions and lift tickets for the Chickadees (ages three and four) for $55; $87 for two sessions on the same day. For Kinderbirds, ages four and five, the cost is $67 for a two and a half–hour session; $135 for a five-hour session with lunch and supervision. Kinderboards, for five- to seven-year-olds, is the same price. Young Riders, to age twelve, and teens have their own programs. Up to two children twelve and under ski the chairs free at Snowbird only, with an adult all-day lift ticket purchase.

Wednesday night the Kids Club is open from 6:30 to 10:00 P.M. for kids ages four to twelve. Admission to the "nightclub" is $38 and includes dinner, entertainment, and craft projects. And parents get a free dessert at one of the restaurants!

Summer brings different activities for Camp Snowbird (ages four to twelve, $45). Kids explore the canyon with nature hikes and science experiments; work on sports skills and arts projects; and swim every day. Children are divided by age into groups of eight to ten campers. Open early June through late August, from 8:30 A.M. to 5:00 P.M.; all days must be preregistered ($25 fee) and campers get a T-shirt and water bottle.

Recreation: Snowbird's Mountain Host program offers free guided skiing tours every day to acquaint guests with the runs and lifts best suited to their skiing abilities. All you need is a lift ticket and a smile to join the group and get better acquainted with the incredible mountain. Snowbird and Little Cottonwood Canyon neighbor Alta offer one lift ticket for both resorts. Made possible by Snowbird's second Mineral Basin chairlift, the Alta-Snowbird ticket provides two of the world's top resorts in one day of skiing.

Almost as famous as the snow, and every bit as great, is the ski school. More than 300 professional instructors offer all-day or by-the-hour private and group lessons. Or, if you want to take your vacation to new heights, try one of Snowbird's specialized seminars that address the specific interests and needs of women, seniors, snowboarders, and experts.

The Activity Center will fill you in on all that goes on: ice-skating, tubing, snowshoeing, and luging. Children must be twelve to book the luge sleds, on Tuesday, Thursday, and Saturday evenings on Chickadee. Want to be the first to make tracks in all that powder? For $20 extra, expert skiers take the first tram with experienced guides, and history is made. Also on the agenda are night skiing, summit snowmobiling, backcountry tours, swimming, and hot tubs to warm you up after all that snow.

In summer the focus of activities is still on the great outdoors. The Snowbird Canyon Racquet and Fitness Club, a short drive away, offers ten indoor and thirteen outdoor tennis courts, racquetball and squash, yoga and kickboxing, along with aerobics classes and a weight room. Try the Oriental rug tours, stargazing, and murder mystery dinner theater; or spend the day pampering yourself at the Cliff Spa. Off-site, you can visit the Winter Sports Park, tour Antelope Island, check out downtown Salt Lake City, or shop in Park City.

SNOWBIRD SKI AND SUMMER RESORT

P.O. Box 929000
Highway 210 Little Cottonwood Canyon
Snowbird, Utah 84092
(801) 742–2222, (800) 232–9542
www.snowbird.com

VAIL/BEAVER CREEK RESORTS
Vail, Colorado

Lots of folks talk of Vail and Aspen in practically the same breath. Granted, several similarities between the two come to mind: Both rank right at the top in excellent skiing, both are high in the Rockies west of Denver, both are chic and sophisticated, and to both have been appended newer developments that are upscale and family friendly—Beaver Creek at Vail and Snowmass at Aspen.

Unlike Aspen's history as an old mining town, Vail grew up in the 1960s. The modern-day careful planning and systematic development give Vail its atmosphere; it is a well-laid-out, Alpine-style village designed with the pedestrian in mind (it's nice that so few cars spoil the scenery). Actually, there are three village areas at the base of Vail Mountain—Golden Peak, Lionshead, and Vail Village—each with its own lodging, restaurants, and facilities, and each within walking distance of base lifts. In practical terms, though, since each abuts the next, most folks think of the tripartite as one friendly town. Beaver Creek is just 10 miles farther down the road. Opened in 1980, Beaver Creek, too, has been planned around a pedestrian village; in addition to the accommodations in the village, some lodges and condominiums are tucked among the grand spruce trees on the mountain. Shuttle-bus lines service the Vail Valley, within each village and between mountain bases. A year-round resort area, the Vail Valley also boasts of its summer beauty and offers art and music festivals, hiking, mountain biking, and more from June through October.

Accommodations: Lodging at Vail can be right at the mountain base a couple of skips from the chairlift and dripping with amenities, or back a few paces and not so loaded with extras, or most economically, a shuttle ride away. Of course, these options are reflected in the rates. Vail Valley's Lodging Quality Assurance program is designed to provide guests with just that: information and quality assurance. A Platinum rating represents the finest accommodations; Gold is upscale, inviting, and stylish; Silver offers comfortable accommodations; and Bronze is acceptable, with no frills. The LQA ratings are for the rooms themselves, not location, costs, or amenities. Vail/Beaver Creek Central Reservations at (800) 404–3535 can help sort it all out for you. The Lodge at Vail is the only ski-in, ski-out hotel in the village itself; additional Gold properties include Lions Head Inn, Lodge Tower, Lion Square Lodge, Manor Vail, and Christiania. Vail Central Reservations at (800) 445–8245 or (800) 525–3875 also can assist with reservations.

With deluxe accommodations and a car-free village, Beaver Creek is a favorite of families. The Park Hyatt, Trappers Lodge, the Inn at Beaver Creek, the Pines Lodge, and Beaver Creek Lodge (all suites) are all beautiful ski-in, ski-out village-based properties. The Park Hyatt offers Camp Hyatt, their own daily, year-round child-care program for ages three to twelve. The new Ritz Carlton, the Charter at Beaver Creek, and loads of condominiums and town homes offer a wide range of lodging and amenities. Nearby Arrowhead and Bachelor Gulch also offer ski-in, ski-out options. Call (800) 427–8308, (800) 404–3535, or (888) 830–7669, or visit www.beavercreek.com for more information and reservations.

Winter is divided into value season (late November to December 21 and again in April), regular season (January 5 to mid-February), and high season (Christmas and mid-February to early April). Summer rates can be as much as 50 percent lower than winter rates. Discounts for children are just about universal and package plans are often a good value. The "Cool Deals" section of www.vail.com offers guests great lodging discounts, and more than 150 properties in the Vail Valley are listed with Vail/Beaver Creek Central Reservations at (800) 427–8308.

Dining: Hungry for a hamburger? Eager to savor a juicy steak? Or is Mexican fare your idea of the perfect après-ski dinner? In the Vail Valley all this is possible, plus Italian, Chinese, French, German, and, of course, American food. With more than 110 restaurants and bars, there are lots of choices. Many restaurants are right in the lodges, such as the Lodge at Vail, Lion Square Lodge, the Landmark, and the Charter at Beaver Creek. Others are in the villages at the base of the lifts or in the pedestrian areas. Larkspur, at the base of Golden Peak, is listed by *USA Today* as a "don't miss while in Vail."

More restaurants are on the mountains and not just quick, cafeteria-style mountainside rest stops: Some hit gourmet standards. Whenever weather permits, outdoor barbecues are planned at the midmountain points. Many of the restaurants have children's menus—just ask.

Children's World: Vail and Beaver Creek both have similar high-quality programs for children. Prices and hours may vary slightly, and reservations are highly recommended for both. At Beaver Creek and at Golden Peak in Vail, the Small World Play School entertains little ones two months to six years old from 8:00 A.M. to 4:30 P.M. daily. The toddlers and preschoolers enjoy games, songs, crafts, and indoor and outdoor play in a colorful nursery/schoolhouse atmosphere. Separate playrooms for ages two to eighteen months, nineteen to thirty months, and preschoolers offer closer supervision. The cost varies by season: from $68 to $85 at Vail, and from $78 to $95 at Beaver Creek. Beaver Creek has half-day sessions from 12:30 to 4:30 P.M. ($62 to $74) or afternoon child care from 2:00 to 4:30 P.M. ($33 to $43). For more information, contact Small World at Vail at (970) 479–3285 or Beaver Creek at (970) 845–5325.

The Park Hyatt at Beaver Creek has its own Camp Hyatt children's program for ages three to twelve with activities offered daily from 9:00 A.M. to 10:00 P.M. Indoor and outdoor play (nonskiing) are featured and kids can attend for an hour, the evening, or an entire day. The price is $13.00 per hour; lunch or dinner is $5.00 additional. Mid-April to early June, Camp Hyatt is available but "on-call" and reservations must be made 24 hours in advance (800–233–1234, 970–949–1234, www.beavercreek.hyatt.com).

The Children's Ski and Snowboard Center operates out of three locations—Lionshead, Golden Peak, and the Village Hall at Beaver Creek (convenient no matter where you're staying!) and divides children into two groups (three- to six-year-olds and six- to twelve-year-olds) for daily lessons from 8:00 A.M. to 4:00 P.M. Both groups have some indoor activities as well as skiing; the older children's schedule concentrates more on skiing. At Vail, programs are $85 to $104, depending on the season, and include lesson and lift; lunch is included for ages three to six only. Equipment rentals are $15 to $18; helmets are recommended and are $10 per day. Snowboarding lessons are available for ages seven to fourteen; cost is the same, except rental equipment is $25 to $28. At Beaver Creek, programs are $95 to $120; rentals are $16 to $20; helmets are $10. Snowboard equipment is $26 to $30. More information on both children's programs is available at (970) 476–3239 or (970) 845–5464 (Beaver Creek).

Adventure Zones are special areas on the slopes just for kids. Chaos Canyon has bumps, jumps, twists, and tunnels. At others, an old fort, a tepee village and ancient Indian burial ground await exploration. On Wednesdays and Thursdays, Night Owls provides a supervised evening of fun at Adventure Ridge. Seven- to twelve-year-olds enjoy dinner and activities atop Vail Mountain from 4:30 to 8:30 P.M. during value and regular season ($55 to $60).

In summer Small World Play School is at Beaver Creek only and starts at two months of age with infant and toddler programs, and special minicamp programs for four- and five-year olds. Hours are Monday through Friday from 8:30 A.M. to 4:30 P.M.

Camp Vail and Pre-Camp Vail offer energetic weekday programs for youngsters ages three to twelve, run by the Town of Vail. Both programs are $60 daily, and have options for five- or ten-day coupons at a reduced rate; hours are 7:30 A.M. to 5:30 P.M. for ages thirty months to five years, and 8:00 A.M. to 5:00 P.M. for kids five to twelve. Campers participate in caving, orienteering, swimming, golf, fishing, and climbing as well as art, drama, and nature discovery. Call (970) 479–2292 for details.

At Beaver Creek, Discovery Camp ($75) is for ages five to seven; and Adventure Camp ($85) for ages eight to twelve. Pony rides, panning for gold, river rafting, mountain biking, ropes course, and miniature golf are some of the activities, all geared toward each age group. Field trips and special evening activities are also planned. For a true Rocky Mountain adventure, the 5-Star Camp ($95) for ages five to twelve, with age restrictions on some activities, does more unusual activities such as kayaking, horseback riding, or go-carts. Call (970) 845–5464 for details and reservations.

Recreation: The name of the game is skiing, and the Vail Valley has all the ingredients for an excellent ski holiday. In the middle of the White River National Forest, Vail Mountain rises to 11,570 feet; at Beaver Creek the summit is 11,440 feet. The vertical drop is more than 3,450 feet at Vail and 4,040 feet at Beaver Creek. An average annual snowfall between 300 and 350 inches (and an artificial snowmaking system) accounts for a season lasting from late November to mid-April.

Vail and Beaver Creek skiable terrain totaling over 6,900 acres (lift tickets for the two mountains are interchangeable) provides variety for all levels of skiers, from gentle beginner slopes to challenging intermediates to exciting mogul and bowl skiing. Vail's Blue Sky Basin provides a unique wilderness ski experience, featuring 645 acres of natural, gladed terrain in two world-class bowls. At Vail the runs are ranked 28 percent beginner, 32 percent intermediate, and 40 percent advanced; at Beaver Creek the breakdown is 34 percent beginner, 39 percent intermediate, and 27 percent advanced.

So that you can cut tracks through the Rocky Mountain powder in style, a very large ski school (1,200 instructors!) can assist you. In addition to the typical group and private lessons for all ability levels, the Vail/Beaver Creek Ski School offers free Meet the Mountain introductory tours: a morning of skiing with guest-services staff who acquaint you with the area's history and topography, classes with videotaped analysis, and high-powered workshops in mogul and powder skiing. Or enroll in lessons in cross-country skiing, which is so refined here that distinctions are made between backcountry skiing, telemark skiing, and track skiing.

Other wintertime sports include ice-skating at Dobson Ice Arena, Black Family Rink in Beaver Creek, or Nottingham Lake; snowmobiling at Piney Lake; and ice-fishing. Snowcat tours to above 10,000 feet offer spectacular views, and if you can walk, you can snowshoe, for an up-close view of winter. The Colorado Ski Museum is here, or relax in one of the three cinemas. An evening outing in a horse-drawn sleigh may be the right way to finish off a perfect day, or enjoy a brisk horseback ride in the snow. Indoor evening entertainment includes nightclubs and movie theaters; favorite haunts for kids are the video arcades and the Vail Youth Center.

Even after the last skier comes down the mountain in late spring, fun in the Vail Valley continues. As in the winter, summertime activities focus on the beautiful outdoors. Hiking through stands of aspens along the trail systems up Vail Mountain and Beaver Creek Mountain, biking on paths through wildflowers, and fishing in mountain streams get you back to nature. Ride horseback at Eagle Ranch, Beaver Creek Stables, and Piney River Ranch, or muster your courage for river rafting.

Vail Valley has eleven golf courses, and more on the way. Some are public, some private or semi-private, and some are connected to various lodging in the Valley. You're sure to find the one that's just right for your skills. With 300 days of sunshine each year, tennis shines here. Free courts at Golden Peak, or for a little Mozart with your game, schedule one of the Ford Park courts at concert time. Target

Tennis is a new teaching concept practically guaranteed to improve your game. Fancy a spa experience? There are at least ten in the area, including the natural Yampah Spa and Vapor Caves in nearby Glenwood Springs. And Beaver Creek hosts weekly rodeos—great fun for the whole family.

Summer Adventure Ridge starts with a scenic gondola ride to the Ridge, where you can spend the entire day. In addition to laser tag, trampoline, orienteering, hiking, disc golf, sledding, guided tours, and mountain bikes, the kids can even hunt for buried bones at the Dino Dig. Admission pass includes lunch at Talon's Deck. Open select dates June to September. The Discovery Center, at the top of the Eagle Bahn Gondola, teaches about our environment through fun, interactive displays and nature hikes. Cultural events are plentiful: the Arts Festival in June, Vail Valley Music Festival all summer, International Dance, the Vail Jazz Festival in August, and Jammin' Jazz, a free concert series at LionsHead Sun Dial Plaza. At Beaver Creek, the Vilar Center for the Arts has children's theater, stand-up comedy, Broadway shows, and musicals. Free movie nights for kids twelve and under, plus costume contests add to the fun. Sunday afternoons, Vail Valley chefs demonstrate their skills. All in all, Vail/Beaver Creek is a tasty resort!

VAIL/BEAVER CREEK RESORTS

Vail, Colorado 81658
(800) 525–2257, (800) 525–3875
www.beavercreek.snow.com,
www.vail.snow.com

WEST

California
Idaho
Nevada
Oregon

THE ALISAL GUEST RANCH AND RESORT

Solvang, California

Okay, so cattle ranches are not the first thing that comes to mind when you think of Southern California or Solvang. Nevertheless, it is the West, and at least one does exist. In the Santa Ynez Valley of southern California is a real working cattle ranch—the Alisal (from the Chumash Indian word meaning "grove of sycamores"). Some things just don't change—cattle have been grazing here for almost 200 years, and century-old sycamore trees line the private entrance road. Fifty-six years ago the current owner's father, a cattleman himself, decided to open the ranch to guests. Today visitors enjoy the atmosphere of an active ranch with the facilities of a resort on this 10,000-acre spread. This is California, after all, so one would expect golf, tennis, first-class accommodations, fine dining, and wine tasting, along with horses and wranglers. And that indeed is what the Alisal delivers. Named a Family Resort of the Year by *Family Circle*; *Sunset Magazine* also ranked it one of the "50 Best Dude Ranches in the West." Only forty minutes from Santa Barbara and two hours from Los Angeles, the Alisal is a welcome haven to harried city-dwellers that is open year-round.

Accommodations: Decorated in classic California ranch design, seventy-three cottages accommodating up to 200 guests are clustered near the swimming pool and tennis courts or overlooking the golf course. All have a wood-burning fireplace, covered front porch, and garden views. Suites offer a sitting room and soaring ceilings. Based on a Modified American Plan, room rates range from $410 to $435 daily; two-room suites are $465 to $495. Children two and under stay free, ages three through six are $50, and six years and older are $80. There's a two-night minimum, and Saturday check-ins are not allowed. Weekdays between early September and early June, a Round-Up vacation package is offered. For the price of a room, the Alisal includes unlimited golf, horseback riding (two-hour rides), tennis, and fishing for two people. The package is also available weekends from November through March.

Dining: The Ranch Room serves breakfast (a lavish buffet or a la carte) and gourmet dinners from a five-item menu that changes every evening. Dinner is a dress-up affair; jackets are required for gentlemen (ties optional), and ladies and children dress appropriately for fine dining. Parents with small children are encouraged to have dinner at 6:30 P.M., before the peak hours of 7:15 to 8:15 P.M. Lunch is not included in the room rate but can be ordered from the Chuckwagon Grill (poolside snack bar) and at the Ranch Course Grill (open from 8:00 A.M. to 3:00 P.M.) on the golf course. The River Grill is open daily from 7:00 A.M. to 8:00 P.M. for all meals. In summer you can saddle up early for a breakfast ride to Adobe Camp or enjoy a seafood barbecue at the lake or a Cal-Mex barbecue at the rodeo arena in the evening. Saturday brings an all-ranch barbecue at the pool lawn. The Oak Room Lounge, an inviting room with a large fireplace, is decorated with warm colors, rustic Western artifacts, and Native American–style rugs. Cocktails and complimentary appetizers are served about 5:30 P.M. and stories of the day's activities are shared. It's adults-only after 8:00 P.M., with live entertainment and dancing that begins at 6:30 P.M. During the summer and holidays, the Waggin' Tongue Lounge by the pool is open daily from 11:30 A.M. to 5:00 P.M.

Children's World: All summer long and at holiday times, counselors conduct an active schedule of arts and crafts, scavenger hunts, volleyball, hikes, croquet, and other outdoor games.

From age seven and up, children can participate in horseback riding on the trail rides ($60 for two hours) or in private lessons. Younger children get corral rides and equestrian-care lessons. Everyone learns more about ranch animals at the on-site petting zoo. Children's golf and tennis lessons are also available. Children love the private lake, where they can participate in fishing, boating, or canoeing ($12 to $50 hour). Summer evenings may include campfires with sing-alongs and stories, which are always better at the lake setting. Kid's Mini Rodeo is staged weekly in the summer—this is every kid's dream of being a cowboy come true. After watching wranglers perform, they get to participate in branding (on leather or wood), roping, and rodeo-style games; a Western barbecue completes the evening.

In the summer the children's program (no charge) runs seven days a week, all day. The arts-and-crafts room is open daily from 9:30 A.M. to 5:30 P.M., where activities are ongoing; there are small charges for materials. Activities such as disc golf, chalk art, relay races and lawn games, dodge ball or kick ball, face painting, and various water games are scheduled during the day—children can drop in and out as they are interested in the activity.

Children ages three to five meet every night but Saturday at 6:00 P.M. for dinner and evening fun until around 9:00 P.M., when evening family activities start. Kids ages six to ten have their nature cookouts, a pool bash, barbecues, and movies from 6:00 P.M.

'Tweens (eleven to twelve years old) share some things, like movies, but have their own dinner activities at the Chuckwagon Grill or Adobe Camp as well. Late night they may have bingo, talent shows, country dancing, or an adventure at the Adobe Camp. The summertime activities for teens involve their favorite things: eating, music, movies, and sports. Teens have their own section of the weekly dinner events, plus off-property movies, late-night campfires, or movies at the ranch.

During the winter, supervised arts and activities go from 10:00 A.M. to 4:00 P.M., with golf,

tennis, and horseback-riding lessons filling in the other times. Although the program is free, some crafts, lessons, and horseback riding do have a charge. Check the daily program.

Recreation: Most recreational activities at Alisal have fees. Family Times allow sharing of two-hour nature walks, archery, a ropes course, and crafts such as tie-dye and creative beading. Evening entertainment begins at 8:30 or 9:00 P.M. Family bingo, comedy, clowns and storytelling, country dancing, and more are offered. 'Tweens and teens have their own programs. Kids and family activities are pretty much nonstop from early morning to late night, with lots of choices.

Be sure to saunter over to the barn to be matched with the perfect mount for the twice-daily trail rides ($60 per ride). A breakfast ride is offered three times a week in summer, twice a week during the rest of the year. More than 50 miles of trails meander through oak and sycamore groves in the rolling hills and along the lake. Wranglers are happy to share a bit of advice about riding, information about the ranch, or maybe even some tall tales along the way.

Trading trails for tees, the gently rambling fairways of two eighteen-hole golf courses are graced with eucalyptus as well as oak and sycamore trees and occasionally a deer or two. Each of the two championship golf courses, the River Course and the Ranch Course, has distinct characteristics shaped by its unique terrain. The driving range, putting green, and practice trap can keep you so busy you'll ride off into the sunset on a golf cart rather than a horse! The resident pro and the pro shop can help with anything from lessons to new equipment. On the tennis courts (seven in all, located in one of the most scenic areas of the ranch) you're likely to find a good game from 8:00 A.M. to 5:30 P.M., or the resident pro conducting private and group lessons.

If your interests are more wet-and-wild, you might swim in the large outdoor heated pool or head to the lake and hop aboard a sailboat, rowboat, paddleboat, canoe, or kayak ($25 to $50). Even beginners find lots of enjoyment in the sailing and fishing lessons offered. The lake—man-made, but mature and encompassing more than ninety-five acres—is stocked with bass, bluegill, and catfish, much to the delight of every angler. A "catch and release" policy protects the fish.

After riding, golfing, playing tennis, swimming, sailing, and fishing, you can always jog, join a guided nature walk, play volleyball, badminton, horseshoes, shuffleboard, croquet, or archery, or take on the new challenge course. Tired yet? Indoors you might play pool or table tennis in the recreation room or relax in the adults-only library with a good book or board game by the fireplace. Be sure to save energy for the evenings, filled with square dancing, cookouts, and movies as well. Every summer Wednesday brings a country fair and rodeo.

THE ALISAL GUEST RANCH AND RESORT

1054 Alisal Road
Solvang, California 93463
(805) 688–6411, (800) 4–ALISAL
www.alisal.com

COFFEE CREEK RANCH
Trinity Center, California

Coffee Creek Ranch, Northern California's only three-diamond dude ranch, is located approximately 300 miles north of San Francisco. Surrounded by National Forest and the Trinity Alps Wilderness Area, the ranch covers 367 acres along Coffee Creek and is home to wranglers and dudes alike. In 1877, Old Charley Henseley staked three claims along Coffee Creek; in 1900 he lost them all in a poker game to Ben Pinkham for $1.00. Mrs. Pinkham started a boarding house for the miners, and it all began then, evolving into a dude ranch in 1946. In 1966 the original ranch house burned completely; built in 1899, Oak Grove Cottage is now the oldest building on the ranch and is currently being restored. The ranch has been in the Hartman family since 1976, being handed down to the next generation; current owner/managers Alicia and Shane Ryan.

Whether you are an old pro at horseback riding or a greenhorn mounting up for the first time, the ranch hands will ensure that your horse and your excursion match your abilities. You can roam this territory all day long or ease into your new cowboy lifestyle more slowly with a half-hour lesson or a two-hour trail ride. Copper Creek Ranch is open from Easter to Thanksgiving.

Accommodations: The sixteen cozy, secluded cottages (one or two bedrooms) are scattered among the trees. Rustic on the outside, all modern and cozy on the inside, each cottage is decorated according to its brand; Circle B for instance has butterflies, bears, and Bigfoot. Spring and fall are geared toward adults; kids are welcome, although there's no specific program or activities for them. In summer, however, families rule. One-week stays are required, beginning on Saturdays. Per person rates for a one-bedroom are $1,025 for adults ($922.50 for ages 55 and up, a nice touch), teens are $1,005, children three to twelve are $905, and the under-three set is $300. Cribs, playpens, and highchairs are complimentary.

The rates only increase by $10 to $20 per person for two-bedrooms, so book early! Rates include your private cabin in the woods, daily maid service, three meals daily, all activities and entertainment, the children's program—just about everything except horseback riding, which has extra fees in the summer. Two-hour rides are $35; a weekly rate of $350 gives you all rides (at least four hours daily) including the overnight pack trip. Friday is departure day, and the horses' day off.

Dining: Recognizing the healthy appetites that fresh air and exercise can generate, the main dining room serves up hearty, nutritious meals with fresh fruit and vegetables, Black Angus beef, and homemade bread from old family recipes. Outdoor barbecues and poolside cookouts are friendly evening events; Mexican and Italian buffets please everyone. For an adventure, ride out to a cowboy breakfast or a picnic on the trial. Beer and wine are served in the Pony Room.

Children's World: In the summer months the youth program, a complimentary service operating from 9:00 A.M. to 5:00 P.M., Saturday through Thursday, attracts children ages three to seventeen. On its fun-filled schedule are archery, nature walks, pedalboating, gold panning, games, and crafts. Ages three to five are designated Cowboys and Cowgirls, and get free pony rides, playtime with the Corral Critters (rabbits, lambs, pigs), lawn games, and story time; and just wait to hear your child tell about feeding the ducks and geese! Junior Wranglers, for ages six to eleven, branch out into canoeing, swimming, and fishing in the pond, and one free riding lesson. Bronc Busters (twelve- to seventeen-year-olds) get to do it all plus their own special roping lessons, overnight campout, orienteering, rifle and trap shoot instruction, plus hiking to the lake. Although there's no formal program in the evening, counselors are generally present at the evening family activities. For children under three, the weekly rate includes baby-sitting while you're out on the trail. If additional baby-sitting is required, you can make arrangements for $6.25 an hour.

Recreation: Saddle up and head into the wilderness for an all-day ride or a two-hour ride. You'll venture up into the mountains and through the wooded landscape along a clear fresh stream; maybe you'll spot a deer or a bear. Even "dudes" will soon experience the friendly spirit of a trail ride.

Try your hand at fishing; you've a choice of stream, river, pond, lake, or wilderness. The locals say that Coffee Creek yields up some mighty fine trout, so an afternoon with rod and reel may turn into a fresh-fish supper. Perhaps you'll test your keen eye on the archery, rifle, or trap range. Hiking trips are an option, and mountain bike trails run through the wilderness area. When not out and about, enjoy the heated swimming pool, volleyball, shuffleboard, basketball, or pedal boating. Doing a lovely bit of nothing is also an option—just let the mountain air work its magic.

Evenings are lively at the ranch, with more activities than days of the week. Hayrides, bonfires, dancing, bingo and talent shows, karaoke and a live band, and even a rodeo liven things up after dark.

COFFEE CREEK RANCH

HC 2, Box 4940
Trinity Center, California 96091
(530) 266–3343, (800) 624–4480
www.coffeecreekranch.com

HYATT REGENCY LAKE LAS VEGAS RESORT, SPA AND CASINO

Henderson, Nevada

In this twenty-one-acre gloriously natural setting of mountains, desert, and lake, it's hard to believe you're only 17 miles from the glitz and glitter of the Las Vegas Strip. It's also just a short day trip to Lake Mead, Hoover Dam, Red Rock Canyon, and the Valley of Fire. Who says you can't have everything? Reflecting the best desert architecture, the Moroccan flavor is apparent in the high arches and deep loggias, the grilled ironwork, and the relaxed, open feeling engendered by mountains in the desert. Comfortably terraced into the hillside, Hyatt Lake Las Vegas rates a Mobile four-star, AAA four-diamond ranking.

Accommodations: The 493 guest rooms and 47 suites reflect the open-air style of the Mediterranean, and most have views of the lake, mountains, or golf course. The theme is Moroccan and features imported furnishings; most rooms have small balconies and all have refrigerators. A real pleasure is that the windows actually open, so you can enjoy the wonderfully clear desert air. Rates range from $129 in the low season to $269 in the high season: January to June and September to November, respectively. Families can upgrade to an Alcove suite for $100 or an executive one-bedroom suite for an additional $175. A resort fee of $10 per room per night covers incidentals.

A sample summer package: Sunshine on Sale includes one complimentary session of Camp Hyatt for up to two children, kids under twelve eat free from the children's menu when dining with an adult, and a 50 percent discount off the second room, plus a free night's stay. Rates are $189 in low season, $299 in high season. Family Fun Experience, from $169 to $219, also offers special options for families.

Dining: Japengo, the showcase restaurant,

features a full sushi bar (rated best in the valley by *Zagat*), a presentation kitchen where you can watch the culinary artistry, and a menu inspired by the Pacific Rim and exotic Asian flavors. Inspired by the Moroccan tradition of cooking in an earthenware pot, Café Tajine, open for breakfast, lunch, and dinner, serves New American cuisine with an international flavor. Dine indoors or out, with the ever-present scenic views. The poolside Sandsabar & Grill keeps you well fed and watered. The twenty-four-hour Marrakesh Express is the place to have that special coffee, shop for the unusual delicacy to take home or enjoy in your room, or indulge in a late-night dessert. Catch your favorite midday game or have a nightcap at the Baraka Bar, inside the Baraka Casino; or people-watch, as a change from the scenery, while sipping a drink at the Arabesque Lounge in the lobby. Restaurants have a children's menu in the summer or during promotions only.

Children's World: The Moroccan theme of Camp Mud Castle fits right into the desert-like environs. Open daily year-round, hours are from 10:00 A.M. to 5:00 P.M. and again from 6:00 to 10:00 P.M. for an evening session. Advance reservations are required. As with other Hyatt Camps, a good-size room is dedicated to camp activities that are diverse, and directly related to the unique aspects and location of each property. Petroglyph art, hula hoop and limbo, sundown fishing, a trip to the "swimmin' hole," summer toad hunts, and playground free time are just some of the things youngsters do here. Evenings bring stargazing and a starlight dinner along with games, movies, drumming, and karaoke contests. Planned for ages three through twelve, the cost is $27 for 10:00 A.M. to 1:00 P.M. or

2:00 to 5:00 P.M. sessions; or $40 until 2:00 P.M. with lunch. The evening session is also $40 and includes dinner. And when they say "daily," they mean "daily"—kids even have their own New Year's Eve gala party!

Recreation: Being ranked twenty-eighth in *Golf Digest*'s "Top 75 Golf Resorts in America" apparently isn't sufficient for this resort. Aiming to be a golf mecca, in addition to the two Jack Nicklaus Signature Golf Courses, they've completed the Falls, a course designed by Tom Weiskopf, and plans are to add a fourth course, designed by Tom Fazio, in 2004/05. The Falls has been voted "Best New Upscale Public Course" by *Golf Digest* and one of the "Top Ten You Can Play" by *Golf Magazine*. All the courses take advantage of the dramatic desert scenery and the largest privately owned lake in Nevada; the Falls even overlooks the famous Las Vegas Strip, seen in an amazing natural setting. Reflection Bay Golf Club is home to the Nicklaus/Flick Game Improvement School if your game needs a boost.

The heart of the resort is the 320-acre lake, with 10 miles of shoreline and beaches for water play and sunning. Take a spin in a paddleboat or kayak, sail, relax, and go fishing in an electric boat or rent a bicycle and ride along the lakeshore.

The daily Spa Moulay membership is included with the resort fee, so take advantage between 6:00 A.M. and 9:00 P.M. You'll find nine treatment rooms to pamper you. After a workout at the fitness center, two outdoor pools beckon you to relax in the tented cabana shaded by palm trees. The children's pool with water slide keeps youngsters happy for hours. Sport Court is the place to play volleyball, short court tennis, or basketball; a putting green, croquet, and horseshoes while away an afternoon. A complimentary bird-watching backpack sends you off with binoculars and an identification book, while a

stargazing kit shows you planets and stars.

The Baraka Casino is European-styled, with gaming tables and, of course, slot machines. The difference here is that it includes scenic views from the two-story windows, unique to casinos in this area. If you want more and bigger, a complimentary shuttle will take you to the Strip. Actually, during the day, and in small doses, Las Vegas is an exciting place for kids too. The various hotels outdo each other for exciting attractions: Walk under and around lions in a glass den at MGM Grand, acrobats fly through the lobby at Circus Circus Adventuredome; a roller coaster circles New York–New York; at the Luxor, learn about ancient Egypt through IMAX movies and ride an elevator almost sideways to the top of the pyramid; knights joust at the Excalibur; Atlantis falls at Caesars and the waters dance to music at the Bellagio—the list goes on and on. This is just a sample, so you see why making several trips is not a bad idea.

Closer to home you'll find MonteLago Village, connected to the resort by walkways and water taxis, and offering dining, shops, and entertainment along the water's edge. Reminiscent of an ancient Mediterranean village, you can stroll the narrow shaded streets or shop on the two-level bridge as if you were promenading on Florence's Ponte Vecchio in Italy.

HYATT REGENCY LAKE LAS VEGAS RESORT, SPA AND CASINO

101 Montelargo Boulevard
Henderson, Nevada 89011
(702) 567–1234, (800) 233–1234
www.lakelasvegas.hyatt.com

THE INN OF THE
SEVENTH MOUNTAIN

Bend, Oregon

A vacation in the woods and mountains of the great Pacific Northwest, the serenity of hiking in the forest, and the excitement of exploring the Deschutes River whisk you away from city life and everyday routines. The Inn of the Seventh Mountain, located on the sunny side of the Cascade Mountains of central Oregon, is a year-round family resort that boasts a cool forest setting and warm hospitality. Nearby Mount Bachelor is the seventh peak in the chain of mountains running south from the Columbia River and the border with Washington State, hence the name. The resort aims to be "a place where you can interact with nature in a hundred different ways, and interact with your family in the only way that really matters." Encircled by peaks, lakes, and meadows, set in the midst of tranquil beauty with all the necessary amenities, the resort makes it easy to accomplish that goal.

Accommodations: You can choose from a variety of accommodations, from a lodge room to a full condominium apartment, depending on the size of your family. Most of the lodge rooms have a private balcony; the condominium units have one to three bedrooms, fireplace, kitchen, and balcony. The architecture is modern yet rustic, and natural-wood facades blend well with the wooded landscape. Rooms range from $75 to $115 depending on the size and season; spring and fall are slightly lower than summer and holiday times. One-bedroom condos are $110 to $165; lofts are $155 to $195, and three-bedroom units are $220 all the time. For a two-night minimum stay between June and September, the resort offers a "See the Sun Again" special for $89 per person per night (based on double occu-

pancy; children under twelve stay free) with two $55 vouchers a day good toward golf, white-water rafting, Kids' Quest, mountain biking, horseback riding, canoeing, and meals at the Gray Hawk Grill or the Mountain Market. Inquire about other packages as well. Improvements are ongoing and the inn plans to "renovate everything but the scenery." Plans for the condominiums include rich textures and earthen colors, brick tiles, and folk art.

Dining: Award-winning chef Christopher Berning has joined the inn and opened a new restaurant, Gray Hawk's Grill, open daily for breakfast, lunch, and dinner. Using local products, the menu is quintessential Pacific Northwest, creatively prepared. Smoked mussels steamed in Oregon chardonnay, or a grilled Black Angus tenderloin served on smoked salmon and morel mushroom ravioli with grain mustard demi-glace is just a small sample of what awaits your taste buds. Gray Hawk's lounge is open nightly. For a light lunch or dinner, stop by the Mountain Market for a sandwich or salad.

Children's World: In addition to individual baby-sitting, which the staff can help you arrange, events are scheduled all day long for your child's enjoyment. In summer and winter the recreation office publishes a flyer, *This Week at the Inn,* to help you keep track of all the activities. From Memorial Day to Labor Day, Christmas, and spring break, Kids' Quest is a supervised play program for children ages five to eleven. A daily charge of $40 buys lunch, arts-and-crafts classes, movies, and more from 9:00 A.M. to 4:00 P.M. each day. Your child might also participate in a tennis clinic, take a hayride or a sleigh ride, search out treasures on a scavenger hunt, or take a field trip. There are also two playgrounds and a wading pool, and two swimming pools for water recreation.

In winter Mount Bachelor Ski School offers day care and ski/board lessons for children.

The West Village Lodge and Sunrise Lodge, at the base of the mountain, have day-care centers for little ones six weeks to ten years old; age-appropriate activities are planned from 8:30 A.M. to 4:30 P.M.; 7:30 A.M. to 4:00 P.M. on weekends. Daily rates are $40 for children thirty months and older; twenty-nine months and younger is $45. An hourly rate (limited space) is $10 or $12, with a two-hour minimum. Children may bring their lunch, or box lunch is available for $5.00, and parents are welcome to eat with their children. For an additional $25, Snow-play is a one-hour introduction to skiing that can be added for three-year-olds. For children four and over, Mountain Masters combines day care and a half-day lesson for $90 not including rentals. Mountain Masters without the day care, to age twelve, is $75 for a full day with lunch; $50 for a half day (two-hour lesson). Rentals are $10.00 and lunch for a half-day session is $5.00. A Guaranteed Kids Package for ages six to twelve ensures beginners learn everything they need to start riding the lifts and enjoying the mountain. An all-day program includes morning and afternoon instruction, lift ticket, and lunch for $75. Children are grouped by age and ability.

Recreation: The recreation department at the inn plans activities for every member of the family, concentrating on water sports, swimming, tennis, and raft trips on the river in the summer; and ice-skating, cross-country skiing, and sleigh rides in the winter. Wintertime also means the thrill of downhill skiing at nearby Mount Bachelor, only 14 miles from the inn.

In summer you just have to discover the beauty of the Deschutes River. Take a relaxing canoe ride and get back to nature, or join a moonlight raft trip. For more daring souls, there are guided white-water raft trips

through the rapids. If you prefer to take in the scenic river from land, horseback riding is a great alternative; group trail rides run along the river and into the Deschutes National Forest. The National Forest is also a picturesque haven for hikers and joggers. For the fisherman, the recreation office arranges trips to the favorite spots with a naturalist guide. Spend an afternoon in sailboarding or water-skiing classes. For a rock-climbing challenge, Smith Rock State Park is one of the best places in the West.

Back at the inn, take a dip in one of the two pools, try the 65-foot water slide, rent a bicycle, play a good game of tennis on one of the four Plexipave courts (group clinics and private lessons are offered), work out in an aerobic-exercise class, try your talents in an arts-and-crafts class, go rollerskating, or get lucky in a bingo game. The rec office organizes all sorts of ball games—softball, volleyball, football, lacrosse, and soccer. Join a hayride, complete with a stop for a marshmallow roast, play table tennis, take in a poolside movie, or head to the video-game room. Then relax in the sauna or one of the hot whirlpool baths.

The Oregon High Desert Museum, just 6 miles south of Bend, discloses the natural and cultural history of this region. The museum makes for a fun as well as educational afternoon.

This part of Oregon experiences beautiful Indian summers, so activities continue well into the fall. During the winter months special treats include ice-skating, sleigh rides, cross-country skiing (with lessons for novices), and horseback riding through the snow-covered landscape.

The inn is the closest lodging facility to the Mount Bachelor ski resort (800–829–2442, www.mtbachelor.com) and provides daily transportation to the mountain base. With 3,365 vertical feet, 71 runs, 3,683 skiable acres, and plenty of dry powder, Mount Bachelor means excellent downhill skiing for all levels of ability. You'll also find snowboarding, cross-country and telemark skiing, snowshoe-ing, tubing, and more. The five lodges at the mountain have restaurants for breakfast, lunch, snacks, and cocktails; ski shops; and the ski school, which offers group lessons for all ranges of expertise as well as private lessons. The season is long here, attracting many visitors late into spring.

THE INN OF THE SEVENTH MOUNTAIN

18575 Southwest Century Drive
Bend, Oregon 97702
(541) 382–8711, (800) 452–6810
www.seventhmountain.com

KONOCTI HARBOR RESORT AND SPA
Kelseyville, California

Konocti Harbor Resort and Spa is a lakeside resort in Northern California, approximately two and a half hours from San Francisco. If you're driving from the city or other points south, your vacation begins with a tour of the Napa Valley wine country on your way to Konocti. Open year-round, the inn sits beneath the 4,300-foot peak of Mount Konocti (an extinct volcano) on the southern shore of Clear Lake, which stretches 25 miles by 8 miles. All this clear blue water of California's largest national lake provides the setting for much of Konocti's recreation: swimming, boating, and fishing. Although today you'll find just happy, active visitors heading to the water, a romantic Indian legend tells of a saddened princess whose many tears formed the lake.

Accommodations: Hotel/motel rooms, apartments, and beach cottages make up the 266 guest units at the Konocti. All have different features, but families like the beach cottages for their convenient location and kitchen, open-air porch, and space. Vista Cloud, close to the marina and a short walk to the Main Lodge is also popular with families for its bunk beds, sitting room, and van-

ity area. Some rooms include a private balcony, and most afford views of the lake. The locations of some make the marina easily accessible, while others are near the tennis courts. Sixteen deluxe apartments are situated near the spa. The apartments and cottages have complete kitchens and living rooms, and many have been recently renovated.

Rates vary not only by size and season but by concert nights. During the in-season, May through October, Beach Cottages are $169 during midweek and $199 on weekends and concert nights year-round. Vista Cloud family units are $99 and $109. Holiday and special event rates are $229 and $119, respectively. Low-season midweek rates are $89 at the Vista Cloud and $129 at the Beach. Children eighteen years and younger staying in their parents' room are accommodated free of charge. Rollaway beds and cribs are available for $10 a night. Tennis, fishing, spa, and golf package plans are offered.

Dining: The Classic Rock Cafe, which is open for breakfast, lunch, and dinner, features California cuisine in at atmosphere filled with fun and music, and memorabilia of the stars. Adjacent to the two pool areas are snack bars so that you don't have to interrupt a lazy day of sunning for refreshments. For evening entertainment, the Full Moon Saloon beckons. Located lakeside with indoor and outdoor seating, Lake County's hottest night-club has live entertainment on Friday and Saturday year-round, and daily from June through Labor Day.

Children's World: Kids at Konocti practically live in the water, with hours spent at the lake swimming, boating, and fishing. They also take hikes and nature walks, play horse-shoes, and putt around the eighteen holes of peewee golf. Little ones particularly like the two wading pools and the playground equipped with a slide, swings, and monkey bars, while those a bit older head to the recreation center for table tennis, pool, and video games. The children's programs are open daily in the summer and the fee is $25 for each session. The events start at 10:00 A.M. Monday through Friday, break at 4:00 P.M., and pick up again from 4:00 to 10:00 P.M. for a night camp. Baby-sitting is not available although supervised care is available on concert nights and holidays year-round.

Recreation: With Konocti's full-service marina, you can take your pick of water sports. Dock your own boat here or rent a paddleboat, Wave Runner, motorboat, or sailboat for an adventure on the lake. Go fishing in these waters where the rewards are many: largemouth bass, trout, crappie, and catfish. There's even a bass-fishing pro to advise you. Water-ski across the lake, or board the *Konocti Princess,* a nostalgic paddle wheeler, for an afternoon excursion. Swim in the lake waters from the small sandy beach, or do laps in one of the two Olympic-size pools overlooking the lake. Two wading pools for children are also available.

The Dancing Springs Health Spa is designed to pamper you a bit. This facility features an indoor pool and capable personnel who will help you relax with a massage, facial, or herbal body wrap. Take a fitness class or work out with free weights or cardiovascular equipment if you're feeling more energetic. Day use of all facilities is complimentary for guests.

The eight tennis courts are lighted for evening play, and lessons with the tennis pro are available. After a good practice session with a ball machine, reward yourself with a new accessory from the tennis shop.

Five area golf courses, all within 20 miles, honor Konocti's golf packages. Round up a fast-paced game of softball, basketball, volleyball, or table tennis, or slow down to a more relaxing tempo with horseshoes and shuffleboard. While jogging and hiking, explore the scenic, hilly terrain that borders the lake.

The Classic Concert Showroom is an intimate, 1,000-seat dinner theater with an all-star line-up. Pat Benatar, Dan Fogelberg, Randy Travis, Loretta Lynn, Hall & Oates, the B-52s, and Kenny G just for starters. The Outdoor Konocti Field Amphitheater is the site of concerts "under the stars, with the brightest of stars." This lakeside venue is configured so that all of the 5,000 seats are within 200 feet of the stage, with comfortable seats and video screens. Stars such as Bob Dylan, Melissa Etheridge, the Beach Boys, B. B. King, and many, many more perform here. Check to see who's there when you are.

Other nearby attractions are Anderson Marsh State Park, Clear Lake State Park, Indian Gaming, Crazy Creek Gliders, and a historical schoolhouse and museum. You can make the kids go to school on their vacation!

KONOCTI HARBOR RESORT AND SPA

8727 Soda Bay Road
Kelseyville, California 95451
(707) 279–4281, (800) 660–LAKE
www.konoctiharbor.com

LA COSTA RESORT AND SPA

Carlsbad, California

Everyone should have at least one spa experience in their life. La Costa is a luxurious resort, a serious spa, and somewhat of a legend. In fact, it was the first establishment to revive the spa regimen as Americans became more health-conscious in the 1960s. Today you can pursue a program of exercise and sound nutrition, redefining your lifestyle after years of sedentary executive matters; or you can indulge in a program of sheer pampering, relieving the stress and tensions of the everyday world.

Located in Carlsbad, just thirty minutes north of San Diego and ninety minutes south of Los Angeles, La Costa enjoys lovely Southern California weather and a picturesque setting of rolling hills. The 400 lush green acres of this four-diamond resort provide an oasis of relaxation.

Accommodations: Four hundred seventy-three guest rooms and suites are all decorated in a Spanish style, and situated around courtyards, near the tennis facilities, adjacent to the spa, and along the golf courses. Room rates are $345 to $520 a night; one- and two-bedroom suites are $630 to $2,400 a night for the Presidential Suite. Children under eighteen staying in their parents' room are free; cribs are provided without charge. Be sure to inquire about the spa, golf, and tennis package plans. A $15 per night resort fee is assessed for incidentals.

Dining: Legends California Bistro features classic California cuisine, along with vegetarian selections from the Chopra Center. It's open daily from 6:30 A.M. to 9:00 P.M.; 10:00 P.M. on weekends, when a jazz trio plays; Sunday brunch is also accompanied by live jazz. Dine indoors or out in the California sunshine. At the Marketplace you'll find your Starbucks morning coffee, TCBY treats, and an Internet cafe, if you need a technology fix. Weather permitting, weekend lunches and drinks are served poolside.

Children's World: Camp La Costa is active year-round and operates from 9:00 A.M. to 4:00 P.M. daily. For five- to twelve-year-olds, the fun includes golf and tennis lessons, swimming, kite flying, and arts and crafts. Kids not only enjoy themselves, they often learn something too, as they experience the surroundings in imaginative and entertaining ways. The fee is $35 for a full day, $20 for a half day. If less time is desired, hourly rates are $7.00 to $10.00. In the evenings Camp La Costa at Night takes over with dinner and entertainment from 6:00 to 10:00 P.M.; the fee is $50 a night. Individual baby-sitting can be requested through the concierge.

Recreation: The spa programs and facilities are extensive. Facials from deep cleansing to mud packs, massages of the shiatsu and Swedish variety, herbal wraps, body scrubs, exfoliation, aromatherapy, reflexology, and hydrotherapy baths are just some of the methods utilized to revive weary guests. Athletic club facilities include swimming pools, a weight room, a cardiovascular room, Pilates, cycling, and a jogging track. You can join one of the many exercise classes offered throughout the day or, with an exercise physiologist, you can devise a personalized fitness program. Individualized analysis also extends to dietary counseling and menu planning.

The Chopra Center is a unique place for healing and deep rejuvenation. Yoga and meditation are offered, along with Ayurvedic treatments and three- to five-day programs. Deepak Chopra, a Western-trained physician from India, has done much to introduce principles of the ancient Indian health system to the West. Ayurvedic refers to the "knowledge of life" and has been practiced for over 5,000 years.

Golf enthusiasts find their exercise on the two eighteen-hole championship courses. At the Golf School the latest technology is used to scrutinize and improve your game. Tennis players have twenty-one courts at their disposal and can choose grass, clay, or hard-court surfaces. Clinics are held daily, and private instruction is easily arranged. The golf and tennis pro shops offer a wide range of equipment and apparel. Croquet, bicycles, and five heated swimming pools complete the picture of exercise potential at La Costa. Rejuvenation potential is unlimited.

San Diego is a paradise for children; among other attractions are Legoland, Birch Aquar-

ium, San Diego Wild Animal Park, Seaworld Adventure Park, and the famous San Diego Zoo. Old Town San Diego and Carlsbad, Village by the Sea, are day excursions the entire family will enjoy.

LA COSTA RESORT AND SPA

2100 Costa del Mar Road
Carlsbad, California 92009
(760) 438–9111, (800) 854–5000
www.lacosta.com

NORTHSTAR-AT-TAHOE
Truckee, California

Tahoe has long been known for the clear deep waters of a 200-square-mile lake, the majestic mountain peaks of the Sierra Nevada, and its proximity to the entertainment and nightlife of Nevada casinos. Northstar-at-Tahoe enables vacationers to partake of all of these. Open year-round, it is a 2,420-acre mountain resort just 6 miles from Lake Tahoe that offers winter and summer family sports activities. Lake Tahoe straddles the California/Nevada state line and at 6,223 feet is the largest alpine lake in North America. It is the second deepest lake in the U.S. (1,645 feet at its deepest point) and so clear you can see a dinner plate at 250 meters. And who do you suppose figured out that if you were to tip Lake Tahoe over, the water would be 14.5 inches deep over all of California?

With the Nevada state line only 7 miles away, side trips to gambling casinos are manageable excursions for grown-ups. But it's not all about glitz. Northstar is dedicated to the environment, and their mission is to treat it with

respect. The championship golf course is a certified Audubon Cooperative Sanctuary, and the resort promotes environmental planning, water quality management, and revegetation practices. Northstar participates in Sustainable Slopes, an environmental charter for ski areas.

Accommodations: The lodging facilities include hotel-type rooms, condominiums ranging in size from studios to four-bedroom units, and three- and four-bedroom homes. With the exception of the lodge rooms, all have a fully equipped kitchen and fireplace; many units have a private balcony overlooking the wooded landscape and the mountains. The wooden facades and rustic designs of the buildings blend well with the natural setting.

Village rooms are $155 to $175 in summer, $209 to $255 in winter. Two-bedroom condominiums are $225 to $255 in summer, $289 to $409 in winter. The Ski Trails lodging is closest to the slopes, ski-in, ski-out on-trail condominiums range from $279 to $329 for a one-bedroom and $365 to $469 for a two-bedroom. Package plans are available throughout the year. The on-site transportation system is complimentary for Northstar guests. Cribs are provided at no additional charge.

Dining: The six restaurants at Northstar mean time off for the family cook. Timbercreek Restaurant, voted one of Tahoe's best for elegant dining, serves dinner in the winter and summer. Mid-December to mid-April, a ski express breakfast buffet and lunch is also served daily and a children's menu and après-ski bar are also available. The Martis Valley Grill is open holiday weeks in winter, and daily for breakfast and lunch in summer months, with a Sunday Brunch. Themed family style buffets (Italian, Southwest, Mediterranean, etc.) are offered. Cippolini's Pizzeria operates in winter only for pizza, soup, and salad bar. You can use the on-mountain pizza phone to call in your order, then ski down to eat.

The two winter restaurants on the mountain are the Lodge at Big Springs, open for breakfast and lunch, and the Summit Deck and Grill, open for lunch. Each offers an informal atmosphere and allows skiers to get back on the slopes quickly. The Summit Deck is really that—set at 8,600 feet on top of Mount Pluto, it has wonderful views of Lake Tahoe and the Pacific Crest from the outside deck. However, to dine here you must be able to ski or ride intermediate runs. And in winter "the party's at the Alpine Bar"; live music, a sports bar with multiple TVs, appetizers, and a full bar tempt skiers off the slope at day's end.

In summer the Turn, at the golf course, has patio dining for lunch and afternoon snacks. Or call your order in while teeing off at the ninth hole, and pick it up on your way through. The Village Food Company, in the Village Mall, is open year-round; with a deli, gourmet groceries, espresso bar, and video rentals, it also provides the supplies for a picnic or snacking in your condo.

Children's World: The Minors' Camp Child-Care Center is fully licensed and accepts children as young as two years old (must be toilet trained). In the winter it is open daily from 8:30 A.M. to 4:30 P.M. Under the guidance of an experienced staff, two- to six-year-olds paint, learn songs, listen to stories, play in the snow, and take walks; with snacks and a hot lunch, the full-day fee is $67; afternoons are $35.

At three years little ones can join the Ski Cubs Program; in addition to the nonskiing activities, these children receive one and a half hours of ski instruction during the day. The fee for child care plus skiing (equipment included) is $77 a day. Five- to six-year-old Super Cubs with some skiing experience receive two and a half hours of ski instruction in addition to indoor activities at a daily rate of $87. The learn-to-ski programs are offered on weekends and holidays. When not with the other Cubs, a child under five skis free with a ticketed adult.

Ski and *Family Life* magazines rank Northstar's family programs and kids' ski school as one of the best in the nation. The ski school is separate from the Minors' Camp program, and the teaching area is at midmountain. Startykes is for ages four to six; most classes start indoors and include plenty of breaks to keep kids energized. A full day with lunch is from 10:00 A.M. to 3:00 P.M. ($72 lesson only, $85 package); a half day begins at 12:30 P.M. ($36 lesson only, $65 package). Starkids, skiing, or skateboarding for ages seven to twelve, has lessons for every ability level that include lesson, snow play (even tubing), lift ticket, and rentals. Prices are the same as for Startykes. On all programs, even Minors' Camp, holiday prices are $2.00 to $8.00 higher.

Paw Parks are six terrain parks for kids, designed with jumps, bumps, and secret snow play areas to kick off skis or boards and just play. Patrolled by ski patrol, they're close to main runs as well. Look for paw prints on the trail map. Another special thing: Mommy, Daddy, and Me is a free program (except Saturday) for ages three to four and their parents, when trained instructors teach you how to teach your kids.

The highlights of the Minors' Camp summer program (mid-June to Labor Day) for children ages two (must be toilet trained) to ten are swimming lessons, nature walks, tennis, arts and crafts, science, and junior ropes course. Day camp is in session Monday through Saturday from 9:00 A.M. to 5:00 P.M. You can reserve a slot for your child for $35 per half day or $60 all day; lunch is included in both. Some field trips/activities may have extra charges or may not be appropriate for children under five years old, so do call ahead. Parents or guardians must remain on Northstar premises while children are enrolled in Minors' Camp. A free half day of child care is provided with more than two nights' lodging.

Recreation: For downhill skiing at Tahoe, you can look forward to 2,280 vertical feet. The Northstar Village is at the base of Mount Pluto, which rises to a summit of 8,600 feet. There are seventy runs and seventeen lifts, and locals boast of sunshine 80 percent of the season. The ski school, with its 200-plus instructors, offers lessons for beginners through experts to help all visitors meet the variety of this mountain. Fifty kilometers of groomed trails attract cross-country skiers; lessons, guided tours, and snowshoe rentals are available at the Nordic Ski Center. Polaris Park begins when the sun drops and most skiers head home. A lighted evening adventure park for skiing, boarding, tubing, and snow toys, plus food, live entertainment, and dancing—it's a happening place! Snow toys are the snowscoot, the skifox, and the snowbike—you figure them out, please.

Après-ski activities may mean taking a sleigh ride or a trip to the Swim and Raquet Club, where you'll find saunas, spas, an adult lap pool, a fitness center, and a teen center, or enjoying a stroll through the Village Mall, which houses shops, restaurants, and bars.

During the summer other activities lure visitors outdoors to the sunshine and clean mountain air. Northstar fully promotes the concept of "recess"; that precious time dedicated to the sole purpose of running around outside and playing that unfortunately is disappearing from our too-busy lives. Well, here's your chance to bring it back. Enjoy golf on an eighteen-hole course that wanders over meadows, past mountain streams, and through groves of tall pines and aspens. The Golf Course Clubhouse includes a pro shop and a restaurant. To work on improving your game, check with the resident pro for tips, or practice solo on the driving range and putting green.

At the Recreation Center, play tennis on one of the ten courts, take a swim in the adult lap pool or junior Olympic-size pool, or just soak up the sunshine on the poolside deck. No one over six years old is allowed in the Kiddie Pool, and families have their own hot tub, one of three. A fitness center is open to guests fourteen and older. The Arcade and Youth Center is a favorite place for kids to "just hang" and have some fun. Foosball, table tennis, and video games—plus the usual suspects of TV and vending machines.

The Adventure Park offers challenge and junior ropes course, outdoor climbing wall, and orienteering courses. Off-road all-terrain vehicle (ATV) tours get down and dirty for those over sixteen. The latest addition, Action Zone, features bungee trampolines, a mountain bike park, and basketball shoot and shower: a timed shoot by which the loser gets soaked. The Northstar stables provide well-groomed horses for riding the mountain trails and offer lessons and guided trail rides. Hiking and biking are also favorite sports in High Sierra country. For adventures in boating and fishing, the clear blue waters of Lake Tahoe await you. And music fills the air every summer Sunday afternoon with free outdoor concerts.

NORTHSTAR-AT-TAHOE

P.O. Box 129
Truckee, California 96160
(530) 562–1010, (800) GO–NORTH
(466–6784)
www.skinorthstar.com,
www.northstarattahoe.com

THE RANCHO BERNARDO INN

San Diego, California

Good news, weary travelers. It is still possible to vacation in the classic style and relaxed atmosphere of an old California ranch. Set in the San Pasqual Mountains of Southern California, the four-diamond Rancho Bernardo Inn is just thirty minutes north of San Diego. Here, on 265 acres, the inn revives the elegance and charm of the early rancheros' way of life, capitalizes on the California sunshine and balmy weather, and adds fine sporting facilities as well—all to provide the perfect holiday for you. The inn is open year-round, and their mission is simple: Treat each guest as a life-long friend.

Accommodations: As you might expect of an old California ranch, the architecture reveals a Spanish influence reminiscent of the area's heritage. The eight red-tiled haciendas house 287 rooms and suites. These are decorated in warm earth tones, highly polished wood, and hand-picked antiques and local art. Every room has a patio or private balcony with valley, garden, or golf course view. Suites offer wood-burning fireplaces and adjoining courtyards. Room rates range from $159 to $299; suites from $309 to $578. Stay and Play packages (based on double occupancy) from $318 to $453 include deluxe room accommodations and your choice of one "play" option (golf, massage, tennis, or local San Diego attraction admission) per person for each night of your stay. Breakfast and dinner may be added to any stay. Children sixteen and under stay free in parents' room; cribs are provided at no charge.

Dining: El Bizcocho is the elegant French restaurant of the inn. This mission-style dining room is open for evening dinner and Sunday brunch; jackets are requested for gentlemen. With consistently high ratings from *Zagat,* one critic calls it "a circus of the senses." More casual and open for breakfast, lunch, and dinner,

the Veranda Grill will lure you with its fresh seafood dishes, such as tiger shrimp Provençale. Alfresco dining was meant for San Diego's several hundred days of sunshine. The Sports Grill serves sandwiches and snacks on its patio, near the ninth hole. Tea, tasty sandwiches, and pastries in the Music Room make a perfect afternoon interlude to tide you over between a lovely lunch and a delicious dinner. For aperitifs and evening entertainment, La Taberna features a piano soloist or dancing.

Children's World: Camp RBI is an active, fun-filled camp offered on holiday weekends throughout the year: Easter, Memorial Day, the Fourth of July, Labor Day, Thanksgiving, and Christmastime; it is also in operation every weekend in August. Minimum age is four years, and there's really no maximum; some activities are planned for older children and teens as well. Between 9:00 A.M. and 9:00 P.M., children share age-appropriate outdoor activities like basketball, swimming, biking, tennis, soccer, relay races, scavenger hunts, and dance contests. Indoor activities such as games, movies, storytelling, and crafts are also scheduled. A full-day session includes lunch, dinner, and a souvenir craft; half-day sessions are also available. Cost is $40 for a half day or $65 for the full day. Each session has a major theme, often connected to the holiday.

Excel Academy is the place for children ages seven to thirteen to learn the basics or prepare for competition in golf, tennis, and swimming. For a day or a week, the time is filled with professional instruction, a little pool time, and a box lunch, plus a T-shirt. Video reviews at the end of the day further develop skills. The Excel Academy operates Monday through Friday from 9:00 A.M. to 4:00 P.M., early July through mid-August; cost is $60 per day or $250 per week.

Destination Science, for youngsters ages five to eleven, is a high-tech, hands-on program where children build and launch a rocket, examine robots and spy technology, or create a UFO flyer and stunt kite. Kids may attend for one day or a full week. It operates Monday through Friday from the end of July to mid-August from 9:00 A.M. to 3:30 P.M.; cost is $40 for a half day and $65 for a full day. On all programs, a discount is offered for the second child in a family.

Recreation: Golf and tennis players are well cared for at Rancho Bernardo. Oaks North, three nine-hole executive courses located ten minutes away, will whet your appetite for the eighteen-hole championship resort golf course. Planted with sycamore, eucalyptus, pine, and olive trees, the lush green fairways roll down the foothills to the valley. With resident pros, individual and group lessons, clinics, tournaments, a driving range, and a well-stocked pro shop, you've got every chance in the world of polishing your game.

Tennis players are found on the twelve outdoor courts including two stadium courts, four of which are lighted for nighttime play. The Tennis College has a thirty-year history of providing programs to players of all skill levels. Stroke development, teamwork, and strategy are just some of the topics covered in the two- to five-day sessions. Private instruction is also available from the five on-site tennis pros.

When you've run out of energy and are ready to relax, head to the full-service Buena Vista Spa. You can enjoy an indoor or outdoor massage, facial, or other relaxing treatment; have a tempting, healthy spa lunch; and unwind in the steam or sauna room. Stop at the spa or gift shop and take your experience home with one of the spa's exclusive, custom-blended skin- and hair-care products. Have a pleasant dip in one of the two swimming pools, or bicycle and jog around the carefully tended grounds. Because of the sunny Southern California weather, these sports continue year-round. As a complement to the spa, the independently owned and operated Salus Heart & Wellness Center will help you learn to nurture your body for optimal health with everything from traditional coronary risk assessments to yoga and spa treatments especially for the heart. Two- to four-day comprehensive programs are offered. Can't miss your daily workout? Drop by the fitness center, where you can also consult a nutritionist or personal trainer.

All of San Diego's attractions are twenty to thirty minutes away. The famous San Diego Zoo, SeaWorld, the Aerospace Museum, and the Wild Animal Park beckon. Enjoy a picnic in Balboa Park, Legoland, or shop at Horton Plaza, a fabulous "mall" like no other. You can even take a quick trip to Mexico—it's an easy forty-five-minute train ride from downtown San Diego to Tijuana for great bargains.

THE RANCHO BERNARDO INN

17550 Bernardo Oaks Drive
San Diego, California 92128
(858) 675–8500, (877) 517–9342
www.ranchobernardoinn.com

SQUAW VALLEY USA

Olympic Valley, California

Squaw Valley—the name itself is synonymous with skiing. From the earliest days (would you believe 1949?), the sunny California weather combined with six high alpine peaks and 4,000 acres of lift-served terrain have made this a world-class ski area. From its beginning in 1949 with one chairlift, a rope tow, and a lodge to hosting the 1960 Olympics, Squaw Valley is now a premier destination resort with year-round recreation and a strong commitment to environmental programs as a member of Sustainable Slopes. Mother Nature deposits an average of 450 inches of snow between mid-November and April. The Sierra Nevada and Lake Tahoe provide a spectacular backdrop, and the vastness of the area contributes to a wide variety of skiing. Squaw Valley is located near the north end of Lake Tahoe.

Accommodations: A central reservation office (800–545–4350) will work with you to find the most appropriate lodging for your family and your needs. Hotels, motels, lodges, and condominiums all have various rates and package plans. Among the closest to the slopes are Squaw Valley Lodge, a ski-in, ski-out condominium ($190 to $1,025); three-day ski packages are available from $414 per person. The PlumpJack Squaw Valley Inn ($185 to $625) is located next to the tram, with sixty rooms and includes a mountain breakfast. The Resort at Squaw Creek, a luxury ski-in, ski-out resort and hotel with a full-service spa, oversize rooms, four restaurants, and an ice rink, sits at the base of the Squaw Creek Lift; rooms are $254 to $3,000. The Olympic Village Inn is a European-style condominium complex about 4 blocks from the base of the mountain; one-bedroom suites, some with fireplaces, are $165 to $385.

Dining: Squaw Valley is certainly the place to eat, drink, and be merry, and choices are plentiful. In the Base Village, the Salsa Bar & Grill has a Southwestern flavor—watch out for those tequila specialties. Start your day off at Wildflour Baking Company for coffee and homemade pastries, Mother Barclay's Café, or grab a bite at the cable car building on your way up. Crepes for breakfast or lunch at Les Crepes de Dion; microbrews and good food (with lots of sunshine vitamin D) at the Sundeck Tavern; and the kids won't be able to walk past Coney Island, offering ice cream, pretzels, and hot dogs. The General Store and Dave's Deli have take-out meals, supplies and sundries; Mountain Nectar offers smoothies, bagels, wraps, and panini sandwiches. Many of the hotels and lodges have fine dining restaurants; and new additions in the Village are PlumpJack Balboa Café, with classic American brasserie fare and take-out, and the upscale High Sierra Grille. See what other wonderful places your family will discover.

On the mountain, the Sunset Dinner at Alexander's ($25 per person) is delightful. Ride the Cable Car to High Camp, winter and summer, and savor views of the valley and Lake Tahoe with your three-course dinner. The Terrace Bar & Deli also offers panoramic views, lunch, and a place to relax at day's end. The Poolside Café, overlooking Lagoon & Spa, has a fun kids' menu, soup-and-salad bar, and hot sandwiches; eat indoors or on the open sundeck. In summer the poolside BBQ and umbrella bar really shine.

The casinos and showrooms of Nevada are readily accessible for dining and evening pleasures. If you want to stay in the neighborhood, however, try the après-ski at Bar One, Le Chamois, or the Plaza Bar, where you'll find entertainment after a strenuous day of skiing.

Children's World: SquawKid's Children's Center is 12,000 square feet of comprehensive programs all for kids ages two to twelve.

Adjacent to the lifts at the base of the mountain, it's designed to be a one-stop center for families with everything kids need and special parking. Parents can even buy their own lift tickets there to save time. Toddler Care is a fully licensed program for children two and three years old. Teachers are specially educated to work with this age group, and trained in CPR and first aid. Arts and crafts, music, snow play, stories, and naps fill toddler's days. One-hour ski lessons are an option for three-year-olds, and also a fun introduction to the sport. Regular season full-day cost is $82; $99 at holidays. Half days are $62 and $79. Snow Sliders, for ages four to six, enhances learning and keeps kids smiling. The full-day program includes several hours on the snow, snack, and lunch; a new magic carpet lift helps with tired little legs. Junior Mountain is for ages seven to twelve, with more focus on safety, skill development, and skiing etiquette—and keeping the kids smiling. The Snowboarding program for ages eight to twelve has the same goals. Nonholidays, the cost is $82 for a full day and $62 for a half day. Holiday times go to $99 for all day, and $79 for a half day. All older children receive lesson and all-day lift ticket; lunch is included in the full-day session.

While summertime has no organized children's programs, many events and activities are planned for kids and families. Old West Weekend, Village Movie Nights, Sunday Family Kite Flying, and Hiking with a Ranger are just a few.

Recreation: The definite wintertime focus of Squaw Valley is skiing. Imagine yourself on an uncrowded run. The sun is shining and you kick up some powder as you stop to check out the scenery. Take off your goggles and look out over glistening white snow to the blue waters of Lake Tahoe. Seventy percent of the runs are for beginner/intermediate skiers. Moreover, Squaw Valley is one of those rare places where this group is not confined to the lower elevations but can ski all day above 8,000 feet in the sunny, sheltered bowls. The vertical drop is 2,850 feet, and challenging slopes for expert skiers are not lacking, as the 1960 Winter

Olympics were held here. Squaw's six peaks are interconnected by thirty-three lifts that include a 110-passenger cable car, a twenty-eight-passenger Funitel (the first of its kind in North America), four high-speed detachable quads, and three six-passenger chairs. The ski school organizes classes and clinics for all levels, from beginners to racing competition. A coin-operated race course allows skiers to perfect their racing styles (and keeps them off the regular slopes!).

Cross-country skiing, offered at the Resort at Squaw Creek, augments the snow diversions of Squaw Valley; the Olympic Ice Pavilion and snow tubing round it out. The Ice Pavilion also operates in summer, if you find yourself pining for winter sports.

In the summertime the cable car operates for scenic tours, hiking, swimming, full-moon hikes, stargazing, mountain biking, and many more events. The High Camp Bath & Tennis Club has a spectacular mountain location at 8,200 feet, surrounded by the beauty of the Sierra's peaks. The Headwall, on the mountain, offers wall climbing, bungee trampolines, and a new experience that promises a thrill, the Skytrek. Climb up a tree, and then trek among the treetops through a series of twenty-five platforms connected by cables, bridges, and zip lines. Tennis, fishing, biking, horseback riding, and nature trails are popular pastimes. Golf is top-notch here, with an eighteen-hole Robert Trent Jones Jr. course that weaves its way through mountains and meadows. Swimming pools, exercise spas, and racquetball/squash courts round out the pleasures.

SQUAW VALLEY USA

P.O. Box 2007
1960 Squaw Valley Road
Olympic Valley, California 96146
(530) 583–6985, (800) 403–0206
www.squaw.com

SUNRIVER RESORT

Nestled in the pines between the towering Cascade Mountains and the high desert, Sunriver Resort encompasses 3,300 acres on the dry side of the Cascade Mountains and enjoys nearly 300 days of sunshine each year. This four-diamond resort has earned numerous awards including *Condé Nast Traveler*'s "Top 50 Ski Resorts in North America," *Family Circle*'s Top 10 Vacation Destinations, and "#1 Family Resort in the Northwest" from *Family Fun* magazine; at least eight golf awards including top one hundred golf resorts in the world and one of the one hundred best women-friendly courses, plus dining and wine awards. It's a unique blend of natural beauty, resort comforts, personal service, and great recreation that makes for a memorable vacation. Sunriver offers three championship golf courses and one of the most complete lists of recreational activities to be found. Experience more than 30 miles of bike paths, white-water rafting, canoeing, tennis, and organized children's, teen, and family programs. In the winter enjoy cross-country skiing, sleigh rides, a covered ice-skating rink, an assortment of shops and restaurants, and world-class skiing at nearby Mount Bachelor. Sunriver Resort has its own shuttle to the mountain that will have you on the slopes within minutes.

Accommodations: Accommodations at Sunriver Resort include deluxe rooms and suites, featuring stone fireplaces and private decks; the suites accommodate two to six people and have a kitchen and dining/living room. River Lodges are close to the main lodge and offer great views; four two-story buildings house deluxe rooms featuring Northwest decor. Lodge Village rooms and suites are also just steps from the Sunriver Lodge. Summer rates range from $179 to $209 for rooms and $239 to $279 for suites in Lodge Village; River

Lodges are $259 to $309 and suites are $600. Higher rates apply on weekends.

Winter rates at Lodge Village average $125 (room) to $169 (suite). Winter packages are available; for example, Family Flake Out starts at $209 per night ($259 holidays), in the Lodge Village suite accommodations with kitchenette, loft, and sitting area. Two adults and two children under ten receive admission to Snowblast tubing park and Sunriver Ice Skating Rink and children eat free in the Meadows at the Lodge with a paying adult. Guests at Sunriver enjoy access to the resort and club membership privileges for golf and dining.

Approximately 270 private homes and condominiums can be rented on a short-term basis. With one to five bedrooms, these can easily sleep up to ten people comfortably. All include a well-equipped kitchen, living and dining areas, and fireplace; some have hot tubs and deck. They are strategically located along the golf course, tucked in among the pines, facing the Cascade Mountains, or overlooking the Deschutes River. Prices for a two-bedroom range from $149 to $279 per night, size and season being the determining factors; summer and Christmastime are the high seasons. The architecture is warm and rustic, modern yet compatible with the surroundings, and individually decorated by owner's taste.

Dining: The Meadows at the Lodge specializes in Northwest cuisine and is open for breakfast, lunch, and dinner daily. Enjoy great views and an imaginative children's menu. The Merchant Trader Café, located on the lower level of the lodge, features snacks and lighter fare for breakfast and lunch, and is open daily. The Grille at Crosswater Club is open during the summer months for lunch and dinner, and in the winter for lunch on Saturdays and dinner Thursday through Saturday evenings. A private club atmosphere, it's open to resort guests and members only. Open daily during the summer months are the Turn at Crosswater and McDivot's Café at the Woodlands golf course, both offering lighter fare and refreshments for golfers.

In addition, Sunriver's Village Mall has a number of restaurants and a grocery store. Whether you cook in or dine out, the variety from quick sandwiches to gourmet fare satisfies almost any mood. For late-night fun, the Owl's Nest Pub in the lodge offers cocktails nightly and live entertainment every Friday and Saturday night.

Children's World: Fort Funnigan gives children ages three through six and seven through ten a chance to develop new skills, interests, and friendships as they create, discover, and experiment in Sunriver's unique environment. Each session revolves around a theme, and includes nature study, adventure, crafts, and games. Fort Funnigan operates daily from mid-June through Labor Day, and on holidays and weekends throughout the year. Spike, the porcupine mascot, hangs out daily at Fort Funnigan; he often makes surprise appearances at other events, and has his own "room" on the resort's Web site. Costs are $50 for a full day, 9:00 A.M. to 4:00 P.M. with lunch. Monday, Wednesday, and Friday evening sessions are 5:00 to 9:00 P.M. with dinner for $30; and Tuesday, Thursday, and Saturday without dinner for $20. No night programs on Sunday.

Guided Adventures is designed for preteens and teens (ages eleven through fifteen) and is held during the summer months. On Tuesday, Wednesday, and Thursday from 9:30 A.M. to 3:30 P.M., activities are geared toward the more independent and adventurous nature of this age group. Prices vary according to the scheduled activity: Wrangler Day features horsemanship and trail rides ($60); Challenge Yourself ($45) is safe but thrilling and involves ropes, cables, tall trees, bikes, and more. Pedal, Paddle, and Fish ($40)—need we say more? Kids are advised to bring their bike, helmet, and lunch every day.

Teens ages thirteen to nineteen have their own summer schedule, generally in the afternoon and evening (much their preference!). Tuesday is indoor rock climbing in Bend ($40); Wednesday is Night Spiker Volleyball, with the unusual effects of black lights and neon ($25); Thursday is white-water rafting ($35); and Friday is cosmic bowling 'til midnight in Bend ($40); often a dance is scheduled weekly. During the rest of the year, loose activities are offered for teens, such as dances or pizza parties.

In addition, youth summer activities include bicycle riding, swimming lessons, canoe or white-water raft rides, games, and tennis. The resident naturalists at the Sunriver Nature Center introduce children to the magic and mystery of the local environment and animals; the Nature Center is open year-round.

In winter the rink at the Sunriver Village Mall makes a great spot for ice-skating. Wintertime also means that all the services of Mount Bachelor are available. Please see the information on Mount Bachelor Ski School for kids, under the listing for the Inn of the Seventh Mountain.

Recreation: Sunriver Resort is proud to offer fifty-four holes of outstanding championship golf. Set amid rivers, meadows, wetlands, pine forests, and spectacular Cascade Mountain views, the Sunriver golfing experience offers incredible variety. Crosswater was designed by Robert Cupp and John Fought and offers play exclusively for resort guests and Crosswater Club members. The Woodlands was designed by renowned architect Robert Trent Jones, Jr., and consistently ranks among the top twenty-five resort courses nationwide. The Woodlands' tree-lined fairways, seven lakes, and strategically placed sand traps have earned Sunriver Resort the distinction of a *Golf Magazine* Silver Medal Award. The Meadows, playing to more than 7,000 yards, has four sets of tees, meticulously prepared bent grass greens, and spectacular Cascade Mountain views; it is also home to the Sunriver Resort Golf Learning Center.

With five Plexipave tennis courts rimmed by tall pines and blue skies overhead, who could possibly have a bad game of tennis? But if your serve or backhand needs some polishing, you can always sign up for lessons. Sunriver Resort offers their own year-round tennis program with three indoor courts. Guests have access to an additional twenty-seven courts.

Two swimming centers each have a heated Olympic-size pool, a diving pool, and a wading pool, providing plenty of variety. The south pool also has a water slide and hot tubs. Also available are the Lodge Village pool and three outdoor spas.

The Deschutes River provides hours of enjoyment for fishermen, who snag brookies, rainbows, and German browns. The Sunriver Marina offers canoe, raft, and kayak float trips down the scenic and calm Deschutes. Marina staff will pick you up downriver and bring you back to the marina; the trips are offered mid-April to mid-October, weather permitting. For the more adventurous, local outfitters offer half-day and full-day white-water rafting trips down more turbulent portions of the Deschutes, leaving from the resort daily during the summer months.

For landlubbers in your party, rental bikes are available for excursions on the 30 miles of paved paths; guides at the Sunriver stables are ready to show off the scenery in rides along the river; the wilderness beckons interested backpackers. Trails past meadows and through the woods await joggers and nature lovers. Surrounding Sunriver Resort is the Deschutes National Forest, offering additional opportunity for back-to-nature serenity and elbow room. The Sunriver Nature Center has been offering extremely comprehensive, very reasonably priced programs for more than twenty-five years. Many nature walks, lectures, and programs are free; there are also archaeology tours, combined biking/bird-watching excursions, spelunking in Lava River Cave, and much more. See galaxies, nebulas, and all of space at the Sunriver Nature Center & Observatory; a nature trail and botanical garden provide earthly fun and learning.

Sage Springs Club and Spa features spa services and hydrotherapy spas; a fitness club with extensive classes in yoga, aerobics (water and other), Pilates, and more; and personal trainers who are available to help with your regimen. The indoor tennis center is here as well.

Sunriver Village has restaurants and interesting shops and boutiques. The Sunriver Music Festival takes place in August; orchestral programs are presented in the Great Hall, originally constructed as an officers' club when what is now Sunriver Resort was Camp Abbot, a training center for the Corps of Engineers during World War II. The Great Hall is composed of 511 logs, totaling 150,000 board feet of lumber and is the only original building that remains. Completely restored to its original beauty, it serves as Sunriver's most popular entertainment venue.

The High Desert Museum, 8 miles from the lodge, is a terrific educational introduction to the cultural and natural history of the Northwest, and a big attraction for kids and adults alike. The otter pond, where you can watch playful otters, is a favorite highlight, as is watching the birds of prey in action.

At Sunriver you'll find a dozen ways to enjoy winter. Mount Bachelor (800–829–2442, www.mtbachelor.com) is one of the West's top-rated ski areas. You'll find breathtaking views, plenty of deep powder, and slopes to challenge skiers and snowboarders of all abilities—from beginners to Olympic champions. You can head cross-country on miles of groomed forest trails or break your own path through snowy meadows. Trek the mountain outback by snowshoe, snowmobile, or dogsled, or take a leisurely tour in a horse-drawn sleigh. And at day's end back at the resort, slip into a steaming outdoor spa for a relaxing soak.

SUNRIVER RESORT

P.O. Box 3609
Sunriver, Oregon 97707
(541) 593–1000, (800) 801–8765
www.sunriver-resort.com

SUN VALLEY
Sun Valley, Idaho

Just saying "Sun Valley" calls to mind fantastic downhill skiing, beautiful powder, and gorgeous sunshine. Located in south-central Idaho, Sun Valley is a Tyrolean-style village perched high in the Sawtooth Mountains. With a ski season that runs from late November to early May, spectacular scenery and mountain air, Sun Valley is indeed a skier's paradise. In 1935 the Union Pacific Railroad sent Count Felix Schaffgtosch to search for the perfect spot for a grand American resort to draw rail travel west. After months of finding nothing that met his strict criteria, he happened upon Ketchum, an old mining town in central Idaho. His response? "This place combines more delightful features for a winter resort than anyplace I have ever seen in Switzerland, Austria, or the U.S." Averell Harriman, then chairman of the railroad, determined to build a resort worthy of the majestic setting, and Sun Valley was born in 1936. Instantly successful, European nobility and Hollywood royalty flocked to the new resort, creating the first destination resort in America. That standard of excellence and style continues today, as families from around the world continue Harriman's vision of "roughing it in style." Sun Valley introduced the world's first chairlift and began the long-running affair between Americans and skiing.

Accommodations: The historic, original Sun Valley Lodge provides upscale lodging and fine dining in an imposing four-story hotel. Each of the lodge's 148 rooms and suites has a French Country decor with marble-appointed baths. The Sun Valley Salon & Day Spa, massage center, heated swimming pool, and bowling alley are located here. Room sizes vary, and Family Suites are one option with three beds in one and a half rooms with one and a half baths. July and August are the highest season and rates range from $199 to $469; winter rates drop slightly to $179 to $429; spring and fall are even lower. The chalet-style Sun Valley Inn is set in the midst of the village and contains meeting spaces, rooms, and suites. There are workout and laundry facilities, open to all resort guests, and the super-heated Inn Pool for year-round swimming in the crisp mountain air. Summer rates are between $159 for a standard room and $399 for a suite; $129 to $169 in winter. Deluxe condos are located near the Lodge and Inn; rates range from $169 for a studio to $449 for a four-bedroom. Standard condos form a horseshoe around the village, all within a ten-minute walk of the Inn or Lodge; rates range from $139 to $329. Both include daily maid service, fully equipped kitchens, and spacious living areas. There is no additional charge for cribs, and children stay free in the room with parents. Ages fifteen and under ski free—one child per adult, with purchase of adult lift ticket.

Dining: Thirteen restaurants at the resort please almost any mood from fancy to family-style. Though many families cook meals in their condominium units, occasional nights dining out mean a real vacation for the family chef too!

The Lodge Dining Room, open for dinner and Sunday brunch, combines excellent service, fine dining with a French flair, and live music in an elegant setting. Also in the lodge, Gretchen's is open for breakfast, lunch, and dinner with a warm, family atmosphere. In summer enjoy the gourmet buffet on the terrace overlooking the famous outdoor ice rink.

In the Village, Konditorei and Sun Valley Deli have sandwiches, pastries, and ice cream; kids love the Bald Mountain Pizza and Pasta. The Ram Restaurant at the Inn is open evenings-only for steak, seafood, and fondues.

On the mountain, Sun Valley's owner considers Baldy a "regal mountain, wearing a crown with three jewels"—the award-winning day-lodges of Warm Springs, Seattle Ridge, and River Run Lodges. Cluster stations ensure that your food is fresh and prepared exactly to your order—baked potatoes, soup, salad, and grills are above-average mountain fare. Lookout at the top of the mountain is cafeteria-style; Roundhouse is more intimate with seating around a four-sided fireplace—it's the first original day lodge. Dollar Cabin suits youngsters just fine and offers their all-time favorites of hot dogs, hamburgers, and fries.

In winter, for an unusual adventure in dining, take a horse-drawn sleigh ride to a rustic cabin nestled in the woods; at the Trail Creek Cabin, enjoy prime rib or Idaho trout near a warm fire. Après-ski haunts include the Duchin Lounge, in the Lodge, known for its "HBR" (hot buttered rum) and a favorite for socializing, live music, and dancing and entertainment. The Boiler Room features comedy and *Forever Plaid,* a family musical. First-run movies show in the Opera House in winter and summer.

Children's World: While Mom and Dad are schussing down Bald and Dollar Mountains, children are not left out of the fun in this winter wonderland. At Dollar Mountain, the Sun Valley Ski School starts three- and four-year-olds in Tiny Tracks introductory classes for $45 for an hour. Dollar Cubs, for four- and five-year-olds of all levels, and Dollar Bears, for ages six to twelve (with ability levels 1 to 4), enjoy a full day of activity (8:30 A.M. to 4:00 P.M.) with four hours per day of skiing instruction for $85. Consecutive day rates are lower. Snowboard clinics for ages seven to twelve are also at Dollar Mountain; same hours and rates apply. All rates include supervised lunch but not lift tickets, and children may ride the lift alone. For the six- to twelve-year-old intermediate to expert skier or snowboarder, Bald Eagles ski clinics strengthen technique and provide the proper amount of challenge. From 8:45 A.M. to 3:45 P.M., classes and sign-up begin and end at River Run Plaza Children's Center.

The Sun Valley Playschool in the village en-

tertains nonskiing little ones six years old and younger, including even infants. The school has games and toys and a nap room for tots who grow weary of all the excitement. There are opportunities for ice-skating and an outdoor playground for romping in the snow. Rates are the same as in summer.

In summertime Playschool school activities for the six-and-under group turn to swimming, arts and crafts, paddleboating, hayrides, and walks around the village.

Recreation: Suitable terrain for all levels of skiers is provided at Sun Valley. With its wide-open spaces and gentle trails, Dollar Mountain (628 vertical feet) is favored by beginners and those who want a few warm-up runs. Bald Mountain, with 3,400 vertical feet, is a challenge and caters to intermediate and expert skiers. Combined, these mountains offer seventy-five runs, nineteen chairlifts, and 2,054 skiable acres. Sun Valley prides itself on lots of good skiing from well-groomed terrain to unpacked powder and short lift lines—the combination every downhill skier seeks. A complimentary bus service operates continuously throughout the day, shuttling guests to the base of both mountains.

The Nordic and Snowshoe Center grooms 40 kilometers of well-marked trails for cross-country skiers through aspen trees, along the creek, and over sloping meadows. There are also 8 kilometers of designated snowshoe trails. Sun Valley was a pioneer in providing Nordic skiing specifically for children. Machine-set tracks designed for a child's stride cover 3 miles of the Nordic Ski Center and in some places parallel adult tracks, allowing an easy family cross-country-skiing experience. Backcountry skiers can tour the mountain from yurt to yurt (Siberian-style huts), finding a warm, welcoming meal and bed at each.

Private and group lessons are available in both downhill and cross-country skiing at beginner, intermediate, and advanced levels. At the ski shops you can rent equipment or purchase all the accessories necessary for either undertaking. With indoor and outdoor rinks, another favorite wintertime sport has become a year-round one here. Ice skates can be rented, and just behind the lodge is an Olympic-size skating rink where such greats as Sonja Henie, Peggy Fleming, and Dorothy Hamill have practiced. Saturday night ice shows are presented throughout the summer, and have been a tradition for over 65 years.

Another year-round activity is swimming; there are two glass enclosed indoor heated pools (one at the lodge and one at the inn) and one outdoor Olympic-size pool. Relax in the sauna or the Jacuzzi, or make an appointment with the masseur in the lodge to ease your overworked muscles. The game room in the lodge offers pool tables, video games, and bowling alleys; or perhaps you'd like to take in a movie at the Opera House. The shops in the village might tempt you with their selections of books, gifts, fashions, jewelry, pottery, and toys.

Summer brings music festivals, parades, antiques and crafts fairs, bicycle races, and much more. Tennis and golf enthusiasts are in their heyday, for there are eighteen outdoor tennis courts, as well as clinics and private lessons with videotaped analysis. An eighteen-hole championship golf course, redesigned by Robert Trent Jones Jr., rolls over gently sloping terrain. Two nine-hole courses provide another option. At the pro shop, you can arrange for lessons and pick up extras in equipment and clothing.

Fishing in Silver Creek makes a pleasant afternoon for novice fishermen as well as experienced anglers; Sun Valley Lake is stocked with trout. Swim in one of three heated pools; or watch the kids play in the children's pool. The mountain trails are open to you for horseback riding and hiking in the wooded wilderness; chairlifts give access to Baldey's Summit. Trap and skeet shooting (instruction available) are also popular with summer visitors. Take a rowboat or paddleboat out on the lake, line up rentals at the bike shop, or plan a white-water raft trip. Whether winter or summer sports beckon you, you'll be captivated by the majestic mountains and the warm, friendly atmosphere of Sun Valley.

SUN VALLEY

1 Sun Valley Road
Sun Valley, Idaho 83353
(208) 622–2001, (800) 786–8259
www.sunvalley.com

THE WESTIN MISSION HILLS RESORT
Rancho Mirage, California

Palm Springs is another name associated with Hollywood stars and elegant living. Its prestigious neighbor, Rancho Mirage, is newer, but making its own name as "the Playground of the Presidents." Set on 360 acres next to the Mission Hills Country Club, the Westin welcomes guests to the California desert. The lush landscaping and verdant golf courses belie its desert location, but the surrounding mountains and canyons, which reflect the sun and shadow and the clear starry nights, are stark and wondrous reminders of what lies beyond the resort's boundaries.

Shopping and art galleries vie with golf as diversions, and natural sight-seeing is varied. Indian Canyons have indigenous flora and fauna in dramatic contrast to the rocky gorges and barren desert; Joshua Tree National Park's 8,000 acres encompass some of the most interesting geological displays in the California desert, and the Living Desert's magnificent botanical gardens provide a fascinating and educative journey. Palm Canyon Drive and El Paseo have all the glitz and glamour you might crave.

Accommodations: Southwestern adobe mixed with classic Moroccan design provides a distinctive architectural achievement. Blue domes reflect the cloudless skies; warm brown arches repeat themselves down a long pathway, framing the desert palms and mountains. The 512 guest rooms are scattered in sixteen low-rise pavilions interspersed with meandering walks, gardens, lagoons, and waterfalls. Guest rooms are of generous size, and most feature a private patio or balcony. Westin has become noted for their "heavenly beds." February to April is the high season, when rooms range from $159 to $450; from June through mid-September, the rates drop to $129 to $209. The remaining months are a midrange of $149 to $365. December 25 to January 31, rates are highest: $179 to $490. Children under eighteen stay free in their parents' room.

Dining: Bella Vista features California cuisine for breakfast, lunch, and dinner. Typically Californian, it blends a sunlit atrium with palm trees. Indoor/outdoor dining is available. If you can't tear yourself or your kids out of one of the three swimming pools, Las Brisas and Las Hadas serve light poolside snacks and drinks; Caliente is the poolside cabana area. For evening cocktails the elegantly casual Lobby Lounge offers drinks and a tapas menu. Sit inside or on the patio with its circular firepit. Westin has prepared a nice list of family restaurants in the area for those who want to venture out.

Children's World: Westin Kids Club is a basic program at Westin resort properties, designed to make family travel safe, convenient, and enjoyable. Children get special age-appropriate gifts upon check-in; parents get a

safety kit, if desired (electric-outlet covers, adhesive strips, ID bracelets, and local emergency numbers); and the room is ready with cribs, potty seats, or bed rails if needed. Jogging strollers, high chairs, and bottle warmers are complimentary, meals can be ordered in advance from a children's menu so that they are ready upon arrival at the restaurant, and a lot of information about local things of interest to families is available. It's a really comprehensive approach, and during the summer special rates and "Kids Eat Free" promotions are generally available.

The Cactus Kids program at Mission Hills bills itself as "the coolest thing in the desert." Operating daily year-round from 8:00 A.M. to 5:00 P.M., it costs $40 per four-hour session (8:00 A.M. to noon and 1:00 to 5:00 P.M.) or $12 per hour. Lunch is additional. Reservations are requested at least one day in advance, and the program will be run for even one or two children. Activities include arts and crafts, volleyball, lawn games, movies, nature walks, and bicycle riding.

Recreation: Two championship golf courses, two practice ranges, and six greens and sand traps keep golfers happy. The Pete Dye Resort Course has his trademark deep bunkers and undulating fairways, while the Gary Player Signature Course is a mosaic of waterfalls, ravines, and lakes. Take lessons from the resident pros, or sign up for a Golf Digest School. Play tennis in the cool of the evening on the seven lighted tennis courts, or join the Reed Anderson Tennis School. Forget something? The pro shops have everything you need. Las Brisas is the largest of the three swimming pools; it was made to resemble the surrounding canyons and has a 60-foot water slide, two whirlpools, and spacious sundecks. Treat yourself to massage, herbal wraps, and facials at the new Spa at Mission Hills; work out at the fitness club; or follow a more leisurely pace with traditional lawn games such as croquet and shuffleboard.

If you need more action, Oasis Waterpark is nearby as well as Camelot Park, where you can enjoy miniature golf, bumper boats, go-carts, or batting cages. Take the Palm Springs Aerial Tramway 8,516 feet to the Mountain Station for a bird's-eye view, and hike through Mt. San Jacinto Wilderness State Park. Weather permitting (meaning when there is snow), Nordic skiing operates from November to April. At the opposite end of the environmental spectrum, explore the desert by four-wheel drive with experienced guides who can show you the secret life of the desert, or have a real Old West experience in a two-hour covered-wagon tour. As a contrast to all this nature, any teenagers in your party might gravitate toward the Palm Desert Town Center, the area's largest indoor shopping mall. Palm Springs and El Paseo shopping are just minutes away.

THE WESTIN MISSION HILLS RESORT

71333 Dinah Shore Drive
Rancho Mirage, California 92270
(760) 328–5955, (800) WESTIN–1
www.westin.com

CANADA

Alberta
British Columbia
Ontario
Quebec

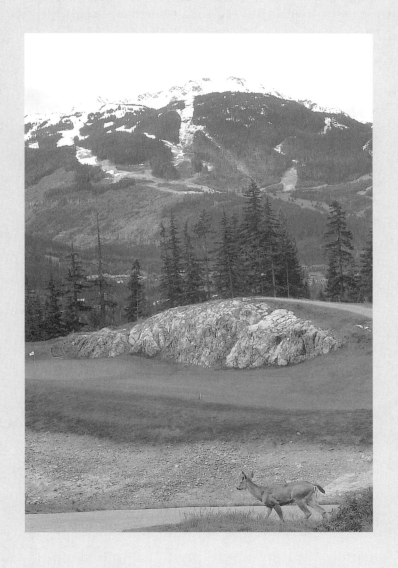

Banff National Park

Banff National Park was the third in the world, and the first in Canada, founded in 1885 after the accidental discovery of a hot springs on Sulphur Mountain. Starting out as a 26-square-kilometer reserve, it is now 6,641 square kilometers of incredible beauty, part of the UNESCO Rocky Mountain World Heritage Site and the most visited park in Canada. Glaciers, snowcapped peaks, lovely Lake Louise, meadows of mountain flowers, wilderness and wild creatures, and the impressive Icefields Parkway make this area well worth many visits.

Because the area is so big, and the Canadian Rockies are great for families, this is a unique entry. We're outlining both the towns of Banff and Canmore, and the Lake Louise area, giving you the choice of a family bed-and-breakfast, an inn, and the Chateau Lake Louise, a luxury resort. We couldn't draw arrows and connecting dots, so read carefully! There's something for kids everywhere, although maybe not your usual nine-to-five supervised program. It's a three-in-one and this one is all about options. And don't forget—the exchange rate is very favorable; we've priced everything in Canadian dollars. (Sunshine Village, another resort in Banff National Park, is discussed separately later in this section.)

BANFF/LAKE LOUISE
Banff National Park, Alberta

Accommodations: Monarch Bed and Breakfast is just right for families. In a private home in Canmore, you have 1,500 feet of private space for one to five people. Canmore is fifteen minutes from Banff (just outside the south boundaries of the park), 45 minutes from Lake Louise, and minutes away from four ski areas. In the house enjoy a recreation area with billiards, TV, and free movies, a family room with fireplace, and a kitchenette. Two private entrances and a deck overlooking the mountains make this a true "home away from home." Decor is simple and comfortable. One bedroom has a queen, the second has two twins; rates range from C$60 to C$115 per night per room.

The Inns of Banff are on the East end of Banff Avenue in Banff. The Hotel is a deluxe property with 180 rooms, all with balconies, many with mountain views. A minifridge and coffee are convenient for families, and children sixteen and under stay free in their parents' room. Family rooms (two queens) with mountain views range from C$115 (January, mid-April to mid-May) to $145 (February to mid-April) to $235 mid-May to mid-October. June through September, two-night Family Fun packages for a family of four are C$520 and include lodging, breakfast for the adults, admission to the Upper Hot Springs, passes to the Lux Cinema, and children twelve and under eat free. Part of the Inns, two-bedroom deluxe condos have a full kitchen; rates range from C$200 to C$330. Four-bedroom condos are also available. Swiss Village Lodge is a deluxe motel just next door to the Inns. Simple, comfortable rooms range from C$95 to C$185, and guests can use the Inns' facilities.

Is there anyone who has not seen an aerial picture of Lake Louise, always with that stunning castlelike structure in the foreground?

The Fairmont Chateau Lake Louise is generally referred to as the "Diamond in the Wilderness." In the National Park, the Chateau sits majestically at the edge of beautiful Lake Louise, 1½ miles long by ¾ miles wide. Views from the hotel across this magnificent glacier-fed lake are truly breathtaking, as the eye takes in the expanse of the lake's turquoise and emerald waters, the blue ice of the Victoria Glacier, and the majestic peaks of the Canadian Rockies, which form the Continental Divide. Dating from 1925, the resort is open year-round, and careful attention to the needs of guests is evident. Elegant yet inviting, the luxury of another era blends with the natural wonders that surround you. Winter and summer both are high season, when nightly rates begin at C$689 for a Fairmont room with courtyard view, C$789 for lakeside view; a junior suite lakeside is C$1,089. In spring and fall those rates are C$339 and C$389 for Fairmont rooms; C$689 for a junior suite lakeside.

Dining: At the Monarch B&B, breakfasts are prepared by Charlie, a professional chef, and can be light or really hearty. Breads and pastries are homemade daily—you can have pancakes, French toast, egg muffins, fruit salad, yogurt and granola, and even a Japanese-style breakfast, all on request. (Charlie's full name is Fumitaka Ogawa!)

At the Inns of Banff, Reflections Dining Room is open for breakfast, lunch, and dinner and serves good food at reasonable prices. Bear's Den Pub has pub food in the evenings; light snacks and beverages are an option at Reflections Lounge, off the lobby. Miki, a Japanese restaurant is open daily for dinner. Or if you just want to kick back, call room service. Banff Avenue in Banff has the market cornered in family dining. The Banff Keg, with two locations, has traditional food with a taste of California, coloring menus for the kids, and a friendly staff. Bumper's Beef House is a popular and fun family restaurant with Alberta beef specialties and an all-you-can-eat salad bar. Earl's is child-friendly, bright, and loud, with Canadian, Mexican, Cajun, and Oriental items on the menu. There's a Hard Rock Café, and Joe Btfsplk's Diner will take you straight back to the '50s with blue-plate specials that are big in size and small in price.

At the Chateau Lake Louise, dinner in the Fairview Dining Room will tempt you with such dishes as Tataki of Bison with daikon radish salad or a caramelized banana Napoleon. Old-world tradition prevails at the Walliser Stube with a classic Swiss menu featuring their famous fondue. In summer dine in the grand manner at the Victoria Room where table-to-ceiling windows overlook lush flowers and the blue, blue lake. Stone fireplaces and wooden beams enhance the setting. Get an early start on your day with breakfast at the Poppy Brasserie, or stop by for lunch or dinner—wonderful international specialties are the order of the day. The Chateau Deli is open twenty-four hours a day so you can eat it there, or get it to go. Early morning coffee and Danish, pack a picnic lunch, or savor a decadent dessert, whenever you want. At the other end of the day, sink in to the thronelike chairs of the Lobby Bar and revel in the glacier, forested slopes, and other glorious views while you sip a sunset. Step through the doors of the Glacier Saloon and into the Old West. Shoot a game of pool, dance to live music, and meet and mingle; pub meals, light snacks, après-ski, and a patio in summer. Warmth and hospitality is what's really served throughout the hotel.

Children's World: At the Monarch B&B, Joscelyne and Charlie have two young children themselves, and are willing to baby-sit and help you with personalized planning. They're well equipped with toys, games, movies—even Nintendo 64!

The Inns of Banff is family friendly, but has no activities especially for children.

There's lots for kids to do in the town of Banff; see below under Banff recreation.

At the Chateau Lake Louise, in winter season the Children's Playroom is available free of charge for children three and older. Open from 9:00 A.M. to 10:00 P.M., parents may leave their children for a maximum of four hours while they pursue other activities within the hotel; they cannot, however, leave the immediate grounds. In summer the hotel will arrange baby-sitting. Five minutes away at the Lake Louise ski area, winter children's programs begin with day care for the wee ones and Kinderski for ages three and four. Chocolate Moose Park combines indoor and outdoor fun; one-hour ski and play is C$15; morning and afternoon ski and play is C$25. Combined with day care, the cost is C$36 and C$46. Kids' Ski for ages five to twelve explores the mountain and increases skill through fun and games. Shreddies, for ages seven to twelve, has instruction in different groups of skiing abilities. A full day is C$69 with lift for either program.

Recreation: Between Banff National Park, Jasper, Lake Louise, and the surrounding townships, it would be practically impossible to do justice to all the recreation possibilities. Web sites that can help are www.canadian rockies.net; and www.skilouise.com. Suffice it to say that every imaginable mountain sport, winter and summer, is here. Torchlight dinners on the mountain, soaking the day away in the mineral hot springs, or heliskiing—Lake Louise guarantees to live up to your expectations or gives you a "snow cheque" to return. The season lasts from mid-November to mid-May, and snow is abundant. *Skiing Magazine* voted it number one for scenery and number two for value in all of North America in 2002. And the wonders of a great National Park surround you; in Banff don't miss the drive through the Bow Valley, or a day trip on the scenic Icefields Parkway. Three other mountain ski areas and four golf courses—the list goes on and on.

At the Monarch, your host, Charlie, snowboards daily in the winter, and is happy to have company in the van; an outdoor skating rink is in the neighborhood. In summer it's five minutes to Cougar Creek, a great path for sunset walks and you're close to Johnston Canyon and Spray and Grassi Lakes for hiking. All summer mountain activities are nearby, and kids enjoy the water-slide pool in Canmore. Galleries, museums, cafes, and shops are all within the 6-block core area of town.

At the Inns of Banff, facilities include a huge outdoor hot pool surrounded by glorious mountain peaks; and an indoor swimming pool, whirlpool, and sauna. Massage and spa treatments are most relaxing. Bike and ski rental shops are also on-site.

The answer to the "what's there to do here" cry for Banff will please most kids. A water slide and pool at the Douglas Fir Resort, a skateboard park at the Banff Community Rec Center, a bowling alley with small arcade, and a movie complex on Bear Street will keep kids happy for a good while. Kinbasket Adventures will take you for a two-and-a-half hour tour floating leisurely through one of North America's most pristine wetlands. Starting in the town of Golden, the Columbia River Wetlands are 1,600 kilometers long and 3 to 16 kilometers wide; visible from the moon, it supports a wide diversity of birds, amphibians, and reptiles.

On-site recreation at the Fairmont Chateau Lake Louise in winter features cross-country skiing, with trails leading right from the hotel and ice-skating on Lake Louise. Evenings are filled with stargazing and stories by the fire-

place. In summer interpretive hiking and mountaineering are the focus. Naturalists and professional mountain guides share the nature, history, and culture; the Lakes in the Clouds is one of the most popular trips. A health club and Escape Spa provide for your physical comforts and well-being.

BANFF/LAKE LOUISE

Banff National Park
Alberta, Canada
www.canadianrockies.net

Monarch Bed and Breakfast
317 Canyonclose
Canmore, Alberta, Canada
(403) 678–2566
www.canadianrockies.net/monarch

The Inns of Banff
600 Banff Avenue
Banff, Alberta Canada
(403) 762–4581, (800) 661–1272
www.innsofbanff.com

The Fairmont Chateau Lake Louise
111 Lake Louise Drive
Lake Louise, Alberta, Canada
(403) 522–3511, (800) 441–1414
www.fairmont.com

DEERHURST RESORT
Huntsville, Ontario

The Muskoka region is Ontario's most popular holiday area. With its clear lakes and beautiful woodlands, it attracts visitors in summer and winter. Deerhurst Resort encompasses 800 acres on the shores of Peninsula Lake and allows guests to experi-

ence all the beauty of the area. And yes, there are still deer at Deerhurst.

The original lodge at Deerhurst was opened in 1896 by Charles Waterhouse, with just eighteen guest rooms. Three generations of Waterhouses oversaw the expansion of the property and today it is one of the largest resort complexes in Canada. In 2002 it was voted the "Best Summer and Winter Resort in Ontario" by e-kidstoronto.com; and the *Toronto Sun* readers survey has voted it the "Best Resort in Ontario" for the past three years. It's a place where families can share the fun together or share the stories about their own adventures.

Deerhurt is two and a half hours by car north of Toronto, or only forty minutes by air from Toronto to the resort's private airstrip.

Accommodations: Today's accommodations are a far cry from the lodge rooms (without baths) of the early days. At that time accessible only by steamboat, the first guests paid $3.50 per person for a week's lodging, with three meals daily! Today, low-rise accommodations for 425 guests are located throughout the resort's landscaped acres. The guest rooms and suites are well appointed and comfortable and are grouped in condominium-style buildings with views of the lake, woods, pools, and golf course. Rates include complimentary access to a wide array of leisure activities, and are higher in summer. A variety of styles suit every need. For families, the Sports Villas are quite popular; a separate sitting area, kitchenette, and patio or balcony allows for more space. Deluxe and Luxury suites have full-size stove and refrigerator. Groceries are obtainable in Huntsville, 13 kilometers from the resort. Low-season rates at the Sports Villas start at C$199 and go to C$349 in July and August. Since standard rooms are C$179 and C$319, the villas are an excellent value. Children under eighteen stay free when occupying their parents' room.

Dining: In the Eclipse Restaurant, no less than eight chefs display their talents with regional bounty; venison, fresh fish, wild mushrooms, and wild berries are often featured in creative dishes. The cuisine is matched by the decor of lake and trees viewed through huge picture windows and set under soaring Douglas fir ceiling beams. Open for breakfast and dinner, it's all family friendly. The signature restaurant, Steamers, is pure Canadian, with

intimate dining rooms in a romantic log house atmosphere designed for adult dining. Open seasonally. The Pub at the Pavilion is casual and well suited for families; soups, sandwiches, pastas, and salads are typical fare here, served all day, from 11:00 A.M. to 10:00 P.M. The Poolside Deck, with views of the lake, serves barbecue favorites in the summer; a golfers lounge is also available for all-day summer dining.

A Modified American Plan is available for adults only. This includes a buffet breakfast and three-course table d'hôte dinner or a la carte selections from the three resort restaurants. Cost is C$59 per night and must be purchased for each day of your stay. There is no meal plan for children, but children's menus are available in the Pub and the Eclipse Dining Room.

Just off the lobby, the Landing Lounge is a good place to meet, unwind, and start the evening. Deerhurst keeps reinventing the critically acclaimed nightly entertainment, which in its twenty-second year is also Canada's longest-running stage show. This lavish performance of music, dance, and exciting visuals is where Shania Twain started performing, so who knows what future superstar you may see? CW's Lakeside Bar & Dance Club, open seasonally in the original Lodge by the lake, is the place to end the evening with DJ, dancing, laser lights, and arcade.

Children's World: Daily through the summer season and school holiday periods, and on weekends throughout the year, Deer Club operates from 9:00 A.M. to 5:00 P.M. Children ages four to twelve swim, hike, make crafts, and enjoy the playground. The fee is C$45 for a full day (including lunch) and C$25 for a half day. Younger children, ages six months to four years, join the Bambi Club, which has its own premises especially suited to little ones. The cost is C$65 full days and C$35 half days. Full day includes lunch for children on regular solid food. Parents should bring food and diapers for infants.

Recreation: The eighteen-hole Deerhurst Lakeside Golf Course was built in 1966 and redesigned in 1988 with many enhancements. Built in 1991, the top-rated Deerhurst Highlands is a magnificent eighteen-hole course winding atop a ridge above the lake, resulting in a combination of challenging play and beautiful scenery. A driving range, practice tees, and target greens make up the seven-and-a-half-acre instructional facility. A team of professionals direct private lessons and group clinics.

The Pavilion, a complete sports complex, consists of two indoor tennis courts, a racquetball court, three squash courts, a fitness room, two pools, and a whirlpool. Also available here is an Aveda Concept Spa, where you can relax in the steam and sauna rooms or schedule a massage, facial, body wrap, or hairstyling service.

If you prefer to exercise in the open air, three more swimming pools await you, and eight more tennis courts are outdoors (tennis lessons are available). Water sports on the lake abound: sailing, waterskiing, kayaking, fishing, and sailboarding. And don't forget to hike and jog along the nature trails in the beautiful Muskoka Woods. Included in the accommodation rates are tennis, squash, racquetball, the swimming pools and beach, hiking trails, and the fitness room. In summer canoes, kayaks, pedal boats, sailboats, and sailboards are all complimentary to guests. Four lakes mean over 60 kilometers of waterways to explore, and replica boats tour where grand steamships used to travel. Water-ski or fish for lake Trout and Northern Pike. Or just sit by the water and drink it all in.

In winter, cross-country ski trails and equipment, outdoor icerink and skates, hockey and broomball equipment, and snow tubing, plus indoor racquet sports, pool, and fitness room are complimentary to guests. Deerhurst is the gateway to over 2,000 kilometers of groomed trails and is right on the Trans Ontario Provincial trail system that connects the entire province, so snowmobilers are in snow heaven. Just next to the resort is Hidden Valley Highlands, open on weekends for a little taste of downhill skiing and snowboarding on eight slopes and thirty-five acres of runs. Group sleigh rides or a spin in an old-fashioned cutter will have everyone singing "Jingle Bells." For something a little more unusual, try dogsledding.

DEERHURST RESORT

1235 Deerhurst Drive
Huntsville, Ontario
Canada P1H 2E8
(705) 789–6411, (800) 461–4393
www.deerhurst.on.ca

FAIRMONT LE CHÂTEAU MONTEBELLO

Montebello, Quebec

You don't have to travel all the way to Europe for a vacation in a French château. Fairmont Le Château Montebello is a luxury resort in a peaceful woodland setting located on the shores of the Ottawa River between Montreal and Ottawa.

Built of over 10,000 massive cedar logs by a team of craftsmen in 1930, Fairmont Le Château Montebello served as an exclusive private club for forty years. In 1970 it became a resort open to the public year-round. Today the Château's old-world charm and contemporary elegance come together as a lovely holiday destination, with the distinction of being one of the world's largest log structures.

Accommodations: The central log chateau shelters all 211 guest rooms and suites, combining rustic elegance with a Swiss chalet–inspired decor. Guests can gather around the huge six-sided fireplace sitting in the center of the soaring three-story atrium for warmth and socializing. The chateau has four wings radiating from the center, affording the guest rooms views to the river, gardens, and forest. Yield management is the rule for rates at most Fairmont hotels. This means that rates depend more on availability than season—room rates seem to range from C$215 to C$309 in general. However, if occupancy were low, rates could drop. Between the end of May and late September, Family Fun two-night packages start from C$359 per night (two adults, two children under twelve; inquire for rates on teens) and include lodging, daily buffet breakfast and dinner, bike rental, miniputt, a pontoon boat cruise, half-day canoeing at Fairmont Kenauk, and the Children's Activity Program. Bed-and-Breakfast packages start from C$220 per night based on double occupancy. Children eighteen and under stay free in the room with parents.

Dining: For dinner, Aux Chantignoles is the rustic yet gourmet dining room of the resort. Menu items such as Rack of Caribou with juniper berries enhance the feeling of a hunting club; the French flavor shows in the cassoulet of snails. The breakfast buffet gives a jump-start of energy to your day; this is also the venue for the Sunday brunch. The Golf Club Terrace is popular for light lunches; a food cart makes the rounds of the greens if you just can't wait. The Igloo Bar is a summer restaurant for outdoor barbecues, ideal for lunch or dinner. The Bistro-Bar la Seigneurie is the place for gathering at the end of an active day; enjoy cocktails at the bar, "pub grub," or a light repast at one of the small tables or the central gazebo-like area while kids are entertained with video games and pool tables; a

house band plays on weekends.

Rue Notre-Dame, where the hotel is located, has many popular eateries. Try the charming Café Terrasse la Lanterne, an ivy-covered roadside inn in Montebello's commercial district with river views and delectable desserts. For lunch, Le Bistro feels like dining at a friend's home; Le Zouk Resto-Pub is a rustic looking joint that's a favorite with locals and tourists alike. At night, the bar is a favorite hangout. For international dining, Le Mar-Lyn, in a beautiful old home, is great for romantic dinners while Le Pot au Feu serves up an eclectic and creative menu in a homey ambience.

Children's World: Daily during July, August, and school holidays, Monte the Beaver presides over the Children's Activity Center from 9:00 A.M. to noon and evenings from 7:30 to 9:30 P.M. Year-round, the program operates only on Friday and Saturday evenings, Saturday from 9:00 A.M. to noon, and Sunday from 11:30 A.M. to 2:30 P.M. Outdoor activities such as hiking and group games are mixed with toys, games, and arts and crafts based on the ages and number of children in the program. The program, for ages three to twelve, is included in the Summer Family Fun package; otherwise, cost is C$32 per session. Outside of regular program hours, day care or babysitting is available at an hourly cost of C$5.00 for one child, $9.00 for two children.

Recreation: Le Château Montebello is quite proud of its golf course, ranked as Quebec's second toughest by *Canada Golf Magazine*. It features a wide range of difficult holes and natural obstacles, so golfers need to be alert with a few tricks in their bag. The golf school provides lessons and organizes clinics. At the Health Club and Sports Complex, you can work out in the exercise room, play squash or tennis, swim laps in the indoor pool, or relax in the saunas or whirlpools. The outdoor pool is a beautiful setting for relaxing, sunning, and swimming. Referee the kids in volleyball and badminton games, then round up the whole crew for bike riding or miniputt.

Other activities include water sports, cruises, jet-skiing, and horseback riding.

The Ultima Spa offers professional services, including full-body massage, facials, body wraps of mud or algae, body exfoliation and polishing, and therapeutic baths using either relaxing pine and rosemary milk or stimulating mineral salts. What a treat after a full day of activity!

The whole family can discover the beauties of Fairmont Kenauk, a 100-square-mile plant and wildlife preserve within 6 miles of the resort, with scores of activities—bird-watching, picnics, hikes with or without a naturalist, mountain biking, or fishing. Explore White Fish Lake by rowboat or canoe, float down the Kinonge River, or rent a motorboat at the marina. It's a great place to laze away summer days enjoying nature. Omega Park provides a slightly different approach to nature. Drive along a 10-kilometer road through 1,500 acres of a woodland corral where native animals small (raccoons, wild boar, and deer) and large (bison, black bears, and wild sheep) roam free. Don't forget your camera! About 10 miles west of Montebello is the Plaisance Waterfall, cascading more than 200 feet

within the Papineau-Labelle Wildlife Reserve; a great spot for a picnic and hike.

Snow brings enchantment to the woods and hills and is the focus of wintertime fun. The familiar activities of ice-skating, ice-fishing, sleigh rides, and snowmobiling compete with the more exotic: dogsledding, curling, snowshoeing, broomball, and deck hockey. More than 27 kilometers of cross-country ski trails beckon, or you may prefer just a walk in the snow and curling up with a good book in front of the huge six-sided fireplace in the château.

FAIRMONT LE CHÂTEAU MONTEBELLO

392 rue Notre-Dame
Montebello, Quebec
Canada J0V 1L0
(819) 423–6341, (800) 441–1414
www.fairmont.com

FAIRMONT LE MANOIR RICHELIEU
Charlevoix, Quebec

In Quebec's Charlevoix County, near Quebec City, the mountains and forests stretching along the great St. Lawrence River create a vista of magnificent scenery and quiet charm. In this rural area, where farming and agriculture are part of daily life, Fairmont has created a historically splendid resort, blending the quiet charm of the countryside with the sophistication of a three-star, four-diamond resort. Tourism in Charlevoix dates back to 1761, when sportsmen came for the salmon

fishing and wilderness. The original Le Manoir Richelieu was built in 1899, atop a cliff overlooking the majestic St. Lawrence River. Destroyed by fire in 1928, it was rebuilt in the style of a French castle, and opened again in 1929. A $140-million renovation and expansion was completed in June of 1999, bringing the hotel back to its original glory.

The Charlevoix region was granted status as a World Biosphere Reserve by UNESCO in

1988, and is the first biosphere reserve to be populated in the world. Within its boundaries are historical gardens, art galleries, a marine museum and eco-center, and many working studios for pottery, papermaking, and fabrics; an amazing variety of wildlife also calls this area home.

Accommodations: Comfort and luxury are offered by 405 guest rooms and 17 one- and two-bedroom suites, and kids love the idea of staying in a castle. Summer is high season, when a Fairmont room with garden view is C$229, river view is C$269. Those same rooms in winter are C$179 and C$119; and in spring the rates drop to C$109 and C$149. Children under eighteen stay free in the room with parents. A summer family fun package includes breakfast and dinner, miniputt, a horse carriage ride, bike rental, tennis, and the kids' club, starting at C$135 per family member.

Dining: For fine dining, the four-diamond restaurant Le Charlevoix, overlooking the St. Lawrence, showcases antiques, local art, and produce from the region. Le Saint-Laurent, the hotel's main dining room, is open for breakfast and dinner. Also overlooking the river, fresh fish, grilled specialties, and buffets will tempt you. Families enjoy Le Bellerive, with a relaxed bistro atmosphere, which serves a casual menu and light buffet. In summer dine alfresco on the sunny terrace. For a romantic evening, the French cuisine at L'Auberge sur La Cote in nearby La Malbaie is a favorite of townsfolk. Sip a cocktail at La Brise Lobby Bar or stroll over to the Bar Le Marie-Clarisse or Salon Murray at the Casino.

Children's World: The "Club des amis," or Friend's Club, is just that, a friendly place for children to gather. A membership card and surprise gift is given when registering. In summer the club operates daily from 8:00 A.M. to 10:00 P.M. for ages four to twelve. Fees are C$12 per hour ($6.00 each additional child) or $70 for the entire day ($50 for second child, $45 for the third), including meals. Daytime (8:00 A.M. to 5:00 P.M.; $55) and evening (5:00 to 10:00 P.M.; $45) sessions

are also available. All rates are in Canadian dollars. Children participate in aquatic games, sports, arts and crafts, treasure hunts, and nature excursions. A mini-cinema for kids has shows from 7:00 A.M. to 8:00 P.M., with popcorn. A giant beanbag and children's playground are always popular.

In winter, weekends for kids begin at 5:00 P.M. Friday and continue almost nonstop until noon on Sunday. Friday and Saturday nights until 10:00 P.M. and all day Saturday are filled with the same pursuits as summer, plus the outdoor thrill of snow shoes, ice-skating, and sledding. Baby-sitting is available for C$6.00 per hour with a three-hour minimum.

Recreation: Golf at the Fairmont Le Manoir Richelieu began in 1925, when President William Taft opened the eighteen-hole course. At the turn of this century it was named "Canada's Golf Resort of the Year" by *Canada's Golf Ranking Magazine,* and was listed one of *Golf Magazine*'s Silver Medal Resorts in 2002. As well, at least three public courses are nearby, so golfers can't get complacent. At the resort itself, enjoy saltwater swimming indoors or out, a wading pool, and water volleyball and basketball. A game room provides evening entertainment for the family. An evening spent at the Casino de Charlevoix, next door to the hotel, may be rewarding—if your luck holds. Horseback riding with gorgeous views, pony rides for the youngsters, and carriage rides at sunset are found at the equine center. Tennis, aqua-aerobics, hiking, a fitness room, and mountain biking will keep you in shape while a whirlpool soothes you at the end of it all. Lawn games and French Bowl are delightful ways to pass an afternoon. AmeriSpa can pamper you with twenty-two treatment rooms, and even a seven-day rejuvenation.

Winter snows bring wonderful outdoor opportunities such as sleigh rides, dogsledding, ice-fishing, horseback riding, and all those sports that require snowshoes, skates, or cross-country skis. Plus you can give the traditional Canadian sport of broomball a whirl.

The Multi-Sports Center can arrange it all. Snowmobiles are so popular that the resort provides parking, if you want to bring your own! Skiers have a choice of Mont Grand-Fonds (15 kilometers from the hotel) with a 335-meter vertical drop and cross-country skiing; or Le Massif, at 770 meters (2,536 feet) the highest vertical drop east of the Canadian Rockies, with an average snowfall of over 250 inches (80 kilometers away). The hotel has shuttles to both ski areas.

Shopping at the hotel or nearby local craft shops and art galleries can be a bargain; a favorable exchange rate and refund of the 7 percent goods and services taxes are an irresistible combination. While American money is generally accepted, often the exchange rate at shops is not favorable. Get all the info at www.ccra-adrc.gc.ca. The Route des Saveurs (Flavor Trail) showcases the regions excellent products: lamb, migneron cheese, and mini-vegetables. The circuit includes restaurants that use regional products in their cuisine; and also a tour of the farms that produce them. It's an authentic glimpse into another way of life, and a great way for kids to make the connections with where food originates

other than the grocery store. The Park of Hautes-Gorges-de-la-Riviere-Malbaie follows the Riviere Malbaie as it winds through some of the most extraordinary valleys between the highest cliffs east of the Canadian Rockies. Here you can participate in biking, canoeing, hiking, and kayaking; or the more sedate can enjoy a glass-bottom boat cruise. A cruise to the mouth of the St. Lawrence to witness migratory whales is a thrilling experience for all; between June and October at least six species of whales also visit. Charming villages dot the coastline. The Tourism Office (800–667–2276) has loads of information. Inquire at the hotel about discounts offered when renting a car from Avis.

FAIRMONT LE MANOIR RICHELIEU

181 rue Richelieu
Charlevoix, Quebec G5A 1X7
(418) 665–3703, (800) 257–7544
www.manoir-richelieu.com,
www.fairmont.com

GRAY ROCKS RESORT
Ville de Mont-Tremblant, Quebec

Just 75 miles northwest of Montreal, in the Laurentian Mountains, you will find a charming four-season, four-star lakeside family resort with a French flavor. Right in the middle of French-speaking Canada, Gray Rocks welcomes American visitors and English is spoken here routinely. You might choose to take the opportunity to brush up on your French, but rest assured that your interests uttered in English in the dining room, on the tennis courts, or during a ski lesson

will be well received with warm French-Canadian hospitality.

Since its beginning in 1906, Gray Rocks has developed into a renowned ski, golf, and tennis resort with hotel and condominium accommodations for all tastes. The hotel sits on the shores of Lac Ouimet. Gray Rocks' own ski mountain, Sugar Peak, rises right behind the hotel; beautiful views of Mont-Tremblant are also impossible to miss. Golf was the first sport in this area, followed by skiing. Today recreational pastimes also include tennis, water sports, horseback riding, mountain biking, or nature hikes.

Accommodations: Fifty-one lakeside rooms with private balcony are available in the hotel's Pavilion and Chalet Suisse; fifty-four regular rooms have lake or mountain views. Fifty-six one-, two-, and three-bedroom condominiums are tucked in among the trees ¾ miles from the hotel, with free shuttle-bus service. Pricing is in three levels: Super Value season is from mid-May to early June and late August to mid-October, when rates are lowest; Value season runs from early June to late July; and Summer is late July to late August. Super Value season rates for hotel rooms are C$113 to C$148; Value season costs from C$136 to C$199. Hotel rates are per person and include two meals daily; stays of four nights or more are discounted further. Condominium rates are C$182 to C$333 in Super Value season, C$265 to C$456 in Value and C$276 to C$481 in Summer; these rates are per unit, per night, with no meals, although meal plans are available.

Summer Vacation packages include hotel accommodations, access to fitness center and private beach, use of kayaks, paddleboats, canoes, rowboats, and sailboats and boards; a social program and nightly entertainment, activities at the Kid's Club, and breakfast and dinner daily. Per person rates are C$144 to C$210. Kids five and under always stay and eat for free. Ages six to ten are C$60 to C$95; ages eleven to seventeen are C$60 to C$105.

In winter guests enjoy a getaway similar to the summer hotel package, with free skiing at Gray Rocks or nearby sister resort Mont Blanc. The most popular winter package is the all-inclusive ski or snowboard week. You will enjoy six nights of lodging; eighteen full-course meals; twenty hours of ski instruction or ten hours of snowboard instruction with the renowned Snow Eagle Ski School; video critique; seven-day lift ticket; races and awards; complete social program for adults, teens, and children; and access to the fitness center with indoor pool. In the regular season, the package is C$1,405 to C$1,720 based on double occupancy. And remember, in U.S. dollars, it's almost half that much! Children eleven to seventeen receive a 40 percent discount, ages six to ten receive 50 percent off, and five and under stay free. Gray Rocks's ski week is considered one of the best ski vacation values in North America.

In winter daily condo rates for a one-bedroom range from C$195 (value) to C$350 (New Year's); a two-bedroom is C$260 to C$465. There are also ski and snowboard packages for condo stays. While there are daily rates for hotel rooms as well, Gray Rocks has such excellent packages for mid-week and weekend getaways that it's hard to resist. Skiing can be an affordable sport, after all. And Gray Rocks is family friendly both winter and summer.

Dining: The main dining room, with its fireplace and picture windows overlooking scenic Lac Ouimet, provides a pleasant ambience during meals. Continental and French-Canadian cuisines are featured; five-course table d'hôte dinners and lavish breakfast buffets keep guests satisfied. Cozy lounges with fireplaces and lake views are perfect to relax and mix with old and new friends; the Thirsty Eagle Bar has evening entertainment in season. In summer, twice weekly barbecues are scheduled on the outdoor patio. There's also a cafeteria at the ski chalet, located midmountain and accessible by car, shuttle bus, or skis. Both golf courses have a club house with snack bar and lounge area.

Children's World: In summer during July and August, the daily children's activity program is in high gear. Youngsters join other children their own ages for supervised morning and afternoon events. Preschoolers ages three to five head to the playground, go on treasure hunts and hayrides, or frolic on the private beach. Kids ages six to nine go swimming and horseback riding, try their talents in arts and crafts, and join hayrides. Preteens (ten to twelve) and teens (thirteen and older) enjoy volleyball, tennis, hiking, canoeing, sailboarding, fishing, and various excursions. For all children ages three to five, the cost is C$35 per child per day and includes lunch. The 8:30 A.M. to 3:30 P.M. programs are included for hotel guests ages six to seventeen as part of the package. Camp is available to condominium guest's children for C$35. Day care for ages six months to two years is also offered, and promises "vigilant supervision and experienced staff"; the ratio of children to supervisor is 2:1 and cost varies from C$17 per hour, C$40 for a half day, and C$65 for a full day with lunch. Private baby-sitting may be arranged, with a three-hour minimum.

Junior Golf clinics run Monday through Friday, for a total of ten hours. The teaching ratio is 5:1 and the fee is C$165. Junior tennis clinics are offered for ages five to ten and eleven to sixteen; C$11 per one-hour session, Monday through Friday. For more serious aspirations, the one- or two-week resident Junior Camp programs in golf and tennis will definitely improve skills.

In winter Gray Rocks's philosophy is to put children on skis as much as possible. Given that the resort's own gentle mountain is just out the back door, this philosophy is easily practiced. The children's ski classes are divided along age lines as well as ability; heaven forbid your first-time thirteen-year-old skier should be in a class with four-year-olds! Camaraderie in a peer group is important in the learning experience. Children and teens can also meet their friends in a variety of après-ski activities, such as cookie baking, face painting, treasure hunts, arts and crafts, table tennis tournaments, parties, movies, water polo, and sleigh rides or bingo with Mom and Dad. You want to have some fun with your kids, too!

Day-care service is available for ages six months to two years as well as private baby-sitting. A Ski 'n' Play program combines day care and one hour of ski instruction per day for three- to five-year-olds. The rate is C$50 per day; $35 for a half day. A special Snow Eaglet program for four- and five-year-olds blends indoor play with more ski time; C$280 for a five-day week includes 8:30 A.M. to 4:30 P.M. daily, Monday evening 5:00 to 6:00 P.M.

while parents have wine and cheese, and again from 6:00 to 10:00 P.M. on Friday, for the ski dinners. On the mountain an exclusive snow park for beginners is close to the day lodge and children's services and is kept secure with an easy-ride "magic carpet" lift and fenced outdoor play area.

The Junior Ski and Snowboard program is designed for ages six to thirteen; it's included with hotel vacation packages, C$280 for condo guests. Two hour ski lessons in the morning and afternoon, plus the special evening hours, have kids schussing down the slopes by the end of the week.

Recreation: Think of Gray Rocks as a university for sports. Its qualified ski, golf, and tennis instructors combine expertise with a sincere enthusiasm for teaching. Improvement of skills and self-confidence go hand in hand, and both are better achieved with ample doses of encouragement and humor. More than 250,000 ski-weekers have enjoyed Gray Rocks's unique teaching methods in a safe, uncrowded ski environment.

The Snow Eagle Ski School has a fine reputation (rated by *Ski Magazine* as one of the top-ten ski schools in North America) and more than fifty years of experience. Skiing is a major wintertime activity. The resort boasts a number of third-generation families who have learned to ski on these slopes and continue to return for their winter holidays. Though Gray Rocks has a modest 620-foot vertical drop, there's variety and, if not long, then challenging runs. Snowmaking facilities cover 95 percent of the slopes, ensuring a ski season from Thanksgiving through early April. Mont-Tremblant ski resort is less than 5 miles from Gray Rocks, so intermediate and advanced skiers can seek additional challenges there. The ski boutique can meet your needs for rentals, repairs, fashions, and accessories. Cross-country skiing is a growing favorite at Gray Rocks. Nearby Domaine St. Bernard offers well-maintained trails through the woods, next to the river. A tour around the area is a lovely way to spend a winter morning, and a sleigh ride with the kids caps off a perfect day.

Summertime opens another whole realm of outdoor sports and activities. There's a private sandy beach along a section of the lake. This is Canada, but summers are hot, so swimmers will be happy. The complete marina near the beach offers opportunity for canoeing, sailboarding, sailing, taking out a paddleboat, or enjoying an afternoon of fishing.

A classic eighteen-hole golf course (La Belle) will take you through lush fairways over diverse terrain framed by the rugged beauty of the Laurentians. Three learning holes are reserved for Eagle Golf Academy players. The combination of time-proven teaching strategies and small class ratios helps players take strokes off their game and turns newcomers on to the joys of the sport. Gray Rocks recently opened an eighteen-hole championship course (La Bête) designed by renowned golf architect Graham Cooke. The course winds its way along Devil's River, offering superb views of the surrounding mountains. With bent grass tees, greens, and fairways, four sets of tees to choose from, and eighteen distinct and challenging holes, you will leave knowing you have played one of Canada's best courses. In fact, it was voted the best family golf resort in Quebec by *Golf Ranking Magazine*.

Tennis buffs enjoy the largest outdoor complex in Canada with twenty-two Har-Tru courts (ten near the hotel and twelve at the golf club). Tennis lessons with videotaping can help you isolate the improvements necessary for a good game. Gray Rocks's golf and tennis academies offer acclaimed two- and five-day clinics.

Jogging along the lake or hiking and horseback riding in the hills are excellent ways to explore the countryside and revel in the clean mountain air. You can enjoy a nice afternoon next to the beach playing lawn games, or get in shape at Le Spa fitness center. Le Spa features an indoor swimming pool, an exercise room, hot tubs, a sauna, and a professional massage service. Many activities are offered free of charge; some, such as golf, tennis, and horseback riding, carry additional fees.

Gray Rocks provides the area's only resort-based pet kennel, and it's free. Now you can really travel with the entire family!

GRAY ROCKS RESORT

2322 reu Labelle
Ville de Mont-Tremblant, Quebec
Canada J8E 1T8
(819) 425–2771, (800) 567–6767
www.grayrocks.com

INN ON THE PARK
Toronto, Ontario

If you're in the mood for a slightly different vacation experience from that offered by most of the resorts we've listed, this is the place. Inn on the Park has the distinction of being a city hotel in a resort setting: Situated on 500 acres of parkland, it's right in the middle of Toronto, one of Canada's liveliest cities. It's the best of both worlds, with shopping, art galleries, and museums offset by the green grandeur of the surrounding park.

Accommodations: A twenty-two-story high-rise with 268 rooms in one tower allows views of the city, the park, or the inner courtyard. Nonsmoking floors, twice-daily maid service, complimentary parking, and terry-cloth robes are some of the amenities offered, and the hotel prides itself on excellent service. Fresh-air windows are also a nice touch. Deluxe rooms are on the higher floors and overlook the city and park (C$120 to C$220) while standard rooms are somewhat smaller and on the first level (C$115 to C$175). Be sure to ask, because some have a patio leading directly to the pool, while others go to the parking lot. Differences in size, location, and view determine room classification and rates; promotions and discounts are available; again, be sure to ask. If you like more space, one-bedroom suites begin at C$225. Children under nineteen stay free in parents' room; cribs and highchairs are available.

Dining: The Harvest Restaurant is casual, with a children's menu of those all-time favorites—grilled cheese sandwiches, hamburgers, and spaghetti. During the summer months the Cabana serves light snacks by the pool. The Terrace Lounge has early evening and late-night snacks. What child doesn't adore room service? Here it's available daily. And all the wonderful restaurants of Toronto are at your doorstep, waiting to be discovered.

Children's World: Innkidz is a very popular and highly organized program that is complimentary for hotel guests. Geared to children ages five to twelve, the program is available from 9:30 A.M. to 4:30 P.M. daily during July and August; weekends-only in May and June. Children gather at the Innkidz Centre on the first floor of the Tower for such activities as puppet making, outdoor games and swimming, and making crafts or clay art. Counselors are often art students

and teachers, so the experience is very creative. Children under five are welcome if parents remain with them. Lunch can be ordered from the Harvest Room menu and charged to the room.

Recreation: At the hotel you can work out in the fully equipped health club and then relax those muscles in the sauna or whirlpool; or try your hand at badminton, volleyball, or shuffleboard. Decide between the indoor and outdoor pools, then decide between swimming and lounging or window-shop the boutiques and gift shop.

Toronto holds many treats for families. Kids like to wander through Ontario Place, by the harbor. Shops, eateries, an IMAX theater, and changing exhibits of dinosaurs or gemstones intrigue everyone. Go to the top of the C.N. Tower, the largest freestanding tower in the world; or check out the planetarium at the Royal Ontario Museum. Let the kids pick out a postcard in the gift shop, then try to find the original in the museum. The Ontario Science Center has a lot of hands-on exhibits, and the Toronto Zoo is a nice excursion on a pretty day. Paramount Canada's Wonderland theme park is forty-five minutes away. And most kids love the medieval dinner with knights and wenches, and no silverware.

INN ON THE PARK

1100 Eglinton Avenue East
Toronto, Ontario
Canada M3C 1H8
(416) 444–2561, (877) 644–4687
www.innontheparktoronto.com

SEVERN LODGE

Port Severn, Ontario

Severn Lodge is beautifully located in the midst of the Georgian Lakelands of Ontario, only 90 miles from Toronto. Georgia Bay forms the northeastern part of Lake Huron and is named in honor of England's King George IV. The area's piney woods, fine fishing, and clear waters attract many vacationers. The geographic features of the Cambrian Shield area where the lodge is located are unique. Spectacular rock formations created during the Ice Age; granite outcroppings, windswept pines, and hardwood forests dot the many islands and inlets. And the Severn Lodge, on the shores of Gloucester Pool, adds to the natural features with its warm pride of being "owned and operated by the same family, for families, since 1937." Severn Lodge is a special place, where the everyday hustle and bustle quiets, and one has time to breathe the fresh air, relax, and do as much or as little as you want. Set in a sheltered cove, the resort encompasses one hundred acres of waterfront property, with over 2,000 feet of private shoreline. The lodge is open from mid-May to mid-October only.

Accommodations: Severn Lodge dates back to the late 1800s. Its early-twentieth-century ambience remains preserved in the many white clapboard buildings, log crisscross railings, and cobblestone sidewalks. All accommodations and facilities, however, are very modern.

Grouped in about a dozen individual buildings set among the trees and along the lake, the accommodations are in three styles. Hotel-style rooms have two double beds with a view of the waterfront; family-size rooms are one large room with two sleeping areas separated by a dividing wall and a sitting area with sofa bed; and two-bedroom units offer more privacy. Three different rate groups reflect location and different amenities. Two- to

seven-day packages are fully inclusive and include lodging, baggage handling, two or three meals daily (according to the season), the children's activity program, evening entertainment, and use of the recreation facilities. Children's rates are based upon age and some weeks during summer are designated "kids free" (under twelve) and 50 percent off for teens. Stays for children two and under are always complimentary. Adult rates are per person and range from C$209 to C$398 for spring and fall (two to three days). Seven days in July and August runs C$922 to C$1,068 for adults, up to C$518 for ages two to twelve, and teens are C$322 to C$644. Cottages and suites are located both on-site and off-site, about five minutes by boat or car from the resort. These rates are per unit, and include the deluxe recreation package but no meals. Weekly rates range from C$1,499 to C$2,129. Remember, that's quite a bit less in U.S. dollars, depending on the current exchange.

Dining: The charming, elegantly rustic dining room has a wood-beamed ceiling and many large windows that capture the views. The Canadian cuisine is accompanied by freshly baked breads and pastries. Severn Lodge has a reputation for delicious foods, and children always have special choices, and even their own summertime buffet. Most summer days feature a poolside barbecue with grilled foods; you can dine either inside or outside. Usually you have four or five choices for dinner; one night each week there's a barbecue, another may be a deluxe buffet. Fresh, high-quality, healthy foods are always used, and vegetarians are not forgotten. Picnic lunches can be prepared for guests who are off hiking or canoeing during the midday meal.

Children's World: The activities program

for children, which runs daily from mid-June to Labor Day and select weekends at other times, includes hikes, crafts, volleyball and baseball games, swimming, diving and boating lessons, picnics, and movies. Add waterskiing, Indian Night, Talent Night, a Fish Derby, corn roasts, and bonfire sing-alongs and you know you have happy kids. No additional charges are applied for these events, and children of all ages are welcome to participate.

Every effort is made to include even very young guests, but also a supervised toddler activity program provides pint-size fun, with specially designed indoor and outdoor play areas for two- to four-year-olds. The program is complimentary and includes arts and crafts, sand-castle building, and other beach and playground activities. This program runs daily except Sunday, and kids eat most meals with their parents. The lodge staff can also arrange an individual baby-sitter for an extra cost. Favorites among the younger set are the sandy beach; the playground, with its swings, slide, sandbox, and climbing equipment; and the dock, for "just fishin'." The Junior Program (ages five to eight) has supervised activities around themes of history, culture or nature. Kids are kept busy with fishing derbies, waterskiing and tubing, island picnics, and scavenger hunts. Ages nine to twelve are in the Youth Program, filled with age-appropriate fun, and teens have just what they like—many things to do and not too much structure. Programs for older children are daily in high summer, but all ages eat most meals with parents.

Recreation: Severn Lodge also knows that creating family memories is an important part of the vacation. Lots of family activities such as picnics, canoeing the coves, horseback riding, and just exploring can be fit into the flexible schedules of the kid's program. Evening entertainment in the Regatta Room is geared toward all ages, and often includes children.

Water sports are an important part of Severn Lodge. Wonderful swimming can be had either in the lake or in the heated swimming pool; perhaps you'd like to try the whirlpool spa at the deepwater dock. Maybe you would prefer to stay on top of the water in a fishing boat reeling in walleye, bass, muskie, and northern pike. Also on top of the water (with any luck, you will stay on top) is the complimentary waterskiing instruction offered several times a week. Free use of the lodge's sailboats, paddleboats, kayaks, and canoes can make an afternoon lazy or exciting, depending upon your skill. The resort has a unique collection of antique runabouts and motor launches. Rental fees are charged on a daily or weekly basis for outboard boats, motors, and Jet-Skis; the lodge offers free island cruises aboard the 37-foot vintage 1922 mahogany motor launch.

On land you can jog or hike on the trails around the lodge's one hundred acres or play a game of tennis. The recreation building, with its library and large stone fireplace, is quite inviting if relaxing is a favorite pastime; here you will find table tennis, a wide-screen TV, card and board games, and a pool table. Nearby sight-seeing (15 to 20 miles) takes you back in history; Sainte-Marie among the Hurons, a Jesuit Mission, and the Huron Indian Village are reconstructions of seventeenth-century settlements. You will also find horseback riding, golf, live theater, museums, casino gambling, and fabulous shopping in nearby lakeside villages. Canada's Wonderland, a major theme park, is one hour away.

SEVERN LODGE

Box 250
116 Gloucester Trail
Port Severn, Ontario
Canada L0K 1S0
(705) 756–2722, (800) 461–5817
www.severnlodge.on.ca

SUNSHINE VILLAGE
Banff, Alberta

High in the Canadian Rockies in Banff National Park is Sunshine Village, one of the best ski destinations in Canada. Perched along the Continental Divide, the peak elevation at Sunshine is 9,200 feet. Located only 85 miles west of Calgary and just 5 miles from the town of Banff, Sunshine is a three-mountain ski resort, Goat's Eye, Mount Standish, and Lookout, constantly being improved. Back in the '20s and '30s, Banff was a summer destination. Those skiers that did come were usually from Europe, and were referred to by the locals as "those people with wooden heads and feet to match." Most had to ski over from Banff—hardly a day trip!

In summer White Mountain Adventures in Canmore provides day trips only, starting you out on the mountaintop for hiking and mountain pleasures. Follow the clearly marked trails on your own, or take a free interpretive walk led by experts. Uncrowded and incredibly scenic, Sunshine Village is a good example of man and nature in harmony.

Accommodations: The Sunshine Inn, constructed in the 1960s and '70s, is still the only on-slope accommodation in the Canadian Rockies; it's right in the middle of the ski area, at an elevation of 7,200 feet. A three-story complex consisting of eighty-four rooms and suites, the inn affords its guests ski-in, ski-out access and a chance at making those coveted "first tracks." Accommodation options include rooms and suites in the main hotel and terrace rooms in an adjoining wing. Check in on a Sunday and stay five nights for special rates that include lodging, lift tickets, and daily ski lessons, and some evening activities. Terrace rooms have separate sleeping areas with doors, but showers only and no TV; per unit rates range from C$1,065 in value season to C$2,450 at holidays and C$2,350 in powder season. Inn rooms have full bath and TV, a queen, and sofa bed. Rates are per person and are C$675,

C$1,050, or C$790 based on season; children ages six to twelve are always C$125. Daily rates always include lodging and lift tickets and begin at C$335 for the terrace unit; C$135 per adult and C$25 for children over six at the Sunshine Inn. Children six years and under always stay and ski free.

Getting to the inn is easy. Check in at the base area, take the gondola to the village, and start skiing. Your bags will magically arrive at your room, and your car will be parked. If you arrive outside of gondola hours, you'll have the thrill of taking "Sunshine Suzy," a cross between an SUV and a tank. She's also available for a fee if you want to escape the mountain at an odd hour, say for an evening in Banff. In the world's longest and fastest gondola, the trip takes twelve minutes; gondola hours begin at 8:00 A.M. and weekday closing is at 5:30 P.M., 7:00 P.M. on Saturday and 10:30 P.M. on Friday and Sunday. If you want to ski Sunshine but don't fancy staying on the mountaintop, central reservations has options in Banff.

Dining: Three locations on the mountain offer amenities. The village, mountaintop where the inn is located, has the largest selection with six restaurants, bars, and lounges. The inn's dining room, the Eagle's Nest, offers fine dining, from rack of lamb to fantastic sirloin steak. The Chimney Corner is a lounge offering cocktails and entertainment in the evenings. In the Daylodge, the Deli and the Cafeteria offer soup and sandwiches; the new Mad Trappers Saloon, located in the original 1928 Sunshine Lodge, is the place to go for drinks and burgers. Goat's Eye is the midstop; the gondola connects to the village at the top and the base area. Goat's Eye Gardens has hot food and drinks as well as snacks, beer, and wine. The base area is where you first arrive, and has a great restaurant for beginning and ending your ski day, serving breakfast and après-ski.

Children's World: Day care and children's

ski schools are in the village at the base of the Clock Tower, where children are carefully supervised in a variety of programs. Be sure to check exactly what is included in the five-day packages, as you may want to adjust the kids programs to fit what is complimentary into a coherent day for your youngster. Tiny Tigers Daycare is a safe, licensed facility for ages nineteen months to six years, with indoor and outdoor play, lunch, and snacks. Cost is C$28 for a half day, C$52 for a full day. Five full days are C$248. Three- to six-year-olds have all the advantages of day care, plus one hour of skiing in the morning and afternoon—it's popular, so reserve early. Cost is C$47 for a half day, C$78 for a full day, and C$352 for the five-day package.

Children from six to twelve years old have the Kids Kampus program where laughter and play go hand-in-hand with learning to be better skiers or riders. A full day is C$69 and a five-day package is C$276, both including lunch.

Recreation: Sunshine Village is located on the Continental Divide, where you can ski the provinces of both British Columbia and Alberta off the same run. The top elevation at Sunshine is almost 9,000 feet and the base elevation is 7,082 feet, yielding skiers more than 3,500 vertical feet. Mother Nature drops more than 10 meters (33 feet) of snow here each year, which results in good skiing from mid-November through the end of May. Of the

103 named runs currently open, 55 percent are intermediate; the remainder are split evenly between beginner and expert. Many of the runs are above the treeline, giving skiers that top-of-the-world feeling. Sunshine Village boasts North America's largest new ski terrain, Goat's Eye Mountain (elevation 9,200 feet), offering extreme-expert-only (Double Black Diamond) chutes and glades, runs, and free fall with an eighty-three-degree pitch. Two snowboarding parks (one half pipe and one terrain park) keep snowboarders happy.

When not skiing, you may want to pursue less rigorous activities in the family games room or relax your weary muscles in the sauna or the Sunshine Inn's giant outdoor hot pool, rated Canada's best by *Ski Canada* magazine. Mad Trapper's is the gathering place to down a few and grab a bite, to trade mountain adventures and tall tales of the trails, and to make new friends from all over the world.

SUNSHINE VILLAGE

Box 1510
Banff, Alberta
Canada T0L 0C0
(403) 762–6500, (877) 542–2633
www.skibanff.com

WHISTLER/BLACKCOMB
Whistler, British Columbia

If you're lucky enough to hear the whistling call of the indigenous marmots, you'll easily recognize how Whistler Mountain got its current name. Originally known as London Mountain, on the old Caribou Gold Rush Trail, this area saw its first settlers in 1914, an adventurous couple who built a fishing lodge on the shores of Alta Lake. Though still attracting fishermen in the summer, Whistler is famous today as an outstanding ski destination. The village has a permanent population of approximately 10,000 people.

Skiers first schussed these slopes in the mid-1960s, and the early 1980s witnessed considerable expansion and development, primarily the opening of Blackcomb Mountain. The two mountains, Whistler and Blackcomb, are serviced by three base facilities. In the Coastal Mountains, Whistler/Blackcomb is just 75 miles north of Vancouver.

Here's just some of what people are saying about Whistler: *Ski Magazine* calls it the number one ski area in North America and the "#1 Dream Vacation Destination"; the *Daily Telegraph* has rated it the number two ski resort in the world. It has the longest ski season in Canada; and in North America boasts the most skiable terrain (more than 7,000 acres), the greatest lift-serviced vertical (5,280 feet), the most slope-side accommodations, and the most qualified ski instructors. *Family Travel Forum* rated it the Top Family Getaway and it was *BC Parent*'s Families Favorite Ski Resort. Whew, that's a lot of mountain!

Accommodations: Hotels and condominiums are found throughout Whistler Resort. In 2003 five Whistler hotels were named on the *Condé Nast* reader's poll of the top fifty ski resorts in North America: the Westin Resort (#1), the Fairmont Chateau Whistler (#2), the Pan Pacific Lodge (#8), the Summit Lodge (#13), and the Delta Whistler Resort (#17) all garnered acclaim. A Four Seasons hotel and resort will open in 2004 in the Blackcomb Benchlands within walking distance of the lift; 2005 will bring the London Mountain Lodge, twenty-five log cabins on ten acres of the western shore of Nita Lake. The larger facilities are the Fairmont Château Whistler at the base of Blackcomb, with 558 units, indoor and outdoor swimming pools, a health club, and indoor tennis courts; the Delta Mountain Inn in Whistler Village, with 288 rooms, an outdoor pool, and two all-season tennis courts; and the Westin Resort, one of the locations for day-care facilities and child care. Midsize properties are the Marriott Residence Inn, with 184 units slope-side on Blackcomb Mountain, or the Crystal Lodge in the village, with 134 rooms. For condominiums, consider Stony Creek, Glaciers Reach, and Aspens, and smaller complexes such as the Hearthstone Lodge, Powderview, Whistler Resort and Club, or Whiski Jack Condos, might also be the perfect choice for your family. Contacting Central Experience at (800) WHISTLER is the first step in

sorting out all these choices. You might want to consider one of the available packages. Inquire about the PEAK rating system to help with consistent, reliable information.

Dining: With almost 100 restaurants and cafes, you'll never have trouble indulging your palate's whim, whether you crave French, Italian, Japanese, Mexican, or Greek cuisine or even fast food. Three restaurants on Whistler and eight on Blackcomb serve hearty soups and stews, burgers, pizza, and pasta to skiers reluctant to leave the slopes for very long. Christine's at the top of Blackcomb Mountain lets you enjoy fine dining in your ski boots, with a view as superb as the menu. The Dubh Linn Gate Pub at mountains' base is an authentic Irish Pub, perfect for day's end. In a ski resort known for fine dining, The Bearfoot Bistro is not just a meal but an experience— five courses served with five different wines. Some of the restaurants favored by families are Black's Restaurant; The Old Spaghetti Factory; Monk's at Blackcomb; and Dusty's at Whistler Creek.

Children's World: Whistler Kids has 500 instructors dedicated to making the mountains a kids' playground. The instructors are highly trained ski and snowboard professionals, specializing in kids' needs. Teaching more than 140,000 kids every winter, Whistler Kids is Canada's premier recreational operation for children. No wonder the kids keep bringing their parents back!

Whistler Kids offers a broad range of programs catering to kids as young as three months; kids first take to skis at three years. Full-day day care at three locations and ski programs for three to four-year olds are C$95; five- to six-year-olds are C$91 for lessons and lift or C$182 for a two-day adventure camp. Seven- to twelve-year-olds can choose ski or skateboard programs for the same cost; and Ride Tribe! for ages thirteen to eighteen gives them lots of action and informal lessons with no standing around (C$91). Adventure Camps include lunch; none of the rates include lift or equipment. Kids Night Out several times weekly provides an evening of fun if parents want to step out.

Late June to late August, summer programs for children are packed with activities that build skills and self-confidence and are just plain fun. Located at various venues throughout Whistler, there's something for kids eighteen months to twelve years. At the Westin Resort, ages eighteen months to four years go on nature walks, visit the fire hall and puppy day care, and have games and nap time (C$79 all day; C$45 half day). At Whistler Village, Adventure Camps for ages eight to twelve run Saturday through Wednesday; C$169 for two days or C$250 for three days with lunch. Also at Whistler Village, ages five to seven have a full day (C$79) in the Big Mountain Adventure Programs; eight- to twelve-year-olds can perfect their mountain-biking skills at all levels for C$89 a day. Kids Night Out evening programs on Thursday and Saturday for ages five to twelve (6:00 to 10:00 P.M., C$45) lets Mom and Dad have a night out too.

MY Youth Centre allows twelve to eighteen-year-olds their own space with all their favorite things, like DVDs, Nintendo 64, air hockey, pool, and table tennis, for only C$5.00. Open Wednesday, Thursday, and Saturday until 8:00 P.M., it's also the center for some planned events such as hikes and overnight excursions.

Recreation: Get introduced to Whistler/Blackcomb in free morning or afternoon guided tours and you'll begin to appreciate the mountains. More than 200 trails, twelve bowls, and three glaciers provide all the variety any skier could hope for. Choose chutes filled with powder, steep runs through trees, broad trails perfectly groomed, or mogul monsters. The average annual snowfall of 360 inches is complemented by sophisticated snowmaking capabilities. Both mountains open in late November, and skiing continues to late April on Blackcomb and to mid-June on Whistler. Blackcomb opens again in mid-June for glacier skiing through August for those who can't get enough of winter. Both mountains average 55 percent intermediate terrain; Blackcomb has about 5 percent more expert trails.

When taking a break from skiing, try ice-skating and snowmobiling, or organize a sleigh ride. Cross-country skiers take to the 10 miles of track-set trails through the forest and valley. For just a little less strenuous exercise, stroll through the village to discover its over 200 shops.

In summer golf is the premier sport, with four eighteen-hole courses, each with fine credentials. The Whistler Golf Course was designed by Arnold Palmer, and the Château Whistler Course was designed by Robert Trent Jones Jr. Jack Nicklaus was responsible for Nicklaus North, which opened in 1994, and the Big Sky Golf and Country Club was designed by Robert Cupp.

Hiking and biking across the Alpine terrain are favorites with summertime visitors. Whistler's intent is to become a mountain-biking meccca. They are well on their way. For family fun, the Meadow Park Recreation Center has an indoor pool outfitted for kids, an outdoor playground and waterpark, and an indoor ice rink for those who miss winter. Adventure Zone is one of those places where you can do everything—wall climbing, minigolf, luge, trapeze, kiss-the-sky trampoline, and horseback riding. Zipline Ecotours gives a twist to outdoor adventure where you spend two and a half hours flying through the trees over a series of cable cords and suspension bridges with a bird's-eye view over gaping gorges and rushing rivers. The five lakes provide fishermen, swimmers, and boaters with ample fun. A variety of festivals and special events are available throughout the year, and actually, more visitors arrive in summer.

WHISTLER/BLACKCOMB

Tourism Whistler
4010 Whistler Way
Whistler, British Columbia
Canada V0N 1B4
(604) 664–5625, (800) 944–7853
www.mywhistler.com

INDEXES

Alphabetical Index of Resorts

Resorts by State/Province

Children's Programs by Season

NOTE: Other resorts not listed here generally have a variety of partial programs, which may include some weekends and holidays. The following resorts are considered family friendly but have limited supervised children's programs: The Arizona Biltmore, El Monte Sagrado, French Lick Springs Resort, Highland Lodge, and Ludlow's Island Lodge. Please see resort descriptions for details.

DAILY, YEAR-ROUND PROGRAMS

SUMMER PROGRAMS

WINTER PROGRAMS

ABOUT THE AUTHORS

JANET TICE grew up in Oklahoma, then spent just as many years in Manhattan. Always a gypsy (although her mother denies it), she considers herself a citizen of the world. Schooled at the University of Oklahoma, with a Master of Science degree from the University of New York, her background in psychiatry prepared her for over twenty-five years in the travel business, which she claims is just another kind of craziness. Proud mother of Fabiana, for many years her inspiration and best field agent, she was a proponent and practitioner of family travel long before it became fashionable. She founded and directed Families Welcome!, a tour company for families, from 1986 to 1995. Currently living in North Carolina, her heart is really in the Southwest.

JANE WILFORD was born and reared in New Orleans, Louisiana. She earned a Bachelor of Arts degree in Art History and History from Duke University and a Master of Science degree in Library Service from Columbia University. After living for several years in New York and London, she currently resides in Connecticut with her husband, D. Sykes Wilford, and sons, Sykes and Paul, and daughter, Sarah. The Wilford family travels extensively throughout the United States and Europe.

HELP US KEEP THIS GUIDE UP TO DATE

Every effort has been made by the authors and editors to make this guide as accurate and useful as possible. However, many changes can occur after a guide is published—establishments close, phone numbers change, facilities come under new management, etc.

We would love to hear from you concerning your experiences with this guide and how you feel it could be improved and be kept up to date. While we may not be able to respond to all comments and suggestions, we'll take them to heart, and we'll make certain to share them with the authors. Please send your comments and suggestions to the following address:

The Globe Pequot Press
Reader Response/Editorial Department
P.O. Box 480
Guilford, CT 06437
Or you may e-mail us at: editorial@GlobePequot.com

Thanks for your input, and happy travels!